Matthew Henry, Samuel Hayward

Seventeen Sermons

On Various Important Subjects

Matthew Henry, Samuel Hayward

Seventeen Sermons
On Various Important Subjects

ISBN/EAN: 9783337160630

Printed in Europe, USA, Canada, Australia, Japan

Cover: Foto ©Lupo / pixelio.de

More available books at **www.hansebooks.com**

SEVENTEEN SERMONS,

ON

VARIOUS IMPORTANT SUBJECTS. Viz.

ON ORIGINAL GUILT—ORIGINAL DEPRAVITY—HUMAN IMPOTENCY—THE TRINITY—THE DEITY OF CHRIST—JUSTIFICATION BY CHRIST'S RIGHTEOUSNESS—THE NATURE AND USE OF FAITH IN THE SINNER'S JUSTIFICATION—ON THE CHRISTIAN'S WARFARE—THE CHRISTIAN'S COURSE—THE CHRISTIAN'S STEADFASTNESS—THE CHRISTIAN'S CROWN—LOVE TO AN UNSEEN SAVIOUR.

BY THE LATE REVEREND
Mr. SAMUEL HAYWARD.

TO WHICH ARE ADDED,

THE PLEASANTNESS
OF A
RELIGIOUS LIFE,

OPENED, PROVED, AND RECOMMENDED TO THE CONSIDERATION OF ALL, PARTICULARLY OF YOUNG PEOPLE.

AND A

CHURCH IN THE HOUSE:

BEING A

SERMON

CONCERNING
FAMILY RELIGION.

BOTH BY THE LATE REVEREND

Mr. MATTHEW HENRY,
MINISTER OF THE GOSPEL IN CHESTER.

A I R:
PRINTED BY JOHN & PETER WILSON.
M,DCC,XCII.
[Price bound Three Shillings.]

TO THE

CHURCH AND CONGREGATION,

LATELY UNDER THE CARE OF

THE REV. S. HAYWARD, DECEASED.

Dear Chriſtian Friends,

YOU, and the Public, are here preſented with a ſmall collection of your late dear and worthy Paſtor's Sermons. Poſthumous diſcourſes indeed, always appear with a conſiderable diſadvantage, as they come out deſtitute of that hand, which alone had a right to make alterations in method or expreſſion. Care has been taken to ſelect ſuch as appeared diſtinct in their ſubject matter, and were moſt full and finiſhed in point of compoſition; yet as they were not compoſed or preached in this connection, ſome coincidence of matter and ſameneſs of thought will occaſionally occur. However, they are publiſhed at your deſire: a deſire which flows from your cordial love to his memory, and genuine eſteem for his labours, which were ſo acceptable and uſeful among you when alive; and with a view to be in ſome degree beneficial to his dear and tender family, now he is removed. Many of you doubtleſs have an agreeable remembrance of the earneſtneſs and affection with which they were delivered from the pulpit, and alſo an experience of inſtruction and profit, as well as of entertainment from them. There needs therefore little apology for the preſent publication,

A 2

nor is there any fear about your kind reception of it. And as to others, even such as are in no degree prepoffeffed in its favour, I cannot but hope, upon their ferious and candid perufal, they will find fuch a plain, fcriptural reprefentation of feveral moſt material and interefting doctrines of our holy religion, and thefe inforced in fo earneſt and pathetic a manner, on the hearts and confciences of men, as will yield them a folid pleafure. If there is any pleafure in perufing the remains of one who appears to have confidered religion as a reality, its doctrines as the appointed means of holinefs and happinefs, principles not merely to be known and maintained, but alfo to be ufed and improved in the divine life; one who confidered himfelf a real friend to the fouls of men, commiffioned to lead them in the paths of peace, and warmly defirous of fuccefs in his work—The truly pious and favoury vein which runs through the whole of thefe difcourfes muſt neceffarily gain a general acceptation, and with the divine bleffing afford both profit and delight. It is proper farther to inform you, that this collection has been made in conformity, in fome meafure, to a plan our deceafed friend had formed a little before his laſt illnefs, which was to lay together in a plain and concife manner, the fcripture evidences for the feveral principal doctrines of the Gofpel, and to employ a confiderable part of each difcourfe in a large and familiar reprefentation of the importance and influence of thefe great truths in the Chriſtian's life of faith and holinefs: the five firſt Sermons were compofed upon this plan; illnefs prevented a farther profecution of it, nor was he able to review them for the prefs, as I know he propofed. Thofe which follow will, it is hoped, appear to have fome degree of conformity to his defign, and yield a fhare of fatisfaction to the intelligent reader.

As to our worthy deceafed friend and brother, it would be but a debt of friendfhip paid to his memory, were I to take this occafion of mentioning fome particulars in his life, which the great intimacy and long continued correfpondence between us have enabled me to lay together; but it may be fufficient juſt to obferve, that he was enabled to fupport the miniſterial character, with reputation and ufefulnefs, for almoſt twenty years. He entered upon the work young, and it pleafed God to own and blefs him, even in his firſt attempts, for the awakening, quickening, and reviving the ſouls of many, eſpecially of young perſons, in the congregation where he miniſtered. From his firſt entrance upon the ſacred office, I have good reaſon to think his heart was very ſeriouſly turned, and in a good degree engaged, upon theſe two great branches of miniſterial care and concern, " The ſaving our own ſouls and them that hear " us." How truly his mind was bent in purſuit of heart religion, how cloſe and affecting his inward exerciſes, how great his ſolicitude about his own intereſt in the great ſalvation, while he was thus ſucceſsful in preaching it to others, will moſt naturally appear by the following extract from a letter wrote in the firſt year of his public miniſtry.

Dear Friend,   *Saffron Walden,* 1739-40,

" I TAKE my pen, but know not what to ſay; I am full
" of complaints and have too much reaſon to be ſo; I
" complain, and yet am unconcerned; I fear, yet am ſtu-
" pid; it will be a mercy if God give me not up to an
" hardened frame. My mercies have made but little im-
" preſſion, love commonly conſtrains, but it ſeems other-
" wiſe with me; mercies are forgotten, and ſins too much gra-
" tified. Therefore if I enjoy any comfort, I fear it is only ima-
" ginary; it is a mercy to diſtinguiſh between the conſolations
" of the ſpirit and the flows of affection; it is pleaſant to have
" the affections raiſed in duty, and I fear I often take this
" for ſomething higher. Duties are pleaſant to God's
" people, but burdenſome to me; ſpiritual mindedneſs I
" know but little of, carnal mindedneſs I am too much ac-
" quainted with, and that we know iſſues in death. In
" ſhort, if I am a child of God, I am ſure I behave not as
" ſuch; if I have an intereſt in Chriſt, the leaſt, the weakeſt,
" the moſt unworthy and contemptible need not to be
" afraid; but if I am an hypocrite! Oh! let every one
" ſearch their own hearts, examine themſelves, and keep a
" diligent watch, leſt, when weighed in the balance, they

"are found too light : for common convictions may carry
"us very far. I bless God my worth'ess labours have been
"beyond expectation blessed, to the good of some souls, but
"I may be a cast away myself, &c."

These deep concerns about vital religion in himself were connected with as genuine a desire, and endeavour, to promote the same in the hearts of others. As he advanced in life, he seems to have been growingly solicitous to advance the interest of religion where providence had placed him. In the course of our correspondence, his letters frequently expressed his great concern about the success of his ministrations. What special methods could be taken to stem the tide of immorality and prophaneness? What, to quicken and revive the spirit of religion amongst professors? What could be done particularly with young persons, to bring them to a serious sense of things? &c. were inquiries, which appeared often to lie near his heart, and were the leading topics of our epistolary converse. In one of his letters, he lays open the result of his own observation, experience, and concern, in respect to a material branch of ministerial duty, with that judgement, humility, and freedom of thought, as rendered it not a little profitable as well as pleasant in the first perusal; it may be so to others, and therefore I hope without offence transcribed.

Dear Brother,   *Pool,* 19 *March,* 1751.

"I Am sorry to find you complain of the state of re-
" ligion amongst you, &c.——Infidelity abounds, and
" Christians grow cold and lukewarm: Ministers labour, and
" in a great measure in vain; sufficient causes of lamenta-
" tion these: Yet both ministers and private Christians have
" reason to be ashamed of their frequent neglect of those
" important duties, a serious and regular discharge of
" which, has a tendency to revive the power of religion;
" though I am fully sensible nothing will do without the
" presence of the spirit of God, yet so far as we live in the
" neglect of any means, so far we are certainly culpable.

" The great defect in serious Gospel ministers in the pre-
" sent day, I apprehend is impertinent conversation, and
" not labouring in private, to imprefs upon the minds of
" their hearers, a sense of what is delivered in public. If
" our visits were more religious, we might hope to find our
" labours more owned When we are in Christian company,
" where we may use the utmost freedom, how backward to
" a serious enlivening conversation! And we can spend
" perhaps an whole evening amongst our less religious hear-
" ers, and not drop a single word that favours of the real
" power of godliness. I speak too much by experience,
" having often lost a disposition to converse about the things
" of God, by impertinent chat, &c. It is a difficult mat-
" ter to retain a serious temper, and an inclination to inter-
" mix with indifferent subjects, serious and suitable reflec-
" tions. We are either ashamed, or afraid, to speak for
" God ; or else our inclination is wanting, or some trifling
" excuse or other keeps us from the discharge of our duty.
" I am often convinced of my neglect, and promise to strive
" against it ; but I am soon overcome with fear, or filled
" with that shameful modesty which is a great hindrance to
" usefulness. It is certainly a minister's duty to preach in
" private and to use plainness and faithfulness : when in-
" stead of inforcing in private what we preach in public
" we readily join in impertinent talk, unrenewed persons
" are hardened in their impenitency, and if they have had
" any convictions, upon this they presume to take encou-
" ragement, either to think well of their state, or to think
" there is nothing in religion ; by which means our public
" performances are despised, or looked upon as a mere form.
" It is necessary then that we use plainness with sinners in
" private, as well as publicly admonish them, and talk with
" them about their souls in the most serious and affec-
" tionate manner, if we would be successful. I am only
" telling you, how it has been with me ; I hope God has
" given some others a greater measure of resolution, and
" grace, to stand up for him : yet as this is too generally
" the case, and you may have found something of it, let us
" resolve, in a dependence upon our great master, to add
" this to all our other endeavours ; hoping to find success
" in a greater measure crowning our imperfect labours in
" the conversion of souls. Infidelity appears more and more

"barefaced; it requires courage and resolution now, to
"confess Christ before men: things cannot continue long
"in the present posture, either a reformation, or some fore
"judgement. God grant it may be the former! I cannot but
"entertain great hopes from those means in town which
"are made use of, to send serious Gospel minister's out,
"&c. I have lately, I bless God, been more deeply impres-
"sed with a sense of the worth of souls, the awfulness of
"death and eternity, than usual, though I could wish it did
"stir me up to greater diligence, in the pursuit of eternal
"blessings: I have such a sense of the awfulness of dying
"in a state of suspence, that I cannot bring my mind to give
"up the point to God, from whom I am sensible I deserve
"no favour, yet I cannot but beg for a cheerful frame in a
"dying hour, to bear a testimony to the truth God enables
"me to deliver. Oh happy case, when the soul is enabled
"to bid a cheerful farewel to time, and boldly ventures
"into eternity, secure of eternal life, through a dear Re-
"deemer."

How far my deceased brother was enabled to conduct himself in after life, according to the excellent and important view of pastoral duty, above expressed, you and others are best able to witness; so far it is evident he did, as to gain your sincere love and esteem, and with such success in connection with other duties of his station, as to be instrumental, of reviving and increasing the interest of religion among you, and of giving a very pleasing prospect of the church's farther enlargement and prosperity.

Amidst the pleasing scene of harmony and usefulness, and at an age of life, which promised much longer public service to his generation, it pleased the wise, the sovereign God, to put a period to his days, and bereave you of so amiable a friend,—so faithful and active a servant, in your best interests. The greater is your loss! A loss which many besides yourselves deplore. But, " The will of the Lord be " done," is the language of filial submission; " And shew " me wherefore thou contendest with me," is the language of humble prayer, which our heavenly father allows, yea which he calls for, from his people under all such mournful and striking instances of his displeasure. And may I not add the well chosen text, at the late funeral solemnity, Job xix. 21. " Have pity upon me, have pity upon me, Oh my "friends, for the hand of the Lord hath touched me;" is still the sorrowful language of a widowed church and interest, which labours under the singular discouragement of this declining age, wherein it is a very difficult thing, fully and speedily to repair so great a breach. Yet as a considerable allay to our grief, and encouragement to our own hopes towards God, it deserves to be remembered, how mercifully the Lord dealt with him in his last illness! What had been matter of his earnest prayers, years before, as expressed at the close of the above letter, was now the matter of his happy experience The evening of his life was serene, and without a cloud; heaven was in his eye, and much of heaven appeared to be in his heart; he was enabled to bear testimony to the truths he had preached, and to take a cheerful farewel of time, comfortably secure of eternal life through a dear Redeemer.

And now my Christian friends permit me to take leave, with reminding you, that Jesus the great shepherd still lives; lives to exercise the tenderest care over his humble dependant flock. The promise yet stands, "I will give you pas-"tors according to my heart." Jer. iii. 15. His power and faithfulness are yet engaged, in the conveyance of that, and every promised good; the residue of the spirit is still with him: he can, and I trust will yet appear for you, will direct and unite your choice, in another useful instrument for your continued prosperity, and the furtherance of your spiritual and everlasting advantage. Only remember your solemn engagements, who are church members, to one another, as well as to the Lord; your Church relation continues, though your ministers are mortal; keep together in God's fear, and cheerfully expect his presence among you. That this may be your constant experience, is the earnest prayer of your

Sincere friend and servant,

for Christ's sake,

Jan. 1. }
1768. }

J. CONDER.

CONTENTS.

SERMON I.
On Original Guilt.
Gal. iii. 22. *But the Scripture hath concluded all under sin*—— Page 17

SERMON II.
On Original Pollution.
The same Text. 34

SERMON III.
On Human Impotency.
The same Text. 51

SERMON IV.
On the Trinity of Persons in the Divine Essence.
1 John v. 7. ——*And these three are one.* 68

SERMON V.
On the Deity of Christ.
Rom. ix. 5. —*Who is over all, God blessed for ever.* 84

SERMON VI.
On Justification, what it is.
Gal. ii. 16. *Knowing that a man is not justified by the works of the law, but by the faith of Jesus Christ, even we have believed in Jesus Christ; that we might be justified by the faith of Christ, and not by the works of the law: for by the works of the law shall no flesh be justified.* 98

SERMON VII.
Man's Righteousness Insufficient.
The same Text. 111

SERMON VIII.
By Chrift's Righteoufnefs.
Phil. iii. 9. *And be found in him not having my own righteoufnefs—* page 127

SERMON IX.
On the Imputation of Chrift's Righteoufnefs.
The fame Text. 142

SERMON X.
Juftification by Faith.
Rom. v. 1. *Being juftified by faith, we have peace with God, through our Lord Jefus Chrift.* 156

SERMON XI.
How Faith Juftifies.
The fame Text. 169

SERMON XII.
The Freenefs of Grace in Juftification.
The fame Text. 179

SERMON XIII.
The Chriftian Warfare and Conqueft.
2 Tim. iv. 7. *I have fought a good fight—* 195

SERMON XIV.
The Chriftian's Courfe.
2 Tim. iv. 7. —*I have finifhed my courfe*— 208

SERMON XV.
Steadfaftnefs in the Faith.
2 Tim. iv. 7. —*I have kept the faith.* 224

SERMON XVI.
The Chriftian's Crown.
2 Tim. iv. 8. *Henceforth there is laid up for me a crown of righteoufnefs, which the Lord, the*

righteous Judge shall give me at that day: and not to me only, but unto all them that love his appearing. page 238

SERMON XVII.
The Christian's Love to an unseen Saviour.
1 Pet i. 8. *Whom having not seen ye love; in whom though now ye see him not, yet believing ye rejoice with joy unspeakable and full of glory.* 254

CONTENTS,

Of the Pleasantness of a Religious Life.

Prov. iii. 17. *Her ways are ways of pleasantness, and all her paths are peace.* 285
Chap. I. The Explication of the Doctrine. 292
Chap. II. The Pleasure of being religious, proved from the nature of true Religion, and many particular instances of it. 305
Chap. III. The Pleasantness of Religion, proved from the provision that is made for the comfort of those who are religious, and the privileges they are entitled to 322
Chap. IV. The Doctrine further proved by Experience. 338
Chap. V. The Doctrine illustrated by the similitude used in the Text, of a pleasant way or journey. 347
Chap. VI. The Doctrine vindicated from what may be objected against it. 356
Chap. VII. The application of the Doctrine. 368

A Church in the House.
1 Cor. xvi. 8. —*With the Church that is in thine House.* 388

SERMON I.

GAL. iii. 22. FORMER CLAUSE.

But the scripture hath concluded all under sin—

OF all kinds of knowledge, that which relates to our everlasting interest is the most important, and particularly that of *one's self*. This is absolutely necessary to our knowing Christ aright, and therefore is so, to our salvation; and is what the spirit gives, when he begins a gracious work in the soul. Yet what is more neglected? How curious are persons to inquire into the works of creation! How diligent in searching into the histories of nations and countries! How careful are many to view and examine this outward fabric the body, with all its various surprising parts! but never inquire into their state God-wards! They never ask, what that guilt is we all lie under, and whether it is removed, but appear to be contentedly ignorant of these most momentous concerns; all which shows the sad effects of the fall, in that blindness and stupidity we are naturally under, and should fill us with the deepest humiliation Nay, notwithstanding our picture is exactly drawn in God's word, and our state represented as awful and deplorable, we will not *believe* it; at least, we will not *attend* to it, though we are in danger of falling into everlasting misery; for *the scripture has concluded us all under sin*.

The great design of the apostle in this epistle was to establish the doctrine of justification by the righteousness of Christ, and to guard the Galatians against a dependence upon the law. He therefore makes use of a variety of arguments for this purpose, particularly in the verse before our text, says, that if there had been a law which could have given us an unquestionable title to eternal life, then there would have been no need of a mediator; as our justifying righteousness would have consisted in a conformity to that law: but this is far from being the case, for *the scripture hath concluded all*, both Jews and Gentiles, *under sin*, and therefore under an incapacity of being justified by any obedience of their own, that so the free promise of life and salvation through faith in Jesus Christ, might be fulfilled to all who should be enabled to believe in him. Thus we have in the words an awful and affecting account of our state by nature, and a glorious intimation of gospel grace; the one to humble, the other to encourage and quicken us. It is the first of these I am now to consider, and may the view of it suitably imprefs each of our hearts, that under a sense of our lost condition we may be thankful for, and may be stirred up cheerfully to embrace the saviour whom God has provided. The great truth then that lies before us is this, viz. *That all mankind are concluded under, or are naturally in a state of sin.* There is not an individual that can be excepted, but all are alike. And this is not a fancy, a human fiction, but is a truth built upon divine testimony, and supported both by the Old and the New Testament. The *scripture* hath concluded us all under sin. To lay open this truth as it appears in scripture, I must represent it under the three following most affecting views.

I. We are all under the guilt of sin.
II. We are all under the pollution of sin.
III. We are all under its power and government.

These three things give us a just view of human nature, and show the miserable state we are all in, from the oldest to the youngest, so long as we are destitute of the grace of God. This is the state in which the Father viewed us when he laid the plan of our salvation, and chose a number of the fallen race of Adam to be his peculiar people. This is the state in which the Son of God viewed us, when he undertook to redeem us, and came actually to accomplish it. And this is the state in which the Spirit finds us, when he comes to apply the blessing of salvation to us. Particularly,

I. We are all under the guilt of sin. This is the case not only with men of years, but with infants of a day old. None are excepted but our Lord Jesus Christ, who descended not from Adam in an ordinary way. To make this truth appear clear, I would

I. Inquire into what is meant by guilt.
II. Prove that we are under the guilt of sin.
III. How it is that we are all guilty. And,
IV. Improve the subject.

I. Let us inquire what is meant by guilt? Guilt is an obligation to punishment on account of sin. When I say, therefore, that we are all under the guilt of sin, I mean, that we are all of us so chargeable with the breach of the law of God, as to be justly bound over by it to punishment. Thus says the apostle, Rom. vi. 23. *The wages of sin is death*, which is agreeable to the threatening which God pronounced upon Adam's disobedience, Gen. ii. 17. *In the day that thou eatest thereof thou shalt surely die.* So that you see, whoever can justly be charged with sin, is brought under an obligation to punishment, by the righteous constitution of God, and according to the nature and demerit of sin. It may not be amiss here to inquire into that punishment which sin renders us obnoxious to. And I cannot give a better description than you have in that excellent form of words, the *Assembly's Catechism*, which gives us this account: *That all mankind by their fall lost communion with God, are under his wrath and curse, and so made liable to all the miseries of this life, to death itself, and to the pains of hell forever.* Let us spend a few thoughts upon this view. And,

1. *By sin we lose communion with God.* Can two walk together except they be agreed? A very important and significant question, which the prophet put to the Jews in the name of God, to convince them of the reason that he had withdrawn his favourable regards from them, Amos iii. 3. When our first parents heard the voice of the Lord God, they attempted *to hide themselves among * the trees of the garden*, sensible of what they had done to prevent all communion with him, and to expose them to his everlasting

---
* Gen. iii. 8.

displeasure. When God did not save his people, nor hear their cries, it was not because he was incapable of doing it, but their iniquities had separated between them and "their God, and their sins had hid his face from them, "that he would not hear*." Sin is so dishonourable to God, that it provokes him to withhold the light of his countenance from the soul, and stop all comfortable communion; an affliction which the Christian too often knows to his grief and sorrow. But,

2. *Sin brings us under the wrath and curse of God.* Every one that believes not in Jesus Christ is under the wrath of God, John iii. 36. And the apostle tells us, Rom. i. 18, that " the wrath of God is revealed from " heaven against the ungodliness and unrighteousness of " men. The curse of the Lord is in the house of the " wicked †;" and therefore you read of the awful curses that were to be brought upon the Israelites, if they did not observe to do all the commandments and statutes of God. Deut. xxviii. 15—20. " Cursed shalt thou be in the city, " and cursed shalt thou be in the field. Cursed shall be " thy basket and thy store. Cursed shall be the fruit of thy " body, and the fruit of thy land, the increase of thy kine, " and the flocks of thy sheep. Cursed shalt thou be, when " thou comest in, and cursed shalt thou be when thou goest " out. The Lord shall send upon thee cursing, vexation, " and rebuke in all that thou settest thine hand unto for to " do." Thus we see that sin imbitters our common mercies, sharpens our afflictions, turns our very table into a snare unto us, and brings down the curse of God upon our persons and upon all we do.

3. *Sin renders us liable to all the miseries of this life, and to death itself.* It is sin that makes man " eat his bread in " the sweat of his brow, till he return into the ground," Gen. iii. 19. Sin brings public judgements and calamities, " famine, and evil beasts, pestilence, and blood, and the " sword," Ezek. v. 17. The righteous themselves shall not escape, or be exempted from trials. Does David sin? David ‡ must feel the smart of the rod too, though a man after God's own heart. There is a difference indeed between the common sufferings of the godly and the wicked,

* If. lix. 1, 2.   † Prov. iii. 33.   ‡ 1 Chron. xxi. 7, 8.   Pf. li.

To the one they are, through diftinguifhing grace, turned into bleffings; to the other they are curfes. To the one they are fanctified, and made a means of preparing for heaven; whereas to the other they are forerunners of everlafting calamities. They all have a fhare in them, and all muft die. And from the account which the apoftle gives us of death, and its relation to fin, we cannot look upon it as a mere neceffary confequence, but the punifhment of fin, Rom. vi. 23, and chap. v. 12.

4. *Sin expofeth us to the pains of hell for ever.* Eternal death, as well as temporal, is the wages of fin. The apoftle appears evidently to carry it farther than death temporal, even to eternal death, becaufe he puts *eternal* life in oppofition to it. And as he eftablifhes it as a general prepofition, *that the wages of fin is death,* without mentioning any particular fin, that by reafon of various aggravating circumftances, may be more heinous than others, fo we may conclude, that *every* fin deferves eternal death. Sin not only renders life uncomfortable, but if not pardoned, death and eternity too; nay, it gives death a fting which will be deftructive of our everlafting peace, and will pierce our fouls through with everlafting forrows. Oh, come and fee the punifhment of fin! An everlafting feparation from all outward * enjoyments. An " everlafting deftruction †
" from the prefence of the Lord and from the glory of his
" power. Weeping ‡, and wailing, and gnafhing of teeth
" in outer darknefs. *A gnawing* worm ||, that dieth not.
" A fire that can never be quenched. Indignation § and
" wrath, tribulation and anguifh. *The fociety of the* devil **
" and his angels. A lake which burneth with fire and
" brimftone †." Dreadful defpair and horror, without one beam of hope. This, all this is the proper defert of fin, what it expofeth us to, and fhall be inflicted upon all thofe who are found out of Chrift. Awful defcription! Such is the punifhment to which fin renders us obnoxious. Let us now,

II. *Endeavour to prove this important point,* viz. *that we are all under the guilt of fin.* It need not take up any of our time to prove the point, was it to be referred only to thofe, who arrive to the years of maturity, fo as to be capable of actual fin; experience fufficiently fhews that there is none, not

* Job vii. 10. † 2 Theff. i 9. ‡ Matt. xxv. 30. || Mark, ix. 44.
§ Rom. ii. 8, 9. ** Matth. xxv. 41. † Rev. xx 10.

even a good man, that liveth upon earth and finneth not.* Therefore, if any are fo infenfible as to efteem themfelves free from fin, they deceive themfelves, and the truth is not in them. We confider not man as grown up, but as he comes into the world, and therefore we include all infants, and affirm that all fuch who have defcended, or fhall defcend from Adam by natural generation, muft be confidered, and are concluded by the fcripture under the guilt of fin. However difagreeable this truth may appear to corrupt nature, it is confirmed by that revelation, which we are to make our guide in all affairs of a religious concern. Thus the apoftle fets the point out in the cleareft light, Rom v. 12, 16, 18. In the twelfth verfe, he abfolutely tells us, " that we all have finned;" and that he does not exclude infants, is plain from the 13th and 14th verfes. In the 16th verfe he fays, " the judgement was by one to " condemnation." The word condemnation is a law term; it fuppofes a charge of guilt, and therefore an obligation to punifhment, the defert of fin. And that this is the cafe with *all*, we are told in the 18th verfe, where it is faid, " judge-" ment came upon all men to condemnation."

This truth is further proved *from the miferies and death of all, even of infants.* See what a train of evils come upon thefe little creatures. They are born to trouble, and therefore feel it as foon as they fee the light. What cries and tears, what pains and agonies, enough to move the hardeft heart! Some foon take their leave, difappoint the wifhes and expectations of their fond indulgent parents, and enter eternity; while others ftay fome days or months to tafte the bitter cup of fufferings, to linger under painful difeafes, till their tender frame is intirely broke, and they yield to all-conquering death. And what can be the reafon of all this but fin? We cannot fuppofe that all this comes by chance to the infant. And, if it come from God it muft be on the account of fin. It would be inconfiftent with our ideas of the infinite goodnefs, love, and compaffion, nay, the infinite righteoufnefs and juftice of God, to confider him inflicting punifhment upon a perfectly innocent creature. Is he a father, and has he no bowels of compaffion? A father indeed takes the rod and corrects his child, but then it is always fuppofed to be for fome inftances of difo-

* 1 John i. 8.

bedience, and where there is a probability of his improving the correction. But in the cafe of infants, they are incapable of reflection, or infenfible of the hand that chaftifeth them, and are not therefore proper fubjects of correction upon that account. It would be confequently afcribing cruelty, feverity, and injuftice to God, whofe character is perfectly contrary to thefe, to reprefent him as putting thefe little helplefs babes to extreme pain and mifery, when they have no manner of guilt. Has this been his ufual cuftom of dealing with innocent creatures? Have the good angels in the courfe of their unfpotted obedience, been under the awful evidences of their Creator's frowns, and felt any kinds of diftrefs; or did our firft parents, when in their innocent condition, groan under any degree of pain? No! it is *fin* that has brought every evil upon us. Befides, if there is any compaffion fhewn to one another, it is to perfons of advanced years, or to infant-children. And therefore it is a fign of the greateft infenfibility and cruelty when a mother, who fhould be all tendernefs, can fo far overpower the ftruggles of nature, as to forget and forfake her fucking child. From the whole then it appears, that an infinitely gracious God would never fuffer affliction and death to feize upon infants, did he not view them under the *guilt of fin*. Thus the fcripture in many places points out *fin* as the caufe of afflictions and death. " Wherefore," fays the prophet, " fhould a living man complain," or grieve; vex, and murmur under his various afflictions, when it is all for the " punifhment of his fins," Lam. iii. 39. The apoftle in the above-mentioned, Rom. v. 12. fays, that " death came into the world by fin," and that the reafon that *all die is* becaufe *all have finned*. Thus it reigned from Adam to Mofes, and has reigned ever fince, even over them that have not finned after the fimilitude of Adam's tranfgreffion. Therefore, as they are fubject to death, and death is upon the account of fin, even as a punifhment, fo thefe infants muft be confidered as *guilty*.

This truth further appears from what the apoftle fays in Eph. ii. 3, that we are " by nature children of wrath, even " as others." That is, that as foon * as we are born, we deferve, lie expofed unto, and are under a law-fentence of

---

* Dr. Guyfe' Paraphrafe. See likewife the note there upon this verfe.

the wrath of God. This is the natural ſtate then of all mankind, not only of the children of diſobedience, but alſo of thoſe who through grace are made heirs of eternal life; not only of grown perſons, but of infant babes. I am now,

III. To inquire *how it comes to paſs that we are all thus naturally under the guilt of ſin.* This can be no otherwiſe than by the imputation of Adam's ſin to us. Now to impute ſin is to charge it upon us, ſo as legally to inflict deſerved puniſhment. We do not mean that the ſin is reckoned to be committed by us; for we did not commit it, but Adam; but it is ſo reckoned ours, upon our being included in him as our covenant-head, that we are puniſhed for it according to the demerit of the ſin. To repreſent this point therefore in a proper light, we muſt conſider Adam as a *public head,* when God made that covenant of life with him, and threatened death upon his diſobedience: the conſequences of that act were not only to affect himſelf, but all that ſhould deſcend from him by ordinary generation. That he was a covenant head appears from his being a figure of Chriſt, Rom. v. xiv. " The figure of him " that was to come." This appears in the following inſtances. The firſt Adam was the head of the covenant of works: the ſecond Adam was the head of the covenant of grace. The firſt repreſented all mankind that ſhould deſcend from him in the common way; the ſecond repreſented all the choſen of the father, all that were given to him. By the one therefore came death; by the other eternal life. You may ſee the parallel fun by the apoſtle in the above chapter. From whence it appears, that if Chriſt was a public head and repreſentative of his ſeed, Adam muſt be ſo of his too, as there are no other inſtances in which he could properly be ſaid to be a *figure of him that was to come.* That it was every way reaſonable that he ſhould repreſent his poſterity, appears, if we conſider, that he was a common parent to all, was perfectly holy, had not the leaſt bias or inclination to ſin, and had a full capacity to fulfil every command, as well as that all would have been put into the poſſeſſion of eternal life, had he continued in his obedience. If the ſcripture repreſent it, we are ſure it is truth, and it is our duty immediately to believe it, knowing that God can do nothing but what is perfectly right.

After the first sin his headship ceased. The covenant broken, all the evils threatened came upon us; so that afterwards, though Adam was a common father, he no longer represented his posterity, but all his after sins were charged upon himself alone. But let us return to what the apostle says in the 5th of Romans for a more direct proof of this truth. Thus when he says, " By one man sin entered into " the world, and death by sin, and so death passed upon all " men, *he adds*, for that, *or* in whom all have sinned." Let but a common reader attend with an unprejudiced mind, and he will easily and readily conclude that the apostles meaning is, that we all have sinned in Adam, and that this is the reason of the death of infants, mentioned in verses 13th and 14th: for, as we have already observed, death is the punishment of sin, and as infants die as well as others, so they must be necessarily concluded to be sinners; but they are absolutely incapable of actual sin, and therefore must sin in their great head, even the first Adam. Thus, verse fifteen, we are said to be dead through the *offence of one*, plainly pointing to Adam mentioned before; and, verse sixteen, judgement was by *one* to condemnation, by *one offence*, or by the *offence of one man*, as in verse eighteen; and, in verse nineteen it is again confirmed, when the apostle says, that by *one man's disobedience* many were made sinners. From the whole of these passages then we may gather this truth, viz. " that in the covenant of works, " Adam represented all his posterity; who were to be dealt " with according as he fulfilled or broke the law; that dis- " obeying the command he entailed guilt upon all his race, " and they therefore have lost communion with God, be- " come liable to all the miseries of this life, to death itself, " and to the pains of hell forever."

But here let it be observed, that " this guilt in all adults " is increased by numberless actual transgressions." We lie not only under the guilt of Adam's first sin, but under the guilt of actual sins which will sink us into an abyss of everlasting misery, unless pardoned through the blood of Christ. We are " transgressors from the womb [*]," have been adding sin to sin, and iniquity to iniquity; so that, if we could reckon them all up, oh how vast the sum! They

[*] Isaiah xlviii. 8.

may fitly be compared to the sand upon the sea-shore for multitude. David says concerning his, that they exceeded the hairs of his head, Pf. xl. 12. Who can draw up the catalogue of his sins, and enumerate every instance of guilt? Who can reckon his sins of omission, and sins of commission, sins of thought, word, and deed, secret and public sins; sins attended with peculiar aggravations, committed against light and knowledge, against conviction and love; sins in every character and relation in life; who can reckon them up? Had we received the desert of our sins, our lives must have been full of misery and wretchedness; nay, we must long ago have taken our dwelling with devouring fire and everlasting burnings. Thus, having taken a view of the doctrinal part of our subject, I come,

IV. And lastly, *to consider what use it may be of to us.* This doctrine appears in a most unfavourable light to many. Some can by no means relish it, and therefore absolutely disbelieve, nay despise and contemn it. Others though obliged to acknowledge it, yet are for treating it rather as a matter of speculation, than of any importance to us. But however disrelishing it may be to flesh and blood, surely it has a tendency to answer some valuable and important purposes, both in promoting the glory of God, and our own present and future welfare; particularly, if this doctrine is viewed aright.

1. *It lays a foundation for admiration, humiliation, gratitude, and obedience.* We must hereby be convinced that our salvation is *perfectly free*, in the contrivance, in the purchase, and in the application of it; because God considered us as fallen, guilty creatures, and therefore as deserving everlasting punishment. And how does this exalt the riches of his free mercy, and call us to stand and admire, and adore! How rich was the grace of the Father, in that whilst we were sinners he laid out the plan of salvation, and cheerfully appointed his own Son to be the Saviour! How inconceivably glorious the love of the Son that he undertook the work, and so readily came to finish it, though attended with so much shame and suffering! How great the love of the Spirit in coming to rescue hell-deserving sinners from unquenchable fire, by leading us to the great sacrifice, and enabling us to lay hold on Jesus for salvation! Here is no room for boasting; that is absolutely unbecom-

ing one who is guilty, and who is saved by free, rich mercy. Under a view of this doctrine then, see how the soul admires infinite grace who has any solid hopes of heaven, and how humble he appears.—" What, says he, " was my name wrote in the Lamb's book of life? Did the " Father look upon me, guilty as I was, and say *deliver* " *him from going down into the pit* * ? And did the son im- " mediately agree, and say, yea, Father, for behold I will " become a ransom for him? What heights and depths, " what lengths and breadths of love! Has the Spirit in " consequence of all this taken possession of my heart? Are " my sins pardoned, and am I an heir of eternal life? " Whence is all this, Oh my soul? A guilty creature par- " doned! A creature deserving hell raised to heaven! Oh " Grace, Grace! free rich mercy to an unworthy wretch! " Lord, I can resolve it into nothing but thy sovereign " pleasure and good-will, and say, *even so, Father, for so it* " *seemed good in thy sight*†! O! what was I, as I came into " the world, but a child of wrath? And why am I not so " now? What was I a few months or years ago, a rebel " against God, increasing, by numberless transgressions, my " guilt? and what am I now? A child of God; Oh, for a " tongue to set forth the praises of God! Oh, for a heart " to love him! what obligations has he laid me under to " him! Why does not a sense of it quicken thee, my soul, " endear the saviour more to thee, engage thee with greater " cheerfulness in his service, and stir thee up to every act, " to every instance of gratitude, and humble and cheerful " obedience? I would chide myself that I am so slothful, " so secure, and that I have done no more for God. Lord " help me to be for ever thine, and to devote that body " and soul which thou hast preserved from the bottomless " pit constantly to thy praise, and bring me at length to " that world, where I shall love, and praise, and worship " thee day and night, for ever and ever." Thus this doctrine may be improved by us But,

2. There is something in this doctrine that tends *to excite us to pity poor sinners, and to use all possible means to open their eyes and bring them to a proper sense of their danger.* Who that has a sense of guilt can forbear dropping a

* Job. † Matth. xi. 26.

tear over the rebellious finner ? Did every minifter fee and confider the ftate, the unrenewed part of his congregation are in, oh how importunate would he be with them to flee from the wrath to come ! With what compaffion would he addrefs them ! Every fentence would come with a peculiar pathos, and he could not certainly be carelefs and flothful. Were but parents properly affected with a view of the ftate of their children by nature, Oh, how would it engage their attention, make every bowel move within them, and put them upon every poffible method to pluck thofe dear parts of themfelves out of everlafting fire ! Come then my hearer, come my child, let me perfonate this minifter, let me act this parent, and expoftulate with thee about thy ftate I muft tell thee this awful truth, that thou art guilty, concluded under fin, and expofed to everlafting burnings, if a ftranger to the Redeemer. Do not think that I tell thee fo out of caprice and humour, out of a cruelty of temper, or merely to affright thee, and render thy life uncomfortable; I only fpeak what the fcripture does, and what thy own confcience often tells thee, wouldft thou but hearken to it; I fpeak it out of tender compaffion to thy foul, and with a fincere view to thy falvation. Believe it, Oh believe it that " thou art a child of wrath," and ferioufly confider it. What are all thy comforts, fo long as thy fins remain unpardoned? How canft thou be at eafe, when every moment thou art expofed to hell ? Is not this " dreadful found " *often* in thine ears * ?" Doft thou not fometimes " flee, " when no man purfueth † ?" Canft thou enjoy a moment's peace, under the guilt not only of Adam's firft fin, but of innumerable actual fins of thy own ? Let me befeech thee to confider thy ftate, confider thy foul, confider eternity and the bar of God ; How canft thou die in fuch a condition ? How wilt thou appear before the fupreme tribunal above ? How wilt thou bear to fee an angry God, or be able to endure that wrath which thou haft deferved ? Oh, to be for ever in the midft of the bottomlefs pit ! The thought one would hope, *fhould*, and thy compaffionate minifter, thy tender parent prays, that it *may* thoroughly ftrike thee. Perhaps thou thinkeft to efcape ; but how can it be ? Did juftice feize upon the Lamb of God, and fill

* Job xv. 21. † Prov. xxviii. 1.

his foul with fo much forrow, and fhalt thou efcape? Doft thou think to pafs unobferved? No; it is impoffible. God is every where prefent *, and nothing paffes unnoticed by him. Thou canſt not poffibly fly from him. Confider this, you who are in the bloom of life; young as you are, you are expofed to hell. You have the guilt of many fins upon you, and if it is not removed you muft be for ever miferable. Art thou old, and yet unconcerned? It is time for *thee* efpecially to awake. How great muft thy guilt be! And fee, the ſtorm is gathering, and all looks black: it will foon break upon thy head to thy everlafting confufion and diftrefs, if fin is unpardoned. Oh, what couldft thou do, were the judge to fummon thee before his bar, and fentence thee to the infernal prifon? Would he be unjuft? Haft thou not finned? Thy mouth then muft be for ever ſtopped, whilſt infinite juſtice is inflicting upon thee that punifhment which is the proper defert of thy fins. The Lord awaken thee therefore before it is too late, and the door of mercy is fhut for ever.

3. This doctrine fhews us *the dreadful nature of fin, and how much we fhould be concerned to guard againſt it*. If one fin ruined Adam and all his pofterity, we may certainly conclude, that nothing is more hurtful than fin. It is an enemy to our temporal and fpiritual comforts, to our peace here and hereafter. It is difhonourable to God, fo difhonourable that immediately upon the commiffion of it, he withdraws his favour and refufes to fmile; the foul is poffeffed with awful fears of an hereafter; the body becomes liable to be diftreffed with painful difeafes, and death comes to feparate thefe two intimate companions, comes with a fting in it, which if not taken away, will fill body and foul with everlafting anguifh. Every fin has an infinite guilt in it, as it is the violation of the law of God, who is a being of infinite perfection. It tends to fink his infinite wifdom into folly; it depreciates his infinite goodnefs, defpifes his omnifcience, and omniprefence, is a contempt of his almighty power, a defiance of his infinite juſtice, a difbelief of his infinite faithfulnefs, offers the higheft affronts to his infinite holinefs, and tends to obfcure all his glory! This, this is fin And can you think lightly of it? or, when con-

* Pfal. cxxxix. 7. 1<.

science is acting a faithful part, and cautioning you against it, can you say, spare it, for it is but a little one? Can you sport with that which cast the angels out of heaven, and our first parents out of paradise, which has slain its thousands and its ten thousands? Can you roll that as a sweet morsel under your tongues, which damned spirits in hell are feeling the sad effects of, and are therefore groaning under the most extreme torments? Oh! consider, when sin entices you, consider and say: " Why should I be thus " foolishly bewitched with sin? Let me not hearken to " this solicitation, and gratify this criminal corruption, let " its pleas be never so powerful. What but sin separated " God and man? And as sure as Adam was ruined by it, " so surely will it eternally destroy my precious soul, if I " pursue it. However beautiful it may appear, and pleas- " ing to flesh and blood, it has the most destructive poison " concealed in it: However sweet it may be in the mouth, " it will be most bitter in the belly; however desirable in " the enjoyment, it will be inconceivably painful in the " review, and ruining in its consequences; therefore, Lord " fill my heart with an irreconcilable hatred of all sin, and " help me by thy grace to be continually upon my guard " that it may not enslave my soul, and cast me into capti- " vity."

4. This doctrine tends to make us *set a peculiar value upon the Gospel, and to stir us up to seek after an interest in that Saviour it reveals.* Are we all guilty, and do we lie naked and exposed to the wrath of God. How pleasing should the tidings of salvation be, how welcome the news of a saviour! How amiable is the gospel! The discoveries it makes are all suited to the circumstances of guilty creatures, not to increase our terror, but to scatter our fears, and enliven our souls with the hopes of eternal life. It brings the news of pardon; pardon bought with the blood of Jesus; pardon for the most unworthy, and those who have contracted the greatest guilt. See, ye the children of Adam, see there is balm in Gilead, there is a physician there to ease your souls. Hear, you whom the law has condemned and cursed, hear the proclamation, and rejoice. " Ho, every one that thirsteth, come ye to the waters, and " he that hath no money, come, buy and eat, yea, buy " wine and milk without money and without price,"

Ifa. lv. 1. If you have nothing to recommend you to God, this is no objection; nay, if you are in the ftate of condemned malefactors, and never fo deferving of death, yet there is encouragement for you in the gofpel, there is free and full pardon: there is a glorious and all-fufficient faviour, who is able and ready to deliver you from the wrath to come; and why do you not rejoice? Why hafte you not to this Jefus, who is holding out the golden fceptre? Is not the news of pardon acceptable to a condemned criminal? does he not receive it with a heart full of joy? Would not every one juftly blame his ftupidity, was he to neglect the profpect of life and liberty? And are not you a thoufand times more reprovable to be fecure under the fentence of eternal death? A fentence which may be executed upon you this very night? Awake, awake ye fleepy dreaming finners, and "turn ye to the ftrong hold as pri-"foners of hope*." The gofpel is now founding in your ears; founding the bleffednefs of pardon, founding the riches of the Redeemer's grace, and the infinite virtue of his blood to deliver guilty fouls from deferved wrath. It is fetting before you a mercy-feat, a throne of grace, and inviting you by the moft endearing motives to feek after falvation. Sure one would think, I need not make ufe of arguments to prefs you to feek after Chrift, when you are " under the wrath of God †." Your hearts fhould leap within you under a confideration of the declarations of the gofpel, a Saviour provided, a facrifice offered and accepted, and a God who can and does " abun-" dantly pardon ‡." Let it be your concern then to have your fouls fprinkled with the atoning blood of the Lamb of God, that the hand-writing which is againft you may be blotted out, and that you may be freed from the condemnation of a broken law.

5. *This doctrine tends to guard us againſt envying the outward condition of an impenitent ſinner, however proſperous, and to make us eſteem ourſelves unſpeakably happy, if our ſins are pardoned.* How inconceivably more happy are the righteous than the wicked? The one, though in circumſtances of outward meannefs and poverty, is truly bleſſed, having " his tranfgreffions forgiven, and his fins " covered ‖ ;" whilft the other is miferable in the midſt of

---

* Zech. ix. 12. † John iii. 36. ‡ Ifa. lv. 7. ‖ Pſal. xxxii. 1.

all his outward abundance, in as much as he is bound over to eternal death.—What means then this envy, Oh my foul, when I view the " profperity of the wicked, and fee " their eyes ftand out with fatnefs? They are fet in flip- " pery places; they fhall be caft down into deftruction. " How are they brought into defolation, as in a moment? " They are utterly confumed with terrors *. They are " referved to the day of deftruction, and fhall be brought " forth to the day of wrath †. Becaufe they have no " changes they fear not God ‡." They are increafing their guilt, and treafuring up unto themfelves wrath againft the day of wrath. But I, though by nature guilty as they, am plucked as a brand out of the fire, am delivered from all condemnation, and have everlafting happinefs in profpect. Ceafe then to envy the poor finner's little all, and rather let my breaft be filled with tender compaffion. " Rejoice, " Oh young man, in thy youth, and let thy heart cheer " thee in the days of thy youth; walk in the ways of thine " heart, and in the fight of thine eyes, but know thou, that " for all thefe things God will bring thee into judgement ||. " What will all thy *carnal mirth be, but* as the crackling " of thorns under a pot §?" Thou wilt make a little flafh, a little noife, and then thy fins will fink thee down into everlafting darknefs and forrow. Ceafe then every angry paffion, and let me rejoice that my ftate is not like theirs.

6 *This doctrine teacheth us to be humble and fubmiffive under all our afflictions.* We are too ready to murmur and repine under the various difappointments, and afflictive difpenfations we are exercifed with, and to accufe God of feverity and injuftice, but a confideration of our being guilty creatures is enough to put a ftop to every reflection, and to forbid the leaft uneafy thought.—' Shall I cenfure ' the conduct of divine providence, or think it hard that I ' am ftripped of this and the other comfort, when, if God ' had been ftrict to mark mine iniquities, he might have ' taken all from me, and have fent my foul to the bottom- ' lefs pit? Do I not deferve it? Why fo angry, my evil ' heart? Why doft thou rife up in rebellion againft that ' God, who has ' punifhed thee far lefs than thy iniquities ' deferve **! I will bear the indignation of the Lord, there-

* Pfal. lxxiii. 4, 7, 18, 19. † Job. xxi 30. ‡ Pfal. lv. 19. || Ecc. xi. 9. § Ecc. vii. 6. ** Ezra ix 13.

"fore,' whatever it is, 'becaufe I have finned againſt him *.'
'Lord, do what thou pleaſeſt with me and my comforts;
'I muſt and will juſtify thee in all thy proceedings, and
'ſubmit with the utmoſt cheerfulneſs to thy various diſpen-
'ſations: nay, I would bleſs thee that thou art dealing ſo
'gently with me; that thou art not taking away my all,
'and giving me an awful view of everlaſting diſtreſs and
'miſery. Do with me therefore whatſoever ſeems good
'in thy fight.'

Thus we ſee how this doctrine may be improved. It may be of uſe to the ſinner, to ſtrike him with a conviction of his guilt and wretchedneſs, and to ſtir him up to ſeek after an intereſt in the Redeemer. It may be of uſe to the Chriſtian too, by filling him with admiration and thankfulneſs for deliverance from the guilt of ſin, by quickening him to all humble obedience, by keeping him from an envious diſpoſition, and by engaging him to behave with the moſt cheerful ſubmiſſion under all the various diſpenſations of providence.

* Micah vii. 9.

SERMON II.

GAL. iii. 22. FORMER CLAUSE.

But the scripture hath concluded all under sin—

WHEN we look into heathen countries, and confider their aftonifhing ignorance, we have the greateft reafon to be thankful for that revelation which God has diftinguifhed us with, and which removes the mifts of darknefs from us, and leads us into the knowledge of truths of everlafting importance. The doctrines of original fin, juftification and falvation by Jefus Chrift, are infinitely above the reach of nature, and would not have been known by us, had it not been for this facred word. The heathens found their minds agitated with a variety of moft ungovernable paffions, and that they were expofed to all manner of pains and afflictions, yea even to death itfelf, as foon as they came into the world, but they were at the utmoft lofs to know the rife and fpring of all this. What they were ignorant of, the fcripture declares to us, fhews us the origin of evil, concludes us all under fin, and tells us how we became guilty, and fo liable to all the miferies of this and a future world.

We have already confidered the fcripture account of original guilt—What is meant by it—That we are all under it—How it came about; and have endeavoured to point out the ufe and importance of this truth both to the finner and the believer. We now come to take another view of original fin, as *polluting our natures*, for this view the fcripture gives us of it. And it is a truth of equal importance with the other, though by no means fuitable to the polite taste of the present age. To set this truth in a clear light, and so, as it may tend properly to affect our hearts, I would take the following method.

I. *Consider what this pollution is, with the extensiveness of it.*

II. *See what proofs we have of it, and how we are to account for it.* And,

III. *Shew the use and improvement of this doctrine,* which I hope will be sufficient to convince us all of its great importance.

I. Let us consider *what this pollution is, with the extensiveness of it.* And now we come to take a further view of the death of the soul. Sin has not only robbed us of the favour of God and exposed us to his displeasure, but it has occasioned a melancholy alteration in us, defaced all the beauty we had, and has rendered us worse than the beasts which perish; sin has destroyed the image of God in us; has depraved our whole nature, and is a constant spring and fountain from whence proceed all the streams of actual transgressions. And this is the sad case with every individual of the human race.

1. *Through sin the image of God is destroyed in us.* We read that when God made man, he made him after his own image. Thus, Gen. i. 26. " God said, let us make man " in our image, after our likeness." And we find he did so, ver. 27. " So God created man in his own image, in " the image of God created he him, male and female cre-
" ated he them." And Gen. v. 1. " In the day that God " created man, in the likeness of God made he him." This image, as the Assembly's Catechism well expresses it, consists in knowledge, righteousness, and holiness, with a dominion over the creatures. It chiefly lay in a resemblance which man had of God in his soul. Thus it consisted in knowledge. Agreeably to which the apostle says, Col. iii. 10. " Put on the new man, which is renewed in know- " ledge, after the knowledge of him that created him." He had a perfect understanding of the law of God, and a large measure of wisdom and knowledge to direct and lead him, which is partly restored when the spirit comes to open our eyes and bring us again into the divine likeness. It consists in righteousness and holiness, as the apostle says,

Eph. iv. 24. " Put on the new man, which after God, is " created in righteoufnefs and true holinefs." He was free at his creation from every blemifh, had not the leaft irregularity in his foul, nor the leaft imperfection, but had an intire conformity to God in every faculty. And to this we may add the dominion he had over the creatures who were all brought to Adam * to yield their united fubjection to him, and to receive their refpective names from him. This image, fin upon its entrance, has fadly defaced. Our gold is become dim, and our fine gold is much corrupted; our beauty is gone, wo unto us that we have finned. We have loft that which was the glory and excellency of the creature, and the crown is fallen from off our heads. Where is that wifdom and light neceffary to difcern between good and evil, to guide us in the way of duty, and to guard us againft every error ? Where is that ready fubjection of foul to God, that fweet acquiefcence and joy in him; that holy awe of him, that care to pleafe him, and that conformity to him that was fo confpicuous in man at his firft formation ? Where is that regularity and harmony amongft all the faculties of the foul, that orderly fubjection of one to the other, and that ready union in divine exercifes, which appeared in our innocent parent ? We have loft our higheft glory, our original rectitude and purity, and our dominion over the creatures too. Inftead of paying their proper homage, and being ready to ferve us according to their ability, they naturally run from us, rebel againft us, and would fet up a fovereignty of their own. And thus we fee the lofs we have fuftained through fin; but this is not all; for,

2. *There is an actual pollution of our whole nature.* It has feized upon the whole man. Body and foul feel the fad effects of it. It has fpread its contagion throughout the creature, and turned every part from that end to which it was directed. Let us take a view of the foul: and we fhall find the underftanding awfully darkened, fo that no true fpiritual light is to be found in it, till the fpirit comes and opens our eyes, and gives us the light of the knowledge of the glory of God in the face of Jefus Chrift. Therefore when God effectually calls a finner, he calls him " out of

* Gen. ii. 19, 20.

"darkness into his marvellous light." 1 Pet. ii. 9. The will, instead of being obedient to the divine will, and choosing that which is good, is full of prejudice and rebellion against God, saying to him, "Depart from me; for I "desire not the knowledge of thy ways. What is the Almighty, that I should serve him? and what profit should "I have, if I pray unto him?" Job xxi. 14, 15. Our affections are sadly depraved, and therefore naturally cleave to nothing but evil, having a distaste to every thing that is of God. Instead of mourning over sin, we lament our wordly disappointments, and are concerned that we have not the opportunities we desire of gratifying our ambition, pride, covetousness, or love of pleasure. Instead of rejoicing in Christ, and in the hope of the glory of God, all our joy lies in the narrow compass of earth and sense, and so ebbs and flows with outward comforts. Instead of esteeming the most amiable objects, we love that which we should hate, and desire and long after that which is dishonourable to God, and ruinous to our immortal souls. Instead of being afraid of sin, and of offending God by it, we are rather afraid of temporal evils, and our greatest concern is to avoid that which is painful and disagreeable to flesh and blood. Once more, instead of fixing our hopes upon the glorious realities within the veil, we confine them to the short-lived happiness of the present state. We are crying out, "who will shew us any good *," and are "spending "our strength for nought, and our labour for that which "profiteth not †." Our affections are upon the whole all carnal, fixed either upon unlawful objects, or else upon those that are lawful, in an immoderate degree. Our memory is depraved too, so that we retain not spiritual things, but soon lose ‡ them, though we can easily remember and are ready to treasure up that which is impertinent and sinful. Our thoughts and imaginations are evil, and are naturally ready to run after things most criminal and displeasing to God. Nay our bodies are partakers of, or are affected with the contagion too, for we "yield our members as instru"ments of unrighteousness unto sin." Rom. vi. 13. Thus our whole nature is defiled; we are all over sin. "From "the crown of the head to the sole of the foot, we are full

* Psal. iv. 6. † Isa. lv. 2. ‡ Psal. cvi. 13, 21.

"of wounds, and bruises, and putrifying sores," in a spiritual sense, so that there is " no soundness in us*." This, this is our state by nature, this our case as we come into the world. And further,

3. *This is a constant spring and fountain in us, from whence proceed all actual transgressions.* These are as so many streams from it: they are so many branches sprouting out from this root. From hence proceed evil thoughts, murders, adulteries, fornications, thefts, false witness, blasphemies and every evil word and work. Every sin is virtually contained in this, and arises from it. It leads one to sensuality and uncleanness, another to pride, another to covetousness, another to infidelity. It pushes one to acts of cruelty and inhumanity, another to blasphemy. It shews itself in an open contempt of divine things in one, in another in hypocrisy and deceit. It is to be found in all the natural descendants, of Adam. It comes into the world with us, and it equally defiles us all. None but the holy one of God was perfectly pure, and he was free from all depravity. He bore our sins, and yet was free from sin. He was tempted by Satan, but the prince of this world found nothing in him; for though he was made of a woman, yet he was conceived by the power of the Holy Ghost in the womb of the virgin, and therefore was absolutely without a spot. Thus we see the deplorable state of all mankind. Let us now,

II. *Inquire what proofs we have of the point, together with the reason of it.* We must go back to our first parents to find out the cause. Adam is not only to be considered as a covenant-head and representative of his posterity, but as their natural root. In one view, guilt is imputed to us, in the other, he conveys a corrupt nature. Defilement therefore has been propagated from father to son in all ages and generations hitherto, and will be so to the end of time. And however we may be at a loss to know how the soul, which comes pure from God, is corrupted, yet it is an undeniable fact, and so, as that he is by no means the author of sin. That this defilement is universal, appears,

1. *From scripture representations of the matter.* Thus it is said that " Adam begat a son in his own likeness, after

* Isa. i. 6.

" his image." Gen. v. 3. It would be a low interpretation to say, that all that is meant by it is this, that he begat a child who had all the features and parts of a human creature. The words appear to be more significant, *viz.* that the son he had came into the world with the same corrupted image which he himself bore after his fall. This therefore seems to be put in opposition to that likeness of God in which man was at first created, and which is mentioned in the first verse. Again, when " God saw that the " wickedness of man was great in the earth," he adds, " and " that every imagination of the thoughts of his heart was " only evil continually," Gen. vi. 5. Who that reads these words but must immediately conclude that there is a corrupt fountain in the heart, else the imaginations that are in the heart could never be *only evil, and that continually.* This is more fully delivered in Gen. viii. 21. where God says, " that the imagination of man's heart is evil from his " youth," from his childhood, so that he comes into the world with a depraved heart. Job therefore represents the impossibility of our being pure, by asking, " who can bring ",a clean thing out of an unclean?" Job xiv. 4. He easily answers it, and says, *not one.* It cannot be. Can an impure fountain send forth pure streams? " Can a corrupt tree " bring forth good fruit? Or, of thorns do men gather figs, " or of a bramble-bush gather they grapes?" We may as reasonably expect this to come to pass, as that from a corrupt root should spring a pure offspring. If Adam had continued innocent, he would have had an innocent and holy seed, but falling, and his nature being tainted with sin, it comes thus from him to all his posterity. And therefore Job again asks, chap. xv. 14. " What is man that he " should be clean; and he who is born of a woman, that he " should be righteous?" Bildad believed this important truth, when he says, Job. xxv. 4. " How then can man be " justified with God, or how can he be clean that is born " of a woman?" David had a deep sense of the sinfulness of his nature, when he says, " behold I was shapen in ini- " quity, and in sin did my mother conceive me." Psal. li. 5. We have no reason to believe that David is here lamenting over some heinous sin that his father and mother had been

* Luke vi. 43, 44.

guilty of. To charge them with a deteſtable crime, only to evade the truth of a particular text, when there is nothing in all ſcripture to ſupport it, is indecent and unbecoming a Chriſtian, and ſhews that we had much rather be guilty of forgery and falſehood, than yield to a doctrine ſo unſuitable to our natural pride. Beſides, David is not in this Pſalm lamenting the ſins of others, but his own ſins, and therefore goes to the root, and ſhews how his very frame was formed in ſin, that it is therefore inſeparable from his nature, and came into the world with him. Theſe paſſages then make this point appear evident to an unprejudiced mind, and tend to eſtabliſh us in this awful truth, the corruption of our nature. " Whatſoever," ſays our Lord, " is born of fleſh is fleſh," John iii. 6. It is a certain truth that *like produceth like.* We cannot ſuppoſe then that Adam's children could be free from corruption, when the ſtock from whence they came was all polluted. They muſt have the ſame nature conveyed to them; from them it muſt come to others, and ſo will be propagated to the lateſt poſterity. But,

2. *This truth is evidently proved by the ordinances of circumciſion and baptiſm.* Circumciſion was not only deſigned as a ſtanding memorial of God's regard and care for the Jews, as long as that diſpenſation continued, but was intended to point out the impurity of the heart, and the neceſſity of its being cleanſed, that they might be the real children of God, and be fitted for the enjoyment of him. As long as this ordinance therefore remained in the church, and was attended to, it was a ſtriking repreſentation of the corruption of nature, even in children of eight days old. Thus baptiſm under the preſent diſpenſation is deſigned to be a ſtanding proof of the ſame important truth. The regenerating and ſanctifying influences of the ſpirit are repreſented by water *; and as water is made uſe of by divine appointment in this ordinance, ſo it has a reference to this ſpiritual bleſſing, and therefore muſt neceſſarily ſuppoſe impurity, and that our ſouls are polluted as we come into the world. But,

3. *This truth evidently appears in the temper and behaviour of children and others.* Solomon ſays, " that fooliſh-

* Ezek. xxxvi. 25. Tit. 3, 5.

'nefs is bound up in the heart of a child," Prov. xxii. 15. and the Pfalmift, " that the wicked are eftranged from the " womb, they go aftray as foon as they are born, fpeaking " lies," Pfal. lviii. 3. If nature was not corrupted, could we fuppofe that all would be led by the influence of example into fin? Some are favoured with the privilege of godly parents, and therefore with a religious education. Their tender relatives early inftruct them in the principles of Chriftianity, and endeavour to inftil in their minds fentiments truly evangelical, recommend the ways of God to them, exhort, intreat, and take every method to guard men againft fin, and lead them to holinefs, inforcing all by a fuitable and becoming example. But you fee how many under all thefe advantages difcover the greateft inclinations to fin, and the ftrongeft prejudices againft God. Cain, notwithftanding the opportunities he had of inftruction, yet difcovered the depravity of his heart by deftroying his own brother, becaufe God had given him fuch teftimonies of his acceptance of Abel's facrifice. Yea, thofe children, who have appeared under the moft early religious impreffions, have yet given many evidences of a polluted nature, and made it manifeft that they came into the world impure. Elfe what means that pride, envy, refentment, and other criminal gratifications fo obfervable in them. It is ftrange if the babe is perfectly innocent and pure, that before he can well form an articulate found, he fhould be paffionate, obftinate, and difobedient, and that not a fingle inftance could ever yet be found, except the holy Jefus, of a child's withftanding the influence of every evil example, and of walking in a perfect courfe of unfpotted holinefs. The reafon plainly is this, that every one has enough in his heart for temptations to work upon, and therefore that all are depraved.

Laftly, *This appears from the experience of the faints.* Thefe fee the odioufnefs of fin, the beauty of holinefs, and are under the influence of the ftrongeft motives, and moft powerful perfuafives to obedience; but fee their numerous backflidings, hear their frequent complaints, their mournful confeffions, all which fhew the fad defilement of nature, which is not perfectly wafhed away. The heart will never be thoroughly pure till the foul gets above. A tree will not be totally deftroyed unlefs you cut it down; to take away a branch will not anfwer the end. ' Sin fays an old divine,

' is like the wild fig-tree, or ivy in the wall, cut off stump,
' body, bough, and branches, yet some sprigs or other will
' sprout out again, till the wall is pulled down." Notwithstanding our high enjoyments, yet sin will discover itself,
and we shall be in danger of being exalted above measure *.
Though we should be engaged in duties, where the presence
of God should enliven us, the fear of God awe us, yet sin
will be there : and what is this but the body of death, the
fountain of corruption, original sin in the heart from which
the believer is not intirely cleansed, whilst he is in the body ?
For the proof of this consult Paul's seventh chapter of his
epistle to the Romans, from the fifteenth verse, and let
every Christian examine his own experience.

Thus I have endeavoured to state and give you some
proofs of this truth, and now come,

III. *To shew the use and improvement of it.* However disagreeable it may appear to our natural pride and self-flattery,
and whatever contempt may be cast upon it as useless and
unprofitable, and only fit for enthusiasts, and persons of
contracted spirits to believe, a serious view of the matter
will easily point out to us, how necessary it is that our
minds should be deeply impressed with a sense of this truth,
because it directly tends to answer the following important
ends.

1. *To keep us ever humble and fill us with self-loathing.*
Humility is an amiable grace, a most beautiful garment, a
robe with which we should be always clothed. And what
tends more to secure us from pride and haughtiness, from
every lofty look and thought, and make us appear low and
despicable in our own eyes, than a serious view, and a suitable sense of our natural depravity ? This keeps the soul
humble in his addresses to God. He dare not now come
in the temper of the boasting Pharisee, but like the penitent
Publican, is ashamed, and smites upon his breast. In his
confessions of sin to God now, how humble! And he does
not only mention and lament over actual sins, but original.
Thus David contented himself not with a mournful acknowledgement of his public sins, but he goes to the fountain head, and laments over its great impurity : " Behold
" I was shapen in iniquity, and in sin did my mother con-

* 2 Cor. xii. 7.

"ceive me," Psal li. 5. As if he had said 'why should I 'dwell upon my actual sins, let me go to their spring and 'source. They are as so many outbreakings of that defile-'ment that cleaves to my heart. Oh let me turn within: 'And see, I am nothing but sin. I brought it into the 'world with me, and therefore have been a transgressor 'from the very womb.' The Christian's petitions are all put up with humility, and accompanied with self-abhorrence, under a sense of his own vileness, and therefore of his great unworthiness to appear before God This keeps him humble under a consideration of that distinction God has made between him and others. "Has the Lord called 'me by his spirit, whilst others remain in darkness and sin? 'let not me ascribe it to any beauty or worthiness he saw 'in me: I am the same by nature with the vilest sinner, 'therefore let a sense of my original depravity be a curb to 'every rising of pride, and keep me continually humble.' This keeps the Christian humble under all his enjoyments and glorious prospects. 'Has the Lord been pleased to fa-'vour me with the light of his countenance, and bring me 'to the top of Pisgah, to give me a view of the promised 'land? Is it day with my soul, whilst it is night with 'many of my fellow Christians? Oh let me yet lie low, and 'not think too highly of myself; let me keep constantly in 'view of the corruption of my heart, and that will 'check my vanity, and make me appear vile and despicable.' Thus likewise, has the Christian been kept from public backslidings; has he walked with God from day to day, made progress in grace, and been careful to maintain good works? Yet so long as he has a proper sense of this truth, he finds enough to lament over, and to convince him that he deserves to be cast out of God s favour and to be separated for ever from him; and thus whilst he is a shining example to others, and is had in reputation among the churches, he is yet kept humble, by a daily view of his own heart. A sense of this truth too guards us against behaving with a haughty and superior air to others, or being lifted up with any outward enjoyments Who art thou that boast-est of thy extraction, thy noble birth, the dignity and antiquity of thy family? Thou wast conceived in sin, and art just upon a level with those thou art ready to despise Who art thou that pridest thyself in thy numerous titles, honours, and preferments? See here is enough to debase thee: and were but thine eyes open to see thy depravity, it would fill thee with self-loathing amidst all thy grandeur; and make thee esteem others equally with or above thyself. Who art thou that art elated with riches, and an abundance of outward enjoyments and cannot stoop to take notice of thy poor neighbour, thou who art ready to look with an air of haughtiness upon all beneath thee, and to claim before others a right to and interest in the favour of heaven? wast thou but to have a suitable sight and sense of the fountain of corruption in thy soul, it would bring down thy loftiness to the ground, make thee look upon all thy riches as empty trifles, fill thee with self-abhorrence, and engage thee to behave with all Christian decency and respect to those who are below thee. Thus in these and all other cases, where there are temptations to pride and haughtiness, a becoming sense of this truth would be a great means of keeping us humble, correcting our tempers and regulating our behaviour. This truth upon the whole, leads us to that poverty of spirit, to which our Lord has annexed real blessedness, and to that excellent frame and temper of mind, which runs through, and is recommended in the whole gospel, and appears so amiable both to God and man, and therefore this truth is of great importance.

2. *This truth greatly enhances and leads us to adore and admire the free grace of God in our redemption, effectual calling, and salvation.* It not only magnifies the grace of God in taking notice of us, who are guilty and therefore unworthy of his favours, but filthy and polluted and so, therefore, contrary to his pure and holy nature. Did the father see us in this condition, when he fixed upon us as the vessels of his mercy? Sure we may well say, why were we not the objects of his abhorrence, having lost his image, and become all over polluted with sin! Did he, who is of purer eyes than to behold iniquity; he in whose sight the heavens are not clean, and who chargeth his angels with folly; did he look upon us in our depravity, and determine our everlasting salvation? Has the Son of God therefore visited this lower world, appeared in fashion as a man, offered up himself a sacrifice upon the accursed tree, and made a complete purchase of all the blessings of salvation for us? Has the Spirit visited our souls, opened our eyes, renewed our hearts,

and partly restored the image of God to us? Did he see us polluted in our blood, and say unto us live? Has God been pleased to manifest himself to us, shed abroad his love in our hearts, and given us the hopes of the everlasting enjoyment of himself? We may surely say, "his ways are not as our ways, nor his thoughts as our thoughts *." Whatever contempt may be cast upon this grace by some, those who have a suitable sense of the evil of sin, and the plague of their hearts cannot but admire the riches of it. The more they view themselves, the more they are astonished at that Grace that chose them, has redeemed, quickened, and given them the hopes of eternal glory. Far, yea very far is this truth from encouraging us to run from God, it leads us to him, fills our souls, when under divine influences, with holy wonder, and presents us with the strongest motives to everlasting love and admiration. Oh, none but the believer can sing the heights, and depths, and breadths, and lengths of the love of God, because none else see properly their own hearts. This makes the mysteries of redeeming saving grace more glorious than all the mysteries of the creation. This engages the attention of angels. ' O, what was I, yea, what was I a few months or years
' ago? In my sins, my understanding a confused chaos, my
' will obstinate and rebellious; my affections all impure;
' nay, what am I now? Does not this body of death still
' continue within me? Do I not find it often leading me
' into captivity to the dishonouring of God? Am I not yet
' carnal and sold under sin? And will God take me into
' his bosom, dwell with and in me? Is he leading such a
' wretch as I am to the top of Nebo, and giving me at
' times a cluster of Canaan's grapes? Oh my soul, for ever
' love this God, admire his Grace and never cease to sing
' his praises."

3. *A sense of this truth tends to convince us of the necessity, reality, and importance of regeneration, and to guard us against a dependence upon an outward reformation.* It is no wonder that he who will not believe the corruption of nature ridicules the new birth, and thinks a change of life to be sufficient to denominate him a Christian. He has never seen the uncleanness of his heart, and therefore in his own

* Isaiah lv. 3.

apprehenfions wants no cleanfing. Has he been a drunkard? If he becomes fober and temperate he thinks it enough Or, has he been a fwearer, or any open or public finner? He is fatisfied by abftaining from thefe notorious immoralities, and more efpecially if he is brought to go through a round of duties, or to a regular attendance upon ordinances; now he cries peace, peace, when he is ftill far from the kingdom of God. Here lies the danger of defpifing this truth Perfons are not aware, how infenfibly a denial of it leads them to a neglect, and often a contempt of real holinefs : whilft on the other hand, when we firmly believe our natural corruption, and efpecially, when we have a becoming fenfe of it, we cannot be contented with an external religion, but muft be feeking after a change of difpofition and heart, as well as a change of life. He who acts confiftently with this belief, and with the voice of this truth, muft reafon in fome fuch manner as this. ' I now fee ' the neceffity of inward holinefs, an inward change, and ' that I may therefore be a hypocrite notwithftanding all ' my fair appearances. Oh, let me fee then that my heart ' be cleanfed. My hopes of heaven cannot be right, if my ' heart is not purified. Let me not then be deceived in a ' matter of fo much importance to my falvation, but feek ' to have the image of God reftored in my foul, which fin ' had deftroyed.' To heal a ftream will not be fufficient ; the fountain itfelf muft be purified. The believer's care is therefore to lay the axe to the root of the tree, and never to be eafy or happy till the body of death is totally deftroyed. Permit me therefore to addrefs you my friends, who are ftrangers to the new birth, and like the Pharifees are only concerned to go through the forms of religion. I muft tell you, and I hope I do it out of real tendernefs and faithfulnefs to your fouls, that you are not fit for the kingdom of God. You may acknowledge that holinefs is abfolutely neceffary to happinefs, but you have never yet been duly fenfible what this holinefs is. You may be outwardly fober and regular, but you have never yet felt the fanctifying influences of the fpirit in your hearts. You have no real knowledge of fin. You fee not its odioufnefs, and how the fad contagion has fpread itfelf through the faculties of your fouls, and thereby rendered you unmeet for the enjoyment of God. You have no true relifh for the fpiritual part of religion, no real love to God in your hearts, no delight in him, and how can you then think of heaven? Can you carry a polluted nature there? Nothing unclean shall ever enter the gates of the New Jerusalem. Besides, could you find admittance, you would have no happiness, because you have no suitableness of soul to the enjoyments and employments of heaven. Let me intreat you to consider, that religion lies not in outward forms. You must be born again. You must have new hearts. Old things must be done away, and all things must become new. You are naturally filthy and polluted, and you must be washed, you must be sanctified by the spirit of God. You must be pure in heart, or else you can never enter into the mansions above. Believe the important truth therefore, and seek with the utmost earnestness to be regenerated, that you may have the image of God in your souls here, and may stand in his presence hereafter, having neither spot, nor wrinkle, nor any such thing.

4. *It is an evidence of the Christian to be made sensible of the fountain of sin in the heart, to mourn over it, and to get it cleansed.* Though the Spirit of God may oftentimes fasten the first conviction upon some actual sin, yet whenever he begins a real work in the soul, he always opens the heart, and gives the awakened creature a view of his uncleanness This you find was the case with Saul when converted. Before, he thought he was blameless, but " when the commandment came sin revived, and he died." Rom. vii. 9. You see therefore how the Spirit opened to him, and set before him the plague of his heart, that though he was chargeable with no public immoralities, yet he had such a view, and such a feeling sense of the corruption within, that he mourned over it, appeared vile in his own eyes, and longed to be delivered from it as that which was his greatest burden. And this you find in a great measure in every Christian. Though he is not all at once led to see what a vile, depraved creature he is, yet as he grows in grace he is more acquainted with himself: and this is his peculiar complaint before God, the darkness of his understanding, the depravity of his will and affections. These lay him low, fill him with real contrition, and warm and earnest desires to be cleansed in the fountain of the Redeemer's blood. With this he struggles as long as he is in

life. The sad remains of sin perplex him daily, lead him often into captivity, unfit him for duties, interrupt him in them, and lay a foundation for deep humiliation, and make him frequently water his couch with tears. 'Oh this body 'of sin, when will it be destroyed? This unclean heart of 'mine, when will it be all pure? I long for deliverance as 'much as a poor captive whose bondage is peculiarly dis- 'tressing. I am burdened, I am burdened; who will take 'off the load? Oh for an understanding free from all dark- 'ness; for every power of my soul to be made perfect! 'Oh for a heart to love God for ever! Blessed be God I 'have the prospect through Jesus Christ my Lord.' We never find that Paul mourned because of his persecutions and afflictions. He was ready not only to be "bound, but "even to die at Jerusalem, for the sake of Christ *;" but when he came to look within, and to see and feel the corrupted fountain, rendering him so unlike God, and filling him with so much coldness, he was grieved; he was cut to the very heart. What can we conclude then from this, but, that all those who are not sensible of the plague and wickedness of their hearts; they who see not their inward depravity, but think themselves perfect, have never yet experienced a saving change. And thus we see the importance of this truth. It is that which the Spirit opens to all his people, as being the great means of bringing them into an evangelical frame.

5. *This doctrine should put us all upon the great duty of examination.* Here let me call upon thee to attend, whilst I put a few questions to thee of everlasting importance. Hast thou ever considered this soul-humbling and awakening truth; or, art thou one of those who cast contempt upon it, as a mere fancy, or art thou passing it by as a matter of speculation? Dost thou believe it as a part of revelation, and hast thou not yet inquired how thou shalt be delivered from it? Hast thou seen and felt this inward corruption, and hast thou been convinced of the necessity of regeneration, and been seeking after it? or, does not a consideration of a loss of God's image, and the depravity of all thy faculties affect thy mind? Art thou apprehending that a mere acknowledgement of this truth is suffi-

* Acts xxi. 13.

cient; and art thou therefore contenting thyself with a zealous vindication of it in opposition to all those who deny it? Doft thou never think of the impossibility of getting into heaven with such a polluted nature, and therefore never inquire how thou shalt get it cleansed? Doft thou never consider that one great part of the Christian's happiness lies in a total deliverance from this body of death? Does it never give thee concern, that thou art unfit for the kingdom of God? What are thy hopes of heaven founded upon; or what encouragement hast thou to hope for eternal life? Is thy soul sprinkled with the blood of Jesus, and art thou in some measure sanctified by his Spirit? A view of this truth will furnish us with a variety of the most important questions to put to our souls, and lay out much work for examination; and therefore it is a truth of great moment, and highly deserving our attention. But,

Lastly, *This doctrine should put the Christian much upon watching and prayer.* We see the Christian is in perpetual danger of falling into sin. We have not only an enemy without us, but we have one within us too. Satan has a friend in our hearts; he sees our pollution, and his concern is to suit his temptations to it; and when sin and Satan are both importunate, it is a difficult matter to stand. How earnest then should we be with God in prayer for his divine presence and assistance, and how watchful over our own hearts, left at any time we should be ensnared? Like sentinels be ever upon your guard, remembering that you are always in danger of a surprise.

Thus we see how important this doctrine is, and what a peculiar tendency it has to be useful to us as to our everlasting interest. I might have mentioned some other instances of its importance; as, that it tends to set off the gospel, and make us highly prize and admire it, for the provision that is made for our sanctification as well as for our justification. It tends to wean the Christian from this imperfect world, and to set him a longing after a better, where all his complaints will be for ever over, and his soul made perfect in holiness. Upon the whole, a right knowledge of original sin is of signal use to us in our way to heaven. It is, says a divine of the last age, the curb of pride, the foil to set off grace, the glass of man, the spur of industry. It is that which makes the best of saints to weep in the best of duties,

G

and the worst of sinners to look pale in their greatest prosperity. Let us not therefore be ashamed of this doctrine, but firmly believe it, and be concerned to get a suitable knowledge of it, that we may not hold it speculatively, but may improve it for the ends and purposes that have been mentioned. Look therefore into the word of God where this doctrine is revealed. Examine your own hearts, and see whether they correspond not with it. And above all, be concerned to look up to the Spirit of God, to open your eyes, and to give you a spiritual discerning of this truth, and to lead you to the blood of Jesus*, *which cleanseth from all sin.* And you who are parents, teach your children early this most affecting doctrine; set before them their pollution; tell them of the necessity of their being born again; and do not take so much pride in seeing them in a gaudy dress, but be concerned to see their souls adorned with the image of God. Not only get them sprinkled with water, and then think you have done your duty, but pray that they may be baptized with the Holy Ghost, that you and yours may be purified and cleansed, and so be fitted for, and at length brought to the mansions above, where you will appear without a spot, and love and praise for ever and ever.

* 1 John i. 7.

SERMON III.

GAL. iii. 22. FORMER CLAUSE.

But the scripture hath concluded all under sin—

THE representations which the scriptures give us of our natural state, though never so just and consistent with truth, are yet highly disagreeable to our corrupt sentiments and inclinations, as they so evidently tend to check our pride and vanity, and to destroy all our self-confidence. The two doctrines we have considered are therefore rejected upon this account: And that we have now in view is equally offensive, and is therefore as much disregarded, though it is never so well supported by the word of God.

The scripture hath concluded us not only under the guilt and pollution, but under the power and government of sin too: so that man *cannot possibly save himself*. This is the great point we are now to prove, and then to improve, or to shew the use and importance of.

That this point may appear clear to every one's understanding, I shall consider man's impotency in two views.

I. *His absolute incapacity to restore himself to the divine favour, and obtain a title to eternal life;* and,

II. *His utter inability to subdue the dominion of sin, and to purge and cleanse his soul from it.* From these views it will appear how weak and helpless man is of himself, and that, had not God graciously undertaken our salvation, we must have perished for ever.

The two great parts of salvation are justification and sanctification; or our being delivered from the guilt of sin, and having a title to eternal life, and our being delivered from the power and being of sin, and so having a fitness for the everlasting enjoyment of God. Man's impotency lies in these two things.

I. *He is absolutely unable to deliver himself from the guilt of sin, recommend himself to the favour of God, and obtain a title to eternal life: Or, he cannot do any thing to justify himself before God.* That we may be justified, two things are absolutely necessary. 1. *That atonement be made for sin.* And, 2. *That we have a perfect righteousness.*

1. *Atonement must be made for sin.* This is the first step towards justification ; and if man is unequal to this, all his attempts to justify himself by a course of obedience will be insignificant, even if he could perfectly fulfil the law. There is a debt that is contracted, and how must this be paid ? We have all sinned in Adam, and have been guilty of violating the law of God in thousands of instances, and how must these breaches be made up ? God has absolutely threatened death upon our disobedience, and how can we escape it ? To say that God will overlook our many past imperfections, if we are but sincere and upright in our walk, is to say that which is contrary to the whole current of scripture, and to reflect upon all the other perfections of the divine nature. The pleas of truth and justice are as powerful and importunate as those of mercy, and therefore demand an equal attention God will not pardon sin, either to depreciate his law, to stain and sink his government, or to sully the glory of his truth, justice, and holiness. He requires a suitable satisfaction therefore, before he will issue out a pardon, that the honour of these may be preserved. The penalty threatened must be borne, and no relaxation granted; and this is his solemn determination, that " without shedding " of blood, there shall be no remission." This appears plainly to be the doctrine of the Old Testament, and therefore represented in the sacrifices that were offered These sacrifices all pointed at the guilt of sin, the demands of justice, and shewed that if we were delivered from the wrath of an offended God, it must be by satisfying these demands : And as they were typical of the great sacrifice, the Lord Jesus Christ, so they plainly represented this soulhumbling truth. Man's weakness and inability to atone for sin by any sacrifices he should offer, or any sufferings he

should endure. " Wherewith shall we come before the Lord,
" and bow ourselves before the high God ? Shall we come
" before him with burnt offerings, with calves of a year
" old ? Will the Lord be pleased with thousands of rams,
" or with ten thousands of rivers of oil ? Shall we give our
" first born for our transgression, the fruit of our body for
" the sin of our soul ?" Mic. vi. 6, 7. All these, were they
in our power, would be absolutely insufficient to repair the
honour of law and justice, so reflected upon by sin. You find
the apostle therefore representing us as " without strength,"
when " Christ died for us." Rom. v. 6. It is evident, that
if man could have made satisfaction to the demands of justice, so that God could have been glorified in our pardon
and salvation, he would not have sent his son to be a propitiation for us. All thy tears and sighs, then, all thy signs
of sorrow and humiliation; all thy sufferings of whatever
kind ; all thy mortifications, thy wasting thy body by ab-
stemiousness and fastings, all bear no proportion to the infinite evil and demerit of sin, and therefore cannot redeem
thy soul from the curse of a broken law. Thus man being
a sinner, is weak and helpless, and therefore lies naked and
exposed to the awful threatening denounced against sin. But,
2. *Besides atonement for sin, we must have a perfect righteousness, or we can never be justified before God.* There
are the same terms of justification now as in the state of innocency. " Do this and live." The law will not admit
of any thing less, neither will infinite justice. That the
obedience that justifies us may be complete, it must be universal, free from all sin, and perpetual. Unless it has these
three properties, it cannot lay any solid foundation for our
expectation of eternal life.

It must be universal. Every divine command must be
obeyed, and none neglected. Therefore the Pharisee's
righteousness was greatly defective, as all he had to say was,
that he was " no extortioner, unjust, adulterer, or so vile
" as the poor Publican ;" that he had " fasted twice in the
" week, and given tithes of all he possessed." Luke xviii.
11, 12. No wonder that our Lord said, " Unless your
" righteousness exceeds the righteousness of the Scribes
" and Pharisees, ye shall in nowise enter into the kingdom
" of God." Mat. v. 20. They paid tithe of mint, and anise,
" and cummin, but they neglected the weightier matters

"of the law, judgement, mercy and faith: Thefe they "ought to have done," as well as "not to leave the other "undone." Mat. xxiii. 23. The curfe of God ftands in full force againft all thofe, who continue not in "all things "that are written in the book of the law to do them." Gal. iii. 10. If one command is laid afide, all our obedience will prove infufficient to juftify us.

But, our obedience muft be *abfolutely perfect too, or free from all fin.* Every command muft be perfectly obeyed in thought, word, and deed. We are greatly miftaken in our natural conceptions of the law. Saul the Pharifee thought himfelf blamelefs, becaufe he had endeavoured ftrictly to obferve the letter of the law, not knowing its full meaning and extent. It requires purity of thought, as well as purity of life; and according to the explanation which our Lord has given us of it, he is not only a murderer in the eye of the law, who actually kills his fellow creature, but who entertains malice and refentment in his heart againft him, or indulges angry paffions: and fo of other things. Matth. v. Thus, "whofoever fhall keep the whole law, *and yet* offend "in one fingle point, he is guilty of all," and therefore is as far from juftification, as if he had broke every command of the law, James ii. 10. Law and juftice will admit of nothing lefs than an abfolutely perfect righteoufnefs as our juftifying righteoufnefs. Again,

Our obedience muft be perpetual. We muft "continue "in all things written in the book of the law to do them," Gal iii. 10. A fingle act, or a few acts of obedience, a day or a year's watchfulnefs againft fin and obfervance of the law will be of no avail to us. Our obedience muft be perfect and complete, and therefore perpetual, elfe we fhall find it intirely infufficient to juftify us before God.

If this then be the cafe, who can ftand before God? Who can fay, he is free from fin? Who can perform fuch an obedience; and, who then can juftify himfelf? "In many "things," fays the apoftle, "we offend all," James iii. 2. If every one would but take a view of his own heart, he muft acknowledge with the affembly of divines, that *no meer man fince the fall, is able in this life perfectly to keep the commandments of God, but daily doth break them in thought, word and deed* *. Who can, who dare fay, that his fervices

* Affembly's Cat. Q. 82.

are perfect? What a mixture of sin is in our best duties, and therefore how insufficient to justify us before God? The believer cannot perform a religious duty without some imperfection. An apostle was obliged to say, that " when " he would do good, evil was present with him," Rom. vii. 21. And how then must it be with a person, in whom the power of sin is not subdued? If the church esteemed her righteousnesses all as filthy rags, and an unclean thing, and therefore every way unable to intitle her to the divine favour, oh what must the duties and services of a poor unrenewed sinner be, which are never animated with a sense of the love of God, neither are ever performed with a view to his glory. Upon the whole, as our nature is sadly and universally polluted, so our services must be polluted too, and consequently insufficient to justify us before God. And thus we see man's impotency in the point of justification.

To this we may likewise add, that he is so much under the government of sin, as to be unable to believe on the Lord Jesus Christ for justification, and therefore would remain for ever in a state of condemnation, did not God graciously impute to him the righteousness of the great Mediator, and his spirit enable him to receive and rest upon it for eternal life. But,

II. *Man is of himself utterly unable to subdue the dominion of sin, and to purge and cleanse his soul from it.* This is absolutely necessary to be done, else there can be no enjoyment of God; and we shall soon be convinced how unequal man is to it, when we consider what power sin exercises in every faculty of the soul. Particularly,

His understanding is so much blinded, that he cannot discern things as he ought. He is therefore said to be " Darkness," Eph. v. 8. He is so dark that he cannot see himself to be that guilty, odious, and despicable creature that he really is represented to be in the scriptures. He sees not the plague, the wickedness of his own heart, but is ready to speak of his goodness, his soundness, his cleanness of heart, as if he had no sin. He is ignorant of the spirituality of the law, and therefore esteems an obedience to the letter of it sufficient to intitle him to the favour of God. Thus * Saul was alive without the law once, and never saw himself such

* Rom. vii. 9.

a transgressor, till the Spirit came and set the commandment before him.

He sees no amiableness in Jesus Christ, no excellency in his person, his righteousness, his fulness, his titles, and offices. He sees no need of the sanctifying and renewing influences of the Holy Spirit, and therefore is ready to look upon all representations of these things as enthusiastic fancies, and wild chimeras of a disordered brain. " He calleth " evil good and good evil," Is. v. 20. " The natural man " receiveth not the things of the Spirit of God: for they " are foolishness unto him, neither can he know them, be- " cause they are spiritually discerned," 1 Cor. ii. 14. This is the case with all, " for there is none that understandeth," Rom. iii. 11. Thus we see one of the noble faculties of the soul, even the understanding, robbed of its native beauty, and so far enslaved by sin, as to be turned into darkness itself; so that all the representations which are made of sin, of holiness, of Christ, and of spiritual things to a natural man, are absolutely lost, and therefore without any saving effect, as he sees no real importance, excellency, or suitableness in them. But again,

His will is absolutely in subjection to sin. He chooses nothing but sin, can delight in nothing else, and is full of the bitterest enmity to, and strongest prejudices against the ways and things of God. " The carnal mind is enmity " against God; for it is not subject to the law of God, " neither indeed can be," Rom. viii. 7. " *His* understand- " ing is *not only* darkened, *but he is* alienated from the life " of God, through the ignorance that is in him, because of " the blindness or hardness of his heart," Eph. iv. 18. Sin has gained such a dominion over the will, that it is obstinately prejudiced against the way of salvation by Jesus Christ, so that the sinner will not come to him that he may have life *. The heart is called a " heart of stone †;" so hard that nothing but an almighty power can make a saving impression upon it. The sinner is represented as *stout hearted.* He walks in the ways of his heart, and in the sight of his eyes, and will not be controlled by man. " He " stretcheth out his hands against God, and strengtheneth " himself against the Almighty. He runneth upon him,

* John v. 40. † Ezek. xxxvi. 26.

Serm. III. ORIGINAL GUILT. 57

" even on his neck, upon the thick boffes of his bucklers." Job xv. 25, 26. Thus his will is determined for and bound to evil, and averfe to all good. He cannot bear to think of plucking out his right eye, and cutting off his right hand fins, and of fubmitting to the yoke and government of Chrift. His heart rifes therefore againft God, and difcovers its implacable enmity by defpifing gofpel truths, by perfecuting God's people, and by running into every act of rebellion againft him. But further,

The affections of the foul are abfolutely under the power of fin. They are intirely enflaved, fo that you find no moaning for fin, no joy in God, no fear of him, no love to him, but every affection turned from its proper object, and going afide readily and fully from God. The finner is abfolutely infenfible and ftupid, a lover of pleafure, a hater of God, ftands in no awe of fin or hell, choofes the way to everlafting darknefs, and is like the wild afs ufed to the wildernefs that fnuffeth up the wind at her pleafure, he will not bear reproof.

His memory is led captive by fin. He likes not to retain God in his mind, but his memory is fet againft every thing that has a tendency to be really ufeful to him, whilft it carefully endeavours to ftore up things, that are of the moft polluting and hardening nature to our hearts, and the moft deftructive to our fouls.

The confcience is hardened through fin. It ftands out againft every awful threatening, and defperately out-braves hell and damnation. In fine, the whole foul is not only polluted, but led captive by fin. It binds us with the ftrongeft fetters; it governs us like a law *; it commands us like a tyrant: it reigns in us, and exercifes a fovereignty, which none can fubdue but that power, which brought all things out of nothing. The foul and body are both in fubjection to it, and ready to execute it's orders, however ruinous to our everlafting peace. We are naturally fo under the power of fin, that no calls, no exortations, however preffing will move us, no awful reprefentations of the terrors of the law, and of the bottomlefs pit will awaken us, no human rhetoric will perfuade us, no invitations and intreaties, though delivered with all poffible endearment, will

---
* Rom. vii. 23.

H

win us, no defcriptions of the love of Chrift, though never fo ſtrong, will melt and captivate our fouls, and bring us into obedience. Our paffions may be moved, whilſt our hearts remain ſtill hardened and impenitent. Like Agrippa we may be almoſt perfuaded to be Chriſtians; or like Felix we may be made to tremble, but ſtill continue under the dominion of fin. Not all the afflictions we meet with can really awaken our ſtupid fouls, or foften our rocky hearts: nay, not even the views of death itfelf can bring us really to God. We may be in fome meafure alarmed, and through fear of hell, promife and vow, and bring ourfelves under the moſt folemn engagements to amend our lives, and return to God; but after all our refolving, and re-refolving, we juſt continue and die the fame, unlefs God is pleafed to enlighten and fave us. We are reprefented as paſt feeling, Eph. iv. 19. and as dead in trefpaſſes and fins, Eph. ii. 1. Which fhews evidently our inability to do any thing in, or even towards the fpiritual life, fo as either to renew our hearts, fanctify and cleanfe them, or prepare ourfelves for the reception of divine grace, as fome have imagined. We are not fufficient of ourfelves, to think any thing as of ourfelves, 2 Cor. iii. 5. Without Chriſt we can do nothing. John xv. 5. Who can put forth an act of faving faith in the Redeemer? Who can exercife real repentance towards God? Who can crucify one corruption, get the dominion over it, and at length eradicate it out of the heart? Who is fufficient for thefe things? The believer readily owns his utter inability to do it: and we may therefore without hefitation conclude that the unrenewed finner muſt be every way unfit for a work fo important.

Thus we have a view of man's impotency. But let it be confidered, that this impotency is voluntary. Though man is naturally carried out after nothing but evil, yet he purfues it willingly: he choofes his flavery, is pleafed with his condition, and therefore ſtifles every conviction that is not accompanied with a faving power, and does all he can to harden his heart againſt God, and get above all impreffions. This, this is the fad and awful ſtate we are all of us in; thefe are the dreadful confequences of fin's entrance into the foul. We are all of us bond-flaves and captives, fold under fin, and thereby have given Satan an opportunity of more eafily feducing our fouls, keeping us from God, and increasing our bonds. If man converts himself, he must conquer not only flesh and blood but principalities and powers, and spiritual wickednesses in high places He must enlighten his understanding, turn the bias of his will, the edge of his desires, and choose, pursue, and delight in that which sin and Satan have given him the deepest enmity to, and the strongest prejudices against This is the doctrine of our Bible, and it is suitable to our experience, and is readily acknowledged by those who have been led by the Spirit of God into a saving acquaintance with their own hearts, however it may be despised by others.

We now come to the use and improvement of this doctrine. I would here shew how much it tends to be useful both to the sinner and to the real Christian.

This doctrine may be of peculiar service to the sinner.

I. *To stir him up to the use of all necessary and appointed means.* Some will conclude, that as man is absolutely unable to convert himself, it is a discouragement to the use of means, and opens a wide door to carnal security, negligence, and sin. Whilst persons entertain this unhappy thought, they are enemies to the doctrine, and lose the advantages that arise from the mind's being impressed with a suitable sense of it But, though man cannot either justify himself by his own obedience, or turn to God by his own power, but this is the work of God alone, yet he does it in the use of means, and therefore it is the creatures duty to attend upon them. Man is not an unthinking stock or stone: He has his faculties still, though enslaved by sin, and he may do more than he does None will have it to say, they have done all they could. We may attend public ordinances, we may read the word, we may converse and pray, and exercise our thoughts about things of everlasting importance. These are the various means which God makes use of to begin, and carry on a work of grace in the heart. Might you not have gone to the house of God, my friend, the last Lord's Day, instead of spending it in walking in the fields, or in sloth and idleness at home? Might you not the other night have spent your time in the exercises of prayer and reading, instead of being at the playhouse, or revelling at a tavern? or could you not have spent that hour lately in religious company for the edification of your soul, which you wantoned away with the sons of Belial? Do not therefore take encouragement from what you have heard of this doctrine, and lull your conscience asleep, by saying that you can do nothing: there are many things you can do. When your mind was laid under some convictions, and you found some emotions of soul, under that awakening sermon you heard the other Lord's Day, or under that afflictive providence, God lately exercised you with; instead of stifling these, as you have done, might you not have gone to God by prayer, and made use of means to cherish and strengthen them? Oh, remember your pleading your impotency, your inability to work out your own salvation, will stand you in no stead at the great day, whilst you lived in the neglect of those means, which you might have attended. Are you under a necessity of ridiculing the gospel, despising the Saviour, reproaching his people, running into all excess of riot, and neglecting ordinances, and the means of salvation? For your souls sake, consider what you are doing, how you are deceiving yourself, and how Satan is leading you on to everlasting darkness. Has not conscience often told you, that you were wrong? Has it not often whispered you in the ear to go to public worship, to read the Bible, to pray, and the like? Oh, let me beseech you to attend the means of grace. Who knows but the Lord may command a blessing upon them, and make them effectual to your salvation. The * impotent man could not get into the pool himself, but he would be in the way to be put in. Do you be in the way of God's blessing; for out of the way of it you cannot expect it. What if the judge at the last day should say, because I called, and thou didst refuse, I stretched out my hand, and thou didst not regard; but hast set at nought all my counsel, and wouldst none of my reproof; I also will now laugh at thy calamity, and mock now thy fear cometh: What would you say but, Lord it is true. I refused to comply with thy calls. I would not hear. I stifled conscience, neglected means, and despised salvation, and thou art righteous in refusing to succour me, now distress and anguish are come upon me.—Oh, think of these things, and if you have any regard for your souls, attend, carefully attend the means of grace. But,

2 *This doctrine is of use to caution the sinner against carnal security and self-dependence.* To cry up the dignity of human nature, and represent man as equal to the great work

* John v. 5.

of converſion and ſalvation, has a moſt dangerous tendency. Upon this many a ſinner has ſtifled preſent convictions, ſilenced conſcience, and preſumed to put off the great concerns of eternity to the decline of life, apprehending it is ſoon enough to think of religion, and promiſing they will hereafter ſet about it in good earneſt, repent, and turn to God. Is not this the caſe with thee, thou young, gay, unthinking creature? Did I not ſee thee the other day under ſome convictions, ſome thoughtfulneſs of ſoul, and how is it removed? How is it thou canſt follow thy pleaſures again with ſo much greedineſs? The caſe is plain: Thou haſt ſucked in that naturally ſweet, but really poiſonous doctrine of man's ſufficiency, and this has lulled thee into a dangerous doze: Thou canſt now ſin again, becauſe thou haſt aſſured thy conſcience that by and by thou wilt certainly leave off thy ſins, and give up thyſelf to God. Methinks I ſee thy inward ſtruggles to get rid of thy convictions. How didſt thou ſtrive before thou didſt hit upon the happy method to appeaſe conſcience, and quietly purſue thy ſins again. But this at once ſet thee at liberty, and now I hear thee ſaying calmly and cheerfully to conſcience, as Felix did to Paul, Go thy way for this time; " when I have a convenient ſeaſon, I will call for " thee." Acts xxiv. 25. What a dangerous ſnare is this! That it is really the caſe, I appeal to the conſciences of thoſe, who are ſo ſelf-ſufficient. Thouſands have ſplit upon this dangerous rock, and, preſuming they could repent when they pleaſed, put off the things of eternity, till it was abſolutely too late to think of them, and their ſouls were lodged in the bottomleſs pit. Could you but hear the reflections of poor ſouls in hell, I dare venture to ſay, you would hear ſome crying out with unutterable anguiſh.—' Oh curſed, ſoul-ruin-
' ing doctrine, that of man's ability, &c. I believed it, and
' was lulled on, thinking I could turn to God, and one day
' or other would do it, till I ſunk into this bottomleſs gulph
' where I muſt lie for ever. I ſtifled every conviction, by
' making reſolutions of doing ſomething hereafter. I with
' zeal propagated this deſtructive notion, and am now ruined
' for ever by it.' Thus it is dangerous to ſet up the power of the creature. I am ſure I have been repreſenting the ſad experience of many poor infatuated ſinners. On the other hand, the doctrine of man's impotency tends to ſtir up the ſinner to make no delay, but now to ſeek the Lord

whilst he may be found, and to call upon him whilst he is near. Permit me to address you then in the language of this doctrine, by which you may judge of its use and importance—' Now is the accepted time; behold now is the 'day of salvation;' do not put off the great concerns of eternity to an hereafter: Remember your impotency, which will increase through sin, and so you become more unfit to 'think about your souls, and your hearts grow harder. 'Now go to God by prayer, and attend the means. Why, 'Oh why do you sleep? Remember the work is great, and 'you are unequal to it. Go to the throne of Grace there- 'fore, and endeavour to engage the almighty arm of God 'to undertake the work, and do not disregard it, left you 'provoke God to withdraw his Spirit, take his final leave, 'and so you perish for ever. Are you under any convictions, 'or divine impressions? Oh consider your weakness and ina- 'bility to revive them, if they are once stifled and lost. Be 'therefore importunate with God to fasten them deeply 'upon your souls, and bring you effectually to himself. 'Tell him of your own weakness, the greatness of the 'work, the worth of your souls, and your dependence 'upon him, and not be careless, and so be eternally ruined.' This is the language of this doctrine; thus it calls upon all sinners.

3. *This doctrine is of use to convince the sinner of the folly and danger of depending on his own duties, and of the necessity of going elsewhere for help.* We are naturally ready to think well of our duties, and to place a peculiar confidence in our own righteousness as if it were absolutely pure, and every way such as the law required. The poor pharisaical creature therefore is elated and alive, though he is actually dead, and exposed to everlasting condemnation. Art thou, my friend, this Pharisee? Art thou thinking favourably of thy righteousness, concluding that thou canst do every thing that is required of thee, and so building thy hopes of heaven upon thy duties? Come and let us reason a little upon this important head, and see what foundation thou hast for self-confidence. Let me bring thee to the law, and see if thou canst stand thy ground. Read over the commands one by one, and then ask whether thou hast perfectly observed them all. Hast thou worshipped none other but God? Has not thy heart been often divided, and gold, honour, or some

earthly enjoyment been fet up as an idol in thy foul? Thou haft then broken the firft command. Haft thou been careful to preferve the worfhip of God pure and free from all fin? Haft thou never been guilty of a vain thought in religious duties, never found any coldnefs or formality, or wanderings from God, never been chargeable with any irreverence? Here thou muft lay thy hand upon thy mouth, as having broken in numberlefs inftances the fecond command. Haft thou not often taken the name of God into thy mouth in a thoughtlefs, carelefs manner, without that ferioufnefs and awe with which it fhould have been done? Haft thou been careful to devote thy Sabbaths to God in the duties of the family, the clofet, and the fanctuary? Haft thou perfectly watched over thy frame, thy words, thy actions that day, fo as not to err in one fingle point? Here thou muft ftop, and cry guilty, and fo thou haft broken the third and fourth commands. Thus I might run through every other command, and fhew how thou haft broke the whole. And where is thy boafted power and fufficiency now? Where are thy hopes of eternal life? Canft thou venture to carry fuch an obedience to the bar of God, and plead it there? Sure, this is enough to convince thee of thy helplefs condition, of the neceffity of a better righteoufnefs, and of making thee abundantly thankful for the Gofpel, in pointing thee to a righteoufnefs which is abfolutely perfect and fufficient to recommend thee to God, and directing thee to an infinite fulnefs, where every want of the creature may be fupplied. Many apprehend they are equal to the whole work of religion, and therefore fet forward in their own ftrength, and foon give up. This is the reafon why there have been fo many apoftates, fo many ftony ground hearers, who under a fudden flow of affection have made a profeffion, but having never feen their own hearts, and been fenfible of their own weaknefs, their zeal has foon grown cold, their fins have revived, they have returned again to folly, and walked no more with the people of God. The Lord grant we may not thus appear to begin in the fpirit and end in the flefh. This doctrine tends to guard the finner againft fuch an attempt, by fhewing him his utter inability to conquer fo many enemies, withftand fo much oppofition, and go through the whole of the Chriftian life.

Thus this doctrine of man's impotency may be of ufe to

the sinner. It tends to empty him of self, to curb his pride, to guard him against a dependence upon his own power, and to stir him up to seek for help in another, finding that he has ruined himself, and that he is absolutely unable in all respects to intitle himself to the divine favour, or restore to his polluted soul that amiable image which he has sadly lost.

But this doctrine is of peculiar service to the Christian, and has a loud and paricular voice in it to him. As,

1. *It tends to fill him with, and calls him to Humility and admiration.* This doctrine takes all boasting from the creature, because it represents him as absolutely weak and helpless in the great business of salvation. Thou didst not gain that spiritual discerning of divine things, by any diligence or labour of thy own. Thou didst not give thy will its present submission to God, or conquer that enmity, thou didst find in thy heart once to him, by any art of reasoning, any power of eloquence, or any strength of resolution. Thou didst not give thyself those holy desires, thou now feelest; that hatred of sin, that delight in Christ, and that readiness to obedience which now appear in thee. It is not by any righteousness of thy own, that thou hast been introduced into the favour of God, and continuest in it. Hadst thou been left to thyself, thy hard heart would never have been softened; thy soul would never have been raised to God, thy affections would never have been freed from the entanglements of sin; thou wouldst never have felt one real desire after Jesus Christ, or ever have had any solid ground of hope for eternal life; but sin and Satan would have kept thee in thy slavery and bondage, till death had ushered thee before the bar of God, and an awful sentence had adjudged thee to regions of everlasting darkness. Keep these things in constant remembrance, and they will bring down every proud lofty thought, preserve thee from an ostentatious spirit, fill thee with deep humility, raise thy thankfulness and admiration, and enable thee to give all the glory where it is most justly due Be often saying therefore, ' who opened my eyes, and ' dispelled the darkness of my mind ? Who removed those ' deep rooted prejudices I once had against Christ and his ' ways ? Who conquered the power of sin, turned Satan ' out of his strong holds, and set my poor captive soul at li-' berty ? What is it that has secured to me the favour of ' God, and given me a title to eternal life, when I was so

'unable to do any thing towards it? O my soul, I was abso-
'lutely without strength, and never should have taken one
'single step towards heaven, if I had been left to myself.
'Learn therefore to be ever humble; ascribe not the
'change to thy own power, skill, or diligence, but learn
'more of this soul emptying truth, that thou art nothing,
'and admire the work that is done in thee, and give God
'all the glory.'

2. *This doctrine tends to keep the Christian from rash and hasty resolutions, and a dependance upon his own strength.* We are too ready to lose a sense of our weakness, and to act as if our strength lay in ourselves and not in Christ. This is the case pretty much with young Christians. Their zeal puts them often upon hasty resolutions, and so brings them into great difficulties. Peter did not consider his weakness, when he so boldly determined even to face death itself, and not desert his master. It was a noble resolution, had it been made in a proper manner. He is full of himself, and thinks nothing can shake his faith, and stagger his soul, and therefore if all the disciples forsook their Lord, he would stand steadily by him. He was left to fall, that he might be more sensible of his own insufficiency, and guard more against a rash imprudent zeal. Many have made great resolutions without considering their utter inability to execute them, and therefore breaking through them, they have thereby been filled with great distress of soul. To make resolutions is not inconsistent with our duty. But then they must be made under a proper sense and impression of our own inability to perform them if the Lord does not help us, and not in a dependance upon our own strength. The making and breaking of resolutions have wounded many a soul, and made him walk uncomfortably a great part of his days, whereas a due sense of this doctrine would set him right, guide his zeal, guard his resolutions, and keep him from that dependance upon self, which is so dangerous and hurtful. We are never farther from danger than when we see most of our own helplessness. When we are * weak, then we are strong: a paradox this to the sinner, but the Christian knows its meaning. In a word, this doctrine is peculiarly useful to the Christian, to humble him, quicken

---

* 2 Cor. xii. 10.

him, bring him into an evangelical temper; to keep him from leaning to his own underſtanding, from being lifted up with his own duties, his progreſs, and advances in grace, and to lead him to a dependance upon the Lord Jeſus Chriſt, that ſo he may be ſafe in a time of danger and temptation, may get the victory over his ſpiritual enemies, be ſupported amidſt the vairous difficulties of life, and perſevere even unto the end. A proper ſenſe of this doctrine has a tendency to bring about theſe deſirable ends, and ſo to promote and ſecure the Chriſtian's comfort and holineſs.

Thus we have taken a view of man's natural ſtate, and have conſidered the uſe and importance of being properly impreſſed with a ſenſe of original guilt, pollution, and moral impotency. Theſe doctrines are ſelf-debaſing and humbling, but not foul diſcouraging doctrines. They bring down our pride, but they do not drive us to deſpair. They happily prepare our minds for receiving the news of the goſpel, make us more thankful for it, and when improved, ſtir us up to ſeek after an intereſt in and acquaintance with the Lord Jeſus Chriſt, whom to know is eternal life. They are doctrines, which indeed for theſe very reaſons, nature cannot bear, and therefore are ſo much ridiculed and deſpiſed. To tell man of the dignity of his nature, the noble powers of his ſoul, and his great ſufficiency to do every thing that is required of him: to praiſe his gifts and abilities, commend his works of charity, and feed him with the hopes of heaven, would be to gain his eſteem, and to eſtabliſh the reputation of an ingenuous preacher; but to tell him that he is guilty, polluted and even worſe than the beaſts that periſh; to repreſent to him his miſery and wretchedneſs, that he is a child of wrath, and is expoſed to everlaſting condemnation, and that he can do nothing to merit the favour of God, or procure eternal life, but is abſolutely helpleſs and without ſtrength. To do this would be highly diſpleaſing, and you cannot expect any kinder treatment than that of ridicule and reproach, and no better a title than that of bigot and enthuſiaſt. But I hope better things of you, my dear friends. You will not reproach me for ſetting theſe truths before you, and preſſing them upon your conſciences, but I truſt will each be concerned to examine what ſenſe and experience you have of them in your own ſouls, and to get a greater acquaintance with them.

Ask your souls these important questions.— 'Do I not only
' acknowledge man's impotency and weakness, but have I felt
' it? Do I not only see it by the light of God's word, but
' have I seen it by the light of his Spirit? Have I found it by
' my experience to be an infallible truth, that I can do
' nothing? Am I no more the proud Pharisee, esteeming
' myself with Saul to be blameless; and boasting of and
' depending upon my own righteousness; but do I see the
' imperfections of my best duties, and loath myself and them
' too? Am I thoroughly sensible that I cannot fulfil one
' promise, subdue one corruption, withstand one temptation,
' exercise one grace, and perform one duty in a spiritual
' manner of myself? Have I seen my understanding to be
' darkness, felt my will to be rebellion, and found my affec-
' tions polluted, and my soul under the power of sin?' These
and such like questions are of the utmost importance, as they
relate to and point out the work of God in its beginnings,
and in its progress in the soul. The more we grow in grace,
the more we see of our own emptiness and impotency: But
if we are strangers to these things, and have seen and felt
nothing of them, we have too much reason to conclude that
we are strangers to the grace of God, and that all our
religion is no more than an empty form. Be concerned
my dear friends, whatever you do, to get a true sense of
your own weakness, and endeavour to have your minds constantly impressed with it, for then you will be in least danger
of falling; be most watchful over your own hearts, and depend most upon the Lord Jesus Christ for all strength and
righteousness.

SERMON IV.

A TRINITY OF PERSONS IN THE UNITY OF THE DIVINE ESSENCE.

I JOHN V. 7. LATTER PART.

—And thefe Three are One.

THE doctrine of the Trinity is one of the glories of revelation, and therefore highly deferving our particular confideration and efteem. However it may be treated with ridicule, and viewed as an abfurdity by many, becaufe it is myfterious and incomprehenfible, it is one of the capital articles of the Chriftian's creed, it enters into the very effence of his comfort, his holinefs, and his falvation, and therefore he receives it with the utmoft readinefs and cheerfulnefs.

The apoftle in the verfe before our text is fpeaking of the Saviour, and telling us that when he came into the world to execute the important work he had undertaken, he came not by *water* only, when he was publicly baptized, but by *water* and *blood*, which appeared when he was upon the crofs, and which were fymbolical reprefentations of that deliverance from the guilt and defilement of fin, which we fhould have through his death. That Chrift is thus a complete and able faviour appears from the Spirit's application of the virtue of his death, to our fouls Nay, there are teftimonies fufficient to his incarnation and the efficacy of it: for not only one, even the Spirit, but the three glorious perfons who inhabit eternity, bear witnefs to Jefus the

Mediator. The Father not only at his baptifm * and tranffiguration † gave a public proof of his approbation of him, but ‡ declared him to be his Son, by his refurrection from the dead. The Son often bare witnefs of himfelf whilft he was upon earth; and if the people would not believe his own teftimony, he appealed to his various works, his many miracles, as inconteftiable proofs of his divine miffion. The third divine witnefs is the Spirit, who defcended upon him at his baptifm, and ever fince his afcenfion has come in a glorious manner, in confequence of his fatisfaction and purchafe, to apply all the bleffings of falvation to the elect of God, and will continue to do fo till the whole number is completed, and all the purpofes of divine grace are fully anfwered. Thefe three divine witneffes, thus giving their diftinct teftimony, and perfonally diftinct from each other, are yet but one. It is not faid of them as it is of the witneffes on earth, that they agree in one, but that they are one; not one perfon but one thing, or one effence. The truth then that appears from this part of God's word is this, viz. (which the Affembly's Catechifm has fully expreffed) *That there are three perfons in the Godhead, the Father, the Son, and Holy Ghoft, and thefe three are one God, the fame in fubftance, equal in power and glory.* I fhall confider this in its feveral parts, fo that the whole may appear clear and evident, as,

I. Prove that there are three in the Godhead.
II. That thefe are three diftinct perfons.
III. *That thefe three perfons are the one Supreme God, equally partaking of one common undivided nature or effence.* And then,
IV. *Confider the ufe and improvement of this truth.* I would defire to fpeak of this divine myftery with the greateft caution and with the utmoft reverence, knowing how infinitely it tranfcends all our ideas, and how much ferioufnefs it requires in us, when we are reprefenting the nature, the perfonal properties, and the perfections of the glorious Jehovah.

1. *We are to fhew that there are three in the Godhead,* or *that there is a plurality in the Godhead.* You will eafily

* Mat. iii. 17.   † Mat. xvi. 5.   ‡ Rom. i. 4.

see that my business is not to attempt to give you clear ideas of the Trinity; that is impossible for man to do: but to prove the various truths from scripture; and where our reason falls short in comprehending the truths, let not this stagger our minds, but let us cheerfully embrace them, so far as we find a divine warrant for it. Take your bibles then into your hands, and examine, whilst I go through the proofs of each doctrine distinctly. We have some intimation of a plurality in the Deity in Gen. i. 1. where. the word *God* is put in the original in the plural number, and so it runs throughout the chapter. And when God came to make man, his form of speech upon that occasion, implies a consultation, and signifies that more than one were concerned in man's formation. Gen. i. 26. " And God " said, let us make man in our own image, after our like- " ness." Accordingly, in Job xxxv. 10. the word *maker* is in the plural number, and so should be read, *where is God my makers?* Thus the word *creator* in Eccl. xii. 1. is in the plural, and so it should be, *remember thy creators.* Again, that there is a plurality in the Godhead, appears from Gen. iii. 22. " And the Lord God said, behold the " man is become as one of us." Thus the same hint is given, Gen. xi. 7. " Go to, let us go down." The same truth appears in If. vi. 8. " Who will go for us?" These things are so plain that he that runs may read the doctrine contained in them. Thus the Old Testament shews us there are more than one in the Godhead. The New Testament is more particular in the account of the persons in the Godhead, representing their number, their names, and characters, and the different offices they have undertaken to execute in the redemption and salvation of fallen man. Thus in Matth. xxviii. 19. we are told there are three, and we have an account of their different names, viz. *Father, Son,* and *Holy Ghost.* In John xiv. 16. they are again mentioned. Christ speaks of himself under the personal pronoun *I;* he mentions the *Father* too, and represents the *Holy Ghost* under the character of a *Comforter.* So verse twenty-six they are distinctly spoken of: " But the Comforter, which is the " Holy Ghost, whom the Father will send in my name." You meet with these glorious three again in John xvi. 13, 14, 15. In the doxology mentioned by the apostle, 2 Cor. xiii. 14 you have them distinctly represented. " The grace

" of the Lord Jefus Chrift, and the love of God, and the
" communion of the Holy Ghoft be with you all." Here
is the Son reprefented under his office character, the Father
called God, which fometimes is a name peculiarly appli-
cable to one of the divine perfons, and fometimes includes
all, and here is alfo the third perfon, or the Holy Ghoft.
Again, the apoftle fpeaks of them all in Gal. iv. 6. Where
he fays, " God," that is the Father, " hath fent forth the
" fpirit of his fon into your hearts." You meet with them
again in Eph. ii. 18. " For through him," that is Chrift,
" we have an accefs by one fpirit unto the Father." Thus
in Hebrews ix. 14. the apoftle fays, " How much more
" fhall the blood of Chrift, who through the eternal fpirit
" offered himfelf without fpot to God," &c. And once
more we have the facred Three mentioned in Rev. i. 4, 5.
" John to the Seven Churches which are in Afia, Grace be
" unto you, and peace, from *him which is, and which was,*
" *and which is to come, and from the Seven Spirits, which*
" *are before his throne, and from Jefus Chrift,* who is the
" faithful witnefs." The Father is here reprefented by his
eternity and immutability, the Spirit by the variety and perfection of his fpiritual gifts and operations, and the Son by his
mediatorial character. And thus we fee from fcripture that
there is a plurality in the Deity, viz. Three, whofe diftinct
names, characters, and offices are reprefented. I now come,

2. To fhew from the fame facred word of truth, that thefe
are three diftinct perfons. And here I readily own myfelf at
a lofs to entertain fuitable conceptions of divine perfonality.
When we apply perfon to one another, we take in the idea
of diftinct being, but this muft be abftracted from perfonality when we are confidering the facred Trinity. They are
not diftinct beings nor diftinct Gods; this is the greateft
abfurdity and impoffibility. And yet they are more than
different names of the fame perfon; to look upon them in
this light would take away a great part of the glory of this
doctrine, and introduce the greateft confufion. They have
a diftinct manner of fubfiftence, and therefore are diftinct
from each other. The Father is not the Son, nor the Holy
Ghoft. The Father did not die, does not intercede, neither is he *that Comforter* who is promifed. Here let it be
obferved, that the diftinct perfonality of Father, Son, and
Holy Ghoft is not the refult of the divine will, nor does it

arise from their distinct offices in the work of redemption or scheme of salvation, but is necessary and eternal, and therefore to be considered as laying a foundation for those distinct parts they have undertaken in the gospel œconomy, and not as produced by them. That they are three distinct persons appears from their being spoken of as distinct. The Father is a divine person, so is the Son, and so is the Spirit, else there would have been some marks of distinction put upon them, to let us know that they were only the different names, qualities, or attributes of the Father. But they are mentioned as distinct from him, and in such a manner as to give us the utmost reason to believe that they are persons as well as the Father, distinctly subsisting as such. Thus the Son is spoken of as distinct from the Father. 1 John i. 1. "In the beginning was the word, and the word was with God, and the word was God." As he was with God, he must be distinct from him, and not that person with whom he was. Thus in the form of baptism the Son and Spirit are spoken of as distinct from the Father. And what is said of the Father to denote him to be a divine person, is said of these two. Is the Father spoken of under the personal pronouns, *I*, *thou*, and *he*, so are they. Thus Christ says, "I was set up from everlasting." Prov. viii. 23. Again says the Father to the Son, "Thou art my Son, this day have I begotten thee," Ps. ii. 7. And again, John i. 10. "He was in the world, and the world was made by him." Thus it is said also of the Spirit, "When he is come." John xvi. 8. As these pronouns are characters of a real person, so they shew the Son and Holy Ghost to be persons. Again, are works and actions ascribed to the Father, which are peculiar to persons, so they are equally to the Son and Spirit. Thus the Son is said to create not only the natural world, but to create anew to good works, John i. 3. He is our mediator, and stands between God and us. He is our prophet, and therefore a divine teacher. Acts iii. 22. He is our priest, and so made atonement for our sins on earth, and is now making intercession for us in heaven, Heb. x. 12. And chap. vii. 25. He is our king, and as such rules and defends us, restrains and conquers all his and our enemies, Psal. ii. 6. He is our shepherd, and as such watcheth over us as his flock, provides for us, restores us when going astray, gathers the lambs in his arms, and carries them in his bofom, and gently leads all thofe that are with young, Pf. xxiii. 1, 2, 3, and If. xl 11. Thus I might go through the various characters, works, and offices of Jefus Chrift, all which are fo many characteriftics of a perfon, and cannot with any manner of propriety be afcribed to a quality or an attribute of the Father. Thus works and acts equally defcriptive of a perfon are afcribed to the Spirit of God, and therefore prove that he is no power of the Father, but a perfon diftinct from him. Thus he is faid to *teach*, John xiv. 26. He glorifies Chrift, by taking of his things, and fhewing them unto his people, John xvi. 14. He brings things to the remembrance of his people, and leads them into all truth, John xiv. 26. and chap. xvi. 13. He renews and fanctifies us; quickens us when dead in trefpaffes and fins; fubdues the power of fin, mortifies our corruptions, and brings us into the image of God, Tit. iii. 5. John iii. 6 He is a fpirit of prayer, and helps his people in that duty; makes them fenfible of their wants, fills their mouths with arguments, and helps them to plead with God, and to come in the exercife of faith in Jefus Chrift, Rom viii. 26. Zech. xii. 10. He is a comforter, and as fuch cheers the fouls of his people, helps them to claim a covenant relation to God, and fills them with joy and peace in believing, John xiv 26. Gal. iv. 6. Now are not all thefe demonftrative proofs of the Spirit's being a divine perfon? Befides, we have him reprefented as being tempted, Acts v. 9. as being vexed and grieved, Eph. iv. 30. As being lied unto, Acts v. 3, 4; as fpeaking to Peter, Acts x 19, 20; and to others, and fending forth, Acts xiii. 1, 2, 4. Thefe things are all defcriptive of a real perfon. Once more, are perfonal properties attributed to the Father? So they are to the Son and Holy Ghoft. Has he underftanding and wifdom? So has the Son, Col. ii. 3. and fo has the Spirit, 1 Cor. ii. 10, 12. Has the Father a will? The Son has fo too, and alfo the Holy Ghoft, John vi. 38 1 Cor. xii. 11. Does power belong to the Father? It does fo to the Son and Spirit, If. lxiii 1. Mic ii. 7. Thus from the whole, thefe three, Father, Son, and Holy Ghoft are three perfons, diftinct from each other. If they are not fo, how can we underftand the diftinct characters and offices that are afcribed to them? If they are only different names of one perfon, then, fuch as thefe are the confequences, viz: The Father, inftead of sending his Son into the world, sent himself: instead of the Son's praying to the Father, the Father prays to himself: the Father suffered, obeyed, satisfied for sin, and is the great mediator of the new covenant Instead of the Father's sending the Holy Ghost as the comforter, he sent himself. In a word, when the Father mentions the other persons, he all the while means himself, only represented under different characters, so that to destroy distinct personality would be to introduce inextricable difficulties. I now come

3. To shew *that these three persons are the one supreme God, the same in substance, equal in power and glory.* I am not here to shew how they are one. It is absolutely impossible for the highest angel in heaven, whose grasp of thought must be vastly superior to ours, to point out or conceive the modus of the Trinity, and therefore it would be vain for a poor weak man to expect it. We readily acknowledge it to be a great mystery, a mystery in which we are entirely lost. However some may esteem it a reproach upon their understandings to believe what they cannot fully comprehend, I desire to esteem it none, and therefore freely own my ignorance, how the sacred three are distinct as to personality, and yet *one* essentially. These are subjects of an infinite nature, and therefore cannot come within the reach of a finite mind. Nothing but infinity can take in infinity, and therefore it discovers the greatest pride and vanity in a short sighted mortal to refuse to give credit to a doctrine so immediately relating to deity, because it is incomprehensible. If we must believe nothing but what we can entirely account for, we must turn absolute sceptics. We must question our own existence, because we know not how we exist; we must deny there are any such things as sun, moon, and stars, though we see them, because we can give no account of their matter and formation: nay, we must deny that there is a God, because we cannot fully know him. We are lost in his eternity, immensity, omniscience, omnipresence, and yet we readily believe these perfections belong to him; because not only all nature gives us some hints of it, but the scriptures particularly and clearly reveal it as an undeniable truth. Why then can we not as easily give credit to revelation, when it represents a Trinity of persons in the Unity of the divine nature? Here we say we cannot

understand it; but in the other cafe, though we cannot understand it, we yet believe it, becaufe it is fo demonſtrable from nature and fcripture. This doctrine is not *contrary* to reafon, though *above* it. We do not fay that three perfons are one perfon, or that they are three diſtinct Beings or Gods, but that the three perfons are one God. The Father is almighty, the Son is almighty, and the Holy Ghoſt is almighty, and yet there are not three almighties, but one Almighty. The Father is eternal, the Son is eternal, and the Holy Ghoſt is eternal, and yet there are not three eternals, but one Eternal.

That this is the doctrine of Scripture, appears plain both from the Old and New Teſtament. Some have thought that it appears in Pfal. xxxiii. 6. where it is faid, that " by " the word of the Lord were the heavens made; and all " the hoſt of them by the breath of his mouth." By the word fome fuppofe is meant Chriſt, who is called *the word*, John i. 1. By the Lord is the Father, and by the breath of his mouth is meant the Spirit, which fignifies breath. Some likewife think that the bleſſing which Aaron and his fons were to pronounce upon the children of Ifrael, fignified the Trinity and Unity, Numb. vi. 24, 25, 26. " The Lord " blefs thee, and keep thee; the Lord make his face to " fhine upon thee, and be gracious unto thee; the Lord lift " up his countenance upon thee, and give thee peace." It is apprehended that the Lord in the twenty-fourth verfe, fignifies the Father, in the twenty-fifth verfe the Son, and in the twenty-fixth verfe the Holy Spirit. But however fuitable this explication of the words may be to this doctrine, as contained in other parts of Scripture, I would not produce thefe paſſages as direct proofs of it. What we have in If. vi. 3. feems more peculiarly defigned to fpeak this great truth. " And one cried unto another, and faid, " Holy, holy is the Lord of Hoſts: the whole earth is full " of his glory." There is no impropriety in faying that this thrice holy refers to the Trinity. This glorious Lord of hoſts Ifaiah faw in his vifion, is in one place referred to the Son, and in another to the Holy Ghoſt, John xii 41. and Acts xxviii. 25. And the fame Lord, in verfe eight, fays, " who will go for us? So that it appears as if the Prophet had a vifion of the facred Three, and heard the Spirits furrounding the throne celebrating the praifes of each; and if fo, it evidently fhews that they are the One

Supreme God, equal in all divine glories, and therefore demanding equal praises from all creatures. But this appears more particularly in the New Testament. Thus it is a truth evidently contained in the order of baptism. In this form the Son and Holy Ghost are equally mentioned with the Father, without the least appearance of inferiority. If they are not one in essence, it is strange that those who are baptized should be as much given up to the Son and Spirit as to the Father; that they should thereby be brought under an equal obligation to pay religious honours to all, and that by a divine appointment, when all revelation is against it: so if the opinion of one supreme and two subordinate Gods were true, we cannot, therefore, from hence but conclude a Trinity of persons in the Unity of the divine nature. This I apprehend the apostle plainly shows in the above-mentioned doxology, 2 Cor xiii 14. It evidently points out an equality, as well as a distinction of person But this truth will be more fully proved, when we come to consider the Deity of the Son and the Holy Ghost; for if all that belongs to God the Father belongs equally to them, then they are the same in substance, equal in power and glory. I shall therefore now proceed to consider.

Lastly, *The particular use and improvement of this doctrine.* It is not a mere matter of speculation, and therefore not a point of indifferency; it is useful, though mysterious, and however above the reach of our limited understandings, it cannot but be of great advantage, when we are enabled to attend to, and to apply it aright. Too many throw all mysteries out of religion, representing them not only as absurd, but as no way tending to be useful; as if it were absolutely necessary to an improvement of a doctrine that we should fully comprehend it. Wherein does the necessity of our perfectly taking in this doctrine lie? Does our happiness depend upon the thing itself, or upon the modus of it? Does its remaining a mystery lessen our comfort? Or cease to promote our holiness? Whilst we believe the glorious Three to be equal in all divine perfections, we are satisfied the foundation upon which we build is safe; we know our salvation is hereby secured: we see the motives, how powerful to all obedience, all which would be no way increased by knowing how these Three are distinct as to personality and yet one God. Therefore it is vain curiosity for any to pry into those things which are unsearchable; and great arrogance for any to say this glorious myſtery can anſwer no valuable purpoſe, becauſe it is a myſtery, when it appears evident that the myſteriouſneſs of it is no way eſſential to our comfort and happineſs, any more than our comprehending the eternity, and other perfections of God is. Let us then conſider what this doctrine teacheth us. And,

1. *It teacheth us thankfulneſs for a divine revelation.* The light of nature would never have inſtructed us in ſo important a truth. There are no hints of it to be met with in the creation. None of the ancient philoſophers could ever find any foot-ſteps of the Trinity, even if they ranſacked all nature. A God the whole creation proclaims, nay the moſt minute part of it clearly ſpeaks this great truth: but a Trinity, where is it to be found, but in the book of God? You had never heard of this important doctrine, if you had been born, and had lived where the goſpel has never come! See how it is with the poor heathen. Look into thoſe countries where there is nothing but Pagan darkneſs, and from thence learn your obligations to bleſs God for the ſcriptures, and be concerned to prize and eſteem this ſacred volume. This word is a *light unto our feet, and a lamp unto our paths*, Pſ. cxix. In it the great myſteries of Chriſtianity are revealed; the object of divine worſhip is clearly repreſented, every thing relating to God, ourſelves, and eternity that is neceſſary is mentioned, and therefore a foundation laid for peculiar thankfulneſs and praiſe. Is it not then a privilege to have a revelation? Is it not deſirable to be reſcued from a ſtate of darkneſs and wretched ignorance, ſuch as poor heathens are in? Is not the Bible to be valued becauſe of the glorious views it gives us of God? Shall we not be thankful that he has revealed himſelf in his perſonal properties, characters, and perfections, with which our comfort, our happineſs is ſo much connected? Is it not an inſtance of infinite grace and condeſcention in God to make himſelf thus known to us? Shall we deſpiſe this revelation, repreſent it as unneceſſary, or ridicule it for thoſe ſacred myſteries it contains? How ungrateful would this be, how inſolent, how unſuitable to our obligations? What, to eſteem our privileges, no privileges, to deſpiſe that word, in which ſo much invaluable treaſure is laid up; ſurely, Sodom

and Gomorrah will rife up againſt thee, thou infatuated foul! Ethiopia and Sheba will condemn thee; the whole heathen world will upbraid thee with fhameful ingratitude; and the devils themſelves will reflect upon thee for thy ſtupidity It is exceeding awful that there ſhould be any found in this land of goſpel light, who treat the ſcriptures with contempt, when all our light and knowledge, comfort and holineſs are derived from them. O let us bleſs God for that word which gives us ſuch ſtriking views of thoſe glorious myſteries, we ſhould for ever have remained ignorant of, had we been left to the mere light of nature.

2. *Hence we are taught humbly to adore the unfearchable Jehovah.* When Job had a view of God he abhorred himſelf, Job xlii. It is enough to keep us for ever humble under a fenſe of our weakneſs, when we conſider the infinite glory of the ſupreme God. Three diſtinct perſons equally partaking of the ſame incomprehenſible eſſence; the Father God, the Son God, the Holy Ghoſt God, and yet not three Gods, but only one God? Is this the object of our worſhip, is this the God that ſupports us, ſupplies, protects, and ſaves us? Glorious Being indeed! Well may angels adore him! Well may devils tremble before him! What a diſproportion between him and us! He is infinite, but we are finite: he is immenſe and unlimited, but we are confined and contracted: he is eternal, but we are of yeſterday. He can eaſily graſp ſuch creatures as we; but it is only a little that we know of him. And ſhall not this curb our pride, and ever keep us low, when we conſider how ſcanty our knowledge, how narrow our underſtandings? Some are for explaining this doctrine, and to ſhew how theſe three are one, borrow ſimilitudes from nature; but attempts of this kind ſhew too great boldneſs with Deity, and only tend to give us improper ideas of the Trinity. We ſhould ever view it as an inexplicable truth, and therefore a ſenſe of it ſhould fill us with a holy awe and reverence of God, and engage us to adore his infinitely tranſcending greatneſs and glory. In fine, this doctrine gives an occaſion for ſuch reflections as theſe.—' Oh how glorious is Jehovah, Father, Son, and
' Holy Ghoſt! This one ſupreme God, ſubſiſting in three
' perſons, is abſolutely incomprehenſible. Who by ſearch-
' ing can find out God, who can find out thee the Al-
' mighty unto perfection? Such knowledge, Lord, is too

'wonderful for me, it is high, I cannot attain unto it. Oh
' all ye angels that excel in strength, that do his command-
' ments, hearkening to the voice of his word, adore this
' unsearchable Jehovah! All ye his hosts, ye ministers of
' his that do his pleasure celebrate his praises. All ye
' creatures in all places of his dominion, according to your
' several capacities, bless your adorable Creator; yea, bless
' him, oh my soul, stand and for ever admire the mysteries
' of his nature; fear, obey, and continually praise him."
Thus this doctrine tends to keep us in a constant, humble,
and adoring temper.

3. *Hence we see the foundation that is laid for distinct communion with the Father, Son, and Holy Ghost, and for distinct ascriptions of praise and glory to each.* As their distinct personality has laid a foundation for their undertaking distinct parts in the salvation of sinners, so likewise for distinct communion with each according to their respective characters, and offices in the œconomy of the gospel. We read therefore of having *fellowship with the Father, and with his Son Jesus Christ,* 1 John. i 3. And our Lord tells us of his and the father's *coming unto us, and of making their abode with us,* John xiv. 23. He speaks of his *coming in to us, and supping with us, and we with him,* Rev. iii. 20. Now, communion with God lies in carrying on a sweet, free, and intimate converse with him, as with a friend, and is maintained in the exercise of faith, love, hope, joy, and in the duties of prayer, meditation, praise, and in public ordinances. In these duties and exercises there is a happy meeting of God and the soul, and the sweetest intercourse is often maintained, even with each person. Thus the Father is mentioned as the object of faith John xiv. 1. *Ye believe in God.* Honour is paid to him in particular. Eph. iii. 14, 15. Blessing is ascribed to him. Eph. i. 3, 4. The Son is likewise represented as the object of faith, John xiv. 1 *Believe also in me.* As the object of love, 1 Pet. i. 8. *Whom having not seen ye love.* Praises are particularly ascribed to him, Rev. i. 5, 6. We read of the communion of the Holy Ghost too, 2 Cor. xiii. 14. This communion with one person distinctly, does not exclude the others. For instance when I have distinct communion with the Father, I do not exclude the Son, for it is through the Son that I have communion with the Father. When again, I

have diſtinct communion with the Son, I do not neglect, or reflect upon the Father; for the exercife of all faith and joy in Chriſt is the effect of the Father's free, everlaſting love. So my communion with the Spirit is the effect of the Father's love, and the Son's purchaſe. Thus diſtinct communion with each is to the glory of all. When with the Father, it is to the honour of the Son and Spirit: when with the Son, it is to the glory of the Father and Spirit: and when with the Spirit, it is to the glory of Father and Son. In this communion lies the very effence of our comfort, the fweetnefs and power of religion. The Chriſtian would be much more happy did he converfe more with the facred Three. The fcheme of falvation is all the life and joy of our fouls, and to view the various characters and offices of Father, Son, and Holy Spirit, which their diſtinct perfonality lays a foundation for, would fill our fouls with unfpeakable pleafure. This communion, were it more maintained, would bring heaven into the foul, fweeten every difficulty, and give that joy which the world knows nothing of. O happy faint that is got above to hold everlaſting communion with God, and to view the diſtinct glories of each divine perfon! Happy Chriſtian that lives much with God here! Let us view the intercourfe he has with each perfon See him then through Chriſt, and by the Spirit approaching the Father, and viewing his perfonal characters, and relations, and the wonders of his love. See, the Father is pleafed to come down and commune with him, and to reveal his love to him. He fhews him how free, how rich, how matchlefs this love; that it was everlaſting, and that it is immutable. He reveals the fecrets of his covenant to him; tells him that his name was written in the book of life. This lays a foundation for the Chriſtian's joy. He feeds upon it; he loves the Father again, and rejoices in him. Father, thou haſt won all my heart, and I give up my all to thee. The Father rejoices in him as his chofen veffel. The Chriſtian rejoices in him as his Father, his reſt. What a fweet complacency, what admiration! " O why did the Father fix
' upon me, why was I chofe to eternal life! Dear Father,
' who am I that thou fhouldſt love me fo as to give me to
' thy Son, to pardon, to juſtify me, to heal my backflidings,
' and to be a Father unto me! Amazing love! Lord enable
' me to give my whole felf to thee, and to live to thy glory."

Again, what sweet communion has the soul with the Son of God? What satisfaction in viewing the glories of his person, the characters he sustains, the work he has already done, and that in which he is eternally employed! The Son rejoices in the Christian as his purchase, tells him how he loved him, how he bled and died, how he engaged principalities and powers, and triumphed over them all, and how he is now engaged above for his salvation. The soul rejoices in Christ as his bridegroom, his husband, his portion, finds his heart captivated and drawn to him, feels the warmest affection for him, and the strongest desires after him. O how amiable is the Redeemer! What endearing expressions does the soul make use of, what meltings of heart, what sweet confidence and holy joy, what admiration, love, and praise at a view of the dear, the blessed mediator! Thus likewise the Christian has the highest pleasure in communion with the Holy Ghost. He is a comforter, and therefore fills the soul with his divine consolations. He seals the children of God, sheds abroad the love of God in their hearts, opens to them the glory of the promises, shines upon his own work in the soul, and lets him see that he bears the image of his heavenly Father, that a saving change is made, that he is sanctified and set apart for God, and is an heir of eternal life. The spirit helps him in prayer, to plead with God, to exercise a cheerful confidence in him, and to call him Father. And these things fill the soul with joy, he views every character of the Spirit and rejoices, he feels the refreshment, and admires. ' Shall ' I grieve this good Spirit? Shall I quench his sacred mo- ' tions? No, this would be the greatest ingratitude. Lord, ' I would admire thy grace in all thy works in me, and ' live to thy praise.' I need not say how your souls would be animated and enlivened, were you but to converse more with these sacred persons, as they are represented in the gospel. Let us then be seeking after communion with God, be often viewing the various glories, works, and characters of these three divine persons, as this will be a happy means of preparing us more for the work and enjoyments of heaven, and contribute much to our comfort and joy, whilst we are here upon earth.

4. *Hence we learn that there must be a constant harmony between these three persons in all their designs, acts, and operations.* As they are one in essence, they must be

harmonious: they muſt have the ſame will, and act in the whole ſcheme of ſalvation with the utmoſt union. What the Father has done, and does, muſt be perfectly agreeable to the Son and Spirit; and what the Son and Spirit do, muſt have the entire approbation of the Father. Thus the forming the plan from eternity, and the execution of it in time, muſt be agreeable to all the three perſons. The ſame things are often attributed to each divine perſon. Creation is aſcribed to all the three. So likewiſe is the new-creation. The Father teaches. John vi. 46. The Son, and the holy Spirit too. The Father quickens, and ſo the ſecond and third divine perſons. John v. 21. Rom. viii. 10. Now this is a very important circumſtance, that the ſacred three ſhould be thus one in will, deſign, and operation. This contributes much to the comfort of a poor awakened ſinner, and to the ſatisfaction of the believer as he paſſes through life. With what pleaſure may a poor ſoul view, depend upon, and plead with the Father the ſacrifice of Chriſt for pardon and acceptance. ' Lord this ſacrifice was of thine ' own appointment, thou didſt approve of it, thou haſt ' accepted it, and ſet it forth as the only refuge for a poor ' guilty ſoul to fly to; Lord I would fly to it and plead it ' for thoſe very purpoſes which thou haſt deſigned ſhould ' be anſwered by it. And wilt thou not look upon it? ' Wilt thou refuſe me acceptance?' Thus we may comfortably depend upon the interceſſion of Chriſt, and conclude that the Father will always hear him. We may now be ſatisfied that the work which the Spirit has begun in our hearts is agreeable to the Father and the Son and that it will therefore be carried on, all our backſlidings be healed, all our corruptions be ſubdued, all our enemies be conquered, and we at laſt be brought ſafe to God in the heavenly Zion. I might here add, that this doctrine *tends to fill the Believer with admiration.* Is this God my God? Is the Father mine? Is the Son mine? Is the Holy Ghoſt mine? O my happineſs! O diſtinguiſhing Grace! What amazing condeſcention, for ſuch a God to look upon me, for each glorious perſon to undertake for my Salvation! Admire, O my ſoul, and long to get above, where I ſhall be ſweetly engaged, in adoring the ſacred three, and in crying Grace, Grace, for ever.

This doctrine commands an awe from the ſinner. And it ſhews the dreadful ſtate he is in to have no intereſt in the

Father, Son and Spirit, nay, to have the Father his enemy, the Son and Holy Ghost his enemies. Melancholy condition! How canst thou eat and drink, and sleep in quiet? What can give thee peace, when God is against thee? Thou wilt not embrace the Son, therefore thou canst expect no pity from the Father, no kindness from the Spirit. Thou art despising the operation, and quenching the motions of the Spirit, and therefore thou canst not look for any mercy from the Father and the Son. They are all united, and if one is despised, they are all despised. O consider this ye that forget God, lest he tear you in pieces, and there be none to deliver.

Lastly, *We should all enquire whether this God is our God.* Is the Father my Father? Is the Son my Saviour? Is the Holy Ghost my Sanctifier and Comforter? Is this God mine in all his relations, persons, characters, offices, and perfections? These are important questions, and which we should all be concerned to put closely and faithfully to our souls.

Thus we see how this doctrine may be improved, how it enters into our comfort, and is useful to us in our way to a better world, though never so mysterious and incomprehensible. The particular improvement of the Deity of the Son and Holy Ghost will be left till we come to a consideration of those distinct subjects; what have already been offered are only a few general hints upon the doctrine of the Trinity.

L 2

SERMON V.

Rom. ix. 5. LATTER PART.

—*Who is over all, God blessed for ever.*

WE have already considered and proved from scripture, a Trinity of persons in the Unity of the divine essence: a glorious doctrine indeed. The Father is God, the Son is God, and the Holy Ghost is God. That the Father is God, all will readily acknowledge; but many absolutely deny Deity to the Son. This therefore is a point of such moment that it will be highly necessary to take it into a particular consideration, that so we may be satisfied whether the Saviour we trust in is God or not. For this purpose I have chosen the words I have mentioned as the subject of our present meditations In the whole verse we have a distinct account of the two natures of Christ, his human and divine. As to his human nature, he derived it from the Jews. He was the offspring of David, and the seed of Abraham. As to his divine nature, he was uncreated, and is infinitely exalted above all creatures, and possessed of all possible blessedness ; *he is over all God blessed for ever.* This, this is the Saviour of poor sinners: a fit person therefore to go through the great work he has undertaken, and a suitable object of our religious trust, reverence, and adoration. That these words prove Christ to be true and proper God, appears very plain. He that is over, or above all, he that is infinitely and eternally blessed in himself, and is the object of everlasting blessing and adoration, must be the supreme God. You therefore find the Father represented under these characters. Eph. iv. 6. *One God and Father of all, who is above all,* And Rom. i. 25. *Who is blessed for ever.* and 2 Cor. xi. 31. *The God and Father of our Lord Jefus Chrift, which is bleffed for evermore.* As thefe are defcriptions of the fupreme God, and as Chrift is reprefented by them, we muft neceffarily conclude that Jefus Chrift is God equal with the Father. But this is not the only text upon which this glorious truth is built; we find it both in the Old and New Teftament. I would therefore,

I. *Confider thefe parts of fcripture, which evidently prove this great truth.* And then,

II. *Shew the importance of this great article of our faith.*

That we may receive this truth upon good evidence, let us,

I. *Examine the proofs we have of it in fcripture.* And here, it would be impoffible for me to go through all the texts of fcripture that prove this doctrine in a fingle difcourfe, there is fuch a fulnefs and variety. I hope what I may confider will be fufficiently convincing. And here let us look into fcripture, and fee how it proves the Father to be God, and we shall find that the very fame things are attributed to Chrift, and confequently he muft be God. Thus incommunicable titles and attributes, as well as thofe works and branches of worfhip which are all inconteftible proofs of deity, are all afcribed to Chrift in Scripture.

I. *Incommunicable titles are given him by a divine authority.* Thus the name *Jehovah* is given to Chrift: a name that muft be peculiar to the fupreme God, as it implies eternity, independency, neceffary exiftence, immutability, infinity, and the like. Therefore the great God takes it to himfelf as his own proper name. If. xlii. 8. *I am the Lord, or Jehovah, that is my name, and my glory will I not give to another.* The prophet Amos defcribing the great God, that formed and fafhioned all things, fays, that *Jehovah is his name.* Rom. v. 8. and ix. 6, and the Pfalmift fpeaking of him fays, *that men may know, that thou whofe name alone is Jehovah, art the moft high over all the earth.* Thus we fee that the name *Jehovah* belongs to none but the true God. This name is in a variety of places given to Chrift. He was *that Jehovah* that fent fiery ferpents amongft the people to wound and deftroy many. Num. xxi. 5, 9. compared with 1 Cor. x. 9. We meet with this name again. If. xl. 3, *Prepare ye the way of Jehovah.* That this was

Chrift, appears from Mat. iii. 3. In that fortieth of Ifaiah, how is that Jehovah fet forth ? What ftriking defcriptions, what grand reprefentations, fuitable to none but to the great God ? Chrift was that *Jehovah*, which Ifaiah faw in his vifion fitting upon a throne, high and lifted up. If. vi. 1, and 2. compared with John xii. 41. He is again called by this name, If. viii. 13. *Sanctify the Lord*, or *Jehovah of Hofts*. This Jehovah in the 14th verfe is called a Sanctuary; but a ftone of ftumbling and a rock of offence to fome; which exactly anfwers the defcription of our Lord Jefus Chrift. 1 Pet. ii. 6, 8, We have the name *Jehovah* given to Chrift in If. xlv, 18, 25. It is very plain from a view of the Saviour that all this is meant of him, and you have full fatisfaction concerning it, if you confult Rom. xiv 10, 11. and Phil. ii. 10, 11. Thus we are thoroughly fatisfied that Jefus Chrift is plainly pointed to in Jer. xxiii. 6. *The Lord* or *Jehovah our righteoufnefs*. Who deferves that fignificant and moft emphatical title but the redeemer? He is again called *Jehovah* in Hag. ii. 6, 7. That this is the mediator appears from Heb. xii. 26. And laftly, you find him called by the fame glorious name in Mal. iii. 1. He who is called *Jehovah*, is the meffenger of the covenant, which is none elfe but our adorable Immanuel. Thus then, if Jefus Chrift in a variety of places bears the title of *Jehovah*, which is a name the great God has himfelf affumed, and which he will not give to any beneath him, it gives us fufficient reafon to conclude that he is *God equal with the Father*.

Again, we find that Chrift has other titles given him which are evident proofs of his deity, as they belong only to the fupreme God. Thus he is called *the great God*, Tit. ii. 13. It is Chrift who is meant, for it is he that will appear and not the Father; it is he who is the hope of his people. Under the fame characters of deity he is reprefented, Pf. xcv. 3. *The Lord is a great God, and a great King above all Gods*. From what the Apoftle obferves, Heb. iii. 7. It is plain that this is the fecond perfon. He is called the *mighty God*, If. ix. 6, the *true God*, 1 John v. 20. The apoftle had juft been fpeaking of Jefus Chrift, and them immediately adds, *this is the great God*. He is called the *highef*, Luke i. 76. *Lord of Glory*, 1 Cor. ii 8. He is ftyled the *King eternal, immortal, and invifible, the only wife God*, 1 Tim i. 17. *The bleffed and only potentate, King of Kings*, *and Lord of Lords*, 1 Tim. vi 15 Now are not all these glorious and pompous titles expressive of deity? Can they with any manner of propriety be given to Christ, if he is only a creature? How must we then distinguish the creator from the creature; If Christ has all the distinguishing names of the supreme God, I apprehend we may readily conclude that he is really God, equal with the Father, for God will not part with those titles which set him infinitely above the highest angels, or give that which is his glory to another. But,

2. *There are perfections given to Christ, which are peculiar to the supreme God.* There are some perfections which are called communicable, that is, they are ascribed in a lower degree to creatures. Thus is God called *wise?* so is man. Is he merciful? so are his people. Is he holy, just, faithful and the like? so are they. There are other perfections which belong to God alone, and cannot be found even in the highest creature, and these are said to be incommunicable: such as eternity, immutability, omnipotence, omniscience, omnipresence. Whoever possesseth these perfections must be God; and therefore Christ is so, because we find them ascribed to him.

1. *He is eternal.* Thus " his goings forth have been " from of old, from everlasting," Mic. v. 2. compared with Matth. ii. 6. He is represented as the " Alpha and the " Omega, the beginning and the end, the first and the last," Rev. i. 8. ii. 17 Chap. ii. 17. chap. ii. 8 He is said to be " before all things," Col. i 17. And to be in the " beginning " with God," John i. 1. An expression which doubtless denotes eternity. Thus he was " set up from everlasting, from " the beginning, or ever the earth was :" and it appears that he was present with the Father when this appointment was made, " Then was I by him as one brought up with him." Prov. viii. 23—31 Thus if Christ was from eternity he can be no creature, but must be true God, for none else inhabits eternity.

2. *He is immutable.* His being called the Alpha and Omega, beginning and end, the first and the last, not only proves his eternity but his immutability. He is unchangeable in his purposes and perfections, and therefore answers the description of the great God. Hear what the Father says to him, Heb. i. 10, 11, 12. " Thou Lord, in the be-

"ginning hast laid the foundation of the earth, and the
"heavens are the works of thine hands   They shall perish,
"but thou remainest; they shall all wax old as doth a gar-
"ment; and as a vesture shalt thou fold them up, and they
"shall be changed: but thou art the same, and thy Years
"shall not fail." What are all these but characters of deity?
He is said to be "the same yesterday, to-day, and for ever."
Heb. xiii. 8. Thus he is immutable.

3. *He is almighty.* He has an omnipotent arm, by which he is able to subdue all things unto himself. He is called the *mighty God*, If. ix. 6.; and is therefore *mighty to save*, If. lxiii. 1. The Psalmist styles him the *most mighty*, Psal. xlv. 3. In Rev. i 8. He is called *the almighty.* And chap. xv. 3. In that song of Moses and the Lamb, sung by the saints above, and especially at the final conquest of every enemy, they cry—*Great and marvellous are thy works Lord God Almighty!* That this is Jesus Christ appears, from its being called the *Song of the Lamb,* from his being called *King of Saints,* a title peculiar to the Son of God.—But,

4. *He is omniscient.* His understanding is infinite, there is nothing but what he knows. He searches the heart of man. Now this is peculiar to God, Jer. xvii. 10. "I the "Lord search the heart, I try the reins. And, 1 Kings viii. 39. "Thou, even thou only knowest the hearts of all the "children of men." This is ascribed to Christ, Rev. ii. 23. "I am he, which searcheth the reins and hearts." You therefore read in the four Evangelists, in many places, how Christ knew the thoughts of his enemies, and the secret reasonings of his disciples. But the apostle Peter puts this point out of dispute in his appeal to our Lord for the reality of his love to him. "Lord thou knowest all things, thou "knowest that I love thee." John xxi. 17. Nothing can possibly be concealed from thine eye, thou knowest every transaction, yea, the very thoughts of the heart, and therefore I can with the more cheerfulness appeal to thee for my love, thou knowest that I love thee. But,

5. *He is omnipresent.* It is an undeniable truth, that no creature can be in various places at the same time, this is peculiar to God. But Christ is in ten thousand places at the same time. Therefore he tells us, that "where two or "three are gathered together in his name, he is in the "midst of them," Matth. xviii. 20. This holds good now, as

well as then when the words were spoken, and therefore supposes Christ present in all the assemblies of his people, in what part of the world soever they may be gathered together. He has also promised to be with his ministers to the end of the world, in the regular administration of gospel ordinances. Matth. xxviii. 20. Consequently he must be in numberless places, even of the greatest distance from each other at the same moment of time, and therefore must be omnipresent. Thus then as Christ possesseth eternity, immutability, almighty power, omniscience and omnipresence, he must be true God, as those are perfections, that cannot possibly be communicated to any creature, but belong to God alone But,

3. *Such works are ascribed to Christ as none but the great God is equal to*—Here I shall not mention what I might, but confine myself to creation work. He that created all things must be God. If we consider what creation was, viz. to bring all things out of nothing. What a variety in the creation, the heavens and the earth, with their respective inhabitants; what a beautiful and exact arrangement of creatures and things, each keeping their proper places : if we consider the sun that rules by day, and the moon which governs the night, we cannot but conclude that he that was equal to all this work must be God, as he must have infinite wisdom, omnipotence, eternity, and uncontroulable sovereignty. You therefore find that creation work is ascribed to God, and to him alone. Neh. ix. 6. *Thou, even thou art Lord alone, thou hast made heaven, the heaven of heavens with all their host, the earth and all things that are therein, the seas, and all that is therein.* He is distinguished upon this account from all other Gods. Jer. x. 10, 11, 12, 15, 16 *. Now creation is ascribed to Christ. Thus John i. 3. *Without him was not any thing made, that was made.* Now if he was a creature, he must be concerned in making himself, and so must be supposed to have a being even before he existed, which is an absurdity. It clearly appears from Col. i. 16. *For by him were all things created that are in heaven, and that are in earth visible and invisible : whether they be thrones, or dominions, or principalities, or powers :* nay, the apostle goes yet further and says, *that all things were* not only

---

* See other places that prove this truth.

created by him, but for him, to manifest his Glory. I might mention other parts * of Scripture that speak this truth, but these are enough, they are so exprefs. Thus by the eternal word were the heavens made He only *spoke and it was done. He commanded and it stood fast* †. He said, *let there be light, and behold there was light* ‡, all which are such proofs of infinite power, and sovereignty, as evidently declare Jesus Christ to be God —But,

4 That *worship which only belongs to the supreme God is given to Christ.* Divine worship is internal and external. Internal worship consists in the various acts of the mind, faith, love, reverence, and the like, external worship lies in prayer and praise, and is performed by suitable gestures, of standing kneeling, and prostration. This worship supposes infinite excellencies in the object, and every thing that lays a foundation for it. Now this worship in its most extensive view is given to Christ He is the object of faith, John xiv. 1. Of love Matt. x. 37. Of Prayer. Acts vii 59 Of praise. Rev. i. 5, 6, and Chap, v 13. All these acts of worship are given him in the Lord's supper. Here he is set forth as a fit object of faith, of love, of praise: here the Christian dedicates himself to him, soul, and body, and all ; and resolves to live to that redeemer who died for him, and rose again. If then religious worship is given to Christ, he must certainly be God. There is no distinction made between him and the Father, but the same praises are ascribed to him as to the Father; prayer is made equally to him, and the poor guilty sinner flies to him, and lays all the stress of his salvation upon him, he then must be equal with the Father, as there is not the least appearance of inferiority —— Besides there are two things, a consideration of which should determine us in this great point, viz. Christ himself has received all religious worship, and the Father has commanded it to be given him.——Christ himself received it when on earth. Thus the woman of Canaan came and worshipped him, Mat. xv. 25. And his disciples worshipped him after his resurrection, Mat. xxviii. 17. Now had he been only a creature, even though of the highest rank, he would not have received divine worship, but would have forbid it as Peter did

---

* 1 Cor viii. 6. Heb. i. 2. Rom. xi. 36. Psal. cii. 25. Is. xl. 12, 25, 26. K. xlv. 18. † Psal xxxiii. 9. ‡ Gen. i, 3.

Cornelius, Acts x. 26 And as the angel did John, Rev. xix. 10. It would not have have been confiftent with his faithfulnefs to his Father to have taken that, which was due to God alone; nor can we fuppofe his Father would have fupported him in it, nay commanded that he fhould be worfhipped. Yet, when he came into the world the Father gave command, that all the Angels fhould worfhip him. Heb i. 6. And in another place it is faid, *he has committed all judgement to the Son, that all men fhould honour him even as they honour the Father,* John v. 22, 23. Which cannot be, unlefs they give the Son the fame divine honour they do the Father. To fum up all, as divine worfhip in all its parts and branches is given to our Lord Jefus Chrift; as he has readily received it without the leaft objection; as it is by the Father's command that he is worfhipped, and as no creature, though ever fo exalted, can be the object of divine worfhip, fo we muft conclude that Chrift is God equal with the Father—

Thefe I apprehend to-be fufficient proofs of this great doctrine. If thefe are the diftinguifhing characters of deity, and they are applied to Chrift, then he muft be God. If they are not, I afk what are fo, and how we muft know the true God from the higheft of his creatures? However the infidel may fneer at thefe hints, I hope they are enough to fatisfy your minds, and to confirm you in the truth. I fhall therefore proceed,

II. *To the improvement of this great article of our faith.* And we fhall now fee the great importance of this doctrine, as for inftance,

1. *It was abfolutely neceffary that Chrift fhould be God, to fit him for executing that work, which he gracioufly undertook.* His work we may confider in a threefold view; that which he was to do on earth—That which he daily does in heaven—And that which he will do at the great day——

2. *He had a work to do on earth, which he never could have gone through, had he not been God.* This was to make fatisfaction to infinite juftice for the fins of his people, to purchafe grace and glory for them, and to gain a complete conqueft over every enemy. And who could do all this but the mighty God? *He could not poffibly have bore up under that load of guilt, which lay upon him, if he had not had deity to*

support him. All the sins of his people lay upon him, and met in him, and were enough to sink him absolutely down, if he had only been a creature. He must be in the utmost distress from his agony in the garden, yea such distress as no being inferior to God could have grappled with; all his body was in a bloody sweat, and the blood dropped upon the ground in clods, being forced through the pores by his extreme torture.—Besides, *he would not have been able to have made atonement for the sins he bore, if no more than a creature.* As sin has an infinite evil in it, so it requires an infinite satisfaction. What was the reason that the blood of beasts could not make this satisfaction, but because there was no proportion between this and sin. And to look upon the sacrifice of Christ as only that of a man, a creature, is only going a few steps higher; still the proportion would not be equal, and therefore it would not declare the glory of God in the pardon of sin, on the account of such a sacrifice.—*If he had not been God, he never could have purchased grace and glory.* Considered as a creature, there could have been no merit in what he did and suffered, especially for others. All a creature can do, he owes to God, in every capacity and relation, and therefore heaven could never have been styled a *purchased possession. He could never have gained a complete conquest over our spiritual enemies if any thing below God* Principalities and powers were not easily spoiled. Death and hell required an almighty arm to conquer them. When he looked, and there was none to help, he must have yielded the victory, and sunk in despair; his own arm would never have brought salvation to him, if it had only been the feeble arm of a creature. And thus our redemption never would have been obtained, the price would never have been paid, and therefore the everlasting gates never have been opened. But, considering him as God, he was equal to the whole arduous work, he finished it in a little time, and had no occasion to lie an eternity under torment; he triumphed over every enemy, and led captivity captive. But,

3. *If he was not God he would not be equal to the work he is daily executing above* He is gone into heaven, to appear in the presence of God for us, Heb. ix 24. He there *makes intercession for transgressors,* Is. l ii. 2. He sits as the exalted king and head of his church, to conquer all our enemies for us, to apply salvation, and bring all his people in, to see that the work is

carried on, that all our wants are supplied, that none he undertook for are loft, and therefore to order and direct all the steps in providence so that his enemies may be disappointed, and the good of his people promoted. Now you will easily see to answer these ends he must have infinite knowledge and wisdom, know all his people, with all their wants and various circumstances: to know his enemies with all their schemes; and to know what methods are best for him to pursue. He must be present every where, that he may be a help in every time of need. He must have almighty power, to crush our enemies, to support, supply and keep us. He must have infinite love and pity, to pass by so many backslidings, and exercise suitable compassion to those that are in distress. In fine, you will easily see, how necessary it is that he possesses every divine perfection ——Lastly, *He must be God to be equal to the work of the great day* He will raise the dead, both small and great, assemble the world, sit upon his exalted throne, pass an equal and decisive sentence upon all, and execute this sentence in the everlasting destruction of some, and in the complete happiness of others. And who but a God can do all this? Can a creature know where the scattered dust of millions lies, raise it and form it into a body fitted for immortality? Can any less than God pass a just and suitable sentence upon all, distinguish the righteous from the wicked, know and remember the secret springs and principles of every action, and produce so many millions upon the stage? Can any but the great sovereign of the world be the judge of it, doom the wicked to everlasting darkness, and immediately execute the sentence upon them, and with uncontroulable authority open the everlasting gates to all his people, and place them at his own right hand?—Thus if Christ had not been more than a creature, he never would have been able to have gone through the work, the execution of which was of so much importance to the glory of God, and to our salvation. Blessed be God we have such a Saviour.——

4. *This doctrine of Christ's deity lays a foundation for, and is a powerful motive to admiration, love and obedience.* How does it magnify the grace and love of the Redeemer in all his works for us! What! did the mighty God undertake our salvation? Did he who was infinitely blessed for evermore, veil his glory in the form of a servant, and ap-

pear in fashion as a man? How amazing the stoop! How inconceivable the love! Had it been a creature's love, it would have appeared great, could he have gone through the work: but it was the infinitely glorious Creator, that gave his life a ransom for us. *Behold the grace of our Lord Jesus Christ; who though he was rich, yet for our sakes became poor, that we through his poverty might be made rich*, 2 Cor viii. 9. Behold it ye angels and wonder and adore. Yea, ye do admire, ye do view this amazing mystery of godliness, and find matter for entertainment and praise. Behold it O my soul, thou art more immediately concerned in it. Behold the heights, and depths, and lengths, and breadths of the love of the Son of God: keep it ever in view, it will warm thee when cold and lifeless; it will humble thee under a sense of thy feeble attempts to love; it will enliven thy services; make thee hate sin, and be a quickening motive to all obedience: it will kindle a secret fire in thy soul, and make thee long to be with thy Redeemer above, to love and praise him for ever without coldness or interruption. Do the saints praise him in heaven? yes, that sacred temple refounds with hallelujahs to God, and to the Lamb. They have the highest, the clearest views of the love of Jehovah the second person. This is the theme they for ever dwell upon, and tune their harps, and touch the loudest string to praise the great mediator. Thou adorable Emanuel, didst thou leave thine exalted throne to come down, and purchase our salvation? Can we make thee more happy than thou really art, hast been from all eternity, and wilt be to all eternity? No, it was thine own free, rich, matchless love, that did incline thee to do all this for us. ‘ Oh love unfathomable!
‘ All glory, honour and praise be to him that thus loved us.
‘ Here we are the fruits of thy purchase, reaping the effects
‘ of thine infinite merit, and we will spend an eternity to
‘ thy praise.’ This love is the strongest and most powerful motive to obedience we have in all the gospel. Come hither, ye slothful souls, who complain that you are like the door upon its hinges, come hither, and view the love of the mighty God, and, if any thing will quicken you, this will, and make you move swiftly on in your Redeemer's service. Come ye, in whom the sacred fire seems faint and low, bring your cold hearts hither, and the love of the everlasting Father will kindle it afresh. Bring your hard rocky hearts hither,

and see if this love will not soften them. Attend ye backsliders; behold the Son of God in the likeness of sinful flesh, and if any thing will melt your souls, and fill you with contrition, this will. Look upon the mighty God becoming a prince of peace, when you are under any temptations to be led into sin, and this will tend to guard you against a compliance, convince you of your obligations to him, and stir you up to all holy circumspection and diligence in the divine life. 'Oh, did God undertake for me? Is God him-
' self become my Saviour? What love is this! What means
' this coldness O my soul, to this divine Saviour? Why so
' dull, and insensible of thy obligations to him? Why so
' worldly, so earthly and sensual? What means this care-
' lessness in thy walk, thy frame, thy conversation! Come,
' let me view the person of my Saviour: See, my soul, who
' is it that has loved thee? It is the high and lofty one that
' inhabits eternity. Oh what motives to praise, to obedi-
' ence! Have this ever in thine eye, that it may keep thee
' from security, endear the mediator more and more to thee,
' and make thee daily active in his service, and for his glory,
' till thou shalt be translated to the world above, where thou
' wilt love and praise for ever.'

5. *What a fund of consolation is there in this doctrine.* It administers relief in every case, and is an inexhaustible fountain and spring of comfort to all in distress. Is the sinner under a deep sense of sin? Does the load of guilt he has contracted lie heavy on his soul? Do his numberless transgressions appear before him with all their aggravations? Does he see his unworthiness of the favours of God, and in his own apprehensions is he upon the brink of hell? It is a melancholy case indeed; but awful as it is, this doctrine affords relief, and opens a door of hope to him at once.
" Shall I despair when I hear of such a saviour? He is not
" a creature, then should I despair; but he is the supreme
" God, and sure he can help me, though never so miserable
" and helpless. He can stand between offended justice and
" my poor guilty soul, therefore will I venture, and cast
" myself upon this glorious, this all-sufficient mediator, not
" doubting but he can pluck me out of the fire, and make
" me, though never so unworthy, an heir of eternal life."
Is the Christian distressed with a sense of his numerous enemies, and his own weakness to withstand them? Is he

afraid therefore that he shall not hold out and persevere to the end? Is he distressed from day to day through fear of giving up the conquest to his enemies? There is enough in this doctrine to set him at liberty, to cheer his soul, and revive his hopes of an everlasting triumph over all opposition. " Why should I be distressed, O my soul, and
" walk in perpetual bondage through fear of my enemies?
" It is true they are too powerful for me ; and was I there-
" fore left to myself I must inevitably fall, and never finish
" my course; but look up and see who is on thy side. God
" himself is for thee, it matters not then who are against
" thee. Thou leanest not upon an arm of flesh, but upon
" everlasting strength. Away then all ye disquieting fears ;
" though I am weak, yet my redeemer is strong ; and I am
" abundantly more secure than Jerusalem itself, though
" surrounded with mountains, for the Lord himself is
" round about me. I will go on my way rejoicing there-
" fore in the midst of every discouragement, and not ques-
" tion my reaching to my journey's end, and getting safe to
" Zion." Oh, it is a glorious truth ? It is upon this that the church * is built, as upon an immoveable rock, and not upon Peter; and therefore the gates of hell shall not be able to prevail against it. Here is something for the Christian under all his fears ; something that tends to fill him with joy unspeakable and full of glory. Whatever his circumstances are ; whether he is discouraged with a sense of his backslidings, or struggling with some corruption, or distressed with his unworthiness : whatever his difficulties are, a view of the mighty God is enough to remove them all, and give him boldness and courage in life and death, and under the prospect of the great day He is now become a fit Saviour. He is a suitable object of a poor sinner's trust and dependence, and we may cheerfully leave our souls with him, as being able to keep them against the judgement day Upon the whole, take this doctrine out of the Bible, and what is it ? This is the glory of the Christian scheme, that God stands at the head of it. It is this that gives life and efficacy to every other doctrine. This makes Christ appear glorious in all his mediatorial characters. This is the foundation of the Christian's comfort. Remove this, and his hopes of

* Mat. xvi 18.

pardon and eternal life ceafe at once; therefore it is a doctrine of the utmoft importance.

6. *Chrift's being God fhould render him infinitely amiable to all, and does fo to his people.* How blind thofe eyes, that can fee no beauty in Jefus Chrift! How hard that heart, that feels no love to him! Is he God? He then poffeffeth infinite glory. Are the angels beings of peculiar excellency; how much more is the Son of God? Come and view him, and fee if there is nothing you can perceive that is captivating in him. How ignorant were the daughters of Jerufalem, when they afked the fpoufe, what her beloved was more than another's beloved, that her heart was fo much fet upon him? She anfwers them by reprefenting the innumerable qualifications and excellencies of our Lord Jefus Chrift. ' What is my beloved, fays the Chriftian? He is
' all I want, all I can defire. He is the Son of God; the
' brightnefs of the Father's glory and the exprefs image of
' his perfon. See, how glorious his perfon, how bright his
' excellencies. How can I but love him, and efteem him
' fairer than all the children of men? Lord, whom have I
' in heaven but thee, and there is none upon earth I defire
' befides thee. Should I be infenfible of fuch excellencies, or
' not love thee, thou glorious Emmanuel, all might efteem
' me funk and loft in the utmoft ftupidity.' How infenfible, and how ftupid muft you be, poor hardened finners, that you can pafs by fo much glory, and fix your hearts upon things that are unworthy of your efteem? Have you yet feen no beauty in Jefus, that you fhould defire him as your friend, your hufband? To prefer the poor enjoyments before the Lord of Lords! This intimates as if you thought there was nothing in him that could render him a fit object of your efteem. What a reflection this upon that Jefus, whom angels adore! Stupid creatures, that the glorious mediator has not yet won your hearts. Let me recommend him to thee as one worthy of thy choice, one worthy of thine efteem; one that can make thee unfpeakably happy, and in whofe friendfhip, whofe favour, thou wilt find the greateft pleafure.

Laftly, *How awful the ftate and condition of thofe who refufe divine honours to our Lord Jefus Chrift, and caft contempt upon his glorious perfon!*

GAL. ii. 16.

Knowing that a man is not justified by the works of the law, but by the faith of Jesus Christ, even we have believed in Jesus Christ; that we might be justified by the faith of Christ, and not by the works of the law: for by the works of the law shall no flesh be justified.

THE great doctrine of justification by the righteousness of Jesus Christ imputed, though of the utmost importance, is become too much the object of contempt; it is no wonder indeed, if we consider, that it is inconsistent with that way of happiness which reason knew in a state of innocency, and which corrupt nature now, only approves; it is in vain to attempt to accommodate the gospel, to the common conceptions of corrupted reason, for reason, when in its highest and purest state, was unacquainted with it; the words *Grace* and *Christ* were unknown, in the state of innocency; no way to eternal life was then revealed but by a personal obedience, to the law. There was no necessity of a mediator, till sin was introduced into the world, therefore there was no revelation of Christ till after the fall; when man had exposed himself to the awful curse of the law, and was absolutely unable to prevent the execution of it. As man was acquainted with no other language when in his perfect rectitude, but *do this* and *live*, no wonder that the way of justification by the righteousness of Christ should now appear new and mysterious, and be represented as the effect of enthusiasm? Have we received any peculiar advantage by the fall? Have we gained any considerable light by it? Or are we more inclined to receive the mysteries God has revealed? No, behold, we have the utmost reason to bewail our apostacy! having felt the sad effects of it, in the blindness of our minds, and hardness of our hearts! The fall has placed us at the utmost distance from God, and filled our minds with the strongest prejudices against the glorious mysteries of the kingdom of God. Thus in all ages, the great and important truths of the gospel have been ridiculed and despised; not only in the darker days of the Old Testament, but under the present dispensation, when life and immortality are brought to life by the gospel. The preaching of the cross of Christ was to the Jews a stumbling-block, and to the Greeks foolishness. 1 Cor. i. 23. The Jews, though favoured with the various prophecies of the Old Testament, which speak of Christ, and his righteousness, yet discovered the utmost aversion to this way of justification, as directly contrary to those high thoughts they had entertained of themselves, and their services, and as absolutely destroying all their favourite principles which they had imbibed, and which they were determined to maintain against all the opposition that should be made to them. Hence we find them uniting their endeavours against Christ and his disciples, to put a stop, if possible to the spreading of a doctrine so repugnant to the sentiments of corrupt nature, and so destructive of those elevated hopes which were built on the apprehended worthiness of their imperfect services. On this account we find the apostles, with a noble zeal, maintaining the great doctrines of the gospel, and particularly this of justification; this glorious truth, however opposite to the dictates of degenerate reason, is of the utmost importance; some have called it the grand prop and bulwark of the Christian religion; it certainly enters into the very essence of Christianity, and is necessary for us to know, as it is the foundation of our hopes of eternal life, is our greatest support in life, and our comfort in a dying hour. Is it not of the utmost importance for the sinner to know how it is he shall be justified before God? How is it, that this is not a more general subject of inquiry? Do you consider that a mistake here may be of the most dreadful consequence? Will it not be inexpressibly awful to live in expectation of a discharge at the bar of God, and an entrance into the everlasting mansions, and to meet with a disappointment? to hear the dreadful sound, Depart, and be sentenced to the bottomless pit! The shame and confusion that must attend such a disappointment cannot possibly come within the reach of human conception: it is no wonder then, that we find the apostle Paul so zealously maintaining the way of justification by the righteousness of Christ, and that he is so large, and so particular, upon this subject. He was well acquainted with the opposition that nature made to this great doctrine, for he was once an enemy to it himself, he was a distinguished Pharisee, was remarkable for his zeal for the law, and for his enmity against Christ and his glorious cause: he was alive in his own apprehensions, and was far from suspecting his title to heaven, till the spirit came and enlightened his understanding, conquered his aversion to the gospel, convinced him of his guilt, and led him to a view of his wretched state and condition without a better righteousness than that he had depended upon. Now he becomes a zealous advocate for Christ, he is unwearied in his endeavours to spread the knowledge of Christ, he labours to convince his countrymen of their ignorance and obstinacy, represents to them the vanity of their hopes, the way, the true way of justification, and presseth them to come to that Jesus, to whom he had committed all his concerns, and on whom he depended for eternal life. In his epistle to the Galatians he particularly enters on the doctrine of justification by faith in Jesus Christ, reproves those to whom he wrote for their departing in some measure from the purity of the truth, and their adherence to the law in this great article; and asserts that neither the works of the ceremonial, nor the moral law, have any hand in the justification of a sinner, it being only by faith in our Lord Jesus Christ. *We who are Jews by nature, and not sinners of the Gentiles, knowing that a man is not justified by the works of the law, but by the faith of Jesus Christ, even we have believed in Jesus Christ, that we might be justified by the faith of Christ, and not by the works of the law; for by the works of the law shall no flesh be justified.* These words naturally lead us to consider this great and important doctrine of justification, so essential to the being and comfort of a real Christian. In hopes that some may be instructed in this glorious truth, and others confirmed and established in their belief of it, let us consider the following things.

I. Let us inquire into the meaning of being justified, or what are the privileges of justification.
II. Show that our personal righteousness is absolutely unable to justify us before God.
III. That it is the righteousness of Christ alone that is the matter of our justification, and the ground of our acceptance with God.
IV. How the righteousness of Christ is made ours, so that we may be really justified by it. And,
V. Make a practical improvement of the subject.

I We are to inquire into the meaning of being justified, or shew what the privileges of justification are. There have been great disputes about the word *justify*; it being evidently taken in different senses in the word of God. Sometimes it signifies our celebrating the justice or righteousness of God, or our vindicating his perfections from any charge that may be brought against them, Psa li. 4. But in the matter of the sinner's justification before God, the word *justify* is to be taken in a forensic sense; the papists plead that it is to be taken in a physical, or moral sense, for the infusion of righteousness, and therefore pointing out that as the matter of our justification: but it is evident we are to take it in a law sense; in several places of scripture, where a judicial process is represented, mention is made of a law accusing of persons guilty, of divine justice requiring punishment or satisfaction given, and sinners absolved and cleared; justification then is a judicial act, an act of justice, as well as of mercy; *who shall lay any thing to the charge of God's elect?* (says the apostle.) *It is God that justifieth, who shall condemn? It is Christ that died.* Rom. viii. 33. Who shall endite them in course of law, or judgement? Who can proceed against them legally? Let him come forth. There is enough indeed, to be charged against God's elect, but who shall condemn them for it? Christ has made satisfaction for them, and God has justified them. They have sinned and violated the law of God, but Christ has made satisfaction for them, on which account God has discharged and freed them from the sentence of condemnation. Thus justification is a judicial act. This being considered, leads us to take notice of the bleſſings contained in juſtification, or what is meant by a ſinner's being juſtified. And theſe two things are ſignified thereby:

1. That the ſins of thoſe who are juſtified are pardoned; and,

2. That they are received into the favour of God, and have a right and title given them to eternal life.

1. To be juſtified, ſignifies that our ſins are all pardoned. This ſuppoſes that we are naturally under a law, that we have violated this law, have forfeited the favour of God hereby, and rendered ourſelves obnoxious to the curſe denounced by the law-giver upon tranſgreſſion.

This is a truth of the utmoſt importance, every where ſo repreſented in the word of God. God gave man a law in innocency, to which he annexed an awful threatening of everlaſting death, to be executed upon us if we violated and broke this law. The firſt tranſgreſſion being an act of a public repreſentative, all mankind are concluded under ſin, and become guilty before God (to this we may add numberleſs actual tranſgreſſions); we are hereby naturally under the curſe of the law, liable to the execution of its condemning ſentence. In ſuch awful circumſtances does God find us, when he comes and actually juſtifies us, by which act he pardons all our ſins, original and actual, blots out the hand-writing againſt us, cancels the enditement, ſtops the proſecution, and gives us a diſcharge from puniſhment. In juſtifying us, God gives us a full pardon of all our ſins, ſo that we ſhall never be brought into condemnation. Hence it is ſaid, *there is no condemnation to them which are in Chriſt Jeſus* Rom. viii. 1 We have the pardon of ſin repreſented in ſuch ſtrong expreſſions in the word of God as ſufficiently ſhews its certainty and fulneſs, ſo that it is impoſſible for ſin ever to condemn the juſtified ſoul. Thus it is ſaid, our ſins are covered. Pſal. xxxii. 1. *Bleſſed is he whoſe tranſgreſſion is forgiven, whoſe ſin is covered.* They are ſo covered that they ſhall never appear before the judicial eye of God to procure our condemnation. Again, in the ſecond verſe pardon is repreſented by a not imputing ſin, *Bleſſed is the man unto whom the Lord imputeth not iniquity.* He reckons it not to him, places it not to his account, and conſequently it cannot procure his condemnation. It is again ſet forth by *a not remembering our ſins any more*, Jer. xxxi.

34. God is said to *caſt our ſins behind his back*, Iſa. xxxviii. 17. *To caſt them into the depths of the ſea*, Mic. vii, 19. Signifying the impoſſibility of their ever appearing againſt the believer more; they ſhall be forgotten never to be remembered, they ſhall be loſt, ſo as never to be found. Again, pardon is ſet forth by blotting out, and cleanſing, Pſal. li. 1, 2. Acts iii. 19. Alluding to a creditor, who croſſes out a debt in his book of accompts, that it may never more ſtand in force againſt the perſon who contracted it. Theſe and various other expreſſions in the word of God, are deſigned to expreſs the fulneſs of pardon, and the happineſs of thoſe who receive it. Thus we find God repreſented as " ſeeing no iniquity in Jacob, neither any perverſeneſs in " Iſrael," Num xxiii. 21. The meaning of which words cannot be, that the ſins of his people are not known to him; nothing can be concealed from his all comprehenſive view. He ſees the ſins his people commit, but not as their judge to condemn them; he deals with them as if they had never tranſgreſſed the law, by diſſolving their obligation to puniſhment, and treating them as children. The ſins of God's people are not ſo taken away, as to deſtroy the demerit of ſin. Though they are delivered from condemnation, yet there is enough in them that is matter of condemnation. The ſins which they daily commit deſerve everlaſting puniſhment, and appear in themſelves infinitely odious in the eyes of God who cannot behold iniquity but with the utmoſt deteſtation and abhorrence. This therefore lays a foundation for continual deep humiliation of ſoul, and admiration at the infinite grace of God, in the pardon of ſins ſo often repeated, and attended with ſuch aggravating circumſtances. Nor does the blotting out of ſin, and the like, ſignify that ſin does not cleave to the ſoul; ſin ſtill remains, and exerciſeth too much power in the ſoul; remiſſion of ſin conſiders it with relation to puniſhment, and not as a quality inherent in the ſubject, therefore the ſtain remains till it is fully waſhed away by the ſanctifying influences of the Spirit of God, which will not be, till body and ſoul are ſeparated: yet there is a full, and abſolute remiſſion of ſin, both as to the guilt and as to the puniſhment: ſo that all the proceedings of God with his juſtified people are in a way of mercy. Here it may be aſked, whether the ſins of the believer, paſt, preſent, and to come, are all pardoned when the ſoul is juſtified? If we conſider remiſſion as to the purpoſe and de-

cree of God, or as to the promife of God in the Covenant of Grace, or as to the merit of Chrift, who gave full fatisfaction to infinite juftice for all the fins of his people, their fins paft, prefent, and to come, are all pardoned. But if we confider remiffion as actually given to the foul, his paft and prefent fins may be faid to be forgiven, but not his future fins; for they cannot be confidered as being actually committed, and a debt cannot be blotted out before it is contracted. No more can our fins be faid to be all at once, and explicitly forgiven, before they are actually committed. However upon the whole, Chrift's righteoufnefs being imputed to us, lays a foundation for the remiffion of all fins; our future fins fhall not be laid to our charge, nor iniquity prove our ruin: and here God has wifely made it our duty, to beg daily for the forgivenefs of our fins, and to bring forth fruits meet for repentance; to fhew his hatred to fin, the character of thofe on whom he beftows forgivenefs, and to evidence to the foul that his fins are forgiven. Thus we fee how important a bleffing juftification is; whilft we are ftrangers to Chrift we have no reafon to conclude that our fins are forgiven, the fentence of the law ftands open againft us, we are expofed to the wrath of God, and have the utmoft reafon to fear the dreadful execution of it, according to the awful demerit of fin. Bleffed therefore is the man whofe tranfgreffions are forgiven, whofe fins are covered; bleffed is the man unto whom the Lord imputeth not iniquity; but there is a further bleffing contained in juftification: for,

2. Thofe who are juftified are received into the favour of God, accepted as righteous, and have a title given them to eternal life. To juftify is more than to pardon: a king may pardon a rebel, but not take him into favour. Adam was under no obligation to punifhment when he was in a ftate of innocency, yet he was not juftified, *i. e.* he was not declared righteous fo as to have a title given him to eternal life, that depended on his continuance in obedience. As juftification is a declaring righteous, fo it fuppofes a righteoufnefs in us, or in another, by which we are declared righteous. There is certainly a pofitive righteoufnefs required by which we muft be declared righteous; becaufe the law requires obedience, as well as fuffering: the one to free from punifhment in cafe of offence, the other to entitle

to life. Thofe who cannot be declared righteous, cannot be entitled to eternal life. In juftification therefore the righteoufnefs of Jefus Chrift being imputed to the believer, he is pronounced righteous, accepted as fuch, and entitled to a glorious immortality, for that righteoufnefs by which he is juftified is perfectly anfwerable to the demands of the law and juftice. If therefore this righteoufnefs be properly reckoned to the believer, he muft be neceffarily acquitted, be introduced actually, into the divine favour, and have a juft and indifputable right to eternal life. And that this righteoufnefs which Chrift has wrought out, may be reckoned to the believer fo as to fecure to him thefe important bleffings, will be confidered more particularly when we come to inquire how the righteoufnefs of Chrift becomes ours. Some there are who apprehend that juftification is imperfect in this life, as depending upon our continuance in obedience; according to them when we firft believe, we have all our paft iniquities forgiven, are at prefent delivered from condemnation, and have a title to eternal life, provided we continue in the performance of obedience, to the end of life. This makes our right to life not immutable and perfect, but changeable, as it depends upon the perfonal performance of certain conditions, the fulfilment of which muft be precarious; our title therefore may be loft, and we deprived of the glorious inheritance above Juftification, according to this uncomfortable fcheme, only makes our falvation poffible, not certain; it does not in this fenfe fuppofe the law to be fulfilled, therefore it does not include a proper title to eternal glory; for if we confider juftification as giving an immutable title to life (as certainly it does) it neceffarily fuppofes the law to be fulfilled, which threatned death; confequently there remains nothing now, but (as man is declared righteous) that he be put into the poffeffion of that glorious inheritance, to which God hath given him a title. In juftification then the finner not only receives the pardon and forgivenefs of his fins, but a right and title to eternal life; thefe two are diftinct bleffings, though infeparably connected; where there is one, there is likewife the other. Every one who has his iniquities forgiven, has likewife a right to all the bleffings of the everlafting covenant; they were both purchafed by Jefus Chrift, and are confequently given to all thofe to whom he imputes his perfect righteousness. Adoption is a part of justification; and " as many as received him to them gave he power to " become the sons of God, even to as many as believed on " his name." John i. 12 Christ came not only to redeem us from the curse of the law, but to favour us with the adoption of sons, Gal. iv. 4, 5. He covers our guilt with the robe of his righteousness, and he makes our persons accepted of God; he renders all the awful threatnings of the law absolutely void, gives us a discharge from eternal death, and presents us with the glorious prospect of an heavenly inheritance; he gives a right to all the promises in the word of God, gives us an interest in all the divine perfections, and makes us heirs of God and joint heirs with himself.

Such are the blessings of justification, blessings of the greatest importance. To be freed from the obligation to everlasting punishment, to be made heirs of eternal life. Who can represent the excellency of such blessings? they are more than all the honours of the present life.

To close the present discourse with some useful instructions deducible from the point: as,

1. Hence we learn how necessary it is for us stedfastly to believe *Original Sin*, with all its consequences. To deny this important truth, is, to open a door for that latitude of thought, which has had so dreadful a spread to the ruin of immortal souls. Many who have fallen off from the gospel, have begun here: it is well to have our hearts established in those divine truths which have so strict a connection with our salvation, and which have such an influence upon it. It is a disagreeable thought to proud man, ' that ' we are all under the guilt of sin, and have our souls tainted ' with its pollution, as we come into the world,' though it really is the cause of that condemnation the law placeth us under, as well as those many actual transgressions with which we are chargeable, which are all pardoned in justification. This truth, of all mankind's being in a state of sin and condemnation, hath a near concern with justification in a gospel sense. The apostle Paul therefore, in treating of that great doctrine, mentions this first, as what is necessary to be first considered; as you may see, in the first, second, and third chapters, of the epistle to the Romans. And in the fifth chapter of the same epistle, ver. 12, &c. he proves this truth, by a regular course of most conclusive arguments.

Wherefore, as by one man sin entered into the world, and death by sin; and so death passeth upon all men, for that, or *in as much as all have sinned.* Experience likewise adds its testimony to put the matter beyond all doubt. There are early discoveries given of the loss of original rectitude, and of the guilt we are under; and whilst we believe stedfastly this important truth, we are led to adore infinite wisdom and grace in the method of salvation revealed in the gospel; to value the great blessings included in justification, and cheerfully and thankfully to depend upon that righteousness which Jesus has provided, and by which alone we can be justified in the sight of God.

2. Hence we learn to adore the infinite grace of God, in bestowing upon creatures so unworthy, such an invaluable and important blessing. When we consider our apostacy from God, and how justly we have deserved his everlasting indignation, we have just reason to cry out, Lord, what is man that thou art mindful of him, or the son of man that thou visitest him!

Does God justify the ungodly? Lord, says the sensible humbled sinner, what astonishing grace! Is there forgiveness with thee that thou mayest be feared! May such a guilty creature as I draw near unto thee! Rejoice, O my soul and wonder at sovereign grace: there is room for *me* to hope; behold God justifies guilty sinners who lie naturally under the condemnation of the law, and might have been made the everlasting monuments of infinite wrath! See the blessings he confers, he pardons, freely and fully pardons every transgression, and gives a glorious and sure title to eternal life; he makes sinners heirs of an inheritance to come, an inheritance that is incorruptible, undefiled, and that fadeth not away, an inheritance that far exceeds all the glory of this lower world. Oh surprising grace! When God gives, he gives like himself. He is himself far above our comprehension, and so are his dealings towards his people. Do not your hearts burn within you? Are not your souls filled with unspeakable wonder, to hear of God justifying the guilty? God, who has been offended in innumerable instances; that God who, for an act of rebellion, cast the sinning angels down from their exalted happiness to everlasting misery? Does this God pardon guilty man, receive him into favour, and make him an heir of everlasting blessings? Who can be silent under such glorious views of divine grace and mercy! Were we to be insensible of such grace, the very stones would cry out against us, and upbraid us with ingratitude. Oh may we unite in ascribing everlasting praises to him, who passed by the fallen angels, but determined to exalt his grace and mercy in the justification and salvation of fallen man, and fulfils his gracious designs by making the heirs of wrath to be heirs of heaven. It is the Lord's doing, may it ever be marvellous in our eyes! Not unto us, O Lord, not unto us, but unto thy name be all the glory.

3. Hence we see the difference, between justification and sanctification. They are both blessings of the everlasting covenant, and inseparable Those who are possessed of the one are also of the other, they cannot possibly be separated, yet they are different: the one is a relative change, the other a physical or moral change. The one frees us from all obligation to punishment, and gives us a title to heaven; the other cleanseth our souls from the pollution of sin, makes us holy, and so fits us for the enjoyment of eternal life. By justification we stand in a different relation to God from what we before did, then we were to be considered as children of wrath, under the curse of the law, and could claim no special interest in the divine favour, but rather had reason to look upon God as offended, and as obliged by his own threatning to execute the sentence of the law against us: now we are related to him as children, he is our father, and we may joyfully expect to enjoy all the happy consequencs of such a relation. Thus justification changes our state, sanctification, our tempers, and dispositions. It is justification gives us the title of children, so sanctification gives us the temper of children, and makes us behave ourselves in some measure agreeably to such a relation In justification we have a righteousness imputed to us; in sanctification we have a righteousness inherent, a righteousness infused; the one is an act of God's free grace through the righteousness of Christ in changing our state, the other is the work of his spirit purifying our hearts. Thus we see they are different, and yet they are both absolutely necessary to our full and complete salvation; and always meet in the soul that gets safe to glory; what God hath thus joined let no man attempt to put asunder. If there are no evidences of the

grace of God changing your hearts, you may conclude that you are still in a state, of condemnation ; you must shew you are justified, by your love to Christ, your hatred of sin by your serious, humble and heavenly conversation, else all your hopes of an interest in the divine favour are vain and deceitful. Sanctification indeed is not perfect in this life as justification is, it is a work that is of a progressive nature, it is gradually carried on in the soul, and not fully perfect till body and soul are separated ; yet as in justification the believer receives a full discharge from the curse of the law, hath a sure title given him to eternal life, and shall never come into condemnation, so likewise, in sanctification where the work is begun in the heart, it shall be carried on till it is perfected ; hence the lowest degree of sanctification is an assurance of the whole, an earnest of heaven. Glory be to God, such provision is made as is every way necessary to secure our everlasting salvation : that we may not be deceived at last, and be deprived of the promised inheritance.

4. Hence we learn that all the afflictions God is pleased to bring upon his people, in the present life, are not curses or punishments for sin, but paternal chastisements and fruits of love. As by justification our sins are all forgiven, and we are taken into the favour of God, so all God's dealings with his justified one's are agreeable to that relation which he stands in to them, and consequently the effects of love and mercy. Sin was indeed the original cause of every affliction ; on the account of sin man gets his bread by the sweet of his brows; when sin was introduced into the world, immediately man became liable to innumerable afflictions and calamities, and if we view afflictions as they are considered in the covenant of works, we must view them as curses, as parts of that punishment which God threatned, and consequently as the effects of his just wrath and indignation: but let us look into the new covenant and there view them in a different light; there they are not considered as curses but as fatherly corrections, and real blessings Psa lxxxix 30, 34. If his children forsake my law, and walk not in my judgements; if they break my statutes, and keep not my commandments : then will I visit their transgression with the rod, and their iniquity with strip s Nevertheless my loving-kindness will I not utterly take from him, nor suffer my faithfulness to fail. Those

that are justified may look upon all their afflictions as mercy and truth; they have a right given them, to all the blessings of the covenant of grace, and therefore afflictions are brought upon them as they are considered in this covenant, which are fatherly corrections. Thus David sinned greatly, and God afflicted him for it, but though his afflictions were on the account of sin, yet they were not as curses, but the effects of a father's displeasure; as such they are likewise designed for our everlasting good, and so are out of love and compassion. As a prudent serious parent not only corrects his disobedient child to shew his displeasure at his sin, but out of love to him to promote his real good and advantage, and to put a stop if possible to that which would prove his ruin: thus God not only shews his detestation of sin when he afflicts his people, but shews his love to their souls, inasmuch as he takes this method to humble them for sin, to quicken them in their way to Zion, and to fit them more and more for a better world. Isaiah xxvii. 9. ' By this therefore ' shall the iniquity of Jacob be purged, and this is all the ' fruit to take away his sin.' What agreeable news must this be to the mourning soul, who is ready to draw rash conclusions from his long and tedious afflictions! Fear not, your troubles have not the dreadful bitterness of the curse in them, see them sweetened by a consideration of that love that is the cause; view them as the gentle corrections of your heavenly father, who takes such measures with you, to promote your everlasting advantage; call not your sonship in question, ' for whom the Lord ' loveth he chastneth, and scourgeth every son whom he ' receiveth If ye endure chastning. God dealeth with ' you as with sons: for what son is he whom the Father ' chastneth not? But if ye be without chastisement, where- ' of all are partakers, then are ye bastards and not Sons.'

5. Does God bestow such invaluable blessings upon his people in justification, This should keep them from envying the prosperity of all the worldly great, and reconcile them to every dispensation of providence.

GAL. ii. 16.

Knowing that a man is not juſtified by the works of the law, but by the faith of Jeſus Chriſt, even we have believed in Jeſus Chriſt; that we might be juſtified by the faith of Chriſt, and not by the works of the law: for by the works of the law ſhall no fleſh be juſtified.

WHEN we conſider the worth of an immortal ſoul, and the tendency which the glorious myſteries of the goſpel have to promote and advance the glory of God, and our everlaſting welfare, we have abundant reaſon to adore infinite grace, for that revelation which he has given us, and readily to receive whatever is contained therein. Had we not been favoured with this, we ſhould have grovelled in perpetual darkneſs and remained perfectly ignorant of thoſe ſublime and exalted truths which are ſo nearly connected with our preſent and future comfort. Original ſin, juſtification by the imputed righteouſneſs of Jeſus Chriſt, and the other great and important truths of the goſpel are pure matter of divine revelation; they lie far above the reach of nature, and would never have entered into the heart of man; nay, now they are revealed, they appear far beyond our comprehenſion we are all ſurpriſe and aſtoniſhment when we view the myſteries of infinite grace, and are loſt amidſt the glorious ſcenes that open to us in our ſalvation by Jeſus Chriſt.

We have entered upon the confideration of the great doctrine of juftification, a doctrine of the utmoft importance, which lays a foundation for the moft glorious expectations, fecures the Chriftian from the awful fting of death, and brings him fafe at laft to the glorious and everlafting embraces of his exalted redeemer. To fet this doctrine in fuch light as may inform the ignorant, comfort the dejected, and confirm the Chriftian in his attachment to it, we propofed to confider,

I. What is the meaning of the word juftify, and what are the blefling of which juftification confifts.

II. Shew that our own perfonal righteoufnefs is abfolutely infufficient to juftify us, before God.

III. That it is the righteoufnefs of Jefus Chrift which is the matter of our Juftification and ground of our acceptance with God.

IV. How this righteoufnefs becomes ours fo that we may be legally and really juftified by it.

We have already confidered the firft thing, and have fhewn the word juftify is to be taken in a law, or forenfic fenfe.—When a finner is faid to be juftified it fignifies,

1. That all his fins are pardoned.

2. That he is introduced actually into the favour of God, accepted as righteous, and has an immutable right and title to eternal life given him. We now come to fhew,

II. That our own perfonal righteoufnefs is abfolutely infufficient to juftify us before God. This is a truth plainly and exprefsly contained in our text, in which the apoftle afferts, that no flefh can be juftified by the works of the law, by which works he means not only thofe of the ceremonial but alfo of the moral law; had there been any juftification by outward works he muft have been juftified; but notwithftanding all his boafting whilft he was a Pharifee, yet when the fpirit of God came, and enlightned his underftanding in the myfteries of the gofpel, he immediately renounced all felf dependance, and committed his foul to Jefus alone, depending entirely on his righteoufnefs. We, fays the apoftle, who are Jews by nature, and not finners of the Gentiles. We are not of the finful Gentiles who have nothing to boaft of, but we are of the race of the Jews, that ancient, and diftinguifhed people of God, who can boaft of the greateft privileges; we are of thofe, to whom the oracles of God, and the means of grace are committed; we have many duties to produce, many works which we have performed, yet being convinced that a man is not justified by the works of the law, but by the faith of Jesus Christ, even *we* have renounced all our privileges and duties in point of justification, and have believed in Jesus Christ, that we might be justified by the faith of Christ, and not by the works of the law, for by the works of the law shall no flesh be justified. This testimony of the apostle, especially when we consider him as directed by the Holy Ghost herein, is sufficient to convince us of the vanity of all dependence upon our own righteousness, and stir us up to seek after justification by the righteousness of Jesus Christ. But as it is so natural to man to go about to establish a righteousness of his own, and as it is a matter of such moment to the soul, so it may not be unprofitable particularly to shew the absolute impossibility of being justified by any righteousness of our own: and I pray God it may be made effectual to convince some self righteous sinner of the vanity of his self dependence, and quicken him to give up himself and his everlasting concerns into the hands of Jesus.

Now in order to make it appear, that our own righteousness, in any state whatever, is unable to justify us before God, I shall shew the necessity of a perfect righteousness, and then consider how far short ours comes, of such a righteousness.

I. Let us consider the necessity of a perfect righteousness to our justification before God—And that a perfect righteousness is absolutely necessary to our justification before God appears, if we consider the infinite justice and holiness of God, and the explanation our Lord himself has given us of the law.

1. Let us consider the infinite justice and holiness of God, and his awful majesty and glory. If we consider the infinite perfections and glory of him who justifies, it will appear that a perfect righteousness is absolutely necessary. The whole creation proclaims the infinite glory of God, and tends to fill us with awe and reverence of him; all the representations we have of God in his word have the same tendency, they forbid every proud exalted thought of ourselves, and fill the most perfect creatures with the most profound humility. Thus the angels who surround the glo-

rious throne of God above, lofe, as it were, all fenfe of their own excellency, when they view the infinite furpaffing glories of their great Creator; they therefore in the moft admiring and adoring ſtrains cry out, Holy, holy, holy Lord God Almighty! God is fo fpotlefs and holy himfelf, that the heavens are not clean in his fight, and he charges even his angels with folly, Job. iv. 18. Chron. xv. 15. Who can ſtand before him without a perfect righteoufnefs? Is it not moſt agreeable to the infinite holinefs and juſtice of God that the righteoufnefs he accepts of, and on the account of which he introduces creatures into eternal life, fhould be a perfect righteoufnefs? It is certainly moſt confiſtent with thofe views we have of the infinite purity and glory of God, with the revelation he hath made of his fpotlefs perfections, as well as with the ends and defigns he has in view in the falvation of his people, which are to exalt his righteoufnefs and juſtice as well as his grace and mercy: if we take but theſe things into our confideration we ſhall fee immediately the neceffity of a perfect righteoufnefs to render us accepted of God. It is indeed eafy for man when elated with pride, in the time of health and profperity, to extol the worth and excellency of virtue; to perfuade himfelf and others, that it is perfectly confiſtent with the juſtice of God, to accept of the righteoufnefs which man is capable of performing; and below him, to take notice of thofe trifling excurfions of nature which are efteemed and reprefented as the neceſſary effects of our conſtitution; it is eafy for the finner to perfuade himſelf that all is well, when confcience is afleep and death appears at a great diſtance; but fuppofe the finner ſtanding upon the brink of an unchangeable world, with confcience awake, his mind impreſſed with a fenfe of the glory and majefty of that God before whom he is going to appear; fuppofe him taking his everlaſting farewell of all mortal converfe, and convinced he is going to the tribunal of that God before whom the angels fall down with the moſt profound reverence, going to receive a fentence that will determine his everlaſting condition; will he not ſtart back at the awful view? Will he not fufpect the fufficiency of his own righteoufnefs, and be ready to cry out with the great Bellarmine, It is fafeſt to truſt in the righteoufnefs of Chriſt? However light and trifling our thoughts may be, of the way of a finner's juſtification before God, an awakening confcience and the views of death will make a great alteration in our fentiments, and fill us with a ferioufnefs and awe, to which we were before in a great meafure ftrangers. Befides, God has brought himfelf under an exprefs obligation to proceed with man according to the law, either to give eternal life upon perfect obedience, or to punifh difobedience with everlafting death. As perfect obedience only is agreeable to the tenour of this law, fo if man is faved, confiftent with the divine juftice and faithfulnefs, it muft be by fuch an obedience. But,

2. It appears from the explanation which our Lord gives us of the law, that an abfolutely perfect righteoufnefs is neceffary to our juftification before God. That a law by which God may govern his creatures, neceffarily flows from the relation in which they ftand to each other, from the infinite perfections of the Creator and the capacities of the creature is felf evident. That a law was given originally to man made capable of moral government, and that this law required fpotlefs and perfect obedience, is likewife as plain. Hence the law doth eternally and unchangeably oblige man unto the fame fpotlefs obedience; for though man has by an act of his own, weakened himfelf fo as to be incapable of paying perfect obedience, yet as there is ftill the fame relation fubfifting between God and us, fo there is the fame obligation upon us, though not the fame capacity in us. Our want of capacity to fulfil the law, is no reafon why the law muft abate of its demands: therefore we find our Lord in the 5th and 6th chapters of Matthew reprefents the law as not only requiring a conftant uniformity of action, but an abfolute regularity and perfection, in the thoughts, will, and affections. I need not repeat what Chrift fays in thofe chapters, as it muft be known to all that attentively read the Scriptures, but we may afk the queftion, why does Chrift himfelf thus open the law? Does it not fignify that the law requires more than an outward obedience, even a perfect conformity of heart and life? and why has he explained the law thus, in our degenerate circumftances, while we are incapable of paying fuch a finlefs obedience? Does it not fignify that the law has fuftained no alteration, that it is as extenfive in its demands as ever, and that nothing but a perfect righteoufnefs will be accepted, as our juftifying righteoufnefs? Chrift's explanation of the law thus has a

tendency to convince the finner of his numberless imperfections, to humble him under a sense of them, to make him despair of ever obtaining eternal life by his own righteousness and to stir him up to seek with the utmost earnestness and diligence, after an interest in that perfect righteousness, which alone is commensurate with all the demands of the law, and can give a soul boldness and confidence at the bar of God. Having thus mentioned the necessity of a perfect righteousness to our justification, we may proceed to shew that man's righteousness, in whatever state or capacity we view him, is absolutely insufficient to justify him before God as being imperfect. And,

1. It is evident that the righteousness of the unrenewed finner must be every way imperfect—or that works before conversion are so—therefore these cannot justify us. If the fountain be corrupt the streams must, if the tree be corrupt the fruit will be so too. You cannot gather grapes of thorns, and figs of thistles." It is as irrational to expect a perfect righteousness from those, who are absolutely under the power and government of sin: none of the works of which the finner is ready to boast, can be called spiritually good: they flow not from a good principle; hearts must be renewed before we can produce the amiable fruits of righteousness in our lives; we must be first united to Christ and ingrafted into him. Unless the branches are in the vine, they cannot flourish and bring forth fruit, they must receive nourishment from the root by which they become productive of proper fruit. Thus must the soul be in Christ, or he cannot bring forth the fruits of righteousness. None of the finner's pretended good works are directed to a good end: they have not the glory of God in view in the performance, and therefore they cannot justify: to suppose it, is to reflect upon the infinite purity of God, or his wisdom and knowledge, for either he must not be so holy as he is represented, or he cannot, consistent with his glorious perfections, connive and wink at sin; or else he must be deceived by the appearance of a splendid profession, and not know the springs, principles, and ends from whence the finner acts: but who dare presume to entertain a thought of God so unbecoming his divine and glorious perfections? Besides, the righteousness of the finner being imperfect, the law, instead of justifying, condemns him, " Cursed is every one that continueth not

"in all things which are written in the book of the law to do them," Gal. iii. 18. May thefe awful words be deeply impreffed upon the minds of the felf-righteous finner! and be made a happy means of leading him to Jefus, who only has fatisfied the law, and is able to deliver the guilty foul from the wrath to come!

2. Our habitual or inherent righteoufnefs is imperfect, and therefore cannot juftify a foul. This is the work of the fpirit upon the heart, and therefore far exceeds all the works of the unrenewed finner; this fuppofes the fountain of fin to be in part cleanfed, the dominion of fin to be in part deftroyed, and the image of God to be in fome meafure impreffed even on all the powers and faculties of the foul; yet this work being imperfect, lays no foundation for the foul to build his hopes of acceptance with God upon; it is abfolutely neceffary to fit us for the enjoyment of God, as it gives a fuitablenefs in the heart to heaven, without which there could be no happinefs; but we muft not put it in the place of a perfect juftifying righteoufnefs. Nothing fhall meet with the divine approbation that is not agreeable to his appointment, and is fitted to anfwer the ends for which he has appointed it; it is plain the work of fanctification is imperfect, the word of God fufficiently attefts it, and fo does the Chriftian's experience. The apoftle Paul makes a melancholy complaint of the remains of fin: he viewed not only with the deepeft humility his various backflidings, but the *Body* of *fin* he ftill found within him. He went to the root, to the fountain head, and was concerned to have that more and more cleanfed and purified. "O wretched man "that I am, who fhall deliver me from the body of this "death?" Rom. vii. 24. And is not this oftentimes your language, Chriftians? are not your fouls often deeply humbled at the melancholy view of the remains of fin in every faculty, which render your fanctification imperfect? And can you then with a comfortable fatisfaction depend upon what God has wrought in you for your acceptance with him? A confideration of that body of fin, that ftill in part remains, forbids your dependence, and fets you upon an inquiry after a perfect righteoufnefs.

3. Good works, or works after converfion, are imperfect, and therefore cannot be our juftifying righteoufnefs. From our habitual and actual righteoufnefs we may be pronounced

just and righteous persons, but not justified. Considering iniquity is in every faculty, there must be iniquity cleaving to every duty. As the works of unrenewed sinners can in no respect be said to be spiritually good, so the good works of real believers are but partly so; how can it be otherwise, when the heart is but partly renewed? if the fountain be not perfectly pure, the streams that flow from thence cannot. Consequently all the good works of the believer cannot justify him before God. The Ephesians were esteemed holy persons when the apostle wrote to them, and yet he tells them they were not saved by works, which must be works after conversion. " For by grace are ye saved; " through faith; and that not of yourselves: it is the gift of " God: Not of works, lest any man should boast. For we " are his workmanship, created in Christ Jesus unto good " works, which God hath before ordained that we should " walk in them." Eph. ii. 6, 9. 10. But it is alleged by some that Christ came not to furnish us with a perfect righteousness of his own, but to fulfil certain conditions agreed upon between the Father and him, by which a valuable consideration should be given to God, that he might not execute the law of works, but disannull it, and new terms of acceptance with God be established for man—viz. a new and much easier law of faith, and repentance, and sincere obedience, which, though imperfect, yet should be accepted as our justifying righteousness. If there is a possibility of our being justified by a righteousness of our own, this certainly stands the fairest for it; and as it is so natural, to espouse sentiments prejudicial to our everlasting comfort, and this is an affair of so much moment, it may not be amiss to endeavour to remove this imaginary foundation, lest we should be unwarily led aside from the truth as it is in Jesus, or fluctuate in our minds about things of such great importance. Accordingly, in opposition to this specious allegation we answer, such a way of justification is contrary to the word of God, and the experience of the saints recorded there. It lays an evident foundation for boasting: It opens a door to the greatest discouragements, and our own righteousness is put in direct opposition to that righteousness by which we are justified.

1. This way of justification is contrary to the word of God, and the experiences of all the saints recorded there. The

Psalmist was a man really renewed, and in part sanctified; he was doubtless sincere in his obedience, and yet he cries out, Psal. cxxx. 3. "If thou, Lord, shouldst mark iniquities, "O Lord who shall stand?" Intimating that as there are none who are without iniquities, so these are sufficient to render all our righteousness, though never so sincere, unfit to stand the trial of infinite justice, and consequently incapable of justifying us. A consideration of the infinite perfections of the judge, keeps the believer from depending upon any thing he himself has done. David intimates that he was a servant of God, he feared and obeyed him, he was eminent for his zeal in worshipping, and is styled a man after God's own heart, and yet I hear his humble language, and see the sense he had of his own imperfections, and of the infinite purity and rectitude of the divine nature. Psal. cxliii. 2. "Enter not into judgement with thy ser- "vant, for in thy sight shall no man living be justified." Behold now he lies humble in his own eyes, and under an awful sense of the glorious perfections of the deity. Does he boast? No, Lord, says he, when I consider thine infinite and spotless excellencies I am lost, my obedience appears every way unworthy of thy acceptance; wast thou to enter into judgement with me, I must give up all hopes of thine everlasting favour, for none can stand before thee when thou art angry. David appears to be absolutely ignorant of a way of justification by faith, repentance, and new obedience; had this been the way, though he could not have pleaded justification by the law, he might by the gospel have pleaded with God his sincerity, &c. Yet see, he intreats that God would not enter into judgement with him; and why? Because in his sight, or before him, no flesh can be justified. We may appeal to God for our sincerity and integrity, and in some cases plead it: thus Hezekiah pleads his integrity for sparing his life; "remember now, O Lord, I beseech "thee, how I have walked before thee in truth, and with a "perfect heart, and have done that which is good in thy "sight: and Hezekiah wept sore." Isa. xxxviii. 3. He had been so zealous a reformer of worship, that had he been cut off in the midst of his days, idolaters might have represented it as the judgement of God upon him. Job maintained his sincerity with the utmost confidence before his friends who suspected it, but when God came to call him to an at-count, behold with what humility he appears! he is entirely filent and cannot plead any thing with God which may entitle him to his favour, but lies at his footstool and " abhors himself and repents in duft and afhes." Job. xlii. 6. The apoftle gives us his own fentiments in the text and in Phil. iii. 9. And " be found in him, not having my own " righteoufnefs, which is of the law, but that which is " through the faith of Chrift, the righteoufnefs which is of " God by faith." Ifaiah perfonating the church fays, lxiv. 6. " But we are all as an unclean thing, and all our righteouf- " neffes are as filthy rags, and we all do fade as a leaf, and " our iniquities like the wind have taken us away." But the apoftle James fays, that Abraham was juftified by works when he offered Ifaac his fon upon the altar, James ii. 21.: true, but this cannot be meant of juftification before God. For the defign of this chapter is to fhew the excellency of juftifying faith, that it is a vital principle in the foul, and is productive of all good works. It could not be meant that Abraham when he offered up his fon, was then and by that action juftified before God, for he was juftified long before, when he believed God, and it was imputed to him for righteoufnefs. That act of Abraham's was indeed a fufficient evidence of his faith, and thus is faith faid to be made perfect by works, James ii. 22. " Seeft thou how faith " wrought with his works, and by works was faith made " perfect." By this act of Abraham's the apoftle fays the fcripture was fulfilled: " and the fcripture was fulfilled " which faith, Abraham believed God and it was imputed " to him for righteoufnefs, and he was called the friend of " God." James ii. 23. i. e. The fcripture before declared Abraham to be juftified by faith, and now it evidently appears that the fcripture was true, for behold he withholds not his own fon when God calls.

2 If we are juftified before God either in whole or in part by our own righteoufnefs, it lays a foundation for boafting. Chrift is the fole author and finifher of our falvation; if we are juftified by his righteoufnefs in oppofition to our works, then he muft have all the glory; accordingly we find the happy fpirits above all adoring him that fitteth upon the Throne, and the Lamb, their glorious mediator, who redeemed them by his own blood, and made them kings and priefts unto God, Rev. v. 9, &c. But if Chrift

came only to procure eafier terms of acceptance, if he came to open a way for the acceptance of our faith and fincere obedience as our juftifying righteoufnefs, this furprifingly leffens that praife that is his due, while it attributes part to the creature: for fo far as refpect is had to our righteouf- nefs in juftification, fo far we have a fhare in the glory, and that no fmall fhare if we are indebted to Chrift only for *making way* for our juftification, while our own righteouf- nefs is the immediate caufe of it. But this is contrary to the whole tenour of Scripture, which gives all to Chrift. It is evidently juft what the apoftle fays, " If Abraham was " juftified by works, then he would have whereof to glo- " ry," Rom iv 2 But the fcheme of falvation is fo ad- mirably contrived, that it lays no foundation for our boaft- ing, but leads us to give all the praife to God, and to ad- mire the aftonifhing riches of his grace, in defigning and bringing about our falvation, fo that no flefh fhould glory in his prefence. " But of him are ye in Chrift Jefus, who " of God is made unto us wifdom, and righteoufnefs, and " fanctification, and redemption. That according as it is " written, He that glorieth, let him glory in the Lord," 1 Cor. i. 29, 30. Pride is very unbecoming in thofe who are indebted to free grace for all they have. God has ef- fectually put it out of the power of thofe that are faved to afcribe any glory to themfelves, by undertaking the whole himfelf. It is the evident defign of the gofpel fcheme to keep the foul humble and to magnify the riches of fove- reign grace; whatever therefore does not debafe the crea- ture, and exalt God; whatever lays a foundation for men's glorying, is inconfiftent with the whole tenour of revelation, difhonours God, and is unworthy of our credit.

3. Juftification by faith, repentance, and fincere obedi- ence deftroys the Chriftian's comfort, and lays a founda- tion for great, and diftreffing fears. Upon this fcheme we can be fure of nothing, becaufe juftification depends upon a continuance and perfeverance in obedience till death, and this perfeverance is not abfolutely fecured to us, neither by the covenant engagements of God, nor by the purchafe of our Lord Jefus Chrift; hence arifes a great uncertainty of our falvation, for though Chrift has purchafed eternal life, it is only for thofe who believe and obey unto the end, and there is no abfolute purchafe of ftrength to enable them to

believe, or to continue in faith; thus the whole mediation of Christ may be rendered fruitless, the end of his death unanswered, and the soul that has believed may fall away and be eternally lost. O uncomfortable doctrine, says the Christian! What, is this the gospel which God has revealed, is this all the encouraging news it brings? Is this all the prospect I have of eternal life? I must then sit down and absolutely despair; for how can I expect salvation? It is true this scheme says, if I will believe, and repent, and obey unto the end of life, then I shall be justified; but how can I believe, says the awakened soul? How can I conquer those deep rooted prejudices with which my mind has been so long filled against Christ and his gospel? Or how shall I be able to stem the tide of sin and corruption, and to persevere in the midst of the most powerful temptations? I am told indeed the terms are easy, that if I will do a part God will do the rest for me, but alas! I find I can do nothing, if God does not begin the work, and carry it on, I must perish. O melancholy thought! If I have not sufficient strength purchased for me I am undone, and all my hopes are absolutely vain. If this be the case, I can at best have no certainty of my salvation; for could I say with the apostle Paul, that Christ loved me and gave himself for me, yet what satisfaction would it give my soul, so long as Christ has not absolutely secured my perseverance in obedience, upon which depends my justification? I can never say I am justified. Whilst indeed my purposes and resolutions are strong, whilst my sincerity appears clear and evident to me, I may entertain hopes of heaven; but when I shall backslide, when my lusts prevail over me, how shall it then be? I must then give up all hopes, till I have again repented, formed fresh resolutions, and turned to God; then I may venture to entertain a distant hope again. Thus uncomfortable would this scheme be, was it the scheme of the gospel; but blessed be God! I have a better foundation to build upon, the everlasting engagements of God, the full and perfect satisfaction, and glorious purchase, and therefore the constant and prevailing intercession of my great Redeemer. Here my soul can sweetly rest, here I find all I want, here is all my salvation and all my desire. Upon the whole, in this scheme, there can be no justification in this life, we cannot with comfort say there is no condemnation, till we have finished our courſe and got ſafe above; and how muſt this diſtreſs the awakened ſoul? What relief can it be to a ſoul burdened with a ſenſe of ſin and ſenſible of his own weakneſs? I ſhall cloſe this head with a paſſage out of a worthy author upon this ſubject.

'This argument, ſays he, is much uſed by our firſt re-
'formers, Luther, Melancton, Chemnitius, and others, and
'they thought it unanſwerable, viz. That however men
'inſenſible of ſin might diſpute for the influence of their
'works in juſtification; yet when men have ſore terrors
'of conſcience neither their works paſt nor their promiſes
'and purpoſes of what they will be for the future will com-
'fort them; but only the doctrine of free grace and par-
'don, by hoping in the mercy of God. Our Martyr Mr.
'Bilney hearing a rhetorical preacher lay a great ſtreſs upon
'repentance and obedience, as the only ground of hope,
'was offended, and ſaid how uncomfortable would this
'doctrine have been to me, when I was in great terrors
'for my fall.'

4. Our own righteouſneſs is put in direct oppoſition to that righteouſneſs by which we are juſtified. The apoſtle is very explicit in mentioning the works of the law as having no concern in our juſtification, Rom iii. 28. "Therefore we conclude, that a man is juſtified by faith without the deeds of the law," Rom. iv. 5. "But to him that worketh not, but believeth on him, that juſtifieth the ungodly, his faith is counted for righteouſneſs."—Rom. xi. 6. "And if by grace then it is no more of works, otherwiſe grace is no more grace; but if it be of works, then it is no more grace; otherwiſe work is no more work." And in our text the apoſtle poſitively aſſerts, that no fleſh can be juſtified by the works of the law. That by the law in general and eſpecially touching juſtification, is meant the moral law is plain, for after he has told us that he had believed in Chriſt, that he might not be juſtified by the works of the law, he ſays, ver. 19. That "he through the law was dead to the law." Alluding to Rom. vii. 9, which muſt be the moral law. Again he gives another reaſon why juſtification cannot be by the law, becauſe by the "law is the knowledge of ſin," Rom iii. 20, which is the moral law, that being the means of the apoſtle's conviction, Rom vii. 7. "What ſhall we ſay then? Is the law

"fin? God forbid. Nay, I had not known fin, but by the
"law; for I had not known lu.t, except the law had faid,
"Thou fhalt not covet." It is this law that is eftablifhed
by faith, which the apoftle excludes, Rom. iii. 31. "Do
"we then make void the law through faith? God forbid:
"yea we eftablifh the law." The law that brings under its
curfe, Gal. iii. 10. "For as many as are of the works of the
"law, are under the curfe," &c. From all which it is plain,
that all the works of the moral law are put in oppofition to
that righteoufnefs by which we are juftified. And furely
the apoftle fays enough to put it out of all difpute, when he
fays, that he "defired to win Chrift, and be found in him,
"not having mine own righteoufnefs which is of the law,
"but that which is through the faith of Chrift, the righ-
"teoufnefs which is of God by faith,' Phil. iii. 8 Here his
own righteoufnefs, and the righteoufnefs by which he was
juftified, are put in direct oppofition; if the righteoufnefs
which is faid here to be by faith, is that holinefs of life, &c.
which faith is productive of in the Chriftian, that would be
the fame as our own righteoufnefs, which the apoftle dif-
claims. The righteoufnefs of faith then is a righteoufnefs
without us, even the righteoufnefs of him, who is God as
well as man, and is received by faith, for our juftifying
righteoufnefs. Thus we have reprefented the infufficiency
of our own righteoufnefs, &c. and fhall clofe with a reflection or two

. We fhould each be concerned ferioufly to examine,
what is the foundation on which we are building our hopes
of eternal life Is it not a matter of the laft importance?
Ye negligent fouls that never make the important inquiry,
whether you are built upon a folid and gofpel foundation;
but take it for granted that all is well, fhould you be fud-
denly removed into an everlafting ftate, fummoned before
the bar of God, and meet with an awful difappointment, how
melancholy muft be your cafe! to be got at once, in a moment, beyond the reach of mercy and the found of falvation,
to find a miftake, which can never be rectified! Oh! the
fad felf reflections which the foul muft too late make upon
his former ftupidity! Infatuated creature! I went on in a
conftant round of duties, and never imagined but I was in
the way to a better world, I never examined my heart, and
it has now deceived me? Now it is too late to recal paft op-

portunities for reflection ! My Sabbaths are concluded ! The gospel has ceased its sound ! and a scene of eternal darkness inexpressibly awful presents itself before my distracted mind, and fills me with the most dreadful anguish and despair ! How inconceivably melancholy must the disappointment be ! May we therefore now seriously ask our souls these important questions, what is my dependence for justification ? Is it the righteousness of Christ or my own ? What have been my thoughts of this important point ? Have I only renounced my own righteousness in judgement, or have I been able actually to do it ? Convinced of its unworthiness, have I actually made application to Jesus Christ ? There are two acts of justifying faith, viz. An act of the understanding, and an act of the will; or an assent of the mind to the truths concerning Christ, and a real application of soul to him as he is represented. Have we been enabled in reality to look to another righteousness and not our own ? It is certainly time to make an inquiry. You who are in the bloom of life, cannot too soon inquire into this important point, or too early come to a satisfaction that you are justified, and have peace with God Can we pass our days in busy cares, or in gayety and pleasure, without a serious reflection upon the state of our souls ! See how the moments fly away, and is there no inquiry made ? May we defer an affair of such moment no longer, but now put the question faithfully and seriously to our souls, looking up to the eternal spirit, to help us in our inquiry, and to give us a view of our state and circumstances.

2. How melancholy is their case, who are going about to establish a righteousness of their own, in opposition to that which God has revealed ! Infatuated souls that fondly think your own imperfect duties sufficient, to entitle you to the favour of God. Did you ever seriously consider the infinite perfections of that God before whom you must appear ? and by whom your righteousness must be strictly tried ? Did you ever consider what the apostle, under the immediate influences of the Holy Ghost, says, that other foundation can no man lay, than that is laid, which is Jesus Christ ? 1 Cor. iii. 11. Did you ever seriously weigh the worth of an immortal soul ? and view the awfulness of a disappointment ? It cannot be, if you are depending upon a righteousness of your own. Think well upon the matter, it is of the utmost

importance. Confider the divine authority of that word that fays, by the works of the law fhall no flefh living be juftified. The law cannot juftify, it condemns, it is as a fchoolmafter to lead us to Chrift. Oh may it be made fuch to our fouls, that we feeing the infufficiency of our own obedience to juftify us, may fly wholly to that righteoufnefs which alone is perfect, and can alone deliver us from condemnation, and entitle us to eternal life.

SERMON VIII.

ON JUSTIFICATION.

PHIL. iii. 9.

And be found in him, not having mine own righteousness which is of the law, but that which is through the faith of Christ, the righteousness which is of God by faith.

THE apostle is evidently in this chapter, representing the way of a sinner's justification, and he gives us his own sentiments while he was a Pharisee, and the different conceptions, frames, and temper of mind he discovered, when he was savingly enlightened by the Spirit of God. If there is a possibility of being justified by works, privileges, or duties, the apostle stood the fairest for it; he exceeded all his countrymen, in his zeal for outward, moral, and ceremonial duties, and in privileges he exceeded many : if " any other man thinketh," says he, " that he hath where- " of he might trust in the flesh, I more," I can go beyond them all if they come to boasting. " I was circumcised the " eighth day;" at the exact time that was appointed of God. " I am of the stock of Israel," that ancient distinguished people, and of a favourite tribe, " the tribe of Ben- " jamin ;" both my parents were Hebrews. And thus none exceeded me in privileges, and as to my character, temper, and behaviour, I have in these outshined most of my countrymen; I was of the strictest sect amongst the Jews, viz. a Pharisee; I was warmed with the highest zeal

for the law, and was tenacious of the various rights and ceremonies of the Jewish religion; and as to my life it was agreeable to the letter of the law; thus, if any think they may have confidence in outward privileges or duties, I certainly may: and therefore I boasted of these, my heart was lifted up with pride, and filled with a vain expectation of eternal life, apprehending I had done enough to recommend me to God; but oh when God was pleased to enlighten my mind, to set his law before me in all its purity and spirituality, and to reveal his Son in me, how was I astonished to find I was a vile unworthy sinner! I saw myself miserable and wretched, with all my pretended duties and privileges! I found there was no other refuge for a poor guilty sinner but in Jesus Christ; In consequence of which, what I before esteemed gain; what I before prized and fondly thought would recommend me to God, now I renounced, parted with, and counted it loss for Christ. "Yea doubtless, and
" I count all things but loss, for the excellency of the know-
" ledge of Christ Jesus my Lord; for whom I have suffered
" the loss of all things," all my righteousness, my name, and reputation, the esteem of my countrymen, and my worldly prospects. I have suffered the loss of all for Christ, and
" do count them but dung that I may win Christ;" I look upon them as mean and contemptible, when compared with Christ, he is all and in all to my soul, I will let go all the world, life, and righteousness, and all, may I but win Christ, and " be found in him not having my own righteousness," &c. Oh what an alteration did grace make in this man! from a persecutor, an enraged enemy, a fiery bigot, he becomes a zealous advocate for, and an affectionate admirer of Jesus Christ, and his righteousness! " and be found in him," &c. He is here evidently shewing the ground of a sinner's acceptance with God, that it is on the account of a righteousness; that this righteousness is not our own, either wrought in us, or performed by us, but it is the righteousness of Jesus Christ received by faith. This is the righteousness on which the apostle had placed all his dependence for justification, the righteousness therefore which he desired to appear in at the bar of God, being sensible that no other righteousness would be accepted and honoured there. The apostle has his eye to some future season of solemnity, either when his soul should appear before God dismissed

from the body, or when body and soul should be united at the morning of the resurrection, and stand before the bar; by which he does not intimate that a person is not justified till then, or that there is a second justification then; no, the soul is justified as soon as he believes, his sins are then forgiven, and he receives a title to eternal life; at judgement his justification is manifested to all the world, he is openly received and publicly acknowledged as the person whom God has clothed with the righteousness of Jesus Christ, and so admitted into the full possession of that glory, to which he had before given him a title It was the apostle's earnest desire to be found thus arrayed, that he might be owned and acknowledged, as one the Redeemer had purchased, and so be introduced into the actual possession of eternal life; and therefore he made the righteousness of Christ his dependence, committed his soul, and his everlasting concerns into his hands, and counted all things but loss for him. Thus then it is evident, that the apostle speaks of that which is the ground of our acceptance with God, and the matter of justification, that is not our own righteousness, but the righteousness of Jesus Christ, here called the righteousness of God, and is said to be by faith, that is received, or apprehended by faith. We have made some small progress in the great doctrine of justification— have considered what is meant by a sinner's being justified, have likewise endeavoured to shew that our own righteousness is absolutely insufficient to justify us before God. This is abundantly evident, because a perfect righteousness is absolutely necessary to our justification, and our own righteousness, in every state and capacity in which man is considered, is imperfect, whether it be works before conversion, habitual or inherent righteousness, or works after conversion. We have likewise shewn, the insufficiency of faith, repentance, and sincere obedience to justify us before God; that this way of justification is directly contrary to the experiences of all the saints, recorded in the word of God— That it lays a foundation for boasting, that it deprives the Christian of all solid comfort, and fills him with distressing fears, and that our own righteousness is put in direct opposition to that righteousness by which we are justified. We might now, according to our proposed method, have proceeded to consider the third thing, viz. That it is the righ-

R

teoufnefs of Chrift that is the matter of our juftification, and the ground of our acceptance with God. But as there are some parts of Scripture which are brought in as favouring juftification by our own righteoufnefs, and which may appear fomewhat perplexing, fo it may not be altogether amifs to take fome notice of them, and efpecially of thefe two. The firft is Matth. xxv. 34 where we have fome general account of the proceedings of the laft day, and where Chrift the judge is reprefented as introducing his people into the poffeffion of eternal life, faying, " Come ye bleffed ". of my Father, inherit the kingdom prepared for you, " from the foundation of the world, for I was an " hungered," &c. Where we find the good works of the believer, and particularly thofe of charity and beneficence, feem to be introduced as the reafon why he inherits the kingdom of God, and confequently good works give a title; but this is only a defcriptive account of the perfons that are admitted into the kingdom of God, and not a reprefentation of the caufe why they are admitted. The word *for*, as a judicious divine remarks upon this paffage, does not always point out the caufe but fometimes the effect: thus, fays he, we fay the fpring is come, for the trees bud. Good works are the fruits and effects of God's beftowing fpiritual bleffings, but not the caufes or conditions for which he does it. God juftifies the finner freely by the righteoufnefs of Jefus Chrift; but in the laft judgement, he will proceed according to works, by which it will appear who they are that really believed in Jefus Chrift, and were juftified by him; by which God will act agreeably to his character as a righteous judge, in beftowing eternal life upon thofe who have brought forth the fruits of righteoufnefs, and dooming to everlafting darknefs all thofe who are ftrangers to real holinefs.

There is nothing in this paffage that is inconfiftent with free juftification, or the peculiar doctrines of the grace of God. For our Lord intimates that the kingdom of heaven was prepared for his people from everlafting, they were fuch as had believed; for love to Chrift which is mentioned as the principle from whence their works of charity proceeded, is the effect of faith. Upon the whole, the words appear to bear this fenfe: " Come ye happy objects of my Father's everlafting love, ye heirs of God, come and inherit the kingdom, for you have made it abundantly manifest that you are the persons for whom it was prepared, by your love to me and to my poor people; come, possess the inheritance which my Father designed for you, the inheritance you were long ago made the heirs of; come, and possess full and everlasting happiness." Thus the transactions of the last day throw no reflection on the grace of God in freely giving eternal life, or on the righteousness of Christ in justification, but are every way consistent therewith, and will show the righteousness of the judge in owning and honouring those, who owned and honoured him, and his people here on earth; and this will lead us into the true meaning of all those passages, where God is said to give to every one according to their works, and the like.

The other passage is in Matth. xix. 16, 17, where we have an account of a young man coming to Christ, and saying, " Good master, what good thing shall I do that I may " have eternal life?" To which our Lord answered, " if " thou wilt enter into life keep the commandments." From whence we may observe that the young man had no knowledge of the way of justification by the righteousness of another: he comes not humbled under a sense of the guilt of sin, and his undone condition, but under the apprehension that he could do something, by which he should have eternal life. Our Lord answers according to the general intent of the question, if thou wilt enter into life keep the commandments, which we may either understand to point out the way to eternal life in general, as a way of holiness and obedience to the commands of God; or to signify to him the mistaken apprehensions he was under as to his obtaining eternal life of himself; in order to enter into it, he must keep the commandments: this was enough, one should imagine, had he had any sense of his own weakness, to have convinced him, that he was miserable without a better righteousness than his own. But behold his stupidity! He tells our Lord, that he had kept all these from his youth: to convince him of which mistake, our Lord bids him go sell all that he had, and give to the poor, and come and follow him: but here he falters.—Thus then if we consider the nature of the question, the answer Christ gave to it, and the whole passage, we cannot but see, that it was a way of treating the young man, which, had he seriously attended to, had a tendency to convince him of his mistake, in apprehending that he could do every thing himself, that was necessary to eternal life, and to lead him to inquire after a better righteousness than his own. Wherefore serves the law now in our state of degeneracy? It is not only to be the directory of our obedience, but by its purity and spirituality to shew us the vanity of our dependence upon it, and to send us to Jesus in whom alone we find a perfect righteousness. Thus the law is called " a school-" master to lead us to Christ," Gal. iii. 24. Upon the whole, the young man inquires not how he shall be pardoned, accepted, justified, from a sense of sin; therefore Christ answers him according to the general intent of the question. How different was the question the jailor put! Here is a sinner deeply humbled, convinced of sin, and in great distress, crying out for salvation, therefore the apostles direct him at once to Jesus, " Believe on the Lord Jesus " Christ and thou shalt be saved," Acts xvi. 31. From whence we learn, how just the observation of our Lord is, that " the whole have no need of a physician but those that " are sick," Matth. ix. 12.

Thus we have shewn the insufficiency of our own righteousness to justify us before God; none will be so weak as to conclude from hence, the uselessness and unprofitableness of sanctification and good works in our salvation. There is a great difference between the necessity of holiness in order to salvation, and depending upon it for acceptance, and eternal life. Good works cannot justify us, but they discover our justification, they are the necessary effects of saving faith, and a means of carrying on and advancing the divine life in the soul. But this will be more particularly considered hereafter Let us proceed,

III. To shew that it is the righteousness of Jesus Christ alone that is the matter of our justification, and the ground of our acceptance with God. *Not having mine own righteousness.*——Here for our better understanding of this subject we may inquire,

1. What the righteousness of Christ is, or of what it consists.

2. Why it is called the righteousness of God.

3. Why is it that we are justified by the righteousness of Christ only.

I. Let us confider what the righteoufnefs of Chrift is, or of what it confifts. The righteoufnefs of Chrift, which juftifies us before God, is that righteoufnefs which he wrought out in his human nature when he was upon earth, confifting of his active and paffive obedience, or that obedience which he paid to the commands of the law, and his fufferings and death; fome have been for feparating thefe two, and reprefenting the fufferings and death of Chrift alone as fufficient for our juftification before God, but they are to be joined; and thus united are confidered as that righteoufnefs by which we receive the forgivenefs of our fins and a title to eternal life; the neceffity of both will appear, if we confider the original intent and meaning of the law, and the power which the law has now over us as finners.

The original and primary defign of the law, was a perfect obedience; this appears from the command, " Do this and " live:" And from the curfe which the law pronounces againft all thofe who are guilty of a breach of it. " For it is written " curfed is every one, that continueth not in all things which " are written in the book of the law to do them." Gal. iii. 10. Had man continued in perfect obedience to the law, he had enjoyed the favour of God, and poffeffed a happy immortality. This leads us then to conclude that the original defign of the law was an active perfect righteoufnefs. The law had no other obligation upon man in a ftate of innocency. But now the law is broke, it has a frefh power, a power to condemn the finner for tranfgreffions; in our prefent guilty circumftances then, two things are neceffary to be done in order to our juftification. 1. That the power which the law has over us to condemn us fhould be diffolved: and, 2. That a perfect obedience fhould be yielded to the commands of the law to entitle to eternal life, and therefore the righteoufnefs of Chrift muft confift of his active and paffive obedience.

1. The fufferings and the death of Chrift are a part of that righteoufnefs by which a guilty creature is juftified before God. Man having broken the law, and confequently fallen under its condemnatory fentence, the firft thing that is to be done towards his juftification is to reverfe that awful fentence, or to make fatisfaction, by which God may, confiftent with his juftice, pardon the rebellious creature, and not put

the law in execution againſt him; unleſs we ſuppoſe God can diſpenſe with his law, and ſet aſide his threatning, without taking notice of tranſgreſſion; but wherefore then did he annex a threatning to the law or covenant which he made with man, if he did not determine to execute it? Is it not opening a way for the ſinner to encourage himſelf in every act of rebellion, upon a preſumption that the threatnings of God, however awful, will not be executed againſt him? Nay, is it not inconſiſtent with the revelation which God has made of his infinitely glorious perfections, his juſtice and holineſs, which are perfections of his nature, as well as his mercy and goodneſs? Is it not inconſiſtent with the obligation God brought himſelf under to deal with man according to the law? Did he determine that the violation of the law ſhould be puniſhed with death? It muſt be ſo then, either in the perſon of the ſinner, or his ſurety; for God is not mutable like us, but whatever he has ſaid ſhall be done; ſatisfaction muſt be made by ſuffering and death, that the demerit of ſin might plainly appear, and God be honoured in his truth and faithfulneſs, in the ſalvation of the guilty: this was ſignified by ſhedding of blood in the ſacrifices of old, the meaning of which was, that God would not pardon ſin without death, without blood; and whoſe blood was ſufficient to expiate ſin? Was the blood of beaſts? No, the daily repetition of them could not bear any proportion to the demerit of ſin, therefore they were only typical of what was to come; man was abſolutely incapable of making any ſatisfaction, for all he can do he owes to God; here then appears evidently the abſolute neceſſity of the ſufferings and death of our Lord Jeſus Chriſt, to which all the ſacrifices of old pointed. We therefore find Chriſt repreſented as " the lamb of God, which " taketh away the ſin of the world." John i. 29. We find him called the *High Prieſt*, and the like. The ſufferings of Chriſt are part of the righteouſneſs that juſtifies us, thus it is ſaid, " by his ſtripes we are healed;" Iſ. liii. 5. and theſe ſufferings belong not only to his death, but likewiſe to his life, they include all thoſe afflictions he was exerciſed withal, thoſe buffetings of devils he was ſubject to, all the mockings, perſecutions, and cruelties, he endured from man, all the ſhame and ignominy he bore, and in ſhort, all that wrath of God which his people deſerved by their ſins: all theſe make up the ſufferings of Chriſt, which were neceſſary to make atonement for ſin and open a way for its full pardon. And here, stop a while O my soul, and view the exquisite agonies, the painful sufferings of thy dear Redeemer! Stop and take a view of his love in suffering and dying, and then say if thou canst any longer doubt his willingness to receive thee, or his care to save thee! Bring your fearful unbelieving hearts Christians, to the cross of Christ, and see whether a view of the dying Saviour will not speak peace, and raise your languishing hopes! Bring your hard hearts hither, sinners, and see whether such astonishing love will not mollify and soften them! Look upon a suffering Jesus, ye slothful souls, this may quicken your diligence, convince you of your ingratitude, and fill you with a growing zeal in your Redeemer's service!

2. There must be a perfect obedience paid to the commands of the law to entitle us to eternal life. It appears from the nature of justification, which consists in pardon of sin, and a right to eternal life, that we must have a righteousness perfectly answering all the requirements of the law, else we cannot enjoy both these blessings. When a man suffers the penalty of any law, the law can exact no further punishment of him, but he cannot be said by his suffering the penalty, to deserve the rewards promised by the law to those that obey it. He that suffers the penalty certainly cannot be put upon the same footing with those that have continued in obedience. The sufferings of Christ made satisfaction for the breach of the law, and therefore stopped the execution of its sentence; but eternal life is not promised to the sufferings of Christ, he therefore came and obeyed the law, that by his obedience imputed to us we might have a title to life everlasting. This is plainly intimated to us in various passages of the New Testament. Thus, Rom. v. 19. "For as by one man's disobedience many were "made sinners: so by the obedience of one, shall many be "made righteous." What was Adam's disobedience, but an actual transgression of the law? What must that obedience be then, that is put in opposition to it, but an active obedience or fulfilling the commands of the law! Again, Rom. viii. 3, 4. "What the law could not do, being "weak through the flesh, God sending his own Son in the "likeness of sinful flesh, and for sin, comdemned sin in "the flesh: that the righteousness of the law might be

"fulfilled in us, who walk not after the flesh, but after the "spirit," which evidently points to a righteousness answerable to the commands of the law.—Again, Rom. x. 4. " Christ is called the end of the law for righteousness to " every one that believeth." Here the apostle clearly intimates that the primary end of the law was obedience; in dying, Christ did not answer the primary intent of the law: therefore in the justification of his people it was necessary that he should obey the law, which having done, in the room and stead of his people, and this being imputed to them, and received by faith, the end of the law is answered in their justification, which is a perfect righteousness. Does the law, says the believer, require a perfect righteousness? Will it admit of nothing less? Here it is, in my glorious surety, he has wrought it out for me! Thus Christ is the end of the law, &c. And thus we see his active and passive obedience, or his obedience to the law, and his sufferings and death, both make up that which is our justifying righteousness. We find in some places indeed, a particular stress is laid upon the death of Christ, but this cannot be understood to exclude his obedience; we might with equal propriety say, it excludes likewise all the sufferings of his life : his death may indeed be particularly mentioned, as that was the last act of his obedience, all was consummated in his death. We now proceed,

2. To consider upon what accounts the righteousness of Jesus Christ is called the righteousness of God. The reasons appear to be obvious, and a consideration of them tends greatly to raise the hopes of the believer, and strengthen him in the belief of this way of justification. It is the righteousness of God.

1. As it is of God the Father's appointment. Our Lord tells us, " He came not to do his own will but the will of " him that sent him." John vi. 38. And again, " Lo I " come to do thy will, O God." Ps. xl. 8. If we consider now the errand Christ came into the world upon, and that he was sent upon this errand by God the Father, we may from hence conclude, that the righteousness which Christ has wrought out for us, is entirely agreeable to the pleasure of the Father; it was by his appointment and it was with his approbation that Christ came to " make an end of " sin, to make reconciliation, for iniquity, and bring in ever-

"lasting righteousness." What a glorious circumstance is this in favour of justification by the righteousness of Jesus Christ! And how much does it tend to fill the souls with the highest hopes of the eternal blessings, which depend upon this righteousness! Remember whenever you come to plead this righteousness with God, that it is of his appointing, his own free, gracious appointing! This is enough to fill your souls with holy boldness at the throne of Grace, to ask for all spiritual and eternal blessings: this is enough to encourage your hopes of acceptance with God; for the righteousness you bring to him by faith, and plead with him, is a righteousness of his own appointing. He has appointed it for those very ends and purposes for which you plead it. This is so important a circumstance, that it should be seriously considered by those, who are depending upon their own righteousness. If God has laid your own righteousness, as the foundation of your hopes, you are safe; but remember if it be not of his own appointment, it will not meet with his acceptance. I might add,

2. That it is God that imputes this righteousness to us in justification. This is a further consideration that tends to encourage and strengthen our hopes herein; God imputes it, therefore he will accept, pardon, and save the soul, to whom he imputes it.—Else why does he impute it? But,

3. He that wrought out this righteousness is God as well as man. The deity indeed cannot be said to obey or suffer, but there is so strict a union between the divine and human natures of Christ, that the act of the human nature is said to be the act of the whole person, and thus it appears in the sight of God. On this account it is, that the righteousness of Christ has such a peculiar virtue and efficacy in it, so as to be sufficient to satisfy infinite justice, and to be properly meritorious. For had he been no more than a mere creature, the law of creation would have laid him under an obligation to perform all the obedience he was capable of; and consequently no one act of his life could have been meritorious for himself, much less could it have been so for others. We hence see then, what matter of thankfulness and admiration it is, that he who is our Saviour is God as well as man! God and man so closely united, that what he has done and suffered in his human nature, is reckoned to be done and suffered by God himself, and is

every way satisfactory and meritorious! See you not therefore the excellency of the Christian scheme? Has not the believer abundantly the advantage of every other person? How does a sense of Christ's being God as well as man, encourage the soul in his dependence upon his Redeemer's righteousness? can he doubt of its efficacy? He may cheerfully venture into eternity, and appear with boldness before the bar of God, being clothed with such a righteousness! Well might the apostle Paul be so desirous of being found, not having his own righteousness but the righteousness of Jesus Christ, because it is the righteousness of God. A consideration of Christ's being God, fills us with wonder at his infinite love and condescension in appearing in human nature, and obeying and suffering for us, and is a glorious motive to stir us up, and to quicken us to all holy obedience. I now proceed,

3. To shew why it is that we are justified by the righteousness of Jesus Christ only. We need not say much upon this head, it appearing evident from what has been already hinted, why we are justified by the righteousness of Christ only—because it alone is perfect and satisfactory—because it brings most glory to God,—and because it affords most consolation to the soul in life and death, and is of infinite and everlasting virtue and efficacy.

The righteousness of Christ alone is perfect and satisfactory. Those who have been enabled to make the greatest advances in grace, have yet come far short of perfection, and therefore after they have done all they can, must acknowledge themselves to be unprofitable servants. When you take a review of your many duties, and consider the numberless defects that have attended them, you must humbly own them with the church, to be but as filthy garments, and as an unclean thing. But is the righteousness of your Redeemer so? Can you observe any spot in his obedience? No, it is all perfectly pure and lovely, it is worthy of God's acceptance, it is fit for your dependence, it is abundantly satisfactory to infinite justice, for all your sins Christians, and therefore only capable of being your justifying righteousness; a High Priest became us, who is holy, harmless, undefiled, and separate from sinners; and such an High Priest God provided for us! He was holy in heart and life, he fulfilled all righteousness, he made full atonement for sin, and shall not such a righteousness be thy justifying righteousness? Oh my soul shall I prefer an imperfect righteousness before it? No, Lord take away mine iniquity, and clothe me with this change of raiment!

The law is honoured by this righteousness, and God is glorified. Is it not a peculiar honour done to the law that he who is God should become man, and be made under the law? Could the law have been so much honoured by the spotless obedience of all the race of Adam? Had they been justified by it the law would have pronounced them righteous, but behold, by what Christ has done the law is magnified, and made honourable, and the end of it abundantly answered, and all the perfections of God glorified. With what lustre does his infinite purity and holiness shine forth in our justification by the righteousness of Jesus Christ! What glorious views have we of infinite faithfulness executing the sentence upon the surety, and requiring a perfect obedience from him, before the guilty offender can be pardoned and accepted to eternal life! how infinitely exceeding all human comprehension does the wisdom of God appear in this method of justification! Behold God is just in punishing sinners, and yet in pardoning; he is just, and yet the justifier of them that believe in Jesus. How glorious are the titles he bears! A just God, and yet, through this righteousness, a justifier, a saviour! And can the love and grace of God more illustriously appear, than in this way of justification—in appointing and furnishing the soul with this righteousness? Suppose God could, consistent with his other perfections, have justified the sinner by his own imperfect righteousness, yet would his infinite mercy, would his grace have been so much exalted, as by this righteousness? No, behold God the Father appointing his Son, to come, and bring in an everlasting righteousness! Behold God the Son, cheerfully undertaking the work! See the mighty God appearing in human nature, obeying the law, and suffering death for guilty, unworthy hell-deserving creatures! See him clothing those who are naturally ungodly with his own righteousness! Pardoning and entitling them to eternal life! And is not this grace beyond the comprehension of men or angels! How glorious is this righteousness! The great end God has in view, in the justification and salvation of his people, is his own glory. And is it this righteoufnefs that only fecures and exalts his glory? It is enough to engage us, to make it our only dependence. Lord as we would aim at thy glory in the whole of our falvation, fo we would gladly and thankfully accept of this righteoufnefs, as that which brings everlafting glory to all thy perfections. But further, this righteoufnefs alone, brings comfort to the foul in life and death. This is the only righteoufnefs that is fuited to the wants and neceffities of an awakened foul. See the convinced finner, he is feeking after a righteoufnefs to appear in before God, he goes to duty, apprehending this will allay the fury of an awakened confcience. But the more he looks to duty for juftification, the more he is perplexed, and can find no reft till he comes to Jefus. See, no fooner does the Spirit give him a view of the Redeemer's righteoufnefs, but behold he is fatisfied; Lord, fays he, it is enough; I now fee where my dependence muft be, give me but this righteoufnefs, and I'll rejoice and triumph in life and death Oh glorious and allperfect righteoufnefs! It is the righteoufnefs of God! Here am I fafe! Oh my foul, this righteoufnefs will bear the trial of infinite juftice, this righteoufnefs will bring me off with honour at the fupreme tribunal, this garment of falvation, will hide all my fins and make me appear for ever amiable, in the fight of an infinitely pure and holy God. It is a foul refrefhing righteoufnefs, it comforts the foul under a fenfe of guilt, under all the fears of a mifcarriage, a view of this righteoufnefs fupports and cheers the believer. Why fhould you be difcouraged, Oh my foul, here is a righteoufnefs anfwers all the demands of law and juftice, here is a righteoufnefs of God! Art thou afraid of appearing before the bar of God? Lay afide thy fears, confider he that will be thy judge, has clothed thee with this righteoufnefs, it is his, and will he difown his own righteoufnefs? In fine, the guilty foul finds the righteoufnefs of Jefus Chrift to be the only ground of comfort in life and death, and no wonder then that he makes it his dependence.

To conclude. This righteoufnefs is everlafting in its efficacy and virtue. " Chrift the fame yefterday, to-day, " and for ever." Heb. iii. 8. And his righteoufnefs, like himfelf, remaineth for ever, 2 Cor ix. 9. It is an everlafting righteoufnefs which he has brought in, Dan. ix. 24. In the virtue whereof, multitudes of happy fouls, have been already juftified, and faved, and are now actually employed, in finging the praifes of redeeming love; and its efficacy is not at all diminifhed, it is ftill the fame, for the complete and everlafting juftification of all that fhall believe through grace For the mercy of the Lord is from everlafting to everlafting upon them that fear him, and his righteoufnefs unto children's children, Pfa. ciii. 17. Wherefore comfort one another with thefe things.

SERMON IX.

ON JUSTIFICATION.

PHIL. iii. 9.

And be found in him, not having mine own righteousness, which is of the law, but that which is through the faith of Christ, the righteousness which is of God by faith.

WHEN the Prophet Isaiah had a view of the glory and majesty of God, as seated upon his exalted throne, and seraphs and glorified Spirits surrounding him, crying out, *Holy, holy, holy is the Lord God of hosts,* he was filled with the humblest sense of himself, saying, " Wo is " me, for I am undone, because I am a man of unclean " lips, and I dwell in the midst of a people of unclean " lips, for mine eyes have seen the King, the Lord of Hosts. Isaiah vi. 1. 5. It is well to have our minds impressed with a suitable sense of the infinite majesty and perfections of God, the more we view them and the more humble our souls lie under a sense of the infinite distance there is between God and us, and especially under a sense of our guilt and imperfections the better: as justification is a judicial act, it is necessary for us to consider before, or by whom it is we are to be justified. We are so stupid that we are ready to think God is such an one as ourselves. It is one thing to view him at a distance, when we have ten thousand objects around us to take away the impression, and another thing to view him when we are just ready to appear before his solemn tribunal, or when our souls are filled with a deep sense of guilt and we feel the terrors of an awakened conscience! some represent him as full of mercy, lenity, and compassion, or as having nothing in him to fill the sinner with the least dread and confusion: but behold our first parents guilty of a breach of the divine command, sensible of the threatning which God denounced, and hearing the voice of the Lord in the garden, were struck with terror, and in the utmost confusion attempt to fly and hide themselves, from the presence of the Lord amongst the trees of the garden. Gen. iii. 8. Or they were afraid that justice would put in execution the dreadful sentence, and punish them with everlasting death, and all the views of mercy would give them no relief until a saviour was revealed. How can we form any hopes of the everlasting favour of God from our own services, when we consider how dreadfully they are tainted, how sadly they are polluted! The apostle Paul, when after his conversion, he came to consider the infinite holiness of God, the purity of his law, and so compare his own heart with it, he styles himself *carnal* and *sold under sin*. Rom. vii. 14. In what a strong manner does he express his desire of appearing in Christ and his righteousness? Being taught by the spirit of God that this was the only way of acceptance with him, and of being entitled to eternal life. " And I count all things but dross and dung that I might win " Christ," Phil. iii. 8. When a sinner is savingly awakened and convinced of the worth of his soul, and his need of Christ, how earnest and importunate is he after an interest in Jesus! He looks on the glory of the present world, and counts it all but dung and dross, his soul is all taken up with concerns of everlasting moment and importance, and he treats all the affairs of mortal life as trifles; and with an indifference suitable to their vanity. Such was the temper of the apostle Paul, when he breathed forth his soul in the most ardent and heavenly manner. " Yea and I count all " things but loss for the excellency of the knowledge of " Christ Jesus my Lord," Phil. iii. 8. In our treating upon the great doctrine of justification, we have already shewn what it is to be justified. That our own personal righteousness is insufficient to justify us before God. We have likewise from these words shewn that it is the righteousness of Jesus Christ, that is the matter of our justification, and the ground of our acceptance with God: under which head we confidered what the righteoufnefs of Chrift is, that it confifts of his active and paffive obedience, or his obedience to the commands of the law, and his fufferings to death. We have fhewn why this righteoufnefs is called the righteoufnefs of God. It is of God the Father's appointment; he that wrought it out is God as well as man; it is God that imputes it. We have likewife fhewn, why it is that we are juftified by the righteoufnefs of Jefus Chrift alone, his righteoufnefs alone is perfect and fatisfactory. It alone fecures the glory of all the divine perfections. It alone affords confolation to the foul both in life and death, and it has infinite and everlafting virtue and efficacy in it, and therefore is fufficient to juftify the moft guilty and unworthy in every age and generation. We now come,

IV. To confider how the righteoufnefs of Chrift becomes ours, fo that we may be really and legally juftified by it. This is a point neceffary to be confidered and to be cleared up to the fatisfaction of the humble awakened guilty foul, that he may be thoroughly convinced, that it is not an imaginary foundation he is building his hopes on, but a glorious reality; that fo he may rejoice in the profpect of eternal life, which is every way fecured to him in believing. That the righteoufnefs of Chrift may properly and legally become ours, fo as we may be juftified by it, two things are neceffary.—1ft, That God fhould impute it to us; and 2dly, That we fhould receive it by faith as our only juftifying righteoufnefs, and reft upon it for that purpofe. Thefe two things well confidered will make it abundantly appear, that the foul is built upon a folid foundation that builds upon Chrift, that nothing can deprive him of the expected inheritance, but he fhall receive the end of his faith, even his everlafting falvation. Thefe two things are of fo much moment and importance, that they deferve each of them a particular confideration.

1. That the righteoufnefs of Chrift may become ours, fo that we may be really and legally juftified by it, it is neceffary that God fhould impute it to us. Unlefs this is done, unlefs God has given us fome good grounds to believe that he does it to all that believe, our faith will be in vain, and our falvation very uncertain. Bleffed be God he has not left us under an uncertainty about this neceffary and momen-

Serm. IX.   ON JUSTIFICATION.

tous point, but has given us sufficient intimations of his imputing the righteousness of Christ to all his people, to their everlasting comfort and salvation. To make this point clear, I shall first consider what is meant by imputation, and then secondly, shew that the righteousness of Jesus Christ is made ours by imputation.

1st. Let us consider what is meant by imputation. We have the word *imputed*, occurring various times both in the Old and New Testament, and we find it signifies to esteem, to reckon, to judge, to lay to one's charge, &c. Lev. xvii. 4. Psa. cvi. 31. The great Dr. Owen mentions two sorts of imputation.

1st. To impute that which was our own antecedently to such imputation; this is a reckoning and a passing judgement that the thing is really in us, and a dealing with us according to it, whether good or evil. Thus when we impute learning to a man, he was learned before the imputation, from hence this divine remarks, that when God esteemeth any thing to be ours that was so antecedently, he esteemeth of it just as it is, no more and no less; consequently, says he, this shews the folly and stupidity of those who are for imputation of faith, obedience, &c. for as it is imperfect, so God esteemeth it, and therefore cannot be said to impute it to us for a perfect righteousness. There is, says the same author, an imputation,

2dly, Of that which is not antecedently our own, and of this kind is the imputation of Christ's righteousness, the imputation of our sins to him, and the imputation of Adam's sin to us. In all these imputations what idea does the word impute convey to us but this, to reckon, to esteem, to place to one's account, and to deal with us according to it? We cannot suppose by imputation, is meant that believers are reckoned by God to have done those things which Christ alone performed, or to have suffered those penalties which he endured. Christ and believers are distinct persons, and the actions of one person cannot properly be reckoned the actions of another. The honour of furnishing this glorious and all perfect righteousness belongs to Christ alone, it was he that came and brought it in, and though imputed to us for our justification, yet he is the author of it; but his righteousness is made ours, and that so really, and upon such grounds, as that we are dealt with according to it, so that it

F

answers all the ends and purposes it would have served had we wrought it out in our own persons. When our sins were laid upon, reckoned, or imputed to Christ, he must not be esteemed actually a sinner, though as he appeared our surety, to answer for us, the law treated him as a sinner, by requiring of him the penalty; and thus he actually made satisfaction for sin, and cancelled the hand-writing which was against us as effectually as if he could have done it, and therefore had done it in our own persons. Thus Adam's sin is justly imputed or reckoned to all his posterity, not that they all sinned personally, and actually, when he did, but he being their federal head and representative, his sin is reckoned to them, so that they are as really liable to condemnation on the account of it, as if they had actually in their own persons each committed it. Thus, in the imputation of Christ's righteousness, God accounteth it to have been wrought by him for all his people, and therefore doth receive them into favour, and give them a title to eternal life upon the account of it. His righteousness is reckoned to their account, so that they have all the benefit of it, and are as effectually justified by it, as if they had perfectly obeyed the law in their own persons. When the debtor is discharged he cannot be said to have paid the money himself, it was his surety that did it for him; yet the money being paid for him in his stead, and accepted for him by the creditor, he may be reckoned a clear person, and the payment be placed to his account as really as if he had paid it with his own hands. Thus Christ's righteousness is made ours, or reckoned to our account, thus it was to Abraham, who is the first person that we read of as being justified by imputed righteousness, though he was not really the first, Gen. x. 6. Rom iv. 20, 24. Thus God is said " to im- " pute righteousness without works," Rom. iv. 6. This imputation of Christ's righteousness has opened a way, for its being represented as a robe or garment, and our being said to put on Christ and the like; and doubtless the apostle Paul had this in his eye, when he says, " And be found in " him, not having mine own righteousness, &c." He desired to be found clothed with the righteousness of Jesus Christ, as a garment, that so he might not be found naked at the great day. Thus we see what is meant by imputation, it is a gracious act of God whereby he reckons the righteousness of Christ to his people, and deals with them according to its infinite and everlasting virtue and efficacy. Our next thing is,

2dly, To shew that this imputation is not imaginary but real, by considering the grounds and foundation upon which it is built. A view of this, through the influence of the Spirit, will free our minds from all doubt and hesitation about it, and fill us with a holy joy at the prospect of everlasting blessings: take what may belong to this head in the following particulars. The law which Christ was subject to, is the same law which man broke.—He obeyed the law and suffered its penalty in our room and stead.—He was constituted our surety by the Father, and all he did and suffered for his people in that character was according to his approbation, and met with his acceptance. And lastly, it was all likewise the effect of his own voluntary choice.

1. The law which Christ was subject to, is the same law which man broke, viz. the moral law. Those that deny that the active righteousness of Christ has any part in our justification, say, that Christ was not under the moral law, but under a law of mediation; a peculiar law established between the Father and the Son, in which it was agreed, what Christ was to suffer to open the way for the acceptance of our faith, repentance, and sincere obedience as our justifying righteousness. If then it can be proved that Christ was made under the moral law, and fulfilled it, it will lead us to conclude that we are justified by his righteousness alone, and that the way in which it was made ours, is by imputation as well as faith. Now if Christ was not subject to the moral law, why was he made man? Does not his being made man, especially when we consider the errand he came upon, suppose that he was to fulfil the law which man had broke, and that satisfaction must be made to infinite justice in the same nature that sinned? This is certainly the easiest, most natural, and obvious construction that can be put upon his appearance in human nature: to accomplish therefore this great and important end he was possessed of absolutely perfect rectitude of nature, and his life was every way agreeable to the divine law, that so, in fulfilling all its demands, he might redeem and save his people. After our Lord had been pressing his disciples to the pursuit of holiness, he says, " Think not that I am come to destroy the law or the

"prophets, I am not come to deftroy but to fulfil." Mat. v, 17. Let not the Jews, or any other perfons object to my coming, that it is to fet afide the law or any part of the Old Teftament; 'I am come as the great Antitype to fulfil the ceremonial law, and I am come to pay a perfect obedience to the moral law, and to endure its curfe, that I may make fatisfaction to infinite juftice for my people.' That our Lord had a particular view to the moral law is plain and evident, for he immediately proceeds to the explanation of it, which muft be the fame law he came to fulfil, and is as much as to fay that he came to fulfil all righteouf- nefs. That Chrift was fubject to the moral law appears evident from Gal. iv. 4, 5. "When the fulnefs of time was come, God fent forth his Son made of a woman, made under the law, to redeem them that were under the law, that we might receive the adoption of Sons." Now here we find there is no diftinction made between the law which Chrift was made under, and the law his people were under whom he came to redeem, therefore we may afk,—What law is that we are naturally under? Is it not the moral law as a covenant of works? If fo Chrift alfo was made under the fame, &c. This truth again clearly appears from Gal. iii 10, 13. "For as many as are of the works of the law are under the curfe, for it is written, curfed is every one that continueth not in all things which are written in the book of the law to do them." In this verfe it is plain the apoftle is fhewing, that all thofe that are feeking juftifica- tion by the works of the moral law are fo far from gaining their purpofe, that they are rather under the curfe of it, be- caufe the law will admit of nothing but a perfect obedience; curfing and condemning all that come in any refpect fhort. From whence it is evident that this can be no other than the moral law. In the 13th verfe therefore the apoftle fays, "Chrift hath redeemed us from the curfe of the law, being made a curfe for us, for it is written, curfed is every one that hangeth on a tree." The way we find by which Chrift hath redeemed us from the curfe of the law, is by being made a curfe for us; now that law from the curfe of which Chrift came to redeem us is the moral law: and if fo it is evident, Chrift himfelf was under it, for no other law could make him a curfe. Thus then we fee, that the great defign of Chrift's taking human nature was, that he might be fub- ject to the law; he came and fulfilled all righteoufnefs, by

Serm. IX. ON JUSTIFICATION.

perfectly anfwering all the precepts of the law, and he bore the penalty of the law; he endured its dreadful curfe by hanging on the crofs, by dying the death which God had threatned. This point being determined, therefore the next thing we have to advance to clear the way for imputation is,

2. That Chrift obeyed the law, and fuffered the penalty as his people's furety, in their room and ftead. We have already obferved, that our Lord came into the world "to fulfil " all righteoufnefs." Mat. v. 17. He came to put an end to fin, to make reconciliation for iniquity, and to bring in everlafting righteoufnefs. Dan. ix 24. But could this be for himfelf? Dare any one prefume to fay that he ftood in need of it? Was he not infinitely happy and glorious, before he appeared in human nature or was this neceffary to make any addition to his bleffednefs? No; It was not, therefore, for himfelf, it muft be for his people on whofe account he came into the world: he came to furnifh his people with a righteoufnefs in which they may appear before God and find acceptance. Therefore he obeyed the law in their room and ftead, that fo his righteoufnefs might be imputed unto them. This does by no means make our obedience unneceffary, it is an unfair and unnatural conclufion that is drawn from hence and is abfolutely inconfiftent with the whole gofpel. The gofpel lays us under peculiar obligations to obedience, though we are not to obey the law for the fame ends and purpofes that Chrift did. The law remains as a perpetual directory and rule of life to us, though we are not to look to it as a covenant of works: all thofe who are juftified by the imputed righteoufnefs of Chrift pay the greateft regard to the law, and are labouring after an internal as well as an external conformity to it. Chrift fuffered in our room and ftead. It is evident from a clofe view of his many fufferings, that he was confidered not as an innocent perfon but as guilty. Where there is no guilt there can be no punifhment; to fay otherwife would be to reflect upon the infinite juftice and righteoufnefs of God. Nor can the afflictions and fufferings of Chrift appear only as common, view his agony in the garden, when he fweated great drops of blood, through the anguifh he was in; view his cruel, curfed, and ignominious death; and are thefe tokens of his innocency, do they not plainly point out pun-

ifhment and guilt? But what guilt had Chrift the fon of God? "Was he not holy, harmlefs, undefiled, and feparate "from finners?" Heb vii. 26. Muft it not therefore be guilt imputed, even his people's guilt? view his fufferings, and you muft be convinced, that he had the fins of his people laid upon him, and fuffered and died in their room and ftead! This is alfo perfectly agreeable to the Scripture account of the matter. Thus the prophet Ifaiah is very particular and exprefs in delivering this great and important truth. Ifaiah liii. 5. "He was wounded for "our tranfgreffions, he was bruifed for our iniquities," &c. And verfe 6. "The Lord hath laid on him the iniquity of "us all," and verfe 8. "For the tranfgreffion of my peo- "ple was he ftricken." What ftronger expreffions could the prophet make ufe of to affert this truth, what more direct proofs? Agreeable to this, the apoftle Peter, under the influences of the holy Spirit, fays, 1 Pet. ii. 24. "Who "his ownfelf bare our fins in his own body on the tree." And the apoftle Paul by the fame fpirit fpeaks the fame truth. 2 Cor. v. 21. "He hath made him to be fin for us who "knew no fin, that we might be made the righteoufnefs of "God in him." Now how was Chrift made fin? Sin could not cleave to him, he was not a finner by inhefion; the meaning then can only be, that our fins were imputed to him, and that he fuffered the punifhment due to us for them. Hence we find him called a *ranfom*. Mat. xx. 28. "The Son of man came to give his life a ranfom for many," and 1 Tim. ii. 6. "Who gave himfelf a ranfom for all." Thus he is likewife faid to "lay down his life for the fheep," John x. 15. and 1 Pet. iii. 18. He is faid *to fuffer for fin*, the *juft* for the *unjuft*. All which expreffions clearly fhew, that he came to obey the law, and endure its penalty in our room and ftead. We accordingly find him reprefented under the character of a furety, Heb. vii. 22. Now a furety is one that receiveth the obligation upon himfelf when the debtor for whom he undertakes is not able to pay, fo that the furety becomes bound to difcharge the debt. Chrift then by taking this character has taken the obligation of having the debt of perfect obedience, and making fatisfaction to juftice upon himfelf, and has actually done it in our room and ftead, which the character of a furety neceffarily fignifies. His being God gave an infinite virtue to his fuf-

ferings, whereby they came fully satisfactory though they were but short; for eternity is only accidental to punishment arising from the inability of the creature's sufferings to make satisfaction. And thus Christ, acting as surety, has laid a glorious foundation for the imputation of his righteousness. What did the apostle Paul mean but this, when he opposed the death of Christ to all the accusations that could be brought in against him? What could be the ground of his triumphing, but the suretyship of Christ? Had not Christ died in his room and stead, it would have been but to little purpose to have triumphed so boldly. It is Christ that died, Rom. viii. 33. This transferring of guilt to Christ, and the doctrine of his suretyship was held forth by the sacrifices of the Old Testament: what was the meaning of the offender's putting his hand upon the head of the burnt offering? Did it not signify the transferring of guilt from the offender to the victim? Lev. i. 4. ch. iii. 2. Was it not as much as to say, ' Lord I have transgressed and ac-
' cordingly deserve to die, but I here bring a sacrifice to
' die for me in my stead, accept thereof and spare me.'
Such sacrifices as were of old could not indeed expiate sin; but they were typical of Christ the great sacrifice, and shew us how he was to take away sin, viz. by bearing the sins of his people, and dying in their room and stead. What could be more expressive of this doctrine, than the confessing the sins of the people over the head of the scape goat? Lev. xvi. 20, 21, 22. Here is plainly a transferring of guilt; by which we are taught that our sins were transferred to Christ; that he died in our room and stead; and consequently the way for the imputation of his righteousness to us is clear. This will still more evidently appear if we consider,

3. That Christ was constituted surety by the Father, and accepted and approved of by him in all he did in that character. Thus the Father calls Christ " his elect, in whom his " soul delighteth, Isaiah xlii. 1. pointing out his being chosen to the office of a mediator by him; for the following verses treat of the work he was to do, and his furniture for it. He is said in another place " to be set up from everlasting," Prov. viii. 23. referring to those eternal transactions between the Father and the Son, in which the Father appointed him as mediator and surety. God is said, " to set him " forth, as a propitiation through faith in his blood to de-

clare his righteousness for the remission of sins, &c. Rom. iii. 25. It is again said by Isaiah, "that it pleased the " Lord to bruise him, to put him to grief, and to lay upon him " the iniquities of us all." Isaiah. liii. 6, 10. Which signify to us, that God the Father constituted him surety, was pleased with his undertaking, laid the sins of his people, whom he represented, upon him and therefore inflicted upon him all that wrath which their sins deserved! Our Lord himself tells us that he came in obedience to his Father's will. John vi 38. "I came down from heaven not to do mine own " will, but the will of him that sent me. In various other places he is said to be sent by the Father, and to do the will of the Father, and his laying down his life, was a fulfilling his Father's will. John x. 17, 18. These things manifestly shew, that the great work of Redemption and Salvation which Christ came to accomplish, was in every respect agreeable to the Father's will. He therefore has given the most public and undoubted evidences of his acceptance and approbation of the work which Christ came into the world upon. At the baptism of Jesus, the Spirit descended upon him, and a voice was heard, "This is my beloved Son, in " whom I am well pleased." Mat. iii. 16. The same was repeated at his transfiguration. Mat. xvii. 5. Thus whilst our Lord was upon earth, he had this public testimony that he pleased the Father. And what was his resurrection? What was his ascention? What his reception into heaven? What his exaltation there? What his perpetual and prevailing intercession? What are all these, but so many undoubted evidences of the Father's perfect approbation of the work which Christ has done, the acceptableness of his sacrifice, and the fulness of that satisfaction which he has made for his people? Now then we see Christ appointed by the Father, accepted of and approved by him, and so far we see a way is open for the imputation of his righteousness. We have only one thing more to consider, and that is,

4. All that Christ has done in the character of a surety, is the effect of his own free, voluntary choice. He gives us the plainest indications of his being free and voluntary, and that it was not a task imposed upon him; "his delights are " said from all eternity to be with the sons of men," Prov. viii. 31. Intimating how much he approved of the work he had undertaken. When no creature could help us, he tells

us how voluntarily he offered himself, and "came to do the "pleasure of his Father," Heb x. 5, 6, 7. In fine, he is said, "to pour out his soul unto death," Isa. liii. 12. Which signifies a voluntary and spontaneous act. Thus then, if we consider that Christ was subject to the moral law; that he performed obedience to it, and bore its penalty, in our room and stead; that all this was agreeable to the Father's appointment, and was the effect of his own free, and voluntary choice; we may from hence see how justly the righteousness of Christ is really and actually imputed to us for justification, and that it is not an enthusiastic fancy, there being a glorious and sufficient foundation laid for it. If a person is willing to pay all the debt which his friend has contracted, if he and the creditor are agreed, shall the debtor make any objection to it? Or is there not a real foundation laid for his legal discharge? If the Son was willing to become a surety, and the Father approved of it. If Christ has paid the whole debt, and the Father has accepted of it, shall we object to an imputation of his righteousness? There can be nothing to prevent or hinder such an imputation. God does not dispense with his law by admitting the suretyship of Christ, the law is rather honoured and magnified by it. He was under no obligation of obeying the law for himself, as some have asserted, for it was his own free voluntary act that he was made man; it was by a stipulation with his Father, and it was entirely with this view that he might redeem his people, and furnish them with a perfect and everlasting righteousness: therefore his righteousness is made legally ours by imputation, and is sufficient to free us from the guilt and punishment of sin, to introduce us into the divine favour, and to give us a right and title to eternal life. But, lastly,

This truth appears clear from various parts of scripture, which cannot be so well understood, as by allowing imputation. We find these occurring, both in the Old and in the New Testament; thus the church is represented as saying, "In the Lord have I righteousness and strength." Righteousness and strength are two distinct things; how does God communicate strength or grace? Not by imputation, there is no making us inherently righteous and strong to resist temptations this way, it must be infusion of implantation; but is this righteousness made ours the same way? Then it would be no longer diſtinct from grace and ſtrength, Iſa. xlv. 24. Therefore it is made ours ſome other way, even by imputation, agreeable to the general ſenſe of ſcripture. To this purpoſe Jeremiah ſpeaks when mentioning Chriſt, he ſays, "He ſhall be called the Lord our " righteouſneſs," Jer. xxiii. 6. The apoſtle evidently points to this, when he ſays, " As by the diſobedience of one," &c. Rom. v. 19. As the guilt of Adam's ſin was imputed to his poſterity, whereby they are reckoned ſinners, and are under condemnation; ſo the righteouſneſs of the ſecond Adam is imputed to his people, whereby they are eſteemed righteous, and are entitled to eternal life. Were not the words to be taken in this ſenſe, the parallel would be deſtroyed between Chriſt and Adam. This truth appears with yet greater light if poſſible, 1 Cor. i. 30. " Chriſt is " made of God unto us wiſdom, righteouſneſs," &c. And 2 Cor. v. 21., " Chriſt was made ſin for us who knew no " ſin," &c. Now Chriſt is not made wiſdom, righteouſneſs, and ſanctification in the ſame way and manner, for theſe are bleſſings ſo diſtinct, that it is impoſſible he ſhould: Chriſt is made ſanctification to us as he has purchaſed it for us, and ſends his Spirit to implant his image in us, and ſo carries it on in our ſouls. But is he made righteouſneſs to us in the ſame way? Then righteouſneſs is the ſame with ſanctification, whereas they are here brought in as diſtinct bleſſings; diſtinct in their nature, though never to be ſeparated. As to the other place already mentioned, the natural and obvious meaning is, that as Chriſt was made ſin by imputation, or as our ſins were reckoned to him, ſo his righteouſneſs is made ours by imputation alſo; therefore, as he really ſuffered for our ſins, though he did not commit them, we ſhall as really be juſtified, and enjoy eternal life, through the virtue of his righteouſneſs, though we did not perform it. Thus then we ſee how this righteouſneſs becomes ours; we may likewiſe be ſatisfied that imputation is not a mere imagination, there is the higheſt reaſon for it, it is built upon a ſolid foundation; for if Chriſt came, and perfectly obeyed the law we had broke, and bore its penalty, if he did this voluntarily, and in our room and ſtead, to furniſh us with a righteouſneſs for our juſtification, and if this was accepted by the Father for his people, then who ſhall forbid the imputation of Chriſt's righteouſneſs?

Is it not every way juſt and righteous? Shall the traitor, who ſtands in need of ſuch a righteouſneſs, object to it? God forbid! Bleſſed be God this imputation is his own act, it is God that juſtifieth: this is the Chriſtian's comfort. If God juſtifies, who ſhall condemn? All the cavils of the moſt ſubtle reaſoners ſignify nothing It is not a mere imagination O humble ſoul! What ever ſome may ſay of it, it has a ſolid, and as real a foundation as that upon which the heavens and the earth are built. Chriſt has obeye ! and ſuffered all that was required, and thy heavenly Father has accepted it; fear not then, thy faith is not in vain, thou ſhalt receive the forgiveneſs of thy ſins, and an inheritance among them that are ſanctified through faith that is in him.

SERMON X.

ON JUSTIFICATION.

Rom. v. 1.

Therefore being justified by faith, we have peace with God through our Lord Jesus Christ.

WHATEVER hatred and averfion the apoftle Paul difcovered to Chrift and his caufe, whilft he was a Pharifee, yet when he was favingly enlightened, his thoughts were peculiarly turned upon, and his affections ftrongly drawn to the perfon and righteoufnefs of the glorious Redeemer; and it was his great concern to make known Jefus Chrift, and him crucified amongft the poor Gentiles, that they might be led into an acquaintance with the true way of falvation, and be no longer ftrangers to him, whom to know is life eternal. The great doctrine of juftification by the righteoufnefs of Jefus Chrift, is what he was directed by the Holy Ghoft ftrongly to maintain, and open; we find him therefore in every epiftle, and almoft in every chapter, either anfwering fome objection to this glorious truth, or reprefenting its reality and importance, its happy influences upon the heart and life, and its tendency to advance and promote the glory of all the divine perfections.

This doctrine the apoftle fets forth particularly and clearly in the third and fourth chapters of this epiftle to the Romans, and in the beginning of this fifth chapter fhews the happy effects of it, in peace with God, perfeverance in his favour, hope of his glory, and a holy rejoicing in every difpenfation of providence.

Therefore being juftified by faith, &c. We have been fome time upon the doctrine of juftification; and the importance of the doctrine, its influence upon our prefent and everlafting peace, and our natural readinefs to miftake it; all fhew the neceffity there is of being particular upon it; and therefore I need not make any apology for my enlarging. In our laft difcourfe you may remember we confidered the imputation of Chrift's righteoufnefs which we fupported by the following confiderations:

1. The law which Chrift was fubject to, was the fame which man broke.
2. That Chrift obeyed the law and fuffered death as his people's furety, in their room and ftead.
3. That Chrift was conftituted furety by the Father, and accepted and approved of by him in that character.
4. All that Chrift has done in the character of a furety, is the effect of his own free, and voluntary choice. From all which confiderations it is plain there is a fufficient foundation laid for the imputation of Chrift's righteoufnefs: and this is one way by which it becomes ours. This is God's act; but there is alfo an act of ours that is neceffary to our having this righteoufnefs fo as to enjoy the benefits of it, and that is faith, or believing, by which we receive this righteoufnefs for all the ends and purpofes for which it was provided. We receive it as our juftifying righteoufnefs; we plead it with God and reft upon it entirely for juftification; and thus it becomes legally and properly ours: God makes us willing to receive it as our juftifying righteoufnefs, and he is gracioufly pleafed to impute it to us as fuch Who then fhall fay we fhall not be juftified by it? Who fhall difpute our real intereft in it? Or fay it is not legally ours? "Who " fhall lay any thing to the charge of God's elect?" &c. Rom. viii. 33, &c. As faith is turned from its proper end, and out of its place by many, and as we are every where in fcripture faid to be juftified by faith, fo it will be neceffary to endeavour to fet this weighty and important affair in a true gofpel light; that God may be glorified and our fouls directed, encouraged, and quickened. To do this it may be proper.

I. To confider the nature of that faith that juftifies. And,

II. How, or in what manner it juftifies. Thefe two heads will lead us to fay all that is neceffary concerning juftifying faith.

I. Let us confider what that faith is which juftifies. And to make this the more clear and diftinct let us confider, 1ft. The author of it. And 2d. What it implies.

1. Let us confider who is the author of juftifying faith. It is neceffary to confider this, that we may know to whom we muft look and be indebted for it; that we may guard againft felf-dependence, and be filled with conftant and deep humility. And the author of juftifying faith is God; it is not a common gift as the bleffings of providence are, but the effect of God's fpecial diftinguifhing grace, and wrought in the foul by an almighty hand: it is not the effect of natural ftrength, nor is it produced by the mere power of moral arguments; all the eloquence and rhetoric of man cannot perfuade the guilty foul to put forth one act of faith in Jefus Chrift. How often have our beft endeavours been rendered fruitlefs, and the moft ingenuous and elaborate difcourfes been only as water fpilt upon the ground, that cannot be gathered! whilft the gofpel, preached in its naked fimplicity without human ornaments, has found its way into the hearts of the moft obftinate and ignorant and caufed a faving alteration, to fhew us, that we are not to boaft of, or depend on our own apprehended ftrength, or abilities, but to look to an almighty arm, to make our attempts effectual to bring finners by faith to Jefus Chrift. God generally works by means, and the means which he has appointed, and which he makes ufe of to produce faith, are fuited to anfwer fuch an end, and fhew that God deals with us as rational creatures whilft he addreffes our underftandings in his word and offers a variety of arguments, which, when accompanied with an almighty power, convince us of our need of Chrift, and are a means to quicken and engage us to believe on him. Believing is our act, but the power that enables us to put forth that act comes from God. Faith, we find therefore is called his gift. Eph. ii. 8. And the fame apoftle mentions " the ex-
" ceeding great power of God," that is manifefted in producing faith; even " that glorious power that raifed Jefus
" Chrift from the dead." Eph. i. 19. Until the day of God's

Serm. X. ON JUSTIFICATION.

power comes we continue in a state of unbelief, and all the loud calls of providence, all the arguments that are made use of, make no saving impression. It is a sign we know but little of our own hearts, when we exalt the power of the creature, and make him equal to the great duties of the Christian life. What was the reason that our Lord's preaching was not attended with greater success? upon the supposition of man's ability to believe, who but must have yielded to his importunity? who could have refused obedience who considered, that this was he that came from heaven, upon the most glorious and important errand, the salvation of sinners? Was not this consideration enough to have melted their souls, captivated their affections, and engaged them immediately to believe! Who could resist such arguments? And yet we see how few believed! What is to be expected from creatures who are alienated from the life of God; whose minds are blinded and whose hearts are hardened; who have the utmost aversion to faith, and are absolutely under the dominion of sin! It is easy to talk of believing, but it is a matter of the greatest difficulty to believe! To commit our souls into the hands of Jesus, under a sense of our guilt and misery, requires an almighty power! Christ is therefore represented as the " Author and the finisher of " our faith." Heb. xii. 2. " And the gospel is the power " of God to salvation, to every one that believeth." Rom. i. 16. " The word is mighty through God, to the pulling " down the strong holds of sin and Satan, and the bring- " ing us into obedience unto Christ," 2 Cor. x. 4, 5. The treasure of the gospel is committed to *earthen vessels*, weak imperfect creatures, that in the salvation of those that hear it, " the excellency of the power may be of God and not " of man," 2 Cor. iv. 7. Thus we see the author of justifying faith is God; this is agreeable to the current of scripture, and to the experience of those that believe. Was it not an almighty power that conquered your natural aversion to Jesus? Removed your rooted prejudices, and enabled you to trust your everlasting concerns with him? Was it not the Spirit that convinced you of sin, of the unworthiness of your own righteousness, gave you a view of Christ, and led you to him? Give him therefore all the glory and look up to him to help you in the constant exercise of this faith, that you may continue unto the end. The confidration of God's being the author of faith does not at all discourage the use of means, or open a door for indolence, as some would insinuate; it rather is necessary to keep us from self dependence, a dangerous and destructive sin, and to quicken us to look up to him, who commands us to believe, to give us that faith which he requires, and display his glorious and almighty power in leading us to Christ, for the salvation of our souls. In fine, if we consider the natural enmity and aversion we all have to the way of salvation by faith in Jesus Christ; if we view the tendency which a sense of guilt, and the apprehension of an angry God have to fill us with absolute despair; and at the same time take notice of the nature of saving and justifying faith, we cannot but be convinced of the absolute necessity of a divine and almighty power to enable us to believe, and that God is the author of this important grace. We proceed therefore now to consider,

2. What faith implies— or what is signified by believing in Christ. We may consider saving justifying faith as necessarily implying three things. 1. As including an assent of the mind to the gospel way of salvation, upon a conviction of its excellency and importance. 2. A hearty approbation of the way of salvation by Christ, and a receiving and resting upon Christ alone for it. And 3. As a vital principle of all obedience. These three things are necessary to make up that faith which is required in the gospel.

1. It includes in it an assent of the mind to the gospel way of salvation, upon a conviction of its excellency and importance, made in the mind by the Spirit of God. The real Christian believes in Jesus Christ upon the highest and best evidence; upon a full persuasion of the truth and importance of what is believed. There must be an assent of the mind to Christ, or else there can be no real faith, this assent of the mind to Christ must pre-suppose some knowledge of him, and consequently convictions. How can we believe in an unknown object? " I know, " says the apostle " in " whom I have believed, and I am persuaded that he is able " to keep," &c. 2 Tim i. 12. I am not ignorant of the person to whom I have committed my soul; I know who he is, I am satisfied of his suitableness and ability to save me, and to do all that for me which I trust him for. Many may believe the gospel and be convinced of its truth by a

careful examination into the evidences of its authority: so a real believer may be sensible of the truth of the Christian religion by viewing its outward evidences; but the assent which he gives, and the profession which he makes do not arise merely from such a conviction, but likewise from a conviction made by the Spirit of God, upon the mind, whereby he is fully sensible of the guilty condition he is in, that he is lost without Christ, and sees a real excellency and suitableness in the gospel method of salvation. Such a spiritual saving conviction as this, does not properly belong to a temporary faith, though there may be some appearances of it; there being oftentimes convictions to be found in persons, and yet no saving faith. Simon Magus saw the miracles which Philip performed, and was convinced of the truth of his doctrine, and therefore gave his assent to it, Acts viii. 13. but he soon fell off. The sinner sometimes by the word, and sometimes by a providence, appears under convictions, talks of his guilt, of his being lost and undone, seems to have the most alarming views of everlasting wrath, and calls upon God for a time, and wishes for an interest in Christ; but he has not those peculiar convictions of the imperfection of his own righteousness, his inability to help himself, the suitableness, excellency, and all-sufficiency of Jesus Christ, as are to be found in those that really believe; all convictions therefore, end not in conversion. Yet convictions, even convictions wrought by the Spirit of God upon the mind, are absolutely necessary to saving justifying faith, being always previous to it, and being necessarily implied in it. This is evident both from the nature, from the end, and design of faith. What is the peculiar business the soul has with Christ when he comes to him by faith? Is it not to be delivered from sin and hell, and to be put into the possession of all purchased blessings? And must not the soul be really sensible that he is guilty and deserves hell, and that none but Jesus can save him?, must he not be sensible of this before he comes? Our Lord plainly intimates this, when he says, the " whole have no need of a physician, but " those that are sick," Matth. ix. 12. The apostle Paul was made to despair of obtaining salvation by his own righteousness, before he came to Jesus Christ for it, Rom. vii. 9. These convictions are different in different persons, as to continuance, degrees, &c. Sometimes we shall find the

X

sinner under great legal convictions; for a long time under awful terrors of soul, before he is made sensible of his own weakness, and of the suitableness and all-sufficiency of Jesus Christ; while others, as soon as they are wounded are led to the glorious remedy. But though they are not exactly alike in all, nor do they always regularly succeed one another in the mind, yet they are for substance the same, and are always previous to real faith. Being the means of prevailing upon the sinner to give his ready assent to Christ, as the only way to salvation, and of his being willing to receive him, whatever contempt he cast upon him before. It will not follow from what has been said concerning these convictions as necessarily connected with justification, that they have any merit in them, or have any causal influence on it. There are often legal convictions, or convictions of guilt, fear of wrath, &c. where there is no justification, nor can these convictions properly be called preparations to it; for the sinner who is convinced of guilt, at first generally goes to duty, apprehending that will render his condition the better, so that he is not prepared to receive Jesus Christ, till the Spirit comes and convinces him of his need of Christ, and his suitableness; then there is immediately an assent to him, and a willingness to receive him.

2. Faith implies a consent of the will, and is a direct application of the soul to Christ, in which act he receives him, and rests upon him for justification——To explain and illustrate this, we may take notice of the object of justifying faith, and then consider the essential acts of it.

1. We may take notice of the object of justifying faith. Now true saving faith hath for its subject matter the whole word of God, all divine revelation: he who believes not the word of God, believes not in Jesus, who is the subject matter of gospel revelation. God is the proper object of faith; he who comes to God must believe that he is, and that he is the rewarder, &c. Heb. xi. 6. All the perfections of God are the objects of faith. Thus the Old Testament saints trusted in the mercy of God, Psa. xxxiii. 18. They pleaded his mercy, as David, Psa li. 1. And the penitent publican flies to the mercy of God for relief. Luke xviii 13. " God be merciful," &c. But we must not look upon this as the uncovenanted general mercy of God; God, considered in himself, out of Christ is a con-

Serm. X.   ON JUSTIFICATION.   163

suming fire, and not a proper object of our faith and hope ; considering the awful demerit of sin, the threatening of the law, and infinite holiness and justice of God, we have rather reason to fly from him, as our first parents attempted to do, than hope and trust in him, unless we view him in Christ. In whom alone he is merciful, gracious, and long suffering, &c. It was the mercy of God therefore as it had a relation to our redemption by Jesus Christ, that the Old Testament saints trusted in. This mercy and grace of God, is the grand spring and cause of justification, redemption, and all spiritual and eternal blessings. " We are justified " freely by grace through the redemption that is in Christ " Jesus," Rom. iii 24. In Christ we " have redemption " through his blood, the forgiveness of sins according to the " riches of his grace." Eph. i. 7. The mercy of God in Christ is expressed in the promises, and the substance of all the promises is Jesus Christ, so that Christ, and Christ alone is the immediate object of faith, for pardon and life. It is Christ contained in the promise, that the sinner is to look to for all ; " Believe in the Lord Jesus Christ and thou " shalt be saved," Acts xvi. 31. From the whole it plainly appears, that Christ as sent, and ordained of God, for the salvation of sinners, is the proper immediate object of justifying faith. But as Christ himself is represented under various characters, and discharges various offices, in bringing about the redemption and salvation of sinners ; and as only some of these characters and offices have an immediate relation to justification, so we may inquire, what is the object of faith in that act of it, that relates immediately to justification. Now that act of faith that justifies, relates only to the priestly office of Christ ; this appears from the nature of justification, and the end and design of faith : justification is to be delivered from the guilt and punishment of sin, to be introduced actually into the favour of God, and to have a right to eternal life ; and the end of faith is our justification, Gal. ii. 16. What the business is, the soul has with Christ, when he first comes, our Lord tells us himself, Jo v. 40. " Ye will not come to me, that ye might have life." The soul comes for life ; he sees himself guilty, and he is seeking after pardon, after deliverance, from the wrath of God which he has deserved ; after acceptance with him, and a righteousness to stand in before him ; this shews that the immediate object of faith, as juſtifying is the prieſtly office of Chriſt; that only anſwering the ſinner's want as to juſtification. The prophetical, and kingly offices of Chriſt, are equally neceſſary with his prieſtly, as by them we have ſpiritual light, grace, and ſanctification, are preſerved, and brought off victorious over all our enemies; Chriſt conſidered in every capacity, in every character, is the object of that faith that is ſaving, though conſidered in his prieſtly office he furniſhes a righteouſneſs for our juſtification: it is this that gives ſovereign comfort to the ſoul ſenſible of guilt, and wounded with ſin, thus it is repreſented in ſcripture, and thus it was plainly intimated to the church of old, by the ſacrifices which God appointed; a crucified Chriſt is all the ſinner's comfort and hope, and all his dependence for juſtification. Thus we ſee what is the object of juſtifying faith. Now,

2. What is the eſſential act of it? Believing in Chriſt is an humble application of the ſoul to him, in which he receives him and reſts upon him alone for ſalvation. There is a great difference between believing that Chriſt is the Saviour, and believing on him; the one is only the aſſent of the mind, the other is the approbation and conſent of the will, and the application of the ſoul to him. The firſt, conſidered abſtracted as an act of the mind, may be found in many, who are ſpiritually ſtrangers to Jeſus Chriſt. In the other lies the eſſence of faith, and therefore we generally find ſaving faith repreſented as a believing on Chriſt, Rom. iv. 5. and 9, 10, 11, &c. In true ſaving faith the aſſent of the mind is accompanied with a hearty approbation of the method of ſalvation by Chriſt, a direct application of the ſoul to him, and reſting on him; in which act the ſoul freely renounces his own righteouſneſs, and every other way of ſalvation, and betakes himſelf ſincerely and cordially to the way which God has appointed, acquieſces in it, as the beſt and moſt ſuitable way, and truſts abſolutely and entirely in Jeſus Chriſt for juſtification and ſalvation. We find faith, ſaving faith repreſented and illuſtrated under various metaphors in the word of God, which tend to ſhew its nature, and point out its actings. We find faith repreſented "by " coming to Chriſt." Thus our Lord called the burdened and *heavy laden*, to *come to him*, that is to believe on him, Matth. xi. 28. John vi. 35. " I am the bread of life, he

"who cometh to me shall never hunger," ver. 37. "All that the father giveth me shall come," &c. ver. 45. "Every man that hath heard and learned of the Father cometh unto me," ver. 65. "No man can come unto me, except it were given to him of the Father." To the same purpose our Lord speaks, John vii. 37. "In the last day, that great day of the feast, Jesus stood and cried, saying, If any man thirst let him come unto me and drink." In all these places what must we understand by coming to Christ but believing on him? Is it not a spiritual act that is meant? An act of the soul, under a sense of guilt? And does it not imply a renouncing self-dependence, and a betaking ourselves entirely to Jesus Christ for pardon and justification? The exercise of no other grace can be called a coming to Christ; faith alone must be meant, which has Christ for its object, to whom we go, and on whom alone we cast our souls, and all our concerns. Again, faith is called a receiving Christ, John i. 12. "To as many as received him, to them gave he power to become the sons of God, even to them that believe on his name." Col. ii. 6. "As ye have therefore received Christ Jesus the Lord, so walk ye in him." And unbelief is often represented by a not receiving of Christ.

Again, faith is represented as a flying for refuge. Heb. vi. 18. "That we might have strong consolation, who have fled for refuge to lay hold of the hope set before us." This has a manifest allusion to the cities of refuge, which God appointed of old; where those that had been undesignedly the cause of the death of any, might fly, and be safe from the wrath of the pursuer, and avenger of blood; there he was out of the reach of those he had injured, and might live secure: thus Christ is appointed as a sanctuary, whither poor distressed souls are to fly, and where they will be safe from the sword of infinite justice; this flying for refuge signifies a soul in distress, not able to do any thing himself, he stands exposed to everlasting death, he therefore betakes himself to Christ, to free him from the wrath to come.

Again, faith is represented by looking. Isa. xlv. 22. "Look unto me and be ye saved," &c. Zech. xii. 10. John iii. 14, 15. Num. xxi 8, 9. A brazen serpent was made and fixed upon a pole, that whoever among the Jews were stung, and looked upon this serpent might be healed. Christ, in allufion to this, is faid to be lifted up; he is appointed, fet forth, and held out, as the fpiritual phyfician and faviour, that whofoever looketh to, or believeth on him fhall be faved. This looking to, or believing on Chrift, therefore fignifies a finner wounded under a fenfe of fin, and points out a real application of foul to him. Faith excludes all our righteoufnefs from juftification, and gives all the glory, and afcribes all the healing efficacy to Chrift alone.

Again, faith is reprefented by trufting in Chrift. Thus fays the apoftle, " I kno whom I have believed," or trufted. 2 Tim. i. 12. In trufting the foul commits himfelf and his concerns into the hands of Chrift, and leaves all with him. As Potiphar left all with Jofeph, and trufted him with all. Gen. xxxix. 6. This is a noble act of faith, which the foul is enabled to put forth, he trufts in Chrift though he fees him not; in the midft of the greateft difcouragements and difficulties, he trufts himfelf with, cleaves to, and depends upon a glorious Redeemer; and this trufting fhews that Chrift is the chief, the only object of a guilty foul's dependence for juftification.

Thus by thefe and various other metaphors is faith fet forth in the word of God, all which give us fo many convincing proofs of juftification by the righteoufnefs of Chrift alone, as well as point out to us the true notion of faith. In fine, we fee the object and the nature of faith: confidered in general as faving faith, it hath for its object Chrift in all his characters, God in his nature and perfections, as revealed in the whole of his word, but confidered as juftifying, it looks to Chrift in his prieftly character alone, and is not only a crediting the report concerning him, but a direct application to him, in which the foul fenfible of fin, renounces all his own righteoufnefs, trufts in Chrift, receives him, and refts upon him alone for juftification.

(3.) True juftifying faving faith is a vital principle in the foul, of all obedience—Saving faith is not a dead, inactive, fruitlefs faith. " Faith without works is dead," fays the apoftle That is not the faith which God requires; a barren, unprofitable faith is only difhonourable to God and injurious to the foul " fhew me thy faith without thy works, " and I will fhew thee my faith by my works." James ii. 18. We are juftified by faith alone, but faith is not alone in the foul, it is accompanied with every other grace, it cannot be separated from a principle of life and universal obedience; it virtually and radically contains in it all obedience, as the effect is in the cause, it is a " faith that purifies the heart " Acts xv. 9. " it works by love." Gal. v. 6. It is the grand spring that sets every wheel in motion, it is an active, an enlivening, and quickening grace, it puts the Christian upon the pursuit and practice of every duty; it discovers its reality and excellency, by curbing the power of sin in the soul, by mortifying every lust, by promoting love to Christ, by freeing the soul from every sensual confinement, and by conforming us more and more to the image of Christ. This faith will not suffer the Christian to live a life of indolence and profaneness; it is a living principle, the more it is in exercise, the more the Christian flourishes and prospers in the divine life. See the Christian, when faith is in lively exercise, he not only rejoices in the prospect of eternal life, but he presses forward towards holiness; see how he mourns for sin! How humble in his own eyes! See how warm his desires after Christ, how strong his love to him! how lively in duty! See how spiritual and heavenly in his frame! How patient in tribulation! How active in duty! The more he looks by faith to his Redeemer, the more he is changed into his likeness, grows in grace, and makes advances in sanctification. But we shall speak more particularly to this, when we come to consider the influence which faith has upon holiness, and good works, or the inseparable connection there is between justification and sanctification. Thus we see the nature of justifying faith.

Inf. 1. Hence learn, that assurance is not of the essence of saving justifying faith. We may really believe in Christ, though we cannot see our interest in him. There is a persuasion or assurance that is essential to faith, but that is a persuasion or assurance of the object, *i e.* of the truth of those promises in which Christ is held forth. Thus we are exhorted to come in full assurance of faith to God. Heb. x. 22. " And we are to ask in faith, nothing wavering." James i. 6. The meaning of which cannot be. that we must believe that we shall receive what we ask, or that this is essential to acceptable prayer; but that we come with a stedfast belief of the truth of these promises which God has made, and that he would fulfil them, according to the intention of them. And this persuasion satisfies the mind, and gives the believer a comfortable hope, that God will give him the bleſſings he comes for, if infinite wifdom fee them neceſſary for him; there muſt be a perſuaſion of the reality of the declarations made of Chriſt, there muſt be a perſuaſion of the fuitableneſs and all-fufficiency of Jeſus Chriſt, or elſe where is faith! Nay, there muſt be ſome peradventure Chriſt will ſave us, or elſe there can be no reliance; for how can we conceive of any medium between hope and abſolute deſpair? But there may be true faith in Chriſt, where there is no aſſurance of a perſonal intereſt in him. If we are juſtified by the faith of aſſurance, then a mere propoſition that Chriſt is ours, would be the object of faith and not Chriſt himſelf; and ſo the principal act of faith would be an act of the underſtanding, whereas the principal, the uniting act of faith, we have ſeen, lies in the will; therefore it is called receiving Chriſt, and being drawn to him; would you therefore know whether you have ſaving juſtifying faith, inquire not whether you can ſay Chriſt is yours, but whether you are made willing to receive Chriſt, whether you have been enabled to give up yourſelves to him, to make him your dependence; inquire into the fruits and effects of faith, whether you love Chriſt in all his characters, for he is precious to none but thoſe who believe.

Inf. 2. Is ſaving, juſtifying faith of ſuch a nature and from ſuch an origin as has been repreſented? Then learn the obligation believers are under to bleſs God for ſuch a favour! O bleſs God that he has given you faith in Chriſt! That you have been enabled to look to him for healing, to fly to him for refuge, to ſee his excellencies, and receive him in all his fulneſs! Look up to him daily, to enable you to live more in the exerciſe of this precious grace. Oh may the life we live in the fleſh be by the faith of the Son of God, who has loved us and given himſelf for us!

SERMON XI.

ON JUSTIFICATION.

Rom. v. 1.

Therefore, being justified by faith, we have peace with God, through our Lord Jesus Christ.

THE way of justification and salvation by faith in Jesus Christ, is so contrary to our natural conceptions, that we should have ever remained in the dark, had it not been for a divine revelation: and till the Spirit of God enlightens our understanding, and leads us by faith to Jesus Christ, we remain perfect strangers to him, notwithstanding the revelation we enjoy. We are naturally flying to a course of duties, to make our peace with God, and gain us an interest in his favour, a melancholy evidence this, of the dreadful ignorance and corruption of human nature! As well as a clear intimation of the obligation we are under, to adore the infinite riches of distinguishing grace, if we are brought to believe in Jesus Christ.

We have under our consideration justification by faith in Christ—And to set this subject in a clear light. We proposed,

1. To consider the nature of that faith that justifies. And, 2. How it justifies. We have already considered the nature of that faith that justifies. We have considered, 1. its author, and 2, what it implies,

1. It implies an assent of the mind to the gospel way of

X

falvation, upon a conviction of its excellency and importance, made in the mind, by the Spirit of God.

2. Faith implies a confent of the will, and is a direct application of the foul to Chrift, in which he receives him, and refts upon him alone for juftification. Here we confidered the object of juftifying faith, and the effential act of it. We now come,

III. To inquire how faith juftifies. Now, 1. Faith does not juftify without relation to its object. The fcripture limits faith to its object. " Believe in the Lord Jefus Chrift, " and thou fhalt be faved," Acts xvi. 31. It may be indeed objected in the cafe of Abraham, for it is faid, " A-" braham believed God, and it was accounted unto him for " righteoufnefs," Rom iv. 3. *i. e. The act of believing*. And therefore faith itfelf is our juftifying righteoufnefs. To which we may anfwer, it is a contradiction to fay, that faith itfelf juftifies: faith, though the gift of God, yet is an act of ours. To fay then, that faith juftifies, is to fay we are juftified by an act of our own, and therefore that we are juftified by works. In the forementioned, Rom. iii. 4, 5, 6, verfes, there is a manifeft oppofition between faith and works. " Abraham believed God, and it was counted " unto him for righteoufnefs." It muft be the object that was counted, and not the act, for the next verfe proves it " Now to him that worketh, is the reward not reckoned of " grace but of debt;" this plainly fhews, that Abraham was not juftified by works but by grace. To him that worketh, i e. for juftification, if he can be juftified by his works, then grace has no hand in it, eternal life becomes his juft due. Whereas it is reprefented as a free gift.—But, fays the apoftle, " To him that worketh not, *i. e.* (for juftifica-" tion) but believeth on him, that juftifieth the ungodly, " his faith is counted for righteoufnefs." Thus we fee the apoftle mentions juftification by works, and by Chrift; from what different caufes they arife, one of debt, the other of grace; confequently as there is this oppofition made between faith and works, our being juftified by faith, is not by the act of faith, but the object which we receive by faith : for were we juftified by the act, we fhould then be juftified by works and of debt; but we are juftified by grace. It is common in fcripture to attribute that to the act or habit which belongs to the object. It was not the woman's

touching Chrift that healed her, but the virtue that came from him, Mark v. 25, &c. It was not faith that made perfons whole, but the power and ftrength of Chrift apprehended by faith. Thus it is not faith that juftifies us, but the righteoufnefs of Chrift received and apprehended by it But what is that faith which is faid to be imputed to Abraham; It was a faith in the promife of God Faith that had an eye to Chrift, Gal. iii. 16. " Now to Abra-
" ham and his feed were the promifes made, he faith not,
" and to feeds as of many, but as of one, and to thy feed,
" which is Chrift." For though Abraham lived at fuch a diftance of time from the days of Chrift, yet he " faw this
" day by faith, and he rejoiced, and was glad." John viii. 56. Thus Abraham was an example for us, in this way of juftification, as appears from Rom iv. 23, 24. " Now
" it was not written for his fake alone, that it was imputed
" to him, but for us alfo, to whom it fhall be imputed, if
" we believe on him that raifed up Jefus from the dead." To fay that faith itfelf juftifies, is to deftroy the nature of faith. What does faith do, but prefent the righteoufnefs of Chrift to God for acceptance? Does faith plead works? No, it pleads what Chrift hath done, which makes it evidently appear, that the righteoufnefs of Chrift, and not the act of believing is our juftifying righteoufnefs.

2. Faith does not juftify as accompanied with works. There is indeed a great difference between an empty, dead faith, and juftifying faith: juftifying faith is a faith that produces works, but yet it does not juftify with its works. We muft feparate works and faith in the act of juftifying; though faith in the foul is accompanied with every other grace, and leads on to virtue, knowledge, temperance, patience, godlinefs, brotherly-kindnefs, and charity, yet it doth not juftify the foul, on account of this beautiful train attending it.

3. Faith juftifies as an inftrument, by trufting in Chrift. Sanctification is a progreffive work, and is abfolutely neceffary to our complete falvation: for which we muft look to Chrift in all his offices; but in juftification we muft look to his prieftly office alone, and therefore juftifying faith, is reprefented by trufting in, depending upon, receiving him, &c. to fignify that faith is only an inftrument in juftification, and not the caufe, or condition of it. The righteouf-

nefs of Chrift is a gift beftowed upon us, and received by us: and how is it received by us? By faith: therefore faith in juftification is no more than the hand or inftrument by which we receive the benefit of the Redeemer's righteoufnefs. When we bid a poor creature in diftrefs hold out his hand, and we will give him fome fupply; the holding out his hand is not the condition of our giving alms; though it is the means by which our charity is conveyed, and he becomes poffeffed of it. In fine, though without faith there is no juftification, yet faith itfelf does not juftify; all that is meant by thefe expreffions of being juftified by faith is this, viz. That the bleffing of juftification is conveyed to us in a way of believing, and was not enjoyed before. Thus we fee how the righteoufnefs of Chrift becomes ours, by the gracious imputation of God, and by our faith, he reckoning it to us on the one hand, and we receiving it, pleading its virtue with God for the pardon of our fins, and a title to glory, and entirely refting upon it for juftification on the other. By this means it becomes ours really and legally, and we are juftified by it, and fhall receive the everlafting bleffings and benefits of it in a better world.

We have now gone through what we propofed,—Have fhewn wherein juftification confifts,—That our own perfonal righteoufnefs is abfolutely unable to juftify us before God: that it is the righteoufnefs of Jefus Chrift alone, that is the matter of our juftification, and the ground of our acceptance with God: and how it is, that this righteoufnefs is made ours, that we may be really and legally juftified by it. Let us now attend to a particular improvement of fo great a fubject, and,

Ufe 1. From what has been faid upon this important fubject we learn, that the three glorious perfons in the trinity, are jointly concerned in the juftification of a finner, and therefore are to be equally glorified. The Father is reprefented, as purpofing the falvation of his people; as contriving the glorious fcheme, which has been purfued; as calling Chrift to the important office of a mediator; as fending him into the world, to bring in an everlafting righteoufnefs; as accepting of this righteoufnefs, and, in confequence thereof, as imputing it to his people, pardoning them, and accepting them as righteous upon the account of it. The Son, the Lord Jefus Chrift, voluntarily accepted of the office his Father had appointed for him, came into the world, veiled his glory in the humble form of a fervant, obeyed the law, and fuffered the penalty, by which he furnifhed us with that righteoufnefs we ftand in before God: he is our great High Prieft, who, after he had offered himfelf a facrifice to God, went into the heavens, and fits down at the right hand of God, pleading the virtue of his righteoufnefs for his people. And the Holy Spirit applies the redemption purchafed by Chrift, and particularly in juftification he works faith in the finner, he convinces him of fin, of his loft and undone condition, and of the imperfection of his own righteoufnefs, that it is but as filthy rags, and an unclean thing, and not worthy of God's acceptance; he leads him to Chrift, and he takes of his things, and fhews them to the foul; he, in fine, enables him to believe, helps him to go out of himfelf, to renounce all his own mean, worthlefs fervices, and to caft himfelf upon the Lord Jefus Chrift, and truft in him alone for juftification. Thus the Spirit implants faith in the foul, and enables him to exercife it, and fo has a concern in the juftification of a finner. He, as the comforter likewife, gives the foul a view of his juftification, introduces fweet peace into his mind, removes the pangs of an awakened confcience, and cheers the foul with a view of a reconciled God. Thus equal honours are due to the three glorious perfons in the Trinity, as being concerned in the juftification of a finner. Whilft you are adoring the Lord Jefus Chrift, for the wonders of his love, in providing fuch a perfect righteoufnefs for your juftification, and introducing you by it into the divine favour; forget not to admire the grace of the Father, who called his only begotten Son to the important office of a mediator, and who fent him into the world upon this glorious errand, and who accepts and juftifies you through him; nor neglect to afcribe equal praifes to the eternal Spirit, who brought you to a fenfe of your need of Chrift, and enabled you to believe on him Oh! what honours has God put upon a poor finner, that the three glorious perfons in the Godhead fhould be all concerned in his juftification! and Oh how truly is he juftified! Need I, Oh my foul, fear to appear before the tribunal of God? Will not each glorious perfon own me? Will not the Father view me, as the perfon he has juftified and pardoned? Will not the Son receive me as one for whom he furnifhed a glorious righteousness? And will not the Holy Spirit own that faith in me, which is of his own implanting? Will he not see the marks and traces of his own work in my soul? How happy, how secure am I therefore, and Oh, what honours are due to the glorious three! The saints above, sensible of their obligations, are offering their united and unwearied praises to the Father, Son, and Holy Ghost. Glory be to thee, Oh Father, for thine everlasting love, thine eternal appointment, thy pardoning mercy. Glory be to thee, Oh thou lamb of God, for thy sweet smelling sacrifice, thy perfect and everlasting righteousness And glory be to thee, Oh holy and blessed Spirit, for thy quickening and enlivening operations, thy sacred productions, thine almighty energy. This, this is the delightful employment of the saints above: Oh may we join these heavenly inhabitants at last, and spend an eternity in praising and adoring the grace, the distinct acts and operations of Father, Son, and Holy Ghost in the whole of our salvation.

Use 2. From what has been said upon this subject, we learn that the notion of an eternal justification is without foundation. Justification we have considered as a relative change, actually made when we become personally absolved, pardoned, pronounced righteous, and entitled to eternal life. This justification is said to be by faith, now faith we know is something wrought in us, it presupposes conviction in the mind, and consequently the actual existence of the person who believes. This consideration therefore effectually destroys eternal justification, unless we can suppose an impossibility, viz. That believers existed from all eternity, and believed from all eternity. We acknowledge that all believers were represented in Christ their head, when he made the glorious agreement with the Father from eternity, he undertook to do and suffer for them all that was necessary, he took all their sins upon him, and the Father, well knowing that the debt would be paid, promised eternal life to Christ their head. Titus i. 2. " In hopes of eternal life, " which God, that cannot lie, promised before the world " began." Thus their salvation was insured and rendered certain; but how different is this from actual personal justification? The blessings of salvation were given to Christ, and received by him for us, but we could not be said to be personally possessed of them. Believers were in some measure justified in Christ when he was raised from the dead, for he arose as a public person, they were justified in their head: but there is a great difference between being justified in our head, and justified personally and actually through him: we all sinned in Adam, but we are not actually under the condemning power of the law, till we appear personally on earth. In fine, what is justification but the removing of sin, and giving us a title to eternal life? This necessarily presupposes a state of guilt, condemnation, and death, and a real, actual change from one state to the other; agreeable to the word of God, which styles even believers themselves, before they believe, " children of wrath even as others." Eph. ii. 3 And the believing Corinthians had experienced a change of state as well as of heart. 1 Cor. vi. 11. " And " such were some of you, but ye are washed," &c. In another place we are said to be concluded under sin, and become guilty before God. Rom. iii. 9. " What then are we " better than they, &c. For we have before proved both " Jews and Gentiles, that they are all under sin." 19 verse, " Now we know, &c. and all the world become guilty be- " fore God." Now, are these meaning or unmeaning phrases? Do they not contain an awful reality in them, viz. That we are naturally under the condemning sentence of the law? What is justification then, but a personal discharge? &c. If then there is a time when the people of God are under the condemning sentence of the law, then there is a time when they are not justified: unless we can suppose that to be under condemnation and to be justified are consistent at the same time, which cannot be. The word of God, and not his secret will is to be the rule of our judgement; and whatever the word of God says is perfect truth. Now, as it represents us at one time children of wrath, under the wrath of God, and at another time justified, and the children of God; we learn that justification, personal, actual, gospel justification, was not, cannot be from eternity, but is in time when the sinner actually believes, and no sooner.

Use 3. From what has been said, we learn the dreadful malignity and demerit of sin! Sin never appears more odious, than when we view the sufferings and humiliation of Jesus Christ. Was man unable to make satisfaction for it? Were all the Old Testament sacrifices insufficient to make atonement? Must the Son of God become man? Must he bear the wrath of God? Muſt he pour out his precious blood before ſin could be pardoned and the guilty creature reſtored to favour? Oh what a dreadful evil is ſin, it is impoſſible to ſet forth its real malignity; it is inconceivably odious and dreadful in its nature and tendency. Would you entertain ſome ſuitable conceptions of the awful demerit of ſin, look upon the mighty God becoming man; view him a man of ſorrows, &c. Follow him to the garden, and ſee him in inexpreſſible agonies of ſoul, ſweating great drops of blood; go from the garden to the croſs, ſee him feeling the cruelty of man, the wrath of God, crying out, " My " God, my God, why haſt thou forſaken me?" All this was neceſſary to the pardon of ſin, to the enjoyment of the divine favour, and eternal life. Oh what an evil and bitter thing is it then to ſin againſt God! And can you roll ſin as a ſweet morſel under your tongues, ye careleſs ſouls, who are ſtrangers and enemies to Chriſt! Can you love ſin, which filled the Saviour with ſuch amazing agony! Oh think, if you can, how inconceivably dreadful thoſe torments muſt be which your ſoul will feel on the account of ſin in the bottomleſs pit, if it is not forgiven. And can you ſport with ſin? Ye followers of Jeſus, who have given your ſouls up to him, Oh ſtand at the utmoſt diſtance from ſin. See what Chriſt has done for you! And Oh be not negligent, be not careleſs, be upon your guard, and be concerned to have your ſouls filled with the utmoſt deteſtation of ſin! Was it a light thing for Chriſt to ſweat great drops of blood; was it a trifling matter for the Son of God to bear infinite wrath! To hang upon the croſs and make himſelf a ſacrifice for you! Oh when you are tempted at any time to ſin, when opportunity preſents, and ſinners, or your own hearts, would tempt you to ſin; ſay, how can I do this wickedneſs, Oh my ſoul? It is the blood of Chriſt, how can I love it? It coſt him his life, how can I trifle with it? Oh let me ſtart even at ſinful thought!

Uſe 4. We learn further, the exceeding great love of our Redeemer, and the obligation we are under, to love, honour, and ſerve him. When we confider that Jeſus Chriſt has furniſhed us with that righteouſneſs by which we are juſtified, and what he did, and ſuffered to bring in this righteouſneſs, we cannot but be convinced of our obligations, to love, honour, and ſerve him; eſpecially if we confider the dignity of his person and our unworthiness of such infinite kindness: when we consider the blessings of justification, which we receive through our Redeemer's righteousness, we cannot but be sensible how much we ought to love him, and call upon our souls, and all that is within us to bless his holy name. Hast thou any hope, Oh my soul, of pardon and salvation? It is owing to thy kind Redeemer: I might have dwelt in the bottomless pit forever, had it not been for his infinite compassion, and the virtue of his righteousness! Can I view God reconciled to me? Have I any prospect of deliverance from the wrath to come? Oh unspeakable love of my glorious Redeemer! It is owing to thee, dearest Jesus, that I have a prospect of such exalted blessings! And, Oh my soul, shall I not love so glorious a friend? Am I not under the greatest obligations to him? Has he saved my poor soul? Made me an heir of eternal life, when I might have perished forever? Oh what wonderful and astonishing love! And why then all this coldness to my dear Redeemer! Why is his name no more precious? Why am I so indifferent, so lifeless in his service, why have I no more boldness, no more zeal for his name and his cause! Oh my ungrateful heart, to be no more warmed with love to Jesus! To be no more sensible of my obligations! Lord shed abroad thy love in my soul, that it may kindle mine to thee, that the fire may burn with greater fervour in my cold heart, and my soul be more lively and vigorous in thy service!

Use 5. From what has been said we learn the perseverance of the saints. If we are once justified, we shall never fall into condemnation. Christ, as our surety, made satisfaction for all our sins. Now this satisfaction was either imperfect or full and perfect; if the satisfaction which Christ made to infinite justice for his people's sins was imperfect, if he only partly satisfied. and left part for us, then indeed our circumstances are melancholy, then may the soul be afraid of a miscarriage, and our salvation would be precarious and uncertain: but this satisfaction was full and perfect, all that justice required was paid down; this appears by his discharge from death, his ascension into heaven, his exaltation and intercession there. Christ therefore making full satisfaction for all his people's sins, they must be discharged from hell and wrath, and be put into the possession of life everlasting; consequently the soul that believes on Jesus shall persevere finally, and never be deprived of the purchased inheritance, unless we suppose God to be mutable or unfaithful, which cannot be. He that is once justified then shall never fall into condemnation. Justification is an act wherein God absolves the soul from punishment, cancels and removes the obligation, and gives him a title to eternal life; the believer may fall into sin, but he shall not fall finally from God. There is room for daily repentance by our backslidings, room to plead with God for pardon, room for humiliation; but the soul that is once justified shall stand in the favour of God. Thus says the apostle, " By " whom we have access through faith, into this grace " wherein we stand, and rejoice in hope of the glory " of God," Rom. v. 2. Once access into the favour of God, and we shall continue in it, we may rejoice in hope of full and everlasting glory; for all whom God justifies, he glorifies. O glorious, O comfortable truth! Once actually in Christ by faith, and you shall never, never, never fall into condemnation! Have you believed in Jesus Christ? You shall receive the end of your faith, even the salvation of your souls: the title which God has given you is good, it will stand the trial, and God will never recal it for the gifts, &c. Rom. xi. 29. This by no means sets aside the use of means, it does not lead to sin; it animates the soul with greater courage, enlivens him more in his way, and fills him with joy unspeakable and full of glory.

SERMON XII.

ON JUSTIFICATION.

Rom. v. 1.

Therefore, being justified by faith, we have peace with God, through our Lord Jesus Christ.

WE are upon the improvement of this great and precious doctrine of a sinner's justification in the sight of God, viz By faith in the imputed righteousness of the Lord Jesus Christ. We proceed to,

Use 6 From what has been said, we learn that there are not different degrees in justification. If justification arose from faith and obedience then it must be imperfect, because our obedience is so; but the apostle says, " There is " no condemnation to them which are in Christ Jesus, who " walk not after the flesh but after the spirit," Rom. viii 1. Either a person is pardoned, or he is not, either he has a title to heaven, or he has not, there is no such thing as half a title, or part of a title; there is a full title or none at all. Justification is not a gradual work, though it would be so, was it to arise from our own obedience; upon this foundation there would be no certainty: according to the measure of our faith and obedience, such would be the measure of our justification: an uncomfortable doctrine! But such is not the consequence of justification by imputed righteousness. " The righteousness of God by faith in " Christ Jesus," the apostle tells us, is unto, and upon all "them that believe; for there is no difference," Rom. iii. 22. The weak believer is juſtified equally with the ſtrongeſt, the ſame righteouſneſs is imputed unto them, therefore they muſt be juſtified alike. Their faith is the ſame, though not in degrees yet in nature: believing more ſtrongly or more weakly, makes no difference in the ſtate of believers, though it does in their frames. The weak believer is not ſo lively, not ſo well fitted for bearing difficulties, and withſtanding temptations, as the ſtrong believer; he is ſooner foiled by the enemy, ſooner oppreſſed with doubts and fears, ſooner loaded with anxious cares, but his title to glory is as good as that of the moſt triumphant ſaint, they ſhall both be glorified. You that are weak in faith, rejoice, your ſtrength, your righteouſneſs, your all is in Chriſt, ſo long as his righteouſneſs has any virtue in it, ſo long will you ſtand in the favour of God; you cannot rejoice perhaps as others do, but remember you have the ſame righteouſneſs to truſt to, the ſame Jeſus to guide you and keep you ſafe to glory as they have, and you ſhall reach ſafe to Zion at laſt as well as they.

Uſe 7. From what has been ſaid we learn how exceeding fooliſh all thoſe are, who will not ſubmit to this way of juſtification. And here give me leave to addreſs you, who are ſtrangers and enemies to Jeſus Chriſt, and are building all your hopes upon the ſandy foundation of your own ſervices: let me ſeriouſly aſk you this queſtion, why is it you reject this way of ſalvation by the righteouſneſs of Jeſus Chriſt? Is it a doctrine that is any ways diſhonourable to God? Let us bring it to the trial, and ſee which of the divine perfections it ſullies. Is it the mercy of God? This cannot be, for mercy is glorified, yea highly glorified in the humiliation and ſufferings of Jeſus Chriſt: here is ſuch grace and ſuch mercy as can appear in no other way. Is it the wiſdom of God that is leſſened? No, behold this is likewiſe greatly exalted. Angels admire the way, and glorify infinite wiſdom in its contrivance, Eph. iii. 10. Is the juſtice of God then diſhonoured? Oh no! The juſtice of God appears in all its infinite luſtre and glory, whilſt we ſee God puniſhing ſin in the ſurety, Rom. iii. 26. "To de"clare, I ſay at this time his righteouſneſs, that he may be "juſt, and the juſtifier of him that believeth in Jeſus." In fine, here every divine perfection appears in its utmoſt radiancy and glory, to fill our minds with the greatest awe and reverence, to engage our adorations and praises, and to encourage our faith and hope. And is God honoured by this doctrine? This is enough to engage us heartily to believe it, and earnestly to seek after an interest in imputed righteousness. Why then do you dislike this amiable truth? Does it injure the law? Search and see. The righteousness of Jesus Christ is perfectly agreeable to all the commands of the law, he suffered its penalty, and was made a curse for us, he has laid us under the greatest obligations to obey it, how then is it injured? It is rather honoured, yea greatly honoured, by the infinite stoop of the Son of God, found in fashion of a man, and made under the law, that he might magnify it and make it honourable. Wherefore then do you despise this truth, is it an uncomfortable doctrine? Does it distress the mind, and fill the soul with a melancholy gloom? Ask the awakened sinner, and you will find nothing is more effectual to remove his fears, to quiet his conscience, to raise his hopes, and fill him with a sweet peace and tranquillity. Oh, says he, it is the most comfortable news I have ever heard, it suits my soul, it opens a door of hope before me. Ask the believer that has walked in the truth some years; he has tried it, and can certainly form a judgement of it. You that twenty or thirty years ago, were led to take hold of this truth, what sort of a doctrine have you found it to your souls? Can you recommend it to the sinner as a soul comforting truth? Have you been enlivened, comforted, and encouraged by it? How has it appeared, when conscience has stung you with a sense of guilt? When death has presented itself before you, and eternity has been in view? Some of you no doubt have met with such opportunities to try the excellency of this truth, and have you any thing to say in its favour? Has it not been your greatest cordial, your chief support? Yes, says the believer, I have tried it for a long course of years, nay, I have tried the poor self righteous man's refuge; I have tried every foundation which the sinner is endeavouring to establish, and find *that* of an imputed righteousness the only one to cheer and support a wounded spirit, to brighten my views, support me in the moment of trial, and to fill me with solid consolation. Hearest thou this sinner? Permit me then again to repeat the question: why do you disap-

prove of this doctrine? Is it an unsafe way, is there any uncertainty in it, do you run any risk of your immortal soul? If so, we will all discard it, and renounce it at once, as not fit for our dependence; bring it to the trial then, and give it a fair hearing. And if we take a review of what we have already said upon this subject, if we consider the Father's approbation of Christ as our surety and righteousness; the fulness of his satisfaction, and his answering all the demands, the ends and purposes of the law; that he did all this voluntarily in the room and stead of his people; if we consider all this, we cannot but conclude, that there is the most solid foundation laid for our trust and dependence, and the utmost certainty of our salvation. The representations we have of Christ in the word of God, as the only foundation, the sure foundation, a tried stone, &c. are enough to convince us, that it is the most safe and secure way. Christ is a tried stone he has been proved, God the Father tried him, when he laid our sins upon him and he bore them all. The devils tried him, and he conquered and spoiled principalities, &c. And his people have tried him above five thousand years, and have found him an able saviour. The thousands and ten thousand times ten thousand, who are at the right hand of God singing victory and salvation, and giving glory to the lamb; all these are living evidences of his perfect, and all-sufficient righteousness; nay, not one soul, that trusted in him, ever met with a disappointment. And Oh, what can you now object? Will you not believe in, and rejoice in this way of salvation yet? Think seriously, whether you can answer satisfactorily these questions. ‘ Why is Christ represented as our righteous-
‘ ness? Why as the lamb of God, &c. Why as the High-
‘ Priest! Why is all the glory of our salvation ascribed
‘ unto him?’ Have these things any meaning? Do they not plainly shew the reality of that doctrine we have been vindicating? Think further, how you will appear before God. You may go about to establish a righteousness of your own, and please yourselves that it will do, but sit, and, with the utmost seriousness, think upon the subject for a few moments, labouring to call off your thoughts from all sublunary things; and now suppose all earthly things vanishing, that you are going to leave converse with mortals, and to appear before God, and to receive a sentence which will

determine your everlasting condition! Suppose you were just going to be examined by him, by that God who is of purer eyes than to behold iniquity, that God in whose sight the heavens are not clean, that God before whom the angels fall down with humble reverence! Is not this an awful thought? Is it not enough in such a serious moment to make you distrust your own righteousness? Oh, how will you appear before God! That God whose presence our first parents would have fled, and hid themselves amongst the trees of the garden! Can you venture boldly before his bar, when you come in that critical moment to look back upon so many omissions of duty, so many commissions of sin; Will not your hearts shrink with fear of the consequences? Oh may these considerations be rendered effectual to engage you to come naked and guilty to Jesus Christ for righteousness and peace! and,

What blessed encouragement does this way of justification give the sinner! God is just, yet there is the greatest encouragement to apply to him, he has acted agreeable to his infinite purity and justice, those glorious perfections of his nature; agreeable to his character as the supreme law-giver and governor, in punishing sin in the surety. Oh blessed news to awaken sinners! Let none despair; if their sins are never so great, here is a perfect, a glorious righteousness " Christ is the end of the law for righteousness to every one " that believes." Rom. x. 4.

Use 8. The last use I would make of this great subject is to to point out the freeness of grace in our justification, " being " justified freely by his grace through the redemption that is " in Christ Jesus" Rom. iii. 24. Our redemption is by a price paid, and our justification is in virtue of a righteousness Christ has wrought out, nevertheless to us it is all gratuitous and free: free, distinguishing, sovereign grace is what the believer is indebted to for every blessing he enjoys here, for all that he lives in the expectation of hereafter. This is a truth of no small importance in the Christian life, as it tends to slay all self-dependence, to keep us truly humble under a becoming sense of our own weakness and vileness, and to fill us with the most adoring thoughts of that grace whereby we are saved. Permit me then to conclude the whole subject by the mention of two or three things in support of this point. This will fully appear if we consider,

1. The fixing and appointing this way of justification was the effect of the free, distinguishing, and everlasting love of God. The scheme was laid in eternity, it was contrived by infinite wisdom, it was the effect of everlasting love; there was none to plead for us, the scheme was formed, and the affair settled, before the mountains were brought forth, or ever the earth or the sea were made, even from everlasting: it was the mere effect of God's sovereign pleasure, and sprung from his free undeserved pity, grace, and compassion. Who was it that laid the grand platform of our salvation, in which the way of our justification, and the bestowment of every blessing was settled? Who was it that appointed the blessed Son of God to be the mediator, to come in the likeness of sinful flesh, and bring in a righteousness for his people to appear in? Was it not God the Father, and did it not spring from his eternal love, his free unmerited grace? Who was there with God when he fixed the glorious scheme, when he called his Son to the important office, and settled the grand affair with him? There was no creature formed to plead his pity; he saw us, in his all-comprehensive view, lost, fallen, wretched, and miserable; and nothing but his own will determined him to have mercy upon us. Our justification, though by the righteousness of Christ, yet was first laid in the love, the eternal love of God the Father; here was the grand spring of all God's future acts, his free grace; this was the foundation, and this will be the top-stone. *Grace, grace* will be all the song of the redeemed of the Lord. Grace began and finished their salvation, formed the plan and put it in execution: Christ's righteousness was the way in which the free grace of God discovered itself! Had not God been from eternity gracious, we must have been forever miserable and wretched, for there is no change in him, he is without any variableness, or the least shadow of turning. He was the same from eternity as he is now, and he will continue so to eternity: Christ did not render God gracious by undertaking the work of our redemption; what Christ has done is the effect of divine grace, and was necessary to open a way for the actual conveyance of this grace to the soul of the sinner. See then, we

are juſtified freely by the grace of God in this inſtance, the Father was free, without any obligation in fixing upon, and determining this way of juſtification: it was becauſe he loved us that he ordained this righteouſneſs for us. And why did he love us? becauſe he would do it! He was perfectly free without compulſion; alas! who ſhould conſtrain him, who ſhould oblige him to make ſuch proviſion for us? All were loſt, had forfeited his favour, and deſerved his everlaſting indignation; in this condition he viewed us when he loved us, and gave his only begotten Son for us: in this wretched condition he viewed us when he made the ſettlement concerning our juſtification and ſalvation, his love then was free as it was great. Rom. v. 8. "But God comendeth his love towards us, in that, while we were yet ſinners, Chriſt died for us," Jer. xxxi. 3. "The Lord hath appeared of old unto me, ſaying, yea, I have loved thee with an everlaſting love; therefore with loving kindneſs have I drawn thee."

1. Chriſt was abſolutely free, and diſcovered the riches of his grace in furniſhing us with that righteouſneſs by which we are juſtified. The righteouſneſs by which we are juſtified, is not of our preparing: as it was of God's appointing ſo it was of God's preparing; God the Father determined and fixed it, God the Son wrought it out and both were entirely free. Was the ſecond perſon in the trinity conſtrained to provide for us ſuch a righteouſneſs! He had no obligation upon him but what he freely and voluntarily brought himſelf under; he was not influenced to do it by a view of advantage, or from a conſideration of any merit or worthineſs in us; we lay ruined, helpleſs, and miſerable; it was free, it was generous love, in the Son of God to come and furniſh us with a righteouſneſs to ſtand before God. As it was free, ſo it was rich grace, abundant aſtoniſhing grace, ſuch as entertains angels and raiſes their admiration: the Son of God muſt lay aſide his glory and appear in human nature, he muſt ſtoop ſo low as to be made under the law, be obedient to all its commands, and, what is more, endure its penalty, be liable to all manner of ſufferings, offer himſelf a ſacrifice, bear the wrath of God, and die a bitter, ignominious, and curſed death, even the death of the croſs! This is the way in which juſtice was to be ſatisfied, and heaven purchaſed; this was the righteouſneſs which we are

to be justified by: and is not the grace of our Lord Jesus Christ abundant in providing this righteousness, when we consider that he who was rich must become poor, that we through his poverty might be made rich? 2 Cor. viii. 9. It is an act of uncommon kindness and generosity amongst men, for a person to lay down his life for his friend; but we were not to be considered in that amiable character when Jesus undertook to provide this righteousness for us; we were enemies, traitors, and rebels, and yet behold he loved us, he loved us so as to fulfil all righteousness for us! Oh amazing grace, is not all this the effect of his free and sovereign pleasure! he might have viewed us with contempt; but behold he undertakes for us, and he furnisheth us with a righteousness. It is not your own righteousness, Christians, that will justify you before God, you are indebted to your glorious Redeemer for it; he wrought it out, he has brought it in, he provided it himself, he came voluntarily and did it—He did it all freely without any consideration of reward or advantage. What did the mighty God stand in need of, that he should be found in fashion as a man? Needed he our poor worthless services? No, it was all to shew how much he loved us! It was to shew the riches of his grace in the justification and salvation of his people. Oh that our souls were more deeply impressed with a sense of it, &c.

Thus we see the appointing this way of justification and the providing that righteousness whereby we are justified are both freely from the grace of God.

3. God's actually making this righteousness ours by imputation is freely by the grace of God. We have shewn that one way in which this righteousness becomes ours, is by imputation, which is an act of God's by which he reckons it to us, and deals with us according to its infinite and everlasting virtue and efficacy. In this act of imputation God displays both his justice and his grace, he is just to Christ, just in the fulfilment of his promises, in imputing this righteousness to the believer, yet he is merciful and gracious to us; can we plead a right a personal right to this righteousness, from any qualification in us, or any service done by us? We have rather reason, the utmost reason to acknowledge our unworthiness of the least mercy. Look upon the poor sinner, see what he is by nature, view him in his filthy rags, in his spotted garments all over polluted, from

the crown of his head to the sole of his feet, see him a transgressor of the law, an open rebel, and consequently worthy of eternal damnation; such is the soul before he has actually an interest in this righteousness, such does God find us when he comes by his spirit to enlighten our understandings and lead us to Christ, such does he find us, when he comes by his grace to renew us, to implant fai h in us, and to impute his righteousness to us; therefore we read, Rom. iv. 5. " But to him that worketh not but believeth on him " that justifieth the ungodly, his faith is counted for righ- " teousness."——Not that they remain ungodly, those whom God justifies he likewise sanctifies, but he finds them ungodly, when he comes to them, to give them an actual personal interest in the blessings of the everlasting covenant. Such were you Christians! You were strangers and enemies to God, guilty and included under sin, exposed to the execution of the sentence of the law, and children of wrath. In these circumstances were you when God came and led you to Jesus.

From this view of the sinner then, let any one judge whether God, in imputing the righteousness of Christ to him, is not entirely free!

Oh, says the believer, hast thou, Lord, imputed to me the righteousness of my Redeemer? What an act of grace, free grace and mercy, to such an unworthy polluted guilty creature! All the glory be to thee O Lord. Thus God freely imputes this righteousness to us and we receive it as a free gift. And thus are we justified freely by the grace of God through the redemption that is in Christ Jesus.

4. If we consider that faith, by which we are said to be justified, we shall see that we are justified freely by the grace of God. We need only here mention two things. 1st, The author of faith. 2d, The nature of it.

(1.) How came we to have that faith that justifies? Here we find we have no claim to merit, for faith is wrought in us by the almighty power of God, and is the gift of his special grace; " by grace are ye saved through faith; and that " not of yourselves: it is the gift of God," Eph. ii. 8. It is God that helps us to believe, or else we should remain for ever under the power of unbelief; we have done nothing to entitle us to this faith, nor is it given on the account of the amiable fruits and effects of it foreseen; but it is given freely, it is a free promise of the everlasting covenant, and is the purchase of our Lord Jesus Christ. And the spirit comes at the time appointed, and implants it in the soul, without paying any regard to the character or temper of the person, or expecting any assistance from him; he comes with his almighty power, sets the poor prisoner at liberty, leads him to Christ, and enables him to believe: thus that faith which justifies, is given to us freely, we have nothing to boast of upon that point, but have reason to say that we are justified freely by the grace of God, &c. After the sinner is laid under the strongest conviction, he yet deserves nothing, the giving of faith is an act of his sovereign grace.

2. It appears from the nature, and actings of faith that our justification is free. Faith receives salvation as the purchase of Christ, as a free gift: Faith does not plead the merit of the creature, it pleads nothing but the rich mercy, the free promise of God, and the righteousness of Jesus Christ; the language of faith stands at the utmost distance from pride, and is full of the deepest humility. Lord I am nothing, I am absolutely vile and despicable, I am unworthy of thy favour, it is rich grace to take notice of so guilty polluted a creature, all my dependence is upon thee, for I am altogether helpless, and miserable; I trust therefore entirely in thee, and receive the blessings of salvation as freely coming from thee, Oh what have I which I have not received! Oh what is my righteousness? Nothing but filthy rags, and an unclean thing! Not worthy to be mentioned! It is not for my righteousness sake, God is pleased to pardon my sins, to accept me into favour, and give me a title to eternal life! It is entirely on the account of the righteousness of my dear Redeemer, which he freely wrought out for his people and which God has graciously imputed unto me; to what am I indebted for all my spiritual enjoyments, but to free grace! All my hopes of eternal blessings, all that is done in me, all that is put upon me, is all the effect of free distinguishing grace, and God therefore shall have all the glory. This is the language of genuine faith. No other way so much exalts free, rich, and sovereign grace as the way of salvation by faith in Jesus Christ; no other grace is capable of the office which is assigned to faith in justification; faith receives Christ and his righteousness, leans, depends upon him, and gives him all the glory, which cannot be said of any

other grace; therefore we fee the beauty of the way of falvation by faith, and its perfect confiftency with the grace of God. Rom. iv. 16. " Therefore it is of faith, that it " might be by grace; to the end that the promife might be " fure to all the feed: not to that only which is of the law, " but to that alfo which is of the faith of Abraham, who is the " Father of us all. Juftification is in every refpect *free*, from the laying of the plan to the execution of it; it is by the righteoufnefs of Chrift, and therefore free; we are wholly indebted to free grace for it, and ean plead no worthinefs of our own to it. " To him therefore who loved " us, and wafhed us from our fins in his own blood, and " hath made us kings and priefts unto God and his Father; " to him be glory and dominion for ever and ever. Amen, " Rev. i. 5, 6.

SERMON XIII.

THE CONQUERING CHRISTIAN.

2 TIM. iv. 7, 8.

I have fought a good fight.

THESE words were spoken by the apostle Paul, that able minister of the New Testament, a little before he took his final leave of earthly things, and entered into his master's joy. They give us a view of the character, duty, and conduct of every real Christian; present us with an example worthy our constant imitation; and encourage our faith and hope, our stedfastness and perseverance in the service of our Redeemer, by the prospects of the noblest triumphs at death, and a glorious immortality, after a life of pain, difficulty, and sorrow here. The apostle, knowing that the time of his departure drew nigh, was willing to give his beloved *Timothy* his last and solemn Charge, before he left him; in which he exhorts him to take heed to his ministry, to maintain, with a noble boldness, and becoming zeal, that cause he had espoused; to contend for the glorious truths he had heard and learned, and to take care of the flock over which God had set him: and then he turned his eyes from inferior comforts, viewed with pleasure that world he was hastening to, and rejoiced in the prospect of that crown he was just going to possess. " I am now ready to be offered, and " the time of my departure is at hand."———I am going to fall a victim to the rage of my perfecutors, to fhed my blood for my dear Redeemer; and yet the thought fits eafy upon my mind. I am not ftartled at the apprehenfions of my approaching diffolution: no, my glorious mafter has not left me in this critical and important hour, but gives me the teftimony of my confcience, and the witnefs of his fpirit, that I have, through grace, been enabled to fight a good fight; and am going to enjoy the crown. Thefe words naturally lead us to take notice,

I. Of the pleafing reflections the apoftle Paul was enabled to make upon his paft life.

II. The glorious profpect he had before him, and the triumphant frame of his foul thereon. And may we, in confidering thefe things, fee the excellency of the Chriftian's life, the honourablenefs of his contention in the warfare, in which he is engaged, and be quickened and enabled to enter the lifts in the name and ftrength of our Redeemer, that we may fight the good fight, and enjoy the prize *alfo*.

I. We are to take notice of the pleafing reflections the apoftle Paul was enabled to make upon that part of his life which he had fpent in his Redeemer's fervice. *I have fought*, &c. Here it may not be amifs to premife, that the apoftle's pleafure did not arife from an apprehenfion of any merit or virtue in what he mentioned, as if thefe things could juftify him before God. He renounced all his righteoufnefs in life, and he retained the fame fentiment till death. Our hatred of fin, our love to God, our diligence in his fervice, and all our good works cannot entitle us to the favour of God, and abfolve us from fin; but they are evidences of the reality of our faith and juftification; and when ever the Spirit of God enables us to fee them as the real effects of a fanctified nature, and confequently as evidences to ourfelves and others of our pardon and right to eternal life, they cannot fail of filling us with the fame unfpeakable fatisfaction the apoftle here difcovers under the like view. I have fought, &c. In thefe expreffions he has a manifeft allufion to the Olympic games in ufe amongft the ancient Greeks; fuch as wreftling, running, &c. in which whoever came off victorious, was honoured with a crown, or garland of flowers. Thus the apoftle had been a warrior, he had fought, and had got the victory; he had run, and had the mark in view; he had kept his ftation, and difcharged his office, and now only waited for a much brighter crown, even a crown of righteousness, &c. We shall consider each of these distinctly, as they lead us to something useful and important.

The apostle had fought a good fight. Here we have the Christian life evidently compared to a *Warfare;* to carry on the allusion, and to shew the propriety of this comparison. We shall shew,

1. When this warfare begins.
2. What are the enemies and difficulties, Christians are called to encounter with, in this warfare.
3. The weapons God has furnished them with, in the use of which they are to get the victory. And,
4. The encouragements they have to use them in this warfare.

1. Let us consider when this warfare begins. As it is of a spiritual nature, so it does not actually begin till the soul begins a spiritual life. The natural man finds but little difficulty in the pursuit of his gratifications; only conscience may now and then disturb him with the apprehensions of eternity, and a judgement-seat. In general he quietly enjoys his beloved pleasures, and meets with but little interruption; Satan keeps him as an easy prey; sin governs him without any disturbance. He makes little or no opposition, he loves his captivity, and cannot be persuaded to proclaim war, until the all conquering Grace of God comes, and sets him at liberty. Christians, you knew nothing of this warfare, until the Spirit enlightened your minds and renewed your hearts. Then you entered the lists, were called to encounter with difficulties you were unacquainted with before, and must continue the contention, until death places you at an everlasting distance from every enemy. The contest begins as soon as the grace of God is implanted. Before the sinner could easily run into every excess; but now he finds a powerful check, the enemies take the alarm, summon all their strength, and begin the combat; and now the soul is warmly engaged; he is got into the field, and finds himself surrounded with enemies, who use their utmost skill and strength to prevent his progress Zion-ward, and to lead him into his former captivity. And thus the contest continues till the Christian is proclaimed conqueror, which will not be until body and soul are separated. This war-

fare none know but thofe who are the real followers of Jefus. The inward ſtruggles, the warm contentions the Chriſtian has with his enemies are concealed from the world. This warfare is not attended with noife of drums and outward inſtruments: many a battle is loſt, and many a victory gained, and the world knows nothing of it. It is a ſpiritual warfare between the ſoul and its enemies. As none then can know it but the real Chriſtian; and as it always begins when he really commences that character, fo all your complaints, Chriſtians, your ſtruggles and conflicts, your fears and diſtreſſes, all evidence a warfare, and therefore diſcover you to be the real followers of Jefus, and to have a principle of grace implanted. The unrenewed finner cannot be ſaid to be engaged in a warfare: the Chriſtian's enemies indeed are his enemies; they will be the inſtruments and caufe of his everlaſting ruin unleſs deſtroyed; but he is infenſible of it, he is eafy under it; he has nothing that puts him upon making an oppoſition, but rather every thing tends to prevent it. His underſtanding is darkneſs, his faculties are all polluted, and he chooſes his captivity; all the pleaſure he enjoys lies in a ſubjection to his enemies. This warfare cannot then begin till a principle is implanted that leads him to God and heaven: it cannot ceaſe till the body is diſſolved, and the ſoul is perfectly freed from ſin, and got above the reach of every enemy. Let us now,

2. Conſider who the Chriſtian's enemies, and what his difficulties are which he is called to encounter. Theſe are many; and are ſuch as theſe,—the devil,—the world,—ſin.

1. The devil is the Chriſtian's enemy. The apoſtle mentions " principalities and powers, rulers of the darkneſs of " this world, and ſpiritual wickedneſs in high places," as enemies the Chriſtian has to contend with. Eph. vi. 12. The devil was an enemy to man as foon as he was created, and fo he continues. This is a ſubtle and moſt powerful enemy, he is oftentimes the caufe of great diſtreſs to the foul. He knows human nature, can find eafy acceſs to us, and has a variety of temptations, all which he makes ufe of, as he ſees they will beſt anſwer his purpoſes. No ſooner does he find his goverment diſturbed, but he takes the alarm, and ufes his utmoſt ſkill that he loſe not a ſubject; he appears under a variety of forms; ſometimes he ſhews the moſt

B b

envenomed malice, and is like a hungry lion roaring after his prey, ready to devour the humble finner: thus he is reprefented, 1 Pet. v. 8. His darts, which he throws with the utmoſt rage, are called fiery. Eph vi. 16. Such are thofe dreadful things he frequently fuggeſts to the mind, by which he endeavours to lead the foul to final defpair, and perfuade him in the agony of his Spirit to put an end to his exiſtence. Again Satan appears in a more favourable, but really more deſtructive form, as an angel of light, 2 Cor xi. 15. he comes in the difguife of a friend, as Judas did to our Lord, when he faid, hail, maſter; and kiſſed him. Mat. xxvi 49. So Satan will fometimes appear a friend to religion, if he can by that prevent us from going any further than an external appearance; if he can make us take up with the ſhadow inſtead of the fubſtance. He knows where is our weakeſt part, and he has a variety of ways to introduce his temptations unfeen to us, that he may the more eafily fucceed. He takes notice of the various circumſtances we are in, and fuits his temptations to them, and fo he continues till death, when he makes his laſt onfet, and tries all his fkill. If he cannot break the Chriſtian's head, as a divine fays, fo as to keep him out of heaven; yet he will, if poſſible, bruife his heel, and fend him limping thither; that is, fill him full of fears, and doubts, about his eternal ſtate.

2. Another enemy the Chriſtian has to encounter with is this world. This world may both include the things of the world, and the men of the world.

1. The things of the world are become, through the corruption of nature, fnares to the Chriſtian in his way to Zion. The honours, the pleafures, the wealth and various enjoyments of this world. Thefe are the things Satan made ufe of to tempt our Lord. Mat. iv. 8. " He took him to an ex-
" ceeding high mountain, and ſhewed him all the kingdoms
" of the world, and the glory of them: and faid, all thefe
" things will I give thee, if thou wilt fall down and wor-
" ſhip me." Agur prayed very wifely, when he defired neither poverty nor riches, Prov. xxx. 8, 4. Such a ſtate is leaſt expofed to fnares and temptations. When perfons grow in wealth and honour, they think themfelves above all admonition and reproof, both from God and man; they are above all religion, imagine they have a right to treat facred things with indifference, and act as if they were no ways ac-

countable. "When Jeshurun waxed fat, he kicked." Deut. xxxii 15. This world instead of making us thankful as it increases, it puffs us up; instead of improving it more, we are more closely attached to it. It requires great grace to keep that person humble whom the world smiles upon : to grow in grace and grow in the world are difficult things. The sinner is easily caught by the flattering honours and pleasures of the present life: he sacrifices all to them, esteems them as his God; and the Christian finds them oftentimes great hindrances to him; they are pleasing to corrupt nature, steal away the heart, and leave little for God and religion. The young man esteemed his possessions before Christ and eternal life. We had need to use the utmost caution how we pursue the honour, wealth, and pleasures of this world; they tempt us to neglect God and eternity, take us off from nobler pursuits, promise us complete happiness, but disappoint our expectations, and leave the poor deceived sinner eternally to bewail his folly.

2. The men of the world are enemies to the Christian. There was ever a war between the seed of the woman and the seed of the serpent. It cannot be otherwise. For between corrupt nature and grace, there is the greatest opposition. The heart of man being all over polluted, it cannot entertain the least esteem for holiness, but is filled with the greatest hatred to it: for the very same reason; the natural man cannot esteem the Christian considered as a Christian. This has appeared in every age hitherto, in the persecutions that have been raised against the followers of Jesus, and the cruelties that have been inflicted upon them. Sinners can agree to violate the sacred commands of God, and run into sinful excesses; but when God is pleased to make a distinction, no sooner is one of them convinced and enlightened: no sooner does he begin to set his face Zionward; but his companions take the alarm, their agreement is over, they have lost all their esteem for him, stigmatize him with the most odious names, and do all they can to perplex and distress him in his way to a better world. What cruelties have been invented, what tortures! what racks! what painful deaths! and all to put a stop to the Christian's progress, and to oblige him, if possible, to desert the ways of Christ. It is impossible to represent the venom of the heart against God and his people: it is an unspeakable mercy the

hands of the wicked are not always at liberty to diſtreſs the righteous. There is the ſame ſpirit ſtill prevailing, that appeared in the moſt fiery perſecutions; the heart itſelf is not changed, it only wants power and opportunity to ſhew its malice. If the natural man cannot exerciſe cruelties upon the Chriſtian, he will reproach him, make him the ſubject of his profane ridicule, and do all he can to injure him in his character, reputation, and eſtate. This makes the Chriſtian life a warfare: the apoſtle Paul found it ſo; he met with the greateſt difficulties in his courſe; "In labours " more abundant, in ſtripes above meaſure, in priſons more " frequent, in deaths oft," &c. 2 Cor. xi. 23, 27. Theſe things greatly perplex the Chriſtian in his way to a better world, and ſufficiently ſhew his life to be a warfare.

3. Another enemy the Chriſtian has is ſin. Sin is his worſt enemy: ſin has ſpread its dreadful contagion through every faculty of the ſoul, and thereby furniſhes Satan and the world with fit matter to work upon. The temptations of Satan would not be near ſo powerful; nor the honours and enjoyments of the world ſo decoying if the heart was free from all ſin. But through ſin it is a neſt of unclean birds, it is like tinder, it catches at every ſpark; it is full of all manner of wickedneſs and abominations; " from the " heart proceed murders, adulteries, thefts, and every " thing that defiles a man," Mark. vii. 20. And though the Chriſtian is ſanctified, yet he is ſanctified but in part: ſin ſtill remains in every faculty, and cauſes an oppoſition: how is he wearied with its daily aſſaults? Its ſecret workings? What vain thoughts does it produce, what carnal deſires, what coldneſs and indifference to ſpiritual things, what interruptions in duties? How often does it cool the Chriſtian's love to Chriſt, and his people, and ways? Damp his zeal, weaken his faith, ſtagger his ſoul, and fill him with awful fears of everlaſting judgements? How often does it lead him into captivity, provoke God to hide his face, to chaſtiſe the ſoul, and to bring afflictions upon him to humble and try him? How often does it eclipſe his comforts, diſturb his peace, and darken his evidences, and preſent him with the moſt melancholy proſpects? How often does it lead him to diſhonour God, by murmuring and repining under afflictions, by diſtruſting his goodneſs, queſtioning his power, diſbelieving his promiſes, and diſputing his care?

In short, sin is a perpetual and powerful enemy, it is difficult to curb its power, to subdue its dominion, and keep it in subjection. It is the cause of all the Christian's difficulties, it fills him with innumerable fears, and lays a foundation for great distress, much labour, and continual struggles. Thus the flesh lusteth against the spirit, and the spirit against the flesh: these two being contrary the one to the other, cause a perpetual war, Gal. v. 17. The apostle experienced so much of the power of sin and its sad effects, that he called himself even wretched, and longed and panted after deliverance, Rom. vii. 24, &c. His soul was wearied and fatigued from day to day, and he could not but desire to be delivered. Thus we see what are the Christian's enemies, and consequently what difficulties he must grapple with before he takes his final farewel of this world: his life must be a constant struggle with sin, Satan, and the world; and therefore with innumerable afflictions and temptations, fears and doubts. What is necessary to overcome these things? How shall he get the victory? How must he withstand and conquer? This leads us,

3. To shew the weapons God has furnished his people with in the use of which they are to get the victory. In fighting, the use of suitable weapons is highly necessary: if the enemy take us unarmed, we are easily conquered. It would be madness for soldiers to go naked to the battle, without those weapons which are necessary, not only to defend their own lives, but cut off and destroy the enemy. They have armour therefore provided, and such as is fit for the purposes of fighting, by which the victory is gained. It is a greater warfare the Christian is engaged in; it requires therefore suitable armour to guard against the assaults of the enemy, suitable weapons to maintain the conflict and gain the battle. Such weapons as are every way fit for the purpose God has provided, in the use of which his people though weak in themselves, yet gain the victory and come off triumphant. The Christian's armour we have particularly described. Eph. vi. 14.—18. " Stand therefore having your
" loins girt about with truth, and having on the breast-plate
" of righteousness, &c. This is the armour, these are the weapons that are suited to this spiritual warfare; and in and through which the Christian maintains his ground, and comes off at last a conqueror. Time forbids me to enlarge upon

each of these particulars, yet we shall take some notice of them. And the first thing mentioned is a girdle; which was in common use among the eastern nations to bind their clothes fast about them that they might have less fatigue in walking, or in their employment. There was a military girdle likewise which came about the loins, which was not only an ornament, but a means of strengthening the soldier and preparing him for the battle. The Christian's girdle is truth, soundness of judgement and heart. A necessary character of a Christian. Hypocrisy is not only odious but dangerous, destructive to the soul. Sincerity makes a person appear amiable to others, and is a great means of strengthening the Christian under those difficulties he meets with. Satan is oftentimes ready to charge the Christian with hypocrisy, insinuates to him, that all he has done is nothing but a mere form: thus the sinner also casts the utmost aspersions upon the Christian, stigmatizes him with the name of hypocrite, represents him as acting falsely and deceitfully in the ways of God, and as secretly pursuing all manner of sin. How necessary is truth then to oppose to such a temptation? It casts a lustre upon a person's character, and it strengthens and supports him under all the calumnies and reproaches that are cast upon him. Peter could appeal to Christ for his sincerity, John xxi. 17. Job was charged with hypocrisy by his friends: it was happy for him, under so heavy a charge, that his conscience cleared him, Job. xxvii. 5, 6. When we are accused unjustly, it is a pleasure to a person that his conscience can discharge him. " Satan would often whisper in my ear, that I am but an almost Christian, &c. It is true I have been guilty of many imperfections, repeated backslidings; but I would not mock God with an outward form. Lord thou knowest that I desire to be what I appear to be: I would love thee with all my heart, &c. and so far as I know myself I am sincere and upright " See to it Christians that you have your evidences of your sincerity ever clear, that you may be enabled to say, under every charge of hypocrisy, " Our rejoicing is this, " the testimony of our conscience," 2 Cor. i. 12. The next piece of armour is a breast-plate; what soldiers frequently used to wear, to guard and defend them from the designs of their enemies, and preserve them as much as possible from mortal wounds. Thus the Christian is furnished with a breaft-plate of righteoufnefs : by which the righteoufnefs of Chrift does not feem to be meant, but our own perfonal righteoufnefs. Thus this breaft-plate is faid to confift of love, 1 Theff. v. 8. The heart being purified, filled with love and every divine grace, is thereby defended and guarded againft all temptations to apoftacy, which would prove fatal to the foul. If we have the exercifes of thofe graces which God has implanted ; if we are enabled to keep up our purpofes and refolutions of obedience ; and if we are found careful to maintain good works, Satan will not fo eafily lead us afide, we fhall be in lefs danger of being drawn away by fin and temptations; and we fhall have fome comfortable evidences of our intereft in Chrift and eternal life, to keep us from that defpair our enemies would drive us to, and to comfort our fouls under every affliction. The next piece of warlike furniture is to have our feet fhod with the *preparation of the gofpel of peace*. Shoes are a neceffary piece of armour to keep our feet from being hurt by the pricking thorns, the flinty ftones, or other things that lie in the path in which we walk. The Chriftian's way to a better world is full of difficulties: it is through much tribulation that we muft enter into the kingdom of God, Acts xiv. 22. It is neceffary the mind fhould be fortified againft thefe things : and what has a greater tendency to do it than the gofpel, which fpeaks nothing but peace and falvation ? A mind filled with that tranquillity and comfort the gofpel promifes, by affurance of the divine favour and eternal life, is fitted for the various difficulties of life, and ftands prepared to meet the enemy in the field. The apoftle Paul was thus fhod : he was full of inward peace, being affured of the divine favour, and therefore could triumph over every enemy, Rom viii. 33—39. Thus the gofpel fortified him againft every difficulty by its peaceful difcoveries. If we are comfortably perfuaded that God is for us, we fhall not fear all thofe that are againft us. Oh look into the gofpel in order to have your fouls prepared for the difficulties of the way : view the promifes it makes, the encouragements it gives, the profpects it fets before you ; fee, it is all peace ; labour therefore to have your minds poffeffed of it. Again, the apoftle goes on to another moft important and neceff.-ry piece of armour, which is the fhield : *the fhield of faith*. There is no fighting for the Chriftian with any fuccefs without faith, faith in our Lord Jesus Christ: "This is the victory that overcometh the world even our faith," 1 John v. 4. It was by faith the apostle Paul was enabled to triumph over every enemy: it was by faith that all the Old Testament saints endured so many afflictions and came off conquerors at last: by faith the martyrs endured the fury of the fire, triumphed over death, and nobly maintained their stedfastness. Faith vieweth the all perfect and glorious righteousness of Jesus Christ, and opposeth this to the unworthiness, sin, and guilt of the creature: faith views all strength and grace in the great Redeemer, and sets it against our weakness, and is the instrument by which we derive from our Redeemer, all that grace that is necessary to keep us in every danger, fit us for every duty, carry us through every conflict, and to bring us off triumphant conquerors. Above all therefore take the shield of faith. Again the apostle mentions *the helmet of salvation,* or as it is otherwise expressed, *the hope of salvation,* 1 Thess. v. 8. Faith and hope generally go together, and are greatly necessary in the Christian warfare. The exercise of hope, like a helmet, fills the Christian warrior with courage; he goes to the battle with greater resolution, receives every assault with firmness of mind, and stands undaunted while the fiery darts of the wicked one are sent thick at him. With a lively hope the soul marches against every enemy, his hope encourages him to the conflict; it keeps him from sinking; it is an anchor, it keeps him steady in the midst of every wave, and threatning danger. While he keeps up his hope the enemy in vain assaults him; he presses on till he gets the victory. See therefore that your hope be well grounded and lively, if you think to stand your ground and come off conquerors. Again the apostle mentions " the sword of " the Spirit, which is the word of God:" this is compared to a two-edged sword, nay it is sharper, " it pierces even to the dividing asunder of soul and spirit, and of the joints and marrow; and is a discerner of the thoughts and intents of the heart." One of the soldier's weapons is a sword, an instrument useful in war: the Spirit of God makes the word effectual as a sword to cut the sinews of temptation, to kill and slay the enmity of the heart, to destroy every lust and corruption, and to carry on the work of sanctification and holiness in the soul in spite of all opposition. Converse much with the word of God, believe its importance, and oppose a *Thus faith the Lord*, to every suggestion and temptation of Satan, and to every enemy you meet with. This was the weapon with which our Lord fought when the devil tempted him in the wilderness; he turned him to the word with an *it is written*, Mat. iv. 4, 7, 10. Lastly, the apostle mentions " prayer; praying always with all prayer and sup- " plication in the spirit." Prayer is a most valuable and important duty; it is a means of keeping off temptations, we are therefore to pray against them: in the use of prayer we get strength from above, by which we are enabled to persevere in the way to Zion, and gain a complete victory. Moses' prayer was more efficacious than Joshua's sword: so long as he held up his hands, Israel prevailed, Exod. xvii. 11. The Christian need not be afraid that delights in prayer, and frequently draws near to God; prayer happily fits him for the greatest conflicts; for God who hears prayer, answers his petitions and gives him what is necessary to carry him through all and bring him off triumphant. Thus we see the Christian in his armour; thus fitted for engagement he may cheerfully enter the lists with all his enemies and not be discouraged, all things shall issue well, to the glory of God, the confusion of his enemies, and his everlasting joy and happiness. We now come,

4. To consider the encouragements the Christian has to fight and engage in this warfare. And here we shall only consider three things by which the Christian appears sufficiently encouraged to engage. 1. It is a good fight. 2. He has a glorious captain who will lead him on, stand by him, and strengthen him. And 3. He has an assurance of victory.

1. It is a good fight in which he is engaged. He has no reason to hesitate about the lawfulness of engaging; it appears plainly to be his duty. It is certainly the duty of every intelligent creature to walk in constant obedience to God, and therefore with the utmost strength to resist every thing that would draw him off from his duty. It is a good fight, for it is the cause of God, it is for his glory: God is no ways honoured by a tame submission to every lust or every temptation; he is rather highly dishonoured. The way to glorify God is to oppose every enemy, to hate every sin, to crucify every lust, to shun every snare, and to press

on in a courfe of faith and obedience. It is a good fight, for God calls us to it and approves of us in it. This is the confequence of implanting grace in the heart. It produces immediately an oppofition to every enemy, ftirs up the Chriftian to a moft vigorous contention, and never ceafes refiftance till it comes off victorious. God therefore manifeftly approves of it: for it is by his affiftance that the Chriftian is enabled to ftand his ground, and come off a conqueror. For he, in himfelf, is weak and abfolutely unequal to fo great a work, and unlefs the almighty Redeemer was to give him all fuitable ftrength, he muft fall an eafy facrifice to every enemy. It is a good fight, for it will iffue in the Chriftian's everlafting happinefs, it can be no ways pernicious or deftructive to him: it may be indeed uncomfortable; the contention may caufe him much diftrefs, but it will end well: it is therefore for the Chriftian's intereft to engage in this fpiritual warfare. A fubmiffion to his enemies will be attended with the moft dreadful confequences; nothing lefs than an everlafting banifhment from God, and unfpeakable and everlafting mifery and wretchednefs. Again it is a good fight for it will bear a reflection. There are many things we do that will not bear a review; our confciences, unlefs hardened, immediately rebuke us on a confideration of neglect of duty, or actual commiffion of fin. But every refiftance againft fin, every ftruggle with our fpiritual enemies will bear a reviewing; the review will be fo far from galling our confciences, that it will afford pleafure: and all our uneafinefs will be, that we have not contended with greater warmth, that we have not refifted with greater force, every temptation. The apoftle Paul was juft upon the borders of an eternal world, he had eternity in view, yet behold; he is not ftartled at the profpect, nor uneafy at a confideration of the oppofition he had been enabled to make to every enemy: no, he rather fpeaks it with the higheft pleafure: " I have fought," &c. I am now going to appear before God; going to give an account of my ftewardfhip, and be fixed for ever; and I can, in this important crifis, look back with an undifturbed ferenity of mind upon my Chriftian warfare; the thoughts of my contention with my fpiritual enemies do not give the leaft terror to death; no, I blefs God I have been enabled to fight: it is a good caufe in which I have been embarked, it will bear me out in the views of death, and give me pleasure in my last moments. Not that I have merited any thing: no, all my dependence is upon my dear Redeemer; and I bless him that has enabled me to fight a good fight, which is an evidence of my love to and my interest in him. Thus it is a good fight and this is a sufficient encouragement to engage in it. Christians, you will never be ashamed either here or hereafter of your fighting this good fight; it is the interest of Christ; it is the interest of your souls; it is for the glory of God. Was it a bad cause, or did it want any evidence of its being truly good and excellent, you might hesitate; but hear a dying person, one who had tried it, who had met with many enemies, uncommon difficulties, hear this brave apostle just before he bids all things an everlasting farewel, hear him in this critical moment, pronouncing it, as it were with his last breath, a good fight; worth our engaging in. This is the trying time, the hour of death: now the world appears as nothing: now sin discovers all its odiousness; now the worldling sees his disappointment: the proud rebel begins to start, looks aghast, and wishes he had, like others, fought a good fight: he finds he has been doing wrong and must be ruined. The Christian is the only person that can now on good grounds rejoice—I have fought, &c. Be not discouraged, but continue your conflicts, you will never have reason to repent of it.

2. The captain of your salvation will stand by, encourage and strengthen you. It is a thing of considerable moment in a battle to have a brave commander, a good leader, one who will lead on, stand by, and not desert the men; but encourage and help them in the hour of danger. Such a commander has the Christian warrior: a glorious captain, Jesus Christ, who loves him and will never desert him. Fight under his banner; follow him, and whatever engagements he calls you to, he will encourage and strengthen you in. Christ has promised to be with his people always, even unto the end of the world. He has never yet forsaken any: his people have been oftentimes in great dangers; engaged with powerful enemies, almost ready to be led captive: they have frequently to appearance been upon the point of giving up all hope, ready to stagger and conclude it is all over; when the captain of their salvation has encouraged and strengthened them, stirred them up to a fresh contention and enabled

them to hold on and perfevere with courage and cheerfulnefs. " Fear not for I am with thee, be not difmayed for I am thy God, I will help thee ; yea I will ftrengthen thee, I will uphold thee with the right hand of my righteoufnefs." Ifa. xli. 10. " I will never.leave thee nor forfake thee," Heb. xiii. 5 Thefe promifes have been always, and fhall ever be fulfilled. Will God call his people out to fight not only with flefh and blood, but with principalities and powers, with enemies numerous and powerful, and leave them to grapple by themfelves ? No, his people have always hitherto found him kind and faithful ; and fo they will to the end of the world, when every enemy will be vanquifhed and their falvation be fully completed. What an encouragement is this to enter the lifts, and fight with every enemy? Had we no one to lead us on, to ftand by us, to affift and ftrengthen us, we might then be difcouraged from fuch an attempt : but when we have fo brave a captain to fight under, one who is heartily attached to our intereft, one who really loves us and will never leave us, it is enough to embolden and animate us; to fpur us on, and to quicken us to the engagement. You may truft your Redeemer, he will ftand by you, he may fuffer you to be hard preffed in the engagement; but in the hour of extremity he will help you, he will keep you with his mighty hand, fupport your finking fpirits, and encourage your fouls to perfeverance and fortitude.

3. The Chriftian has a fure profpect of victory. Was the cafe uncertain and dubious the Chriftian might be afraid of a difappointment ; the young beginner might be difcouraged in his entrance upon this warfare ; but there is an abfolute certainty of victory. The moft experienced commanders, the beft difciplined foldiers are not fure of fuccefs, when they enter upon engagement. The battle is not always to the ftrong, nor the race to the fwift ; the wifeft are oftentimes puzzled, and the braveft and moft refolute overcome ; but it is not the cafe here, the Chriftian foldier fights upon fure grounds. Not that the victory is obtained by his own ftrength and prudence ; for who is fufficient for thefe things ? Was he to fight alone he muft lofe the battle, and be led a captive ; but though weak in himfelf, he is ftrong in his mighty Redeemer : " I can do all things," fays the apoftle, " through Chrift Jefus ftrengthening me." He that

loves the Christian will bring him off a conqueror. None shall ever be able to pluck his people out of his hands; the gates of hell shall not be able to prevail against them. What are principalities and powers, what are all earthly snares and temptations, nay what is sin itself, though never so deeply rooted in the soul? All must yield to an almighty power, when that is displayed. The Christian may be led into captivity, the apostle Paul himself was, but though he fall he shall arise again, resume the fight, and conquer at last. Why may the Christian be sure of conquest and victory? Because God has promised it, Christ has purchased it, and he gives him strength to overcome. All the enemies the believer has are not a match for him, considering him as united to Christ, and strengthened by him; he has no reason to despond, but to rejoice and triumph; a little time and his warfare shall be accomplished and the victory be his. This by no means weakens his endeavours or makes him indolent: though the glory is Christ's, yet the victory is got in the use of means. It encourages the Christian then to faith and prayer, and to put on that armour which God has appointed. What can animate the soul more than an assurance of conquest? It will not be always so, oh my soul; Look forward to that day when thou shalt be proclaimed a conqueror. Now I languish at times under fears, I am ready to be pressed down with difficulties, but it will not be long before I shall get above the reach of all my enemies, and sing victory and salvation. Hark the apostle triumphs in his last moments: the trumpet sounds to tell him the victory is his, the battle is just over and his enemies are all vanquished. I have fought a good fight. I have encountered a variety of enemies, I have laboured hard and been pressed sore, but now it is almost over; a few struggles more, and I shall gain the field, a few more conflicts and my warfare will be accomplished: I am now in view of the prize, and in a little time I shall enjoy it. Thus did the great apostle conquer at last, and so shall every real Christian, through his almighty and glorious Redeemer.

1. Hence then we learn, it is not an easy thing to be a Christian. The soldier that is always in the field has hard service, he must be ever upon his guard, lest the enemy should surprise him: he must endure cold, be subject to hunger and thirst, learn to habituate himself to hard-

ness, if he would stand his ground, and discharge his duty. Christians must *endure hardness like good soldiers of Jesus Christ*.

The Christian's life is a warfare, a continual warfare; from the first moment of his spiritual life to his possessing the crown, he must be ever upon his watch; he has enemies continually endeavouring to lead him captive, watching every opportunity to beat him from his ground, he must not be indolent or slothful. Think not a little will do: it is not a few weak desires, or feeble attempts that make a Christian; if you think to meet with no difficulties you will be mistaken, you had best sit down and count the cost. Lusts and corruptions the most pleasing to nature, must be subdued and mortified: Satan and hell conquered: the soul must stand against the temptations of the world, and follow Jesus till death, through all difficulties and opposition: this it is to be a Christian: we had best inquire whether we have only the shadow without the substance, that we be not deceived and meet with a disappointment. It is difficult work to fight the good fight: it costs many prayers and tears, many hard struggles before the Christian comes to Zion. You that are contenting yourselves with only a form, are but almost Christians: the believer has great and difficult work to do, with which you are entirely unacquainted.

2. Hence learn, how it is the Christian overcomes, and to whom all the glory is due. It is not by his strength, but in the strength of Christ that he conquers sin, Satan, and the world. The apostle did not attribute any thing to himself, he did not take the glory of conquering his enemies; for he in many places declares his own weakness, and his dependence upon Jesus Christ for grace and strength to overcome. The armour which God has provided points out to whom the glory of victory is due; faith, hope, and prayer all give the glory to Jesus Christ, to whom it is justly due. We must depend upon him if ever we come off with honour. It is a mistake here that causes many to miscarry: they begin in their own strength, they continue for a little while, but soon tire and faint, give up the conquest and fall a sacrifice to their enemies. We from hence then see how necessary it is that the sinner should have a sense of his own weakness in order to his setting out right in the ways of God, and consequently how needful it is that the gospel

should be preached, as it opens to us the way of salvation, and leads us to the Lord Jesus Christ, by whom alone it is that we overcome. May we learn to depend upon him, apply to him, and give him all the glory.

3. What a difference there is between earth and heaven, and how happy is the Christian when he has got safe above. Earth is a tiresome and fatiguing place; we meet with nothing but difficulties to retard us in our way to Zion; nothing but snares and temptations to entice our affections from God; here we groan under the weight and pressure of sin; our souls hang the wing, and we are oftentimes disconsolate and melancholy. But above there is no enemy to encounter, no difficulties to perplex, no ensnaring objects to lead us from God; there the wicked cease from trouble, and there the weary are at everlasting rest. Oh happy souls that have got the victory, and are introduced into their Redeemer's kingdom; now they have no tormenting cares, their fears are all scattered, their conflicts are for ever over, their enemies are placed at an everlasting distance, and they are triumphing as conquerors; as those who have gained the day, and are now wearing the immortal crown. Oh who would not long to be there? Who would not fight the good fight, to wear so glorious a crown at last? Who would not be willing to put off this earthly tabernacle to be with Jesus? Look within the veil, oh my soul, and see the glory that is prepared; view the place, see how it will be when thou hast got the victory, and rejoice in the vast, the immortal prospect.

SERMON XIV.

THE CHRISTIAN'S COURSE.

2 Tim. iv. 7, 8.

I have finished my Course.

TO die is something solemn and important; the soul had need to have somewhat to support him in the critical moment. To have a juft sense of the worth of a soul, and the importance of eternity is enough to make us sink, unless we can see our sins forgiven, and the Saviour smiling. It is not every one that, like the apostle Paul, can face the king of terrors with boldness and resolution. Nature shudders at the awful shock, and is ready to start back at the boundless prospect, till God comes with his divine consolations, and cheers our fainting spirits, by telling us all is well, and giving us a pleasing view of approaching glory. The apostle Paul had laboured hard in his master's service, and he was well rewarded both in this life and in that to come; he had not only the enjoyment of the prize at last; but he had a comfortable prospect of it here. The thoughts of bidding an everlasting farewel to all earthly things, did not give him the least uneasiness; he received the tidings of death with that bravery, that calmness and cheerfulness which are peculiar to the Christian; and talked of his dying, nay of his awful manner of dying, with all the compofure of a follower of Chrift. He viewed his paft life, and though he could fee many imperfections, yet he rejoiced that God had enabled him to *fight a good fight*, and to bear his teftimony in the midft of enemies, and oppofition to his dear Redeemer; he looked forward and though all was eternity, yet he was not affrighted, for he faw the crown prepared, the judge ready to put it upon his head, and multitudes of glorified faints to be his company, to join him in his everlafting Hofannahs, and fongs of victory and falvation. *I have fought*——From thefe words we propofed,

I. To confider the pleafing reflections the apoftle takes of that part of his life which he had fpent in his Redeemer's fervice.

II. The glorious profpect he had before him, and the triumphant frame of his foul under that amiable view. We have entered upon the firft of thefe; and have confidered that part of our text which reprefents the Chriftian life under the fimilitude of a warfare.

We now come to the apoftle's 2d, reflection. I have finifhed my courfe. Here the apoftle evidently compares the Chriftian life to a race; another of the Olympic games, in which he that firft reached the goal was prefented with a prize, a garland of flowers, which though of no intrinfic value, yet was efteemed a mark of diftinguifhing honour. Thus the Chriftian fets forward in his way to heaven, he runs his heavenly race, at laft finifhes his courfe, reaches the mark and receives the prize. In our further treating upon this I fhall,

I. Confider the way or path in which the Chriftian is to run.

II. How we are to run fo as to finifh our courfe with advantage.

III. The encouragement we have to run this race.

I. We are to confider the way or path in which the Chriftian is to run. This is effential to a race; there muft be a way a path appointed and determined in which perfons were to run. Such there is in the heavenly race; the end is eternal life, the way is appointed and determined by God who gives the prize, and he has marked it out, and revealed it to us in his word. This way we find to be a way of faith and holinefs.

1. The way in which the Chriftian is to run is a way of

faith in our Lord Jesus Christ. Thus Christ calls himself the way, John xiv 6. Christ has opened a way for us into the holiest of all, and he is likewise the way thither. He satisfied infinite juſtice for the sins of his people, appeaſed the wrath of God and opened a way for the conveyance of grace and mercy in the everlaſting ſalvation of the guilty. And had he not undertook this great and important work, we muſt have been in the moſt deplorable circumſtances. None being equal to it but he who gracioully condeſcended to undertake it, and has gone gloriouſly through it. It is accordingly through faith in him that we become partakers of the bleſſings he has purchaſed. Thus God has every where revealed faith in Chriſt as the way to ſalvation. " God " ſo loved the world that he gave his only begotten Son, " that whoſoever believeth on him ſhould not periſh but " have everlaſting life," John iii. 16. " He that believeth " ſhall be ſaved." Mark xvi. 16. " Being juſtified by faith " we have peace with God." Rom. v. 1. " By grace ye " are ſaved through faith, and that not of yourſelves, it is " the gift of God," Eph. ii. 8. " Without faith it is im- " poſſible to pleaſe God " Heb. xi 6. This is the way he has appointed, and he will approve of no other How can we reaſonably expect acceptance with God in any other way but that which he has determined ? This would be ſuppoſing him a weak imperfect being ; defective in his wiſdom or changeable in his nature and purpoſes. It ſuppoſes God to reveal a way of ſalvation by faith in Jeſus Chriſt, that this is the way he has determined and appointed, but yet it ſuppoſes him accepting of a creature who is prejudiced againſt the way of faith, and ſets up one of his own in oppoſition thereto : it is arrogance to attempt to put God upon a level with changeable creatures, he is of one mind and who can turn him ? It is through faith in Chriſt that we muſt be juſtified. The apoſtle tells us it is by that righteouſneſs " which is of God, by faith," Phil. iii. 9. And that is none but the righteouſneſs of Jeſus Chriſt, which is graciouſly imputed to us and received by faith. The apoſtle tells the Galatians, they did once run well. " Who " hindered you, that ye ſhould not obey the truth," Gal. v. 7. Ye once firmly believed the doctrine of juſtification by the righteouſneſs of Chriſt. Who is it, has turned you out of the way ? This is the good old way ; a way that has been tried; a way in which all who have run have reached the mark and got the prize : it is the moſt comfortable way, it gives the Chriſtian the higheſt courage, the greateſt intrepidity in every danger, and the ſweeteſt compoſure in the views of death : it is, in ſhort, the beſt way, the ſafeſt to walk in, we cannot miſcarry here, but muſt finiſh our courſe well, and be put into the poſſeſſion of the crown.

2. The way the Chriſtian is to run is a way of holineſs. " I will run the way of thy commandments," ſays the Pſalmiſt, " when thou ſhalt enlarge my heart," Pſa. cxix. 32 Faith is productive (wherever it is) of univerſal obedience. God, in the everlaſting covenant, determined holineſs to be the way to everlaſting happineſs; thus he hath choſen his people " through ſanctification of the Spirit and belief of " the truth," 2 Theſ. ii. 13. " He hath not called us to " uncleanneſs but to holineſs," 1 Theſ. iv. 7. God has appointed a certain meaſure of grace and holineſs, which every one of his people ſhall fill up before they are introduced into his kingdom above. This is fitly called a courſe; a courſe that is limited and laid out, in which thoſe that are engaged in a race are to run. In a race there is a quantity of ground laid out, at the end of which a mark is fixed, he that runs and firſt reaches the mark receives the prize : Thus with great propriety is the Chriſtian life compared to a race, there is an appointed mark which they muſt through divine grace reach; before they enter into reſt, for ſo it is appointed. Not that this has any caſual influence upon the prize ſo as to merit it; the prize they receive as a free gift; but holineſs is a meetneſs for heaven, and the different meaſures and degrees of it God has fixed, and we find it different in different perſons Chriſtians, in proceeding on this courſe, do it not with the ſame life and vigour; ſome appear cold and indifferent, whilſt others are quick and lively; ſome make great advances, whilſt others go on by ſlow degrees. Some begin the heavenly race ſoon, in the bloom of life, whilſt others loiter till towards the evening of their days. Some make quick improvements and through Chriſt finiſh their courſe ſoon, go off the ſtage of life, and receive the crown of glory; whilſt the race of others is long; they begin in youth, and continue their zeal and patience, their faith and labour of love till a good old age. However all are made holy, and they bring forth the fruits of holineſs:

Not that they arrive at perfection in this life; it is impossible. Neverthelefs we are to feek after advances in holinefs, knowing that the nearer we approach to perfection, the more fhall we be like unto God, in a conformity to whom lies our greateft honour. The way of fin leads down to the bottomlefs pit; it is the way of holinefs alone that ends in eternal life.

II. We now come to confider how we are to run, that we may finifh our courfe with advantage. If we examine the word of God and the Chriftian's experience, we fhall find the following things to be neceffary. 1. That every weight fhould be caft off, as the apoftle expreffes it. 2, That we begin right and continue fo, viz. In a dependence upon Chrift 3. That we are armed with patience, courage, and refolution. 3. That we be watchful and diligent. And 5. That we keep preffing forward and perfevere to the end of our courfe.

1. That we may run the Chriftian race well, it is neceffary that we caft off every weight. A perfon that runs choofes not to be overburdened, becaufe it may retard him in his way, he may foon tire, and faint, and lofe the prize. In allufion to this the apoftle Paul exhorts us, " to lay afide " every weight, and the fin which fo eafily befets us, and " fo run the race that is fet before us " Heb. xii. 1. We have many things that prove as weights to prefs us down, and make our running difficult. The love of prefent things is a burdenfome load; a too clofe attachment to this world is greatly injurious to the Chriftian, it clogs him in his race, makes him run heavily on, and make but little progrefs. The young man feemed fetting out full fpeed towards eternal life, but when he came to find he was to part with his worldly poffeffions he gave over the heavenly purfuit. Mat. xix. 22. Every weight muft be in fome meafure removed; whatever we find to clog, confine, and hinder us in our race we muft lay afide; the fin therefore that fo eafily befets us, what ever it is, whether pride or paffion, covetoufnefs, envy, uncleannefs, &c It muft be laid afide, or there will be little or no progrefs made. There is a fin in every one that is generally diftinguifhed by the name of conftitution fin; that is, it is a fin that appears to be interwoven with our very conftitutions; it is the fin that is moft predominant in us, to which we are moft inclined, and which moft of all leads

us afide. This fin cannot but retard the Chriftian's progrefs, it vexes and frequently difturbs him; and unlefs greatly mortified and fubdued, it makes him almoft ready to faint, ftaggers his foul, and caufes the greateft perplexity. How neceffary is it then to our running well that this, nay every fin be fubdued? unlefs the dominion of fin is deftroyed in the foul, he cannot run to advantage; it will effectually confine and keep him down. Therefore you muft inquire whether fin reigns in your hearts, whether you love it, and your happinefs lies in the purfuit and practice of it; if fo, there is no running this race. A work of fanctification muft be begun, whereby your fouls may be in fome meafure at liberty to fet forward in the heavenly race; this being previous to it.

2. In order to run well we muft begin and continue in a dependence upon Chrift. To begin wrong is the fame as not to attempt it. We are naturally too fond of ourfelves, and too ready to apprehend that we are capable of doing every thing in a Chriftian life by our own ftrength. With thefe imaginations the finner makes fome attempt, begins a reformation, abftains from the practice of various fins, attends the means of grace, reads the word, and perhaps prays, and feems refolved for heaven; but the difficulties he meets with foon overpower him, his corruptions begin again to affault him and to be predominant for him; he retains a pleafing remembrance of former gratifications; a coldnefs in duty, and fo he gives up the conflict, and returns again to folly. If we fhould fucceed in the Chriftian race, we muft fet out right. This is a matter of the utmoft importance. How neceffary is it then that the finner's impotency and weaknefs fhould be reprefented to him, that he may guard againft flattery and felf dependence? How neceffary that Jefus fhould be reprefented as our ftrength, as well as righteoufnefs; that we may go to him for all we want, and walk in a conftant dependence upon him: without him we can do nothing. The difficulties we meet with in our way would perplex and weary us, was it not for our almighty Redeemer. The corruptions in our hearts would foon prevail, cool our affections, ftop our progrefs, and entice us from God, was there nothing to curb and fubdue them. We had need be ever fending up our petitions to our glorious Redeemer; " draw us, we will run after thee." Cant. i. 4. He muft

enliven us with his gracious smiles; he must give us fresh strength continually to strive with and surmount every difficulty; he must quicken our desires, or else we shall loiter in our race, grow faint and weary, and proceed no further. They must be absolutely unacquainted with their own hearts, who imagine they are equal to every duty and difficulty, and will not depend upon the great Redeemer, for his kind and necessary assistance. Christians you must have your eyes up continually to Jesus; your dependence upon him: " run the race that is set before you, looking to Jesus the " author and finisher of your faith," exercising faith in him, and expecting all that strength from him, by which alone you will be enabled to hold on and finish your course with advantage.

3. We must run with patience, courage, and resolution. Thus says the apostle, " run with patience the race that is " set before you." Heb. xii. 1. The ground that is laid out for a race, the path in which they are to run, is not always smooth and even; sometimes there are steep ascents, or the way is rough and rugged; that those that run cannot make that speed they would desire; they may stumble and fall, and be some time before they reach the mark. Thus it is in the Christian race. The way is not so easy and smooth as many may imagine, it is full of difficulties: the Christian must ascend many mountains of opposition, and run through valleys dark and difficult before he gets to the end of his race. He meets with many things that clog him in his way, dispirit and perplex him, try his faith and patience, and call for great courage and resolution: sometimes he that runs in a race is ready to be dispirited, and was he not to take fresh courage at the view of the prize he must give out;' thus it is with the Christian. He is often tossed between hope and fear: sometimes he has the prize in view, and hopes to enjoy it; at other times it is lost in darkness, he cannot see it, his hopes begin to flag, and his soul to be discouraged. And now there is need of patience, fortitude, and resolution to bear up his mind in such a painful dilemma, and to encourage him to wait and hope, and still keep on in expectation of the prize. Patience is a most valuable grace, it is greatly suited to the present difficult and perplexing state, and keeps the soul from sinking under those difficulties it meets with, composes the mind, quiets every tu-

tumultuous paffion, and helps the Chriftian to prefs on in oppofition to every difcouragement. Some meet indeed comparatively, or however apparently with but few obftacles in their way: the path feems fmooth and pleafant, and they hold out with cheerfulnefs, fee the prize before them, and rejoice in the profpect; whilft others languifh along the road, are often ready to grow faint and give over; meeting with a variety of difficulties to try their faith, before they reach the goal. Some finifh their courfe with cheerfulnefs, fmile at the fhady valley of death, and bravely withftand every enemy in their way, until they have reached the mark and got the prize; whilft others droop, hang their harps upon the willows, and ftart at the appearance of that immortality, which will crown their labours with a moft glorious and exalted happinefs. However every Chriftian meets with fomething to exercife his patience and to fhew the neceffity of refolution and courage. Do your fouls hang the wing? Are you ready to faint and give out? You are not the firft: exercife a little patience, and all your difficulties will foon be over. Why do you meet with mountains of oppofition? It is to try your faith, that God may be glorified in your patience, that you may wait and depend upon him for the prize, and receive it at laft with unfpeakable thankfulnefs. Be not difheartened, this is not the way to reach the goal; but be of good courage, " you fhall reap if " you faint not."

4. We muft be watchful and diligent. A perfon who runs a race muft be active and diligent, not flothful and carelefs: he may then lofe the prize. The Chriftian muft be active and fpeedy. To run fignifies as much as fpeedily to go forward, Gal. v. 7. to make hafte, Prov. i. 16. it fignifies readinefs of affection, Thus it points out that diligence and activity we ought to difcover in our Chriftian race: the flothful perfon that hid his talent in the earth, was caft into outer darknefs where there is weeping, wailing, and gnafhing of teeth, Mat xxv. 30. We muft ftrive to enter in at the ftrait gate, Luke xiii. 24. The apoftle was diligent in his race, his mind was bent upon it; having his eye fixed upon the prize, he was active: he forgot thofe things that were behind, he did not loiter and look back, but, as a perfon in a race, kept his eye upon the prize, he looked and he preffed forward; the nearer he came to the

goal the more he pushed, as a runner exerts all his strength, and throws himself forward to reach the mark, Phil. iii. 13, 14. He was upon his guard, lest he should be retarded; he watched over his heart, mortified the deeds of the body, and took the utmost care that he was not hindered in his course, 1 Cor. ix. 24, 27. " Know ye not that they that " run in a race run all,—so run that ye may obtain.—Every " man that striveth for the mastery is temperate in all " things.—I therefore so run not as uncertainly, so fight I, " not as one that beateth the air, but I keep my body un- " der, and bring it into subjection, &c. Take heed to " yourselves," says our Lord, " lest at any time your hearts " be overcharged with surfeiting, drunkenness and the cares " of this life, and so that day come upon you unawares," Luke xxi. 24. A person overloaded with liquor is not fit to run a race : no more are those fit for the Christian race who are full of sensuality. Be upon your guard, Christian, the way you run is difficult, and it is attended with many snares and temptations; Satan, the world and your own hearts will oppose your progress, stand in the way and lead you astray : every fall you have, every stumble you make, every snare you fall into will be a hindrance to you; will harrass and perplex you, and cause you much labour and difficulty. Watch therefore and pray that you enter not into temptation; be up and doing, be not indolent, you may have many steps yet to go, many difficulties yet to encounter before you reach the goal; " gird up the loins of your mind " then, be sober and watch unto the end," 1 Pet. i. 13. See that your minds are more upon the stretch; that you make more speed, that you loiter not; in fine, take care that your loins be girt and your lights burning, that you may be waiting for the coming of your Lord and master.

5. We must keep pressing forward and persevere to the end of our course.——A person that runs in a race, keeps on; if he stumbles and falls, he gets up and goes forward : he is approaching nearer and nearer the mark every step he takes. Running signifies making progress. This is not always visible in the Christian : he sometimes appears to decay, languish and go backward; but there are different ways of growth : the Christian may grow in grace and make some progress though it may not be so visible to himself and

others.——Trees in winter appear dead and wither, but in the spring, revive and flourish: the Christian often meets with winter seasons: he is cold and almost frozen, but when the sun of righteousness begins to arise, and like the sun, in his return from the winter solstice, spreads his glorious beams, the Christian begins to look beautiful and flourishing, " he goes forth and grows up like calves of the " stall," Mal. iv. 2. We should be ever concerned to go forward, and to have it visible to ourselves, and others, that we do so. Christians, if you stumble and fall, lie not still but up and press on. Loiter not, but keep the prize always in your eye, and be moving towards it: you cannot run well unless you hold on and persevere. " He that is faith-
" ful unto death shall receive a crown of life." Rev. ii. 10.
" He that endureth unto the end shall be saved," Mat. x.
22. You may meet with many discouragements, but still keep on, the further you go, the less ground remains to be trod, therefore let not your hearts be troubled, neither be afraid, but keep on one steady course; the nearer you come to the end of your race, be the more active, let the prospect of victory animate and quicken you, and let nothing be in your minds but to finish your course, and to enjoy the prize. We come now to consider,

III. The encouragement Christians have to run this race. It is attended with toil and difficulty, the believer must take perhaps many wearisome steps before he reaches the mark, but this should be no discouragement; let none be alarmed at the prospect of difficulties, there is enough to quicken and strengthen the soul in this race; for instance, 1. There is a glorious crown before us. 2. He that begins aright shall at length certainly finish his course. 3. Every one that finishes his course shall as surely receive the prize.

I. There is a glorious crown in prospect. I shall not here particularly inquire into the nature of this crown, that will be considered when we come to the latter part of our text. I shall only consider now the Christian's crown as glorious, to shew the encouragement he has diligently and patiently to run the race set before him. The prize which the heathen conquerors received in their games, was only a crown, or garland of flowers, or greens: a low prize indeed! of no intrinsic value, only those who gained it were esteemed as victors, and it was reckoned a mark of honour;

though in itself it was a mean, empty, infignificant trifle, not worth contending for. Whereas the Chriftian's prize is glorious, unfpeakably glorious: our Redeemer's fervice is not an unprofitable fervice; he is no hard mafter; he not only fits for his fervice thofe whom he calls to it, but freely rewards them at laft: were they to have nothing but what they really merited and deferved, they muft come fhort of this prize; there is no proportion between our fervices, and the crown of glory. Judge not therefore of its value by the performance of duty: eftimate not its worth according to the manner in which you have ferved your Redeemer: behold it as the purchafe of the great Redeemer, God and man, view it as his gift, given to glorify and exalt the riches of his grace, and you cannot but entertain the moft raifed conceptions of it. The crown we have in profpect is no low earthly trifle; it is not made up of corruptible things as filver and gold; but of bleffings inconceivably more exalted, fuch as eye hath not feen, ear hath not heard, and which the heart of man is incapable of conceiving: bleffings not of a day, not tranfient and fading, but incorruptible, immortal, everlafting. Is not this then fufficient encouragement to run the Chriftian race? Shall the young beginner be difcouraged at a profpect of difficulties? Shall the Chriftian that has long toiled, tire and faint at laft? No, look forward to that day when the Chriftian's crown will be difplayed in all it's glory: look into the veil, where the prize is laid up, and fee its glory And is not this enough to overbalance every forrow, every weary and painful ftep? Mark what the apoftle fays. He had well confidered every ftep of the Chriftian's race, the difficult wildernefs he was to pafs through, the fufferings he was to endure, and the end of his pilgrimage, the glory he fhould at laft receive; he had well weighed every circumftance in his mind, had put this life in one fcale, and glory in another, and found the latter by far to overbalance the former. "I reckon therefore," fays he, "that the fu.T-ings of this prefent time are not worthy " to be compared with the glory which fhall be revealed " in us," Rom. viii. 18. This then is a glorious encouragement to the Chriftian, and fhould quicken him in his way, fupport his fpirits when ready to faint, and bear up his mind under the moft preffing difficulties. Mofes had his eye upon the recompence of the reward above, when he turned his back upon the glory of the Egyptian court, entered upon the Chriſtian race, and made choice of his afflictions: the proſpect encouraged him, amidſt thoſe trials he met with; and he frequently took a view to ſtrengthen his mind, Heb. xi. 25. Thus the Chriſtian has the greateſt encouragement to hold on with the greateſt fortitude; the crown he has in proſpect will make ample amends for every tear, every ſtruggle, every painful ſtep; it will be far above his expectations, far beyond his utmoſt reach of thought. Oh glorious encouragement! What difficulties can alarm the ſoul that has ſuch a proſpect? See, Oh my ſoul, what is before thee: canſt thou think what is laid up within the veil? A glorious crown, a crown immortal and everlaſting: not made of earthly materials: far beyond all ſenſible enjoyments: How then can I think of loitering, or fainting, in my race? Shall mortals, ambitious of a little earthly honour, run with the utmoſt cheerfulneſs and vigour! Shall they deſpiſe the difficulties of the race and preſs on to reach the mark? And ſhall not a proſpect of immortal honour, awaken me to the utmoſt diligence, encourage me under every difficulty, and help me to preſs forward? Can I faint, lie down weary of my toils, and give up the crown? No my ſoul, have thine eye upon the prize, conſider its magnificence and that will quicken thee in thy way, and enable thee to hold on.

2. He that begins his race aright, ſhall finiſh his courſe.— It is a principal thing in the Chriſtian race to ſet out in the right path: too many are ready to miſtake the way, and therefore never come to the mark, and gain the prize. Here we are liable to err; we are enemies naturally to the way which God has appointed, and vainly think that which is moſt agreeable to our own apprehenſions is the moſt agreeable to God and ſafe for us. Thus we miſtake at firſt, in the matter of the greateſt importance, and wander until we are abſolutely and eternally loſt, unleſs God is pleaſed to lead us into the right way. Some there are, that to appearance begin right, but ſoon tire, and faint, and give up. Their zeal abates, their love grows cold, they cannot encounter with ſo many difficulties; they cannot reſiſt the riſings of corruption, they cannot live a life of faith and mortification, they ſoon grow weary and give up the conflict. Theſe, notwithſtanding their appearance, never began

right. Had they really had the dominion of sin subdued, grace implanted, and been enabled to give up themselves really and sincerely into the hands 'of Jesus Christ, they would have continued until they had finished their course and got the prize. This therefore should not be the least discouragement to the humble soul; for where the good work is begun, it shall be carried on until it is perfected, and every one that really begins the race shall reach the mark. The great question is, have you been made sensible of your weakness, your guilt, and unworthiness, and your inequality to the difficulties of the Christian race? And have you been enabled to cast your whole dependence upon the great Redeemer? Have you, under a sense of sin and guilt, been enabled to fly to Jesus Christ as your only sanctuary? Is it your concern to seek to, and depend on him daily for grace, wisdom, and strength to enable you to hold on? In short, is Christ your all? You may then be encouraged, though the way be rugged and difficult; he to whom you have committed yourselves will guide, direct, support, and keep you, and at last give you the prize. It is only those that depend upon their own strength, and are empty professors that faint and give up: not those who are united to Christ depend upon him, and are partakers of his grace, such cannot lose the prize; he has put his spirit within them, to carry on the work of sanctification and holiness in them, to guide and direct them in the way they should go; to quicken and enliven them when slothful, to support them when weak, to encourage them when cast down; and to fill them with fortitude and courage, resolution and faithfulness, and enable them to press forward and hold on their way till they finish their course, and get the prize. Fear not ye humble souls that have set your faces Zion-wards; you shall not faint and give up; the more sensible you are of your own weakness, the more you go to Christ as your strength and righteousness, and the less you are in danger of being drawn aside out of the path that leads to eternal life, be of good courage, you shall so run as to obtain: none in your circumstances ever yet came short. Thousands have been afraid, as well as you, were ready to faint, thought they must tire, stop and go no further; but have been again quickened, set on with fresh vigour, and, through the strength of their Redeemer, finished their course with joy.

Serm. XIV.   COURSE.

Seeing then there is so great a cloud of witnesses, be encouraged to run the race with patience, in hopes that you also, through the same glorious power, shall reach the mark and possess the crown. The apostle Paul was but a man, a weak and frail man like us; he was not equal to the difficulties of the Christian race, of himself: yet he was enabled to hold on till he came to the end: hear him intimating the same just before he took possession of the prize. " I have " finished my course." I have been long sweating and toiling in the Christian race, I have met with many hindrances and obstructions in my way: I have laboured hard, have been often ready to faint; I have had many stumbles; but, blessed be God, I have been enabled to keep on, I have still pressed forward, and now I am just come to the end of my course, my difficulties are just over, a few steps more and I shall reach the mark, and receive the prize. Thus did the apostle triumph; thus did he finish his race well, and now has got the crown in sure possession; be not afraid you shall hold on likewise, he that kept him will keep you, direct, quicken and encourage you, and enable you to persevere unto the end, that you may have eternal life.

Every one that finishes his course, shall receive the prize. This is not the case amongst men; many perhaps run, but there is but one that can receive the prize: he that first reaches the mark has the honour and advantage of the prize; those that are behind, though they come afterwards to the goal, yet they have no part therein, but it is not so in the Christian race; every one that comes to the goal, and finishes his course, whether it is sooner or later has the crown. " Know ye not," says the apostle, " that they which run " in a race, run all; but one receiveth the prize?" Though never so many set out with expectation, all must meet with a disappointment except one; " so run that ye may obtain. 1 Cor. ix. 24. Though our race is not the same with theirs, though not only he that comes first to the mark, but every one that finishes his course shall be crowned; yet it requires the utmost activity and diligence; the case is not indeed who is first at the goal; but the path is full of difficulties, and the great concern in the Christian race is to reach the goal. Many, to appearance set out well, but faint in the way, tire and give out. Therefore the apostle's exhortation is necessary: so run, that is, as those in a race, that strive who shall be foremost, so do ye strive to hold on your course; It is of no importance whether you reach the mark before others or not; if you get thither, whether it is first or last, you shall have the prize. This then cannot but be an encouragement to the Christian in running the race that is set before him: has he an assurance of reaching the mark, and as soon as he reaches the mark shall he be crowned? What should discourage him then in pursuing the track that is marked out for him? Do others finish their course before him? Are many that set out with him in this heavenly race, got to the end of their journey, and rejoicing in the possession of the prize? He shall at length reach the goal himself, and join them in giving everlasting praises to him that enabled them to finish their course well, and has given to each the prize of immortality. Oh happy news! What encouragements are here! the prize is glorious, you shall all, that begin in Christ finish your course, and every one that does so shall be crowned. To conclude, with some improvement of the point.

1. The further we proceed in our text, the more we see the difficulty of the Christian life, and the vanity of their hopes who content themselves with a mere form. The last metaphor wherein the Christian life is compared to the warfare, shews the difficulties of it; and so does this, wherein it is compared to a race; a race signifies much labour and toil; that our minds must be upon the stretch, our souls active and armed with patience; that we must watch and strive, and press forward with all our might. Oh you that imagine a little will do in religion, and therefore are not concerned to be active or diligent in the pursuit of spiritual and eternal things! See the vanity of your hopes, the stupidity of your souls; see how Satan is lulling you into an easy security, when you are in the utmost dangers, will you not believe there is much difficulty in religion, that it requires much labour and toil? Look into our text; and give us a reason, why the Christian life is compared to a fight, and to a race? Do not these and many other similitudes in the word of God point out plainly, that it is not an easy thing to be a Christian indeed? And will you not yet believe? Are you determined to run the venture, when the scriptures are so evidently against you? The consequence must be dreadful! Oh be not content with a few faint wishes, an

external shew of appearance, but examine yourselves. And in earnest seek after eternal life. Mind religion as the one thing needful.

2. How foolish are all those that run eagerly after perishing enjoyments, and neglect the prize of immortality! The prize men generally run for, is of an earthly nature, yet see how many have been willing to contend for it. The Christian's prize is glorious and immortal, as it is expressed, 1 Cor. ix. 25. " They do it to obtain a corruptible crown; " but we an incorruptible." And yet how few aim at this glorious prize!

3. What arguments are there for running this race. Sit down a while and consider; examine the case impartially; view the different objects men are pursuing, and consider what is the issue of their pursuits. See the natural man toiling for a little glittering gold, or a little honour which will soon leave him. See the Christian upon a different pursuit; his face is stedfastly set Zion-wards, he has heaven in his eye, in his aim, and no less than heaven will crown his pursuit: behold what different views these two have at death—One taking an unwelcome farewel——Looking back, and longing to return——looking forward and shudering—unless stupid—See the other, if under the influences of the Spirit, rejoicing that he has just finished his race, and is waiting for the prize.

Consider these things and begin this race ye that are young——To that end look up to the Spirit of God who can enable you to begin, hold on, and at last finish your course with joy and triumph.

4. How should every one that has begun this race rejoice in the encouragements that have been offered!——Whether you have but just entered, or whether you have been long toiling, yet take encouragement to hold on, " for he that " endureth to the end, shall be saved and enjoy the prize, " So run, therefore, that you may obtain."

SERMON XV.

2 Tim. iv. 7, 8.

I have kept the Faith, &c.

BEFORE we enter into the kingdom of heaven, we must pass through much tribulation, Acts xiv. 22. This life is a state of trial; it tries our faith and patience, our stedfastness and constancy in our Redeemer's service, and it calls for the exercise of all those graces which God has implanted. There is a wide difference between earth and heaven: here we are labouring under pressing difficulties, striving with innumerable enemies, and wading through seas of affliction; there the Christian is at everlasting rest, free from every trouble, and triumphing over every enemy. Heaven is not to be got without difficulty: we must strive much, press hard, and cry earnestly. Heaven is to be taken by violence, it is not given to the indolent and slothful. We must run with patience and diligence, fortitude and courage, for the way is mountainous and rugged; full of intricacies and difficulties that call for great care lest we mistake the road, and for great resolution, that we faint not before we reach the goal. We have already considered the Christian life under the similitude of a race, have inquired into the way we are to take; how it is we must run so as to finish our course well, and the encouragements Christians have to run this race. We now come to consider the third reflection which the apostle was enabled to make, I have kept the faith. Here I shall,

I. Shew what is meant by keeping the faith.
II. Shew the necessity and importance of it.

I. Let us consider what is meant by keeping the faith—This may point out two things.

1. That we firmly believe the doctrines God has revealed, and steadily maintain them; and, 2 That we faithfully observe the vows and engagements we have brought ourselves under, to our glorious master, and hold on with integrity and constancy in his service.

1. It may signify that we firmly believe the doctrines God has revealed, and stedfastly maintain them. We read of a " faith once delivered to the saints." Jud. v. 3. This faith includes the various articles and doctrines, which the apostles, under the immediate influences of the Holy Ghost, delivered to the church and people of God. These therefore coming from God are certainly worthy of our credit, deserve our notice, and ought to be stedfastly maintained by us. There is but one faith, which God has revealed in his word; all the various opinions of men, or different doctrines that are industriously propagated in the world, cannot be that faith, being many of them directly opposite to, and inconsistent with one another. That all who enjoy the Scriptures, do not believe the truth of the gospel, is not owing to the darkness of the revelation God has made, but to our natural prejudices against the truth: every part of divine revelation conveys a determinate sense, which it is possible for us to know; else we reflect upon God for giving a revelation which we do not, which we cannot understand. Hence then, as it is possible to come to the knowledge of the truth; we have various exhortations in Scripture, to believe it, to maintain and keep it, to seek after unity and judgement, &c.: keeping the faith must imply, first, our believing it. The apostle himself believed those glorious doctrines he so earnestly contended for. As a minister and as a Christian, he believed the gospel in all its parts, and warmly maintained it; he kept the faith, without giving up any part of it, through fear or cowardice. " He was " not ashamed of the gospel of Christ, for it is the power " of God to salvation to every one that believeth," Rom. i. 16. He boldly faced all opposition, openly defended the gospel, and would not part with one of its truths, on any

F f

pretence whatever: and he pressed others to stand up for it, "not to be like children tossed to and fro with every wind "of doctrine," Eph. iv. 14. "But to hold fast that form "of sound words they had heard and learned." The present time is a time to try our stedfastness in the faith. The glorious truths of Christianity are become the objects of contempt. They are so opposite to the dictates of degenerate nature; so exceed the reach of our understandings; and so much humble and debase our proud hearts, that cannot receive them, but make them the subjects of ridicule, though never so clearly revealed. It is almost a reproach to a person to profess a regard to the peculiar doctrines of grace; it requires therefore courage and resolution in both ministers and Christians, to own and defend the gospel, and not to betray a cowardice of spirit, and so give up the faith for the sake of peace, or through shame and fear. "I have kept "the faith," says the apostle. I have stood my ground and kept my station; I have preached the gospel of Jesus Christ, and have not shunned to declare the whole counsel of God. I have parted with nothing through shame or fear; I have gone through persecutions and reproaches innumerable, and yet I have not deserted the cause I have espoused; but have kept my charge, and am now going to seal the glorious truths I firmly believe, with my blood.

2. The expression signifies, that we faithfully observe the vows and engagements we have brought ourselves under, to our glorious master, and hold on with integrity and constancy in his service. When we en'ist ourselves under the captain of our salvation, we take him for our Lord, our Prophet, Priest, and King, we give up ourselves unto him, and bring ourselves under the strictest engagements to love, honour, serve, and follow him in all things unto the end of life; we engage to sacrifice all for him, and be faithful unto death. This was the case with the apostle Paul, when Jesus called to him from heaven, he fell at his feet, crying out, "Lord what wilt thou have me to do?" Acts ix. 6. Lord, I am sensible of my folly, I have been doing wickedly, but now behold here am I, devoted to thy service, here am I ready to fulfil thy commands; speak Lord what thou wilt have me to do; I will follow thee in all things, &c. Thus the apostle, at his conversion, gave up himself to God, and brought himself under the strictest en-

gagements to him, and he was faithful in his Redeemer's service; he met with a variety of difficulties in the discharge of his duty, enough to have discouraged him, and forbid his continuance had he not experienced an almighty power upholding and supporting him: but see, he is not moved, he will not desert his master's service, whatever difficulties stand in the way. All the persecutions he met with, did not lessen his love or abate his zeal: all the hardships he endured did not weary his soul, or cause him to slacken his pace; he still kept on with a noble firmness and resolution; and he had nothing so much in view as the honour of his great Redeemer. See how cheerfully he submits to be stripped, to be imprisoned, and to endure all manner of cruelties for his master's sake! "He counted all things but "loss for the excellency of the knowledge of Christ Jesus, "for whom he cheerfully suffered the loss of all things, "and counted them but dross and dung," Phil iii. 7, 8. Thus he continued faithful even to the last, and set his face like a flint, cheerfully parting with his blood for Christ and his cause: and thus he kept the faith. We are to "hold "fast the profession of our faith without wavering," Heb. x. 23. You must maintain your allegiance to Jesus Christ, to whom you have given up yourselves. See that you war a good warfare, "holding faith and a good conscience, "which last, some having put away concerning faith have "made shipwreck," 1 Tim. i. 19. You have given up yourselves to Jesus, you are bound to him by oath, by promise, by the most solemn vows, by the most sacred ties, and by the strictest engagements. See then that you follow him: to vow and not to perform is only to mock God, and to deceive your own souls See that you keep the faith; behave with fidelity to the king of righteousness whose professed subjects you are. I have kept the faith, I have met with many enticements many snares, many difficulties, and temptations, but blessed be God I have been enabled to stand fast, I have been enabled, through grace, to persevere, notwithstanding every difficulty, and now have the prize in view.

II. We are now to shew the necessity and importance of keeping the faith. And,

1. It is the distinguishing characteristic of a real Christian. We cannot, we dare not say it is essential to the Christian to believe and maintain all the peculiar doctrines of

the gospel; Christians, according to their standing in Christ, according to their education, according to their different instructions, have different conceptions of the gospel: as there are some whose judgements are sound, but whose hearts are wicked; so there are others whose hearts are better than their heads. Yet Christians agree in that which is essential to their character, they are all united to Christ and are concerned for his glory: they are all such as believe on him for salvation; and they are such as are constant and persevere in his service. Those that turn aside from following the Redeemer, were never his disciples in reality. There are too many who are stony ground hearers; who, through a sudden overflowing of affection, make a profession of the gospel of Christ, but soon return to folly, either through a remembrance of former gratifications; or through some peculiar difficulties they met with in their profession. That profession that is not set upon good principles will never hold. Those whose hearts are established with grace never totally fall off. Fall they may, and oftentimes do, but they shall return to God by deep and humble repentance, resume their integrity, and press on towards the mark. The seed that is sown in the heart grows up unto eternal life: the grace that is implanted keeps the soul in some measure steady; and strength being daily communicated, he keeps on, follows his leader, until he finishes his course; all the temptations he meets with, all the enemies he encounters, are not able to prevail over him. He never absolutely deserts his glorious master, but remains faithful unto death. He does not make vows and never perform them, but is enabled to pay his vows in some measure, and to continue in the service of his Redeemer until he leaves this world, and enters into a better. This is the character of every real Christian. He must maintain his allegiance to his glorious Lord, withstand the opposition he meets with, and keep his fidelity.

2. In keeping the faith, the Christian's comfort is greatly promoted. The glorious doctrines of faith are of the most excellent nature; they abundantly recompence the Christian in his steady belief of and attachment to them, by the unspeakable supports they yield in every circumstance and station of life. A consideration of the person, offices, righteousness, and characters of Jesus Christ; the everlasting

covenant and promifes of God; the perfon and operations of the Holy Ghoft; together with the various other important myfteries of Chriftianity; greatly conduce to fweeten every difficulty, to eafe every burden, to remove every anxious care, to enlighten every affliction, ftrengthen our hopes in life and death, and fill us with unfpeakable joy and fatisfaction. The more we know of the Gofpel, the more we are like to be comforted and ftrengthened under every forrow. Ignorance of and want of attention to fome of the glorious truths of Chriftianity expofe the Chriftian to a variety of fears, difficulties and burdens, which a knowledge of the Gofpel has a tendency to remove. Whilft the Chriftian is ftedfaftly maintaining the faith he has received, he finds it cheering his foul with the nobleft fupports, reconciling him to the greateft afflictions, and enabling him to rejoice when every other refuge and fupport fails. The martyrs experienced the excellency of thofe truths they fealed with their blood; whilft they were fuffering for them, they were fupported by them, and rejoiced more than if they had been raifed to the higheft pitch of earthly honour and profperity. They that keep the faith lofe nothing by it. The gofpel is better than all the world; this and this alone cheers the foul, when nothing elfe can; it heals the wounded confcience, forbids every fear, and gives him living hopes in his dying moments. Oh! Who would be cold and indifferent to the faith God has revealed? Who would give up that which can reconcile them to leave the prefent life, and make their views of eternity glorious? Shall we prefer the low honours of this world before it? Shall we part with the faith through fear of reproach and perfecution? What, part with that which alone can comfort our fouls in life and death? God forbid!———Take the words in the fecond fenfe, to fignify fidelity and perfeverance in our Redeemer's fervice; and we cannot but foon fee how clofely that ftands connected with our comfort. When we are led into captivity, break our engagements, and prove at any time unfaithful; how are our confciences wounded, how is our peace interrupted, and what fears are introduced, that break in upon our comfort and give us awful apprehenfions of death and eternity? Whereas whilft we are enabled fteadily to adhere to our great Redeemer, to hold on in his fervice, and to perfevere, we have thereby fome comfortable evidences of our interest in Jesus and his salvation, to comfort our souls both in life and at death. The more faithful and the more stedfast we are in the service of our great master, the more comfortable. The ways of sin and ungodliness cannot certainly bring any solid satisfaction to the mind: every time we turn aside there must be an interruption of our peace; solid comfort is only to be found in keeping the faith. I have kept the faith; I have not been ashamed of the faith of Christ, but have been enabled to maintain it with a holy zeal. I have lived in the faith, in some measure, as well as stood up for it, and been enabled to persevere in my master's service even unto the end. This was to the apostle a comfortable evidence of his interest in a better world, and therefore a cheering cordial in his dying moments. He could face death in all its various forms with an undisturbed calmness and serenity of mind, and rejoice in the prospect of an approaching eternity. Would you have the same comfortable evidence? you must then keep the faith. Can you expect to be lively in your souls; to enjoy the smiles of God's countenance; can you expect to be free from melancholy fears, from the alarms of conscience; whilst you are cold to the faith, or walk unfaithfully with God? Remember David's fall, how it wounded his soul, provoked the spirit of God to withdraw his special influences, and filled him with anguish and distress: Pf. li. 8. &c. Backslidings darken our evidences, and lay a foundation for distress and melancholy, make us go on heavily through life, and droop our wings when death and eternity appear in view.

3. Keeping the faith is necessary to promote the honour of Christ, and to secure the Christian from those errors and snares to which he stands exposed. Whilst we are indifferent about the faith we are liable to be turned away, and to be tossed to and fro with every wind of doctrine, by the cunning craftiness of men. The many expressions of " buying " the truth, and selling it; not contending for the faith once " delivered to the Saints," &c. shew the excellency of the faith and the necessity and importance of keeping it. The enemy is watching every opportunity to unhinge our minds; how soon is it done when we are not stedfast, but wavering? Oh hold fast the profession of your faith without wavering. Whilst you appear stedfastly resolved for Christ and his gospel, as you have received it, you will be in little danger

of being drawn into error by the moſt crafty inſinuations of thoſe that love not the truth. But if you are unſettled and unſteady, you may eaſily be drawn to receive the doctrines of men, and fall into errors the moſt fatal to the ſoul Whilſt you are unſteady and wavering, the enemy may likewiſe draw your feet aſide into the forbidden paths of impiety; you may wound your conſciences, and diſhonour your Lord. The enemy has but little hopes of ſucceſs, when he finds the Chriſtian reſolved, his heart eſtabliſhed, ſtedfaſtly attached to the ſervice of his maſter, and determined to walk therein. Beſides, keeping the faith is neceſſary to the honour of Chriſt: as we have taken the character of Chriſtians, ſo we ſhould be concerned to walk agreeably thereto. As we profeſs to believe the goſpel of our Lord, and call ourſelves his followers, we ought certainly to keep the faith, otherwiſe we diſhonour Chriſt, bring reflections upon that honourable name by which we are called, and render Chriſt and the goſpel the ſubjects of ridicule and contempt. Who honours his great maſter more than he who ſwerves not from his intereſt, whom no temptations can draw away, but ſtands firm in every danger, reſolutely withſtands all oppoſition, and perſeveres in faith and holineſs even unto the end? Such are ornaments to the cauſe they eſpouſe: they only honour Chriſt, live like Chriſtian's, and glorify God. And wouldſt thou, Oh my ſoul, honour thy Redeemer? would you, Chriſtian's, lay no foundation for reflections on your glorious maſter? Are you tenderly concerned for his honour? Then keep the faith. Stand up like Chriſtians for the goſpel, and part with none of its glorious truths: perſevere in the ways of holineſs; like good ſoldiers fight your way through every difficulty; like good ſentinels be upon your guard, keep your ſtation, let nothing move you from the hope of the goſpel; then will you honour your dear Redeemer, and act conſiſtent with your character and profeſſion.

4. Without a ſtedfaſt perſeverance in the faith our hopes of heaven are vain and deceitful. Perſeverance in the faith does not entitle us to eternal life, but there is no eternal life without it. God has promiſed the crown of life only to thoſe who are faithful unto death. Thoſe that, after they have once made a profeſſion, fall off, are in the utmoſt danger. Every fall ſhould fill us with a godly jealouſy, every backſliding ſhould put us upon the inquiry, whether we have received the grace

of God or not. Thofe appear in dangerous circumftances who once profeffed to receive the faith and to give up themfelves to Jefus Chrift, but are now fallen off, have deferted the ordinances of God, and are ftrangers to good works. How happy is it when we can fay with the apoftle, "but we are not of them that draw back unto perdition, but we are of them that believe unto the faving of the foul!" Heb. x. 39.—How much fhould we be upon our guard? Though where the good work is begun, it fhall be carried on; yet there are many who appear to begin in the fpirit and end in the flefh. The doctrine of perfeverance therefore by no means encourages flothfulnefs and fecurity, it is brought about in the ufe of means. Thofe therefore who imagine that a work of faith and grace is begun in their fouls and grow carelefs and fecure, running into fin, upon a vain prefumption that the feed fowed fhall not die, but grow up unto everlafting life; fuch perfons have the greateft reafon to fear they never were rightly acquainted with the power of religion, and therefore that their hopes of eternal life are abfolutely vain. This fhould by no means diftrefs the humble foul, and fill him with flavifh fears; in a humble dependence upon Jefus Chrift, you fhall perfevere and be faithful unto the end. But you who once felt the force of convictions, made the moft folemn promifes and vows, and an open profeffion for a time; but have loft your concern, forfaken the Lord, and turned again after your former follies; what evidence can you produce of your intereft in Chrift, and your title to eternal life? What then are your hopes? Can you be fo irrational as to expect the glorious crown, becaufe you once to appearance bade fair for it? Can you think that God will welcome you into his immediate prefence, becaufe you for a little while expreffed a concern to walk before him in all righteoufnefs, becaufe you difcovered a few faint wifhes to be his, and made a few feeble attempts towards the Chriftian life? No, you have fince fallen away, renounced what you once profeffed, and will appear every way unworthy of eternal life; unlefs you are united to Chrift and found in him. How melancholy muft it be with the apoftate, when death and eternity appear in view, if his confcience is awake? To look back upon his former profeffion, and compare it with his paft life: to confider his amazing fecurity, his dreadful apoftacy; to look forward and see a righteous judge standing ready to pass the sentence according to his works: Oh awful view! Where are now his hopes? His heart begins to sink his spirits droop; it is a dark and dreadful prospect. May we not suppose him saying, Oh what have I been doing! I can look back to the time, when, like the young man, I bid fair for heaven; I passed under many convictions; like Balaam wished to die the death of the righteous, and appeared determined for heaven; but my zeal soon abated, my pretended love grew cool, I could not continue a life of mortification, faith, and selfdenial; and was therefore soon weary, and turned again by degrees to my former stupidity and folly, yet persuading myself that all was well; but how can I hope? Am I not a hypocrite? Will God own one that has deserted his cause, forsaken his colours, left his station, and turned apostate? Alas! alas! my case is melancholy; I have ruined myself: what can I blame but my own heart? The ways of God I found to be too severe for me, I could not relish closet duties, I have no regard for spiritual meditation, and the other distinguishing duties of the Christian life; Oh foolish creature! I have left God, and he will I fear leave me when I stand in most need of his favour and presence. Oh eternity, eternity; what an awful thought! Oh death, death thou art armed with every terror! Oh that I could fly from thy fatal arrow; but I must submit to thy call, and now take the important consequences. Not such is the language of the persevering Christian, especially if under the refreshing influences of the Spirit of God. I have kept the faith. True, I have been chargeable with many backslidings and imperfections; I have been often beset with Satan and my own heart; and Oh how near was I to being led aside to my everlasting ruin? My feet were almost gone; I had begun to decline; begun to enter upon the borders of temptation, had swallowed the bait laid before me, and often, yea often I repeated the same; thus had I been gone for ever, had not infinite distinguishing grace convinced me of my folly, and recovered my soul, and led me in the paths of righteousness again; Oh blessed be God that kept me from absolutely falling away, and enabled me to return unto him. I have often stepped aside, I have been cold and indifferent, but my God has again quickened me; he has kept me by his mighty power, he has enabled me in some measure to persevere in faith, and holiness; I depend not upon this for salvation, but, blessed be God, it is an evidence of the grace of God in me; it is an evidence of my union to Jesus Christ, in and through whom I hope to be put into the possession of that crown which he has purchased for all his people. Thus without perseverance, our hopes of eternal life are vain and deceitful, and absolutely without foundation. Apostacy is attended with melancholy consequences. Better never to have known the way of righteousness, than after to turn from it, 2 Pet. ii. 21. There is nothing but a dreadful looking for of judgement, and fiery indignation for all such. A word or two of improvement must close.

1. Is keeping the faith the distinguishing character of a Christian? Then how few are there in the present age. It is melancholy to see such numbers casting contempt upon the doctrines of faith: this nation was once famous for a zeal for the purity of the gospel; but now in too many places there is a famine of hearing the word of the Lord. The gospel is become the object of too general contempt; churches and congregations have left the faith once delivered to the saints, and religion is degenerated into infidelity. It is almost become a reproach to a person to profess to believe the gospel, and to stand up for Jesus Christ, and him crucified: how few are there that really love our glorious Redeemer? How many are there that fall off from their profession, desert the cause of Christ, prove unfaithful to him, and turn out no better than hypocrites? The honours of the world lead away some, the sensualities of life ensnare others: some are influenced by a view of riches to leave the Redeemer, others are ashamed to own him, because of the reproaches that are cast upon his followers; too many have but a name to live, and content themselves with a mere form, after they have professedly given up themselves to God. Were our public assemblies to be carefully examined, how many would be found unfaithful? There are not many in this assembly I apprehend, that have escaped convictions, either through the word, or providence; these have, when under convictions, promised and vowed, resolved and determined, to take up their cross and follow Christ, but alas! How few have been faithful? How many have broke their vows, and after a little appearance of zeal, turned again to their old pursuits, or have so

far dwindled as to take up with some outward form? The number of true Christians then must be but small. There may be many who may take the name; but how few are there who keep the faith? How few that hold on and persevere in the ways of God even unto the end? Oh melancholy consideration!

2. Is perseverance in the faith the character of a real Christian? How melancholy must their state be who never yet set forward in the ways of God! How many are there young and airy, whose minds are full of nothing but vanity; who have never yet sat down and seriously considered the great concerns of their souls, whether they are Christians, or whether they are not, whether heaven is worth seeking after; they run carelessly on in the path of pleasure, and spend not one thought upon future things. Melancholy consideration! What, no concern about your immortal souls! No serious inquiry whither you are going, what will be the end of your present pursuits! No desire to walk in the ways of God! No thought about future happiness! This is the melancholy case; young persons greedily swallow the bait that is laid before them, are easily ensnared by the honours and pleasures of the present state, without considering what is necessary to an immortal happiness. Is not this acting a most irrational part? Are you too young to die? Are you sure of life? Will your present pursuits give you complete satisfaction, and secure you everlasting felicity? No, you have not kept the faith, you are unconcerned about it, you think nothing of a future reckoning; you dream of nothing but of pleasure, wealth, and earthly honour; and may be suddenly snatched out of time into a long and miserable eternity; amazing stupidity! your state is melancholy in the midst of your apparent prosperity: your souls are every moment at stake, for you have not so much as thought about keeping the faith. But Oh how much more melancholy is it with those who are come to the decline of life, and yet have not thought seriously about the faith; who have given themselves no time to think about their souls? You are hastening to the grave, and yet have not thought of eternity. Is it not melancholy to see gray hairs in the ways of sin? What, are you going to appear before God, to be called to an awful account, and yet strangers to the divine life! no concern whether you are in the road to Zion? Astonishing

folly! Can you say with the apostle, when in the views of an eternal world, we have kept the faith? No, alas, you will have, if you continue in your present thoughtless condition, no evidences of an interest in Jesus to comfort your souls in your departing moments: you will have nothing but an awful eternity in prospect; nothing but everlasting burnings before you to fill your souls with awful surprise, and inexpressible agonies. None of those that will then be found under the dominion of sin, can say they have kept the faith: they never received it aright, they never gave up themselves in reality to Jesus; sin kept dominion over them, and all they professed was only a mere form; all their religion was only lip service. Such is the state, such the case of every unrenewed soul: they are in the gall of bitterness, and in the bond of iniquity, slaves to Satan, and children of wrath.

3. Is it so important to keep the faith? Then let us seriously examine our own hearts concerning it. Examination is a duty highly necessary: to be nothing but hearers will be but of little avail, if we never look into our own hearts, and inquire whether we experience what we hear. Then let me now sit down and take my heart to task; let me turn within and make diligent search: I have heard this day that it is the distinguishing character of a Christian to keep the faith. And how is it with me? Do I believe the gospel which Christ has revealed? Have I received the great doctrine of faith? Those doctrines that are of such great importance, that enter into the very essence of religion, and are the foundation of all true holiness? And have I kept the faith I have received, amidst the reproaches of infidels, and the sneers of scoffers? Have I not been ashamed of the gospel of Christ? Have I parted with the truth, through fear, or for the sake of the world? Is Christ a stumbling stone, and a rock of offence unto me? Have I given up myself to the Lord Jesus? Have I solemnly dedicated and devoted myself unto God? Have I determined and promised to be the Lord's? Have I vowed, and have I been enabled to perform my vows? Have I been faithful to my Redeemer? Have I been enabled to withstand all opposition; to maintain my ground, to keep diligent watch, and to continue in my master's service? Or have I broke through all my resolutions, and turned again to my former vanities? Have my

lufts and corruptions been too predominant in me? Have they ftifled every conviction, overcome every refolution, and led me again into captivity? Have I been unfaithful to my mafter? Or have I continued ftill refolved for heaven and eternal life? And what is my prefent frame? What are my refolutions? What are my thoughts? Am I preffing forward? Am I ftedfaft and immoveable, and am I refolved, through the grace and ftrength of my Redeemer, to hold on and be faithful unto death? Inquire, Oh my foul, and let me not be a ftranger to myfelf. Examination is difficult work, but it is neceffary; neceffary to our comfort, neceffary to our growth in grace, neceffary to know our ftate, why then are we fo backward? You who make a profeffion of religion, fit down and inquire, whether you have hitherto kept the faith; whether you are hypocrites or whether you are Chriftians indeed? How neceffary is it to have this important point determined? Omit it therefore no longer; " for now is the accepted time, now is the day of falva-" tion."

4. Let me earneftly exhort you to keep the faith. As you value your comfort; as you value your immortal fouls; if you have any concern for your real intereft, fhew it by a fteady belief of the gofpel, and faithful adherence to Chrift.—Oh you that have given up yourfelves to Jefus—Keep the faith—Stand faft—To that end look up to him for ftrength— Be much in prayer—Watch over your hearts—Keep death and eternity always in view.

SERMON XVI.

THE CROWN OF RIGHTEOUSNESS.

2 TIM. iv. 8.

Henceforth there is laid up for me a crown of righteousness, which the Lord, the righteous judge, shall give me at that day: and not to me only, but unto all them also that love his appearing.

IT is the opinion of too many that a religious life is a life of melancholy: they form conceptions of certain austerities in religion which by no means suit their relish, and which give them an entire distaste to the ways of God. The Christian doubtless meets with a variety of difficulties in the service of Christ, it is a warfare; a warfare in which the Christian soldier has many enemies to encounter: it is a race in which we must run, labour, and toil before we reach the mark: yet notwithstanding, it is a comfortable and profitable service. The Christian meets with suitable supports and comforts in his way; God does not leave him to toil by himself, but gives him his presence and favour in life, and crowns him with everlasting life and glory at death. There is a crown at last which will make ample amends for all their labours, difficulties and sorrows, and fill them with full and complete happiness. The apostle Paul met with as many and as pressing difficulties as most; yet he would not have exchanged his condition with the most magnificent prince in the world: he experienced divine supports in the way, and when he got to the end of his race, he rejoiced in the prospect of a glorious crown, which he now enjoys, and will do so for ever. May we like him maintain our stedfastness in life, hold out to the end, have the same glorious prospects before us, and receive the prize of immortality. " I have " fought the good fight," &c. These words give us a view of the apostle's reflections he was enabled to make upon that part of his life which he had spent in his master's service.—And the glorious prospect he had in view, and the triumphant frame of his soul under such a prospect. We have already considered the apostle's reflections, before he left the stage of life. He had fought a good fight,—he had finished his course,——and he had kept the faith. We now come,

II. To consider the glorious prospect the apostle had before him, and the triumphant frame of his soul under that amiable view. We shall divide this into two heads. The prospect itself, and the frame of soul the apostle was in. First the prospect, and secondly the frame.

First, let us consider the prospect itself. " Henceforth " there is laid up," &c. Here we find various things worthy of our observation, viz. the prize the apostle had in view; the person by whom it is bestowed; the time when it shall be given; and the character of the persons who shall enjoy it.

I. Let us consider the prize the apostle had in view, " a " crown of righteousness." Here the apostle may not only allude to a crown which was given to the conquerors in the Olympic games, but to a crown, the ensign of power and dignity; for we find the Holy Ghost has represented the happiness above, under a variety of the most grand similitudes, taken from sensible objects, about which we are conversant, and in which are the highest degrees of human glory, in order to strike our attention, raise our expectations of, and stir up and quicken our desires after, so exalted a happiness. Royalty is the highest pitch of human grandeur. Those that wear earthly crowns are got to the very summit of earthly honour, and are in that station in which centers all worldly glory and happiness. What an idea is this similitude designed to give us then of that glorious world, where every saint wears an unfading, incorruptible and immortal crown? Here, what angry debates, what warm contentions, what bloody contests are occasioned by an over thirst for government, for all cannot reign; but in the bright regions of immortality, all the people of God are of this illustrious rank and character: all stand before the throne as kings and conquerors, bearing the ensigns of royalty and victory, are perfectly freed from every anxious care, and possess a happiness as glorious as their natures are capable of. In fine, this crown points out the whole of the Christian's happiness in a better world, and gives us the grandest ideas of it. It is far beyond our present reach; we fall inconceiveably short in our conceptions of it; it is the preparation of an almighty power, of infinite wisdom and grace; it is the purchase of Christ, and consequently it must be inexpressibly glorious. It is here called a crown of righteousness. The propriety of which will appear if we consider, that it consists of perfect righteousness. It is purchased by the righteousness of our dear Redeemer, and it comes to us, or we are put into the possession of it in a way of righteousness.

1. This crown consists of perfect and everlasting righteousness. The sparks of this crown are perfect holiness and a conformity to God. Here lies the difference between earth and heaven. This is a state of sin and imperfection: while in a state of nature there is not the least spark of true holiness appearing in us. We are nothing but sin. The image of God is every where defaced. The understanding, will, and affections are all polluted; we are nothing but sin; made up of ignorance, enmity, obstinacy, and sensuality. And when renewed by the spirit of God, we are yet imperfect: at first grace is compared to smoking flax and a bruised reed; it is as it were almost smothered by those corruptions that are still in the soul. And when it comes to its most flourishing state here, when it burns up into a bright, even into the brightest flame it can do in the present life, it is far from perfection. Perfection is what the Christian is aiming at, and earnestly pressing after; but it is a blessing reserved for heaven. The Christian when arrived to the highest measures of grace here, yet finds some remains of sin; his duties are but imperfect, and sin cleaves to every faculty. There

is some pride, some ignorance, some carnality, some enmity in the best of God's people in the present state: in heaven they shall receive the sum of all their wishes, in that perfect holiness with which they shall be crowned. This crown has no alloy in it; it is pure without the least mixture. Behold the saint when he has put off the body and arrived in the realms of glory; see him shining in the glorious image of God, placed at an everlasting distance from all sin, and fully possessed of all the beauties of holiness. Behold his understanding no more clogged with darkness; his will no more tainted, his affections no more polluted; he has dropped the body of sin, and is without spot, or wrinkle, or any such thing. "Here we know in part, but there we shall "know as we are known; here we see through a glass "darkly, but there face to face."

Here our services are imperfect, but there all righteous and holy; no vain thoughts, no impure desires, no wanton looks. The soul perfectly loves his glorious Redeemer; God absolutely and entirely possesses his affections; and no other object appears to divide his heart; he worships him who sits upon the throne, with unwearied cheerfulness, and finds no temptation, but an everlasting delight in God and holy subjection to him. Oh happy, Oh desirable state! Who would not long to be in heaven? To be fully delivered from all sin, to be made perfectly holy! This glorious thought fills the Christian with a peculiar satisfaction in this imperfect state, and helps him to wait with patience till that happy day when his desires will be fully satisfied. Such is the crown that is in reserve, such the happiness of heaven: body and soul shall be fully freed from all sin, and be possessed of complete holiness. In such a view is heaven amiable to the real Christian.

2. This crown was purchased by the righteousness of Jesus Christ. It cost a valuable price, and therefore is of inestimable worth. Heaven is a purchased possession. We forfeited and lost it by sin; and before we could have the possession of it, it must be purchased for us. This was necessary to preserve the honour of the divine government, to secure the glory of his perfections, and to magnify the riches of sovereign grace, which was the peculiar end he had in view in the salvation of sinners. For God to have given heaven to guilty creatures, without any satisfaction to his

H h

justice for sin, would have reflected upon his holiness and purity, his truth and faithfulness, which perfections he would exalt and glorify in bestowing eternal life. This then made way for the obedience and sufferings of our great Mediator. For in the second covenant man's salvation was not to be precarious or uncertain, or liable to be lost, but fixed and absolute; and as we were unable to perform the conditions of this second covenant, by which the salvation promised was to be secured; our great mediator has done it in our room and stead; he came as he agreed, appeared in human nature, perfectly obeyed the law, and suffered death; by which the great ends of moral government are answered, the divine perfections glorified, and heaven secured to all his people, inasmuch as Jesus made an absolute purchase of it for them. Though our righteousness could be of no real value, yet his was of infinite worth and excellency. He was under no obligations to take human nature, only what arose from his free and voluntary promise and engagements. The end and design of his fulfilling all righteousness was entirely to make satisfaction to infinite justice, and purchase heaven for his people. He is God as well as man, the two natures being closely united; his righteousness was the righteousness of God as well as man; from thence it derived all its efficacy, and on this account is it a valuable consideration for heaven itself, and all that glory which he will bestow upon his people. Thus we are to receive this crown as the purchase of Christ, and as the free gift of God, hence it is become sure to every believer. If Christ has purchased it, it shall be given; else it would reflect upon the divine faithfulness. That Christ's righteousness was sufficient to purchase it who can doubt? It is a glorious truth. The crown in reserve is a crown secured by the righteousness of our Redeemer; it is purchased by him. Lord we would receive it as such, and adore the infinite riches of our Redeemer's grace, in thus securing it to us.

3. We come to the possession of this crown in a way of righteousness. It's being purchased for us does not lay a foundation for our slothfulness, sin, and security. To give salvation in this way would be inconsistent with the divine perfections: there is an absolute impossibility. Those that represent sin and security as the necessary consequences of salvation by grace, and the righteousness of Christ, have

never yet rightly feen the beauty of thefe truths, nor experienced their power and fweetnefs. There muſt be a perſonal righteouſneſs in order to the poſſeſſion of this crown; it is called a crown of righteouſneſs; it confiſts of righteouſneſs, and how can we be fit to enjoy it, or feel any real pleaſure in the enjoyment, unleſs we are righteous? When there is no ſuitableneſs in the heart to the object we expect to enjoy, our expectations are vain, for happineſs neceſſarily ſuppoſes agreement. We muſt have therefore internal righteouſneſs, or a righteouſneſs wrought in us before we can enjoy this crown: nay, the happineſs above is a perfection of what God begins here in the heart. Heaven is begun in the ſoul when the Spirit ſubdues the dominion of ſin, and implants the divine image. Heaven is fully enjoyed when this work is completed, which will be at death, when the ſoul is introduced into the immediate preſence of God. There muſt be this work of holineſs in the heart: " Verily, " verily I ſay unto thee, except a man be born again, he " cannot enter into the kingdom of God." John iii. 3. " Without holineſs no man ſhall ſee the Lord." Heb. xii. 14. This holineſs is not only implanted in the heart, but it appears in the life; all thoſe therefore who are ſtrangers to good works, are ſtrangers to internal holineſs, and have little reaſon to lay claim to eternal life, for wherever grace is implanted, it will manifeſt itſelf in love to God, in prayer, watchfulneſs, and in walking ſoberly, righteouſly, and godly in the preſent world, in all thoſe ſubjects who are capable of it. Thus we ſee how beautiful the method of ſalvation is; how much it glorifies God, and how well it ſecures the comfort and happineſs of every believer; by the righteouſneſs of Chriſt, the juſtice, truth, and holineſs of God are exalted, heaven is fully purchaſed: by internal holineſs a meetneſs is given for the enjoyment of heaven, and by the fruits of righteouſneſs in thoſe that are ſaved God appears righteous in giving them eternal life, and the mouths of all his ungodly enemies are ſtopped. And this leads us,

II. To conſider the perſon by whom this crown is beſtowed, and his character as a righteous judge. This illuſtrious perſon is every where repreſented to be our Lord Jeſus Chriſt. Thus, Acts xvii. 31. " God hath appointed " a day in the which he will judge the world in righteouſ " neſs, by that man whom he hath ordained; whereof he "hath given affurance unto all men, in that he hath raifed him from the dead." Chrift is the appointed perfon, and he is every way fitted for the great and important work, he being God as well as man: he is abfolutely incapable of committing the leaft miftake or error. He knows all the actions of his creatures, he fees the fprings and motives from whence they proceed: He is not to be deceived by fair pretences; he knows the hypocrite from the believer, can diftinguifh the leaft dram of grace from the faireft profeffion, and cannot be impofed upon. And he is a righteous judge. He will difplay his righteoufnefs in the laft fentence that he will pafs upon every creature. He will appear perfectly righteous in the condemnation of the wicked, and in the falvation of the righteous, in dooming one to everlafting darknefs, and inviting the other into manfions of everlafting felicity. The wicked cannot open their mouths againft the fentence they will receive, or accufe the judge of injuftice. No, they have but what they have deferved. The proper wages or defert of fin is everlafting death. God never determined their minds to evil; he never conftrained them to walk in the paths of impiety; they were advifed and warned to the contrary: he fent his ambaffadors with meffages of peace; he fent his minifters to warn them of the wrath to come; they were told of the nature and defert of fin, the worth of their fouls, and the awfulnefs of falling into the hands of an angry God. They were told of the refuge that is provided, the fuitablenefs of the faviour, and his willingnefs to fave all that come to him; they were invited to come to Jefus, were exhorted to flee from the wrath to come; they had the calls of God's word and providence, and every encouragement was given them to ftir them up to a diligent purfuit of eternal things. This is the cafe with gofpel finners: and will it not be an act of righteoufnefs in the judge to doom fuch to everlafting darknefs? And as for thofe whom he will fentence to the bottomlefs pit, who were deprived of thefe privileges, the rules he will obferve in their judgement will be perfectly equitable and righteous : " for as many as have finned without law, fhall alfo " perifh without law—in the day when God fhall judge the " fecrets of men by Jefus Chrift." Rom. ii. 12. So that every finner muft be for ever filent. Hell cannot reafonably object to, and heaven will applaud the fentence. He will ap-

pear righteous likewife in beftowing the crown of eternal life upon his people. For he purchafed it for them, he gave them a title to it, and he promifed them the enjoyment of it. He purchafed it for them. He laid down his life for his fheep, he fuffered the punifhment they had deferved, bore their fins on his own body on the tree, and fulfilled all righteoufnefs on purpofe to purchafe eternal life. If then the purchafe was abfolute; if he entirely fatisfied juftice, and gave a valuable confideration for heaven; muft not fuch objects of his love be faved? God acts righteoufly to the mediator in giving them faith, and an entrance into this falvation in time, and Chrift will act righteoufly in paffing the glorious fentence upon them at laft. Chrift gives his people a title to this crown here. This he does when he clothes them with his perfect and everlafting righteoufnefs. The title which he gives them is clear and good: it is indifputable, and will bear the teft. Devils cannot fet it afide; and the judge will not: it is of his own giving, and he will therefore accept of it. If the title is good, who can difpute the enjoyment? Chrift gave it, and he will act a righteous part in beftowing the crown of glory and immortality upon them. But further, he has promifed the crown to his people. He has given an actual, abfolute promife to all who wafh their robes in his blood, fight under his banner, run diligently their race, keep the faith, and maintain their allegiance unto death: he has promifed the crown to all fuch, and therefore is perfectly righteous in giving the enjoyment. We hence fee that Chrift the judge does not give his people eternal life for any peculiar merit or excellency there was in their works done on earth. And yet he is righteous in giving them the prize of immortality. We read that the fentence will be according to our works. Rom. ii. 6, &c. " God will render to every man according to his
" deeds: to them who, by patient continuance in well doing,
" feek for glory, and honour, and immortality, eternal life.
" But unto them that are contentious, and do not obey the
" truth, but obey unrighteoufnefs; indignation and wrath;
" tribulation and anguifh upon every foul of man that doth
" evil; of the Jew firft and alfo of the Gentile." Faith is mentioned in juftification without works; as it is by faith alone, and not by works that we lay hold on Jefus Chrift, and are interefted in him: but in the laft judgement, good

works are mentioned and not faith. And why? becaufe good works are the only evidences of a genuine and fincere faith

The reprefentation which is made of the final judgement in the 25th of Mat. &c. is of the vifible church; all profeffing faith, but not all poffeffed of it. Nay, is it not the cafe with all forts, in all nations to hope for future happinefs? And how fhall the good be diftinguifhed from the bad, but by the marks and characters of the real Chriftian? The trial is openly to be made; in order to diftinguifh then, between the hypocrite and the fincere foul, in order to make it appear who really believed in Chrift, and who did not; their works are to be brought to light and examined; Chrift will therefore mention the charity, and beneficence, and other works of his people, publicly proclaiming the fprings and principles of love and gratitude, from whence they proceeded, and confequently will declare them true marks and characters of thofe that really believe on him, and accordingly introduce them into the poffeffion of eternal life, as being purchafed for all fuch : whilft he will mention the works of the wicked and ungodly as the marks of all that are really his enemies, and deferve everlafting condemnation. Thus he will appear righteous in each fentence: free from all partiality and prejudice, perfectly juft and holy, to the everlafting admiration of fome, and to the everlafting mifery of others. We now come,

3. To confider when this crown fhall be completely poffeffed and be fully given. It is here faid to be given *at that day*, viz. The day of Chrift's appearance to judge the world. This is the emphatical day the apoftle mentions more than once; the day that will determine the everlafting ftates of all, put fome into the poffeffion of complete happinefs, and fink others down into everlafting mifery. This is the day when Chrift the righteous judge will give the crown to the conquerors, and make them kings and priefts unto God. This does not imply that the believer will remain indolent and inactive, or be put into a ftate of fleep or infenfibility until that day: or that he fhall remain in a ftate of trial and purgation. At death the foul enters into glory. Chrift told the penitent thief, that that very day he fhould be with him in paradife.

The moment the foul is feparated from the body, it is put

Serm. XVI. RIGHTEOUSNESS. 247

into the everlasting possession of the most exalted happiness. No sooner is the Christian released from his earthly tabernacle, but he is present with the Lord. A place of purgatory to purify our souls, and fit them for the enjoyment of the pure and unspotted pleasures that are above, is only an invention of man, calculated to promote and advance the power of the priest, and to accumulate wealth and riches in the Popish church. We must at death be either immediately sentenced to everlasting burnings, or received into everlasting felicity. But in the state of separation that will ensue at death, there cannot be a complete enjoyment of what Christ has purchased and promised. The body is mouldering in the grave, reduced to its original dust, inanimate and therefore insensible and inactive. The complete possession of this crown will be reserved therefore to that day: that day when Christ the judge will appear, that day when he will raise the body that has lain so long inactive, call all before his judgement seat, join every spirit to its respective body, and place body and spirit thus reunited in an unchangeable state, of misery or happiness. What a day will this be! A day big with terror and triumph! A day full of solemnity! The judge shall come arrayed in all his glory: in his own and in his father's glory, accompanied with a numerous retinue of angels and saints, Dan. vii. 10. " Thousands of thousands will minister unto him, and ten " thousand times ten thousand will stand before him: the " judgement will be set and the books be opened." The heavens dissolving, and the elements melting with fervent heat. All nature trembling at his presence! What a striking scene! " The Lord himself shall descend from heaven with a shout, " with a voice of the archangel, and with the trump of " God, and the dead in Christ shall rise first; then we " which are alive and remain, shall be caught up together " with them in the clouds, to meet the Lord in the air; " and so shall we ever be with the Lord," 1 Thess. iv. 16. 17. Then will the glorious morning of the resurrection appear, when the saints shall be raised; their bodies, which have lain so long in the grave, and been scattered into ten thousand particles of dust, will awake; appear under different qualities, put on glorious forms, after the fashion of Christ's glorious body, and be fitted for the highest enjoyments in the heavenly world. The saints, the apostles tell us, shall be raised first, afterwards the wicked; every body shall be raised, even the same body: with these eyes shall we see God, and with these ears hear the sentence. Oh glorious, yet awful day! What inconceivable crowds must attend the judge in the solemn transactions of it! See infidels starting at the view, saints rejoicing; some filled with fear and confusion, others with unspeakable joy and triumph. Jesus has already made his first appearance; this was to purchase salvation for his people: his second will be to finish it, when he will appear without sin, in all the pomp and splendour of the most exalted character. And now is the time that he will make up his jewels; now will he own and acknowledge his faithful warriors, those that have laboured in his service, have fought the good fight, finished their course, and kept the faith; now will he set the crown of glory which he has purchased upon their heads. Behold them rising therefore from the dust: see this corruption inheriting incorruption; this mortal putting on immortality, and Jesus a smiling Saviour welcoming them into his glorious kingdom, and making them eternally happy both in soul and body. " When he who is our life shall appear, " then shall we also appear with him in glory," Col. iii. 4. We now come,

4. To consider the persons to whom this crown shall be given. "To all those who love his appearing." The apostle was one of that happy number. When the great Redeemer shall stand at the latter day upon the earth; he, the apostle, shall appear, and shall receive from the hands of his divine master this glorious crown. " Henceforth there is " laid up for me." But is he the only person whom Christ will honour with such a gift? No, " and not to me only; but " unto all them also that love his appearing." This is the character of all those whom Christ the judge will honour in that great day. They love his appearing, for then every enemy will be vanquished. Satan the roaring lion will torment the people of God no more; sin that secret destroyer shall cease for ever. The door of the bottomless pit will be eternally shut, and no more shall the Christian stand in fear of its terrors. Death shall then be swallowed up in victory, and no longer confine the body: in short, every enemy shall be fully vanquished. Again, then the Christian's salvation will be perfected. Body and soul be again united,

and both fitted to dwell with the glorious Redeemer, and to ferve him eternally. And laftly, then Chrift the mediator will be glorified. Then will he appear in all his majefty and glory, and be admired by all his faints, whilft finners, who here blafphemed his name, will tremble before him. On thefe accounts Chrift's Redeemed people love his appearing, long after, and wait for it; and this is the character of all thofe upon whom the judge will beftow this amiable crown It was doubtlefs a pleafing thought to the apoftle Paul, that he was not the only perfon who fhould partake of the honours of the laft day. He would not be alone. Every real believer is willing that others fhould be faved and triumph in the enjoyment of an everlafting crown as well as himfelf, the real Chriftian is not like the cruel mifer, who would willingly grafp all to himfelf, and be unconcerned at others ruin, fo he did but profper. The gofpel will not allow fuch a fpirit. It forms us into a moft generous temper, gives us a real love to others, and a true pleafure at the confideration of their falvation as well as our own. Though the flock of our Redeemer appears but fmall when we view it in this imperfect ftate; yet thofe that love Chrift's appearing will make up a glorious number, in that day when he fhall appear with the whole train of his ranfomed people, the general affembly and church of the firft born, who fhall all appear with him and add to the glory, happinefs, and joy of the day, Thus we have confidered what this crown is, &c We have only a few words to add concerning the frame of the apoftle under fo amiable a view. I have fought, &c. How amiable was his frame? How glorious his profpects! He was not terrified either by looking back or looking forward; but triumphed when he was going to bid all things here an everlafting farewel. And how could he but triumph? Had he his evidences of an intereft in the divine favour clear? Had he fuch a vaft, fuch a glorious profpect before him? Could he look forward to the time of Chrift's appearance, and fee the triumphs of that day and a perfonal intereft in them? Oh what could intimidate him? What wanted he more? Was not this enough? Yes, behold he is fatisfied, he is willing to die; ready to part with all earthly things, life, reputation and all: he was willing to give up all fo long as he was happily affured of a glorious crown. He had now nothing to difcourage or affright him He had now no more complaints to make; nothing to fear: death loft all its terror; he could triumph over it, and boldly face eternity, fecure of his Redeemer's love. Was this the frame of all God's people; how happy, how pleafant would it be to die? Then we fhould hear of nothing from the Chriftian's mouth but triumphant fongs. "O " death where is thy fting?" &c. But fuch a frame at death is not abfolutely neceffary to falvation, we may go fafe to a better world, and not be certain of it. It is abfolutely neceffary indeed to our dying comfortably, though it is not to our dying fafely, a want of fuch a frame at death may occafion the moft melancholy fears, fill the Chriftian with the greateft diftrefs; but he is ftill united to Chrift, and fhall be fafely conducted to the regions of bleffednefs. As fuch a frame then is not abfolutely neceffary, fo God does not always give it to his people. We often fee the Chriftian at death under the preffure of doubts and fears. Sometimes not fully certain; fometimes having but little hope; yet all get fafe to a glorious world. A comfortable affurance of an intereft in Jefus is a bleffing which God gives to fome and withholds from others, juft as he fees to be moft for his own glory. In times of public perfecution when his people fall martyrs to his caufe, he generally favours them with the glorious profpects of a better world to fupport and comfort them under their important trials. This was the cafe with the apoftle Paul: he was going to be facrificed for Chrift, therefore his mafter kindly fupported him and enabled him to rejoice in death. But in times of general profperity, with the church; Chriftians are not fo much favoured with thefe extraordinary comforts either in life or death. Yet God does not obferve one conftant and invariable method; he is pleafed to diftinguifh fome of his children by the light of his countenance, and to make their dying hours pleafant and comfortable. And it muft be acknowledged to be a defirable and important bleffing. Death cannot but appear melancholy and awful to thofe who are under an uncertainty about their everlafting ftate. What feafon more folemn, on this fide the grave! What fpectacle more awful, than a perfon juft entering on eternity, and not knowing whither he is going! Impreffed with a deep sense of the worth of his immortal soul, the awful majesty of that God he is going to appear before, and with his evidences all dark; Oh it is impossible to conceive the confusion the soul is in at the awful view, he would willingly be all submission to God, but yet he cannot bear the thought of launching forth in such an uncertainty. How necessary is it therefore for our comfort that we enjoy God in death! Besides it is a glorious confirmation of the Christian religion: when a Christian looks upon death with an undaunted firmness of mind, and cheerfully parts with all present enjoyments to go to God; it is a clear and abundant evidence of the reality, excellency, and glory of Christianity, strengthens the faith of others, and encourages them to continue in the service of their Redeemer, in hopes of a happy immortality. On these accounts it appears to be our duty as well as our interest earnestly to seek, and importunately desire and labour after such a frame as this, when we leave the stage of life. Yet remember we are not to look upon it as absolutely necessary or to be distressed and discouraged on the want of such a favour, but ought to comfort ourselves with the consideration of the unchangeableness of God, the stability of his promises, the suitableness and all-sufficiency of Jesus Christ, and that those who are united to him, and depend upon him shall be glorified and saved by him, whatever be the dying frame. This subject is capable of particular improvement by many useful reflections, such as,—The wisdom of those persons who make it their chief concern to seek this crown. The way in which sinners are directed to seek it, viz. by the righteousness of Christ, which gives the title; and in a way of righteousness, which gives the fitness. How amazing it is, the solemn transactions of the last day have no greater impression and influence upon us. As also the importance of the duty of self-examination, what prospect we have of obtaining this crown, &c. But leaving these things to private meditation, I shall close the subject with one general remark, viz. Hence we see the excellency of the Christian religion, and what encouragement we have to believe and maintain it under all difficulties! Amidst the doubts that may arise in our minds, and the discouragements we may meet with, let us suppose ourselves near the dying bed of a triumphant saint, or view the apostle's frame in the last moments of his life, and we shall soon be convinced of the reality and excellency of the Christian religion, and be encouraged to keep up our confidence in Christ, and our hope of eternal life. The Christian religion is not a fancy; it is not an imaginary dream, however difficult it may be for us to comprehend it. It is a glorious reality; for it supports the soul under its greatest difficulties fortifies the mind against all discouragements, and when every thing else fails; when nature is dissolving, and time and all things disappearing, it then sweetly calms the mind, frees the soul from every fear, and fills him with the highest satisfaction. What season more important than the hour of death? Every thing now conspires to fill the soul with gloom and melancholy, nay with the greatest surprise and consternation; all his riches and worldly honours, are now going to be no more, he is taking his last and everlasting farewel of all earthly things; and was he to be annihilated, it would be nothing: but he must not cease to exist, he is going into an unknown world: he has something within that forbodes something awful. Conscience tells him that he is going before the bar of God to be examined, and there to receive a sentence of everlasting life, or everlasting condemnation: he is going amongst innumerable spirits as yet quite unknown, and to have his dwelling fixed for ever either with devils or saints. What can be more awful than such a view as this! Must not the soul shudder at such a vast and important prospect? Behold him just ready to launch forth, and nothing here to yield him the least support. If he looks back upon his former enjoyments, they give him not the least satisfaction: does he view his friends weeping around him? This instead of cheering him, rather adds to his confusion; in short, every thing looks gloomy, and contributes to render death awful and solemn: but behold in this critical moment, the gospel soon changes the scene, brightens the Christian's prospects, enables him with pleasure to bid all below farewel, and to enter triumphantly the regions of immortality. Death loses all its terror, and whatever awful surprise filled his mind before, now with the sweetest compofure he talks of eternity, the bar of God, and unembodied spirits, and longs for death to make the experiment. How glorious, how excellent then must that religion be, that thus comforts and cheers a dying Chriftian. Is this a fancy, a dream? No, it is an undoubted reality, and receives a noble teftimony from all thofe who leave this world in the comfortable expectation of a better. The Lord grant we may all thus clofe our eyes on time, and open them on eternity!

LOVE TO AN UNSEEN SAVIOUR.

1 Pet. i. 8.

Whom having not seen, ye love; in whom, though now ye see him not, yet believing, ye rejoice with joy unspeakable and full of glory.

THE love of Chrift is a glorious theme to entertain our minds, a quickening fubject to inflame our affections, being attended with the moſt defirable fruits and effects. How aftoniſhing is it, that any ſhould caſt contempt upon that which angels admire and adore ? Wonders far exceeding the reach of finite mortals appear in the fubject of redemption, deferving our utmoſt attention and calling for our higheſt praiſes. Strange that man ſhould be fo ſtupid and loſt to all fenfe of gratitude as to contemn the amazing heights, and depths, and breadths, and lengths of the love of God ! Do we not wonder at the ſtrange phenomena and appearances of nature ? And ſhall we not obferve the more glorious and ſtriking difplays of divine grace in the works of redemption by Jefus Chriſt ? Shall we honour an earthly benefactor, a fellow mortal, who loves us and gives us all the evidences of the moſt fincere and friendly eſteem, and ſhall we not much more love and honour him, who laid down his life for us, and who is the author of eternal falvation to our fouls? The perfons to whom the apoftle wrote were diftinguifhed by their love of Chrift and their faith in him, and were worthy of commendation on this account. As to their outward circumftances they were ftrangers, fcattered about in various parts; they were purfued and hunted like partridges upon the mountains, and fuffered a variety of perfecutions and reproaches for the fake of Chrift. Peter labours to encourage them by the profpect of that glorious inheritance they had a lively hope of, and by the confideration of their perfeverance through the mighty power of God, verfe 3, 4, 5. This they ought to look to, as it would have a peculiar tendency to ftrengthen their minds under every difficulty, reconcile them to every difpenfation, and enable them to bear every affliction with a becoming fortitude and refolution of foul. He told them of the neceffity there was for their prefent trials, that infinite wifdom abundantly appeared therein, as they were defigned to promote the glory of God and their own advantage; the excellency of the Chriftian religion, being greatly confirmed, and their grace tried and improved, verfe 6, 7. Whom having not feen; fays the apoftle, ye love, &c. Thefe Jews had not feen Jefus, confequently they were not at Jerufalem at the feaft of the paffover, elfe they muft have feen Jefus perfonally; but probably they might be there on the day of Pentecoft when under Peter's fermon fo many were converted: however it was as to this, they had not feen Chrift bodily, but they had heard of him, and his word had melted their hearts, they faw him fo diftinctly by the eye of faith, as to be abfolutely certain all was genuine that was reported of him, and as to fill their fouls with the warmeft love to him, and a joy unfpeakable and full of glory. This was not only their cafe, but it is the cafe with every Chriftian, thofe who live at the utmoft diftance from the time in which Chrift appeared upon earth. It is their diftinguifhing character: it is effential to their very being. Love is here put before faith, whereas it is in reality the effect of faith, the genuine and ripe fruit of it. Thefe words prefent us with three things.

 I. The diftinguifhing character of real Chriftians, they believe on him whom they have not feen.

II. The genuine effect of true faith, a spiritual and ardent love to an unseen saviour.

III. The happy consequence of such a faith in, and love to the saviour, it gives the soul joys unspeakable and full of glory. And oh that we may see the glorious excellencies of the great Redeemer, that we may believe in him, and find our souls filled with the most cordial esteem for him, and experience that joy that must necessarily arise from a view of his various characters and offices, and a comfortable persuasion of our interest in him! But the only topic I have singled out, and shall attempt to discourse on, from this text, is,

The believer's love to an unseen saviour.

To produce in us a love to Christ, it is not necessary that we should see him with our bodily eyes, a few persons enjoyed that privilege the little time he was on earth, our apostle was one of them, and this privilege every Christian will enjoy in the last great day. " Behold he cometh with " clouds, and every eye shall see him," Rev. i. 7. Hence says holy Job, " I know that my Redeemer liveth, and " that he shall stand at the latter day upon the earth, and " though after my skin, worms destroy this body, yet in " my flesh shall I see God, whom I shall see for myself, and " mine eyes shall behold and not another," Job, xix. 25, 26. 27. But those who actually saw Jesus and loved him, are comparatively few to those who love him unseen. This is no way necessary to form in the breast this amiable grace: his word, accompanied by his spirit, is every way sufficient to do it, and is the great spring of such warm desires after, and such an affectionate esteem for Jesus Christ. Therefore we find persons in every age possessed of this most amiable grace. This love to Christ consists in entertaining the highest and most honourable thoughts of him, warm desires and strong affection to him: he is the soul's all in all: and all his desires, affections and thoughts, center in him. To make this fully appear, and to evince that the Christian acts the most rational part herein, let us inquire into three things.

1. What are the principal properties of the Christian's love to an unseen saviour.

2. What are the grounds, and reasons of such a love to him.

3. Mention a few things, which will evince the reasonableness of the Christian's love to an unseen Saviour.

I. We are to inquire into the properties of this love. And it has all the excellent properties that are necessary to make it appear amiable, and to shew how much the Christian is devoted to Christ. For it is sincere and hearty.—It is universal or has respect to Christ in all his characters, and titles.—It is superlative, it is constant, and everlasting.—

1. It is sincere and hearty. None questions its reality but the soul himself—except in public falls, and in a long course of backslidings. David gave no evidence of his love to Christ, when he fell so criminally, and so publicly with Bathsheba, and lay so long secure. But when he came to himself, his bitter lamentations for his sin, abundantly manifested his hatred of it, and his real love to God. We must not judge of ourselves nor of others, by one single act in life, but by the habitual frame of a person, and the general bent and tenor in his behaviour. A real concern of mind for offending a friend, is a sign that we esteem him. And it is so here: the Christian loves Christ, yet he sometimes dishonours him; but is it not matter of his deepest humiliation that he should be so unkind and ungrateful; Lord, says he, have I thus offended thee? Oh why was I not more watchful? What! Indulge sin, sin which is so odious to my dearest Redeemer! Sin which has wounded him so bitterly, and tends to open his wounds afresh! Have I indulged sin? Have I been so inconsiderate and ungrateful? Lord, I mourn in dust and ashes before thee. I abhor myself: it is my greatest concern that I have offended thee, and Oh that I could find my soul more humbled: Oh be not angry with me, turn not away thy countenance, enter not into judgement with me: I cannot bear to think that I have provoked thee. Thus the Christian laments over his sins, is affraid he has provoked Christ to abandon him, and therefore is restless until he has cast himself prostrate before him, and given up himself afresh unto him. How often has it been the case with your souls, Christians, though you are so often questioning your love to the great Redeemer? Have you not often mourned in secret before him over your backslidings, your coldness to him, your unfruitfulness and other things by which you have been afraid, you have provoked him? When you have approached his

table, and there remembered his love, has not a remembrance of your sins at the same time filled you with bitterness? And have you not deeply lamented before him, your ingratitude to him? All this was an evidence that you sincerely loved him. Peter, when he was put to the trial, fell most shamefully, and who would have thought that the person that was denying him with oaths and imprecations really loved him? And yet he did; as by his repentance he made abundantly evident, for we read that, " he went out " and wept bitterly," Luke xxii. 62. Again, appealing to God for our love to him, shews the sincerity of it. Peter therefore gave another sure evidence of his love to Christ; our Lord was pleased to interrogate him three times, that he might as often publicly declare his love to him. " Si-" mon, son of Jonas, lovest thou me more than these?" Peter, sensible of his late fall and of his weakness, did not say, yea Lord I do love thee more than these: he did not assert that his love was stronger than others: but he appealed to him for the sincerity of it. " Lord thou knowest " that I love thee:" nay, when the question was put to him the third time; he adds, " Lord thou knowest all " things," I appeal to thee for the reality of my love; thou must know for nothing is concealed from thee: thine eye surveys all things. Thou art perfectly acquainted with the secrets of every heart, and canst easily distinguish between hypocrisy and sincerity: thou therefore knowest Lord the real frame of my soul, and the situation of my heart, better than I know myself; speak then Lord; am I an hypocrite? If I am, let me be exposed; but thou knowest that I love thee sincerely, John xxi. 15, &c. You Christians perhaps cannot at all times speak so positively as this apostle did, being afraid your hearts deceive you. But so far as you know your own hearts, you can make the appeal: however you can say, Lord, thou knowest that we desire to love thee; we would not deceive ourselves, nor mock thee, we would have our hearts more fixed upon, and filled with love to thee. This then is a comfortable evidence of the reality and sincerity of your love. Another evidence of sincere love to Christ is the souls mourning after him, and his thinking upon him. We are ready to be uneasy in the absence of persons we esteem, and to have our thoughts frequently upon them. Thus it is in the present case, the humble soul mourns after an absent Jesus, goes from one duty to another seeking his face, and inquiring and longing after him. Oh what pain it oftentimes gives the soul that he cannot see Jesus? And what satisfaction and joy when he is enabled to see his interest in him? What sweet intercourse? The soul sits under his shadow with abundance of delight, views his various perfections, excellencies and characters with pleasure, and rejoices in him as his all. This is illustrated in the conduct of the spouse, Cant. iii. 1, &c. And is it not your case, Christians? Your many fears, doubts, secret mournings, and longings, make it evident, and therefore you are no hypocrites. Your love is not nominal, it is sincere, it is hearty.

II. This love is universal, or it has respect unto Christ in all his characters and titles. When the spouse had enumerated various of the beauties and excellencies of Christ, she breaks out into an adoration of him as every where full of glory: "yea he is altogether lovely!" Cant. v. 16. What need I go any further in a description of him? He is all over amiable and glorious; in whatever character I view him, I find the strongest affection for and desires after him. Thus it is with the Christian, Jesus appears lovely in every character, in every title which he bears. The sinner bears no love to Jesus in any character; he sees no beauty in him: thus it is represented in Cant v. ix. Strangers to Christ ask the Christian why his affections are so much set upon Jesus: what is your beloved more than another's beloved? Is there any beauty in him more than in other objects, does he possess any peculiar and distinguishing excellency? We can see nothing desirable in him, in any of his characters; and therefore cannot find any esteem for him. No, " we will " not have this man to reign over us. We hate his government, we love not that he should bear the sway, or exercise an authority in our souls. " Depart from us for we " desire not the knowledge of thy ways." The sinner hates Jesus Christ: what contempt therefore does he cast upon him in his person, his righteousness, and all his characters? Some profess a regard to Christ in one character, but not in all, they would be willing to share in the blessings of his priesthood, but will not submit to his yoke, nor take up their cross and follow him. Such is not the Christian; he loves Christ in all that he is, and in all that he has.

As the great prophet he efteems him, adores him in that character, and looks to him for all faving knowledge. As a prieft, the great High Prieft, he honours him, and loves him; values and efteems his righteoufnefs, rejoices in his facrifice, and has the ftrongeft regard for his advocacy and interceffion: and as the king and lord of his people they love him, love his rule and government, think themfelves fafe under his protection, and would have their hearts more in obedience and fubjection to him. As God over all bleffed for evermore they love him; entertain the moft honourable thoughts of him, and caft their whole fouls upon him as the glorious foundation of their hopes of eternal life. Jefus! In whatever character I view him, fays the Chriftian, he is amiable and lovely: all his characters are moft important: fee how he is defcribed, "as the wonderful coun"fellor, the mighty God, the everlafting father, the prince "of peace." All titles the moft glorious. Such is thy beloved, and fuch is thy friend, Oh my foul, how can I then but efteem him? I cannot but entertain the higheft and moft honourable thoughts of him. Sure he is all amiable: what excellencies belong to his perfon? How glorious his qualifications, his titles, his perfections? See him as thy friend to counfel, advife, and direct thee; as thy fhepherd to guide, watch over, and keep thee; as thy brother to love thee, as thy father to pity and preferve thee: fee him as the foundation to fupport thy hopes, as thy dayfman and furety to undertake for thee. See him as the only begotten fon of God, high in his favour and efteem; as Emmanuel, God with us, and therefore as the fon of man appearing in human nature, and fuffering and dying: fee him as the captain of falvation leading his noble warriors to the battle, encouraging them therein, and giving them the conqueft. As the fun of righteoufnefs, enlightening, warming, and quickening the fouls of his people with his cheering and reviving beams. Behold him as the great bridegroom efpoufing his people to himfelf for ever, married to them; rejoicing in and delighting over them. As the bread of life not only giving life but maintaining and fupporting it in the fouls of his children. Nay, fee him as the lion of the tribe of Judah! view him as the great judge of quick and dead, fummoning all before his fupreme tribunal, and paffing a decifive fentence upon each, and he appears amiable and lovely: in whatever character I view him, I see enough to raise my esteem of him, and cannot but be astonished that any should be blind to his excellencies, and have their hearts filled with the least enmity to him. Oh glorious Redeemer thou art all lovely: my soul with wonder and affection stands and views thy person and characters, and with delight gazes upon thy adorable excellencies. Is it possible for any to be so ignorant and stupid as to view thee with the least degree of indifference? Lord certainly it cannot be: it appears to be incredible, did not fatal experience too much shew it: but with concern I see thee despised and contemned by ignorant sinners, thee whom my soul would always love.

III. This love is superlative. It exceeds the esteem which the soul has for all other things. Christ requires the heart: he will accept of nothing less. "My son give me thine "heart." Prov. xxiii. 26. It is agreeable to the command of God. Mark xii. 30. "Thou shalt love the Lord thy "God with all thy heart, and with all thy soul, and with all "thy mind, and with all thy strength," It must be sincere, and it must engage the whole soul. The covetous man we find lays all his heart out upon his beloved idols. He can relish nothing but what is of this world. His thoughts, his affections, his heart, his hands, his time, and his all, are employed about the diligent pursuit of the riches and honours of the present state. And he has nothing for Jesus, "If any "man therefore love this world," that is, set it up as his chief idol in his heart, and pursue it as his chief happiness, "the love of the father dwelleth not in him." 1 John ii. 15. Christ must bear the sway, else your love is partial, and comes short of that which is the mark, and characteristic of a real Christian. The Christian shews that his love to Christ is superlative by his longing after him; by his concern for his own and others ingratitude to him, by his desire to honour him, and his longing after that glorious world, where he shall love and serve him with the utmost perfection. The Christian thinks upon and longs after a dear Redeemer. His thoughts are not indeed so much and so warmly fixed upon Christ as he would desire them to be, the necessary affairs of life must employ his thoughts, and they perhaps too much encumber his mind, and give him uneasiness, lest, whilst he thinks he loves Jesus, he should be deceiving him-

self, and be found to love the world before him. But this is not the case with such dejected souls. They are frequently longing after a dear Redeemer, and it is their greatest joy and happiness when they see his face; but they think themselves wretched when they cannot find him. They cannot give the world all their time and thoughts, they must frequently steal an hour to converse with whom they love. And Oh with what concern are they filled when they see or hear him dishonoured by prophane sinners, when they see the falls of those that profess a real love for him and consider their own ungenerous conduct and behaviour by which they have frequently offended him! They are labouring to honour him more, are tender of his glorious name, and concerned to bring forth the fruits of righteousness to his abundant praise, they are circumspect therefore and watchful; out of a love to Christ they love his people, and are concerned to pay a constant obedience to those commands which he has left them. And Oh how do they frequently long after that glorious world where they will be for ever freed from all sin, and be fitted for glorifying their great Redeemer in the most perfect manner! the views of heaven give a peculiar pleasure to the believing soul; because he there shall no more dishonour, offend, and provoke his dear Redeemer, but have clearer and more glorious views of his love, and make more suitable returns than he can possibly do here. All this shews his love to be superlative, notwithstanding all his fears. How careful should those be that find such a fondness for this world, lest they be found destitute of this divine and amiable Grace? He that loveth this world above Christ is not worthy of him. Nay, he himself tells us, " that who-
" soever loveth father or mother more than him, or son or
" daughter more than him, is not worthy of him." Mat. x. 37. Hard saying this, who can bear it? Not that we must hate parents and children, and such near and invaluable comforts to shew our love to Christ, nor can we in times of prosperity and peace, so well try ourselves by these things. But in times of persecution, whoever out of love and regard to parents and children disobey the commands of Christ, and turn their backs upon him; such are not his disciples We are to honour parents; but when they interfere with our allegiance to Christ, we must leave them and follow Christ, being under greater obligations to obey God than man. A time

of prosperity is a wrong time for the Christian to try his love to Christ by such marks as these; for he but seldom comes off with advantage. We hear him frequently saying I am afraid I cannot part with all things for Christ and follow him, should he call me to it : you cannot judge of this properly, though your present strength may be but small, yet when Christ calls you to trials, he will animate and support you in proportion to them. Therefore say not, your love is not right, as you give those evidences which are true and real, and suitable to the circumstances God has placed you in; so you may conclude that you really and superlatively love a dear Redeemer.

IV. This love is constant and everlasting. It is not like the esteem which we have for our fellow creatures, which frequently stops upon receiving an affront, and is often changed into resentment. Where this grace is once implanted it continues and never ceases. Grace may not be always in the same lively exercise; sometimes it appears cool and indifferent, at other times vigorous and lively; but grace will ever remain in the soul that is renewed : nothing can quench that love which the believer has to Jesus. It will abide through every difficulty, through the remains of life and be greatly improved in a future world. The believer really loves his great Redeemer when he afflicts him, as well as when he smiles upon him. When he takes the rod into his hand to chastise him for his forgetfulness and disobedience, afflicts him in the tenderest part, yet this does not alter the Christian's sentiments of his exalted Redeemer, or change his esteem into hatred : but he casts himself prostrate before him, and humbles himself at his footstool, acknowledges his guilt, and mourns that he has offended him, and provoked him to hide his face and discover his resentment. It is the peculiar property of this love, to be constant and abiding, whatever is the conduct of God towards him. Should his life be nothing but one melancholy scene of sorrows and affliction; should God take one comfort after another from him, till at last he has stripped him of all, even the dearest and most valuable, and thrown him into the most distressing circumstances; nature would indeed be ready to recoil and prompt the believer to rise in rebellion against God, charge him with cruelty and injustice, and put him upon withdrawing his affections from him, but grace teaches him a different leſſon: he humbles himſelf therefore under his mighty hand, is full of concern leſt God ſhould have entirely abandoned him, and cannot be eaſy till he ſees his ſmiles, and has ſome comfortable hope that he has not forſaken him, he may at times murmur and repine, but he quickly checks himſelf for his preſumption, and humbly adores and loves that hand that has ſo much corrected him This was the caſe with Job: his afflictions were remarkably ſore and heavy, he was deprived of children and ſubſtance; every one appeared againſt him; and his body was full of anguiſh through the melancholy diſorder that he was exerciſed with; and now was the time for the trial of his love to and eſteem of God. Did he under all this ſtill keep up the moſt honourable thoughts of God? Did he notwithſtanding all this really love him? Yes, he bleſſed the Lord in taking as well as giving, which diſcovered the higheſt love for and the moſt genuine obedience of ſoul to him. Job. i. 21. Nothing can poſſibly quench this love; nothing can hurt it: the innumerable temptations to which the Chriſtian is ſubject, the many enſnaring objects with which he is ſurrounded, all tend to leſſen his eſteem for Jeſus, and catch his affections. But he ſtands unmoved in the midſt of all; views them all with indifference when put in competition with Jeſus, and continues in his loyalty and affection; no other lords or maſters muſt have dominion over him; he loves his Saviour, and he will love him unto the end. Whatever perſecutions and diſtreſſes ariſe for the ſake of Chriſt, he is not offended like the ſtony ground hearers; he does not turn his back upon his great Redeemer; but continues the ſame eſteem both in life and death; the moſt cruel and painful death has not cauſed him to think ill of Chriſt, but his love has led him through the greateſt tortures, and made him willingly ſhed his blood for his glorious Saviour. Witneſs the martyrs who followed Chriſt unto death, and loved him ſo as to ſuffer the greateſt cruelties human art could invent and an arm of fleſh could inflict: this is that love that diſtinguiſhes the real Chriſtian from the hypocrite: if you once profeſſed to love the Redeemer but now have deſerted him; if other objects have gained all your eſteem, or the reproaches and difficulties you met with in your profeſſion of Chriſt, have cauſed you to change your thoughts of him, you never loved him in reality, and therefore are none of his followers. Thofe that continue not, but turn afide, belong not to Jefus, nor have they any intereft in him: Chrift muft always have your hearts, or elfe you will have no part in him: you that are entering upon the ways of Jefus, and find a defire after him, enquire, do you think to love him unto death? If ever you defert him, all your former profeffion will fignify nothing,: " if any man draw back my foul fhall have no pleafure in " him.". Oh that we may not be " of them that draw back " unto perdition, but of them that believe unto the faving " of the foul." This love is conftant; it is everlafting: death will not remove it, but place the foul where it will be much improved: there is no room for faith and hope, in the heavenly world, but there is for love. Faith and hope will be no more, for the object will be enjoyed; but the enjoyment will greatly increafe the Chriftian's love. Here it is but imperfect, but there it is perfect: here it is often interrupted; the heart feems too often divided between Chrift and the world; but in heaven there are no enfnaring objects to take the affections from Jefus, or cool the Chriftian's love; but the everlafting enjoyment of his Redeemer will keep it in everlafting exercife, and raife it to the higheft pitch the foul is capable of. Oh Chriftian look more to heaven and long more to be with Jefus, for it is there you can only love your Redeemer aright: there your love will have no mixture, nothing to interrupt or check it, but every circumftance poffible to heighten and encreafe it, and make you for ever happy in the exercife of it ——Thus we fee the properties of the Chriftian's love: it is fincere, it is univerfal, it is fuperlative, conftant, and everlafting. All thefe fhew the value of this grace, and how important it is: how effential it is to the real Chriftian, and therefore how neceffary it is that we make a ftrict inquiry into our own hearts whether this grace is implanted in our fouls, and has ever been brought into exercife. Who would not be willing to know that they are Chriftians indeed? Is it not a matter of the utmoft importance to have this weighty point out of difpute? Befides, as Chriftians, thofe that are called to wait upon Jefus at his table, fhould examine themfelves, and then eat of that bread and drink of that cup: let us therefore recollect what has been hinted upon this love to an unfeen Saviour; and let us examine ourfelves, left we fhould be miſtaken. The great queſtion is, do we love Chriſt? Do we love him in ſincerity? Or is our love to him only nominal? Do you love him in deed and in truth? Sinners, it is evident you love not our Lord Jeſus Chriſt, for you love ſin: you hate his yoke, you cannot part with your beloved Dalilahs; you fondly hug them in your boſoms, and will not renounce them for Jeſus and ſalvation. But is this your caſe ye that mourn in ſecret, leſt you ſhould be but almoſt Chriſtians? Is this your character, ye that thirſt after Chriſt at his table? No, ye love our Lord Jeſus Chriſt, and ye ſhew it by renouncing your ſins, mourning over them, and ſtriving againſt them. Do you not long after Chriſt, think upon and rejoice in him? All this then ſhews the ſincerity and reality of your love to him; and is not your love univerſal? Do you not take Chriſt in all his characters? Is he not precious to you in every title? As prophet, as prieſt, and king, and do you not ſubmit to him in every character? Or at leaſt deſire and aim to do ſo? Again, is your love to him ſuperlative? Do you love him with all your hearts? &c.— The ſinner prefers others to him, but the believer cheerfully parts with every thing, every luſt, every idol, every vain and ſinful delight for him, and when called to part with the world, wife, children and ſubſtance, he leaves all and follows Chriſt through perſecutions, and fiery trials.

In fine, is your love conſtant and abiding? Do you continue ſteadfaſt and unmoved? Or has it been only a ſudden flaſh of affection like the Jews, Hoſanna to the ſon of David, and then crucify him? Thus it is neceſſary to inquire how our affections ſtand: "For they that love not " our Lord Jeſus Chriſt, let them be anathema maranatha." 1 Cor. xvi. 22. This is the character of every real Chriſtian, to love Chriſt. Oh that this grace may be implanted in each of our ſouls, that we may grow more and more into the likeneſs of Chriſt, may find his love increaſing ours, and may at laſt be tranſlated into that glorious world, where we ſhall love and praiſe him for ever and ever. We are now,

II. To inquire into the grounds and reaſons why the Chriſtian loves an unſeen Jeſus. Love to one another is generally owing to three things,—either a conſideration of ſome peculiar amiableneſs and excellency a fellow creature poſſeſſes, or ſome near relation which we ſtand in to them, or elſe ſome peculiar obligations we are under from their kind and endearing behaviour to us, and the favours they have conferred upon us. From ſome of theſe, love to one another takes its riſe, and they all appear as reaſons why the Chriſtian loves an unſeen Saviour. Though he has not ſeen him perſonally, yet he has heard of his excellencies, and has ſeen by an eye of faith his beauty and glory. He ſtands in the neareſt relation to him, and has received the greateſt favours from him; all which ſhew the foundation there is laid for the greateſt admiration and eſteem, and how ungratefully the Chriſtian would act, as well as unſuitably to his character, was he not to love Jeſus Chriſt. But particularly,

1. The Chriſtian loves an unſeen Jeſus, becauſe of the excellencies which he poſſeſſes. Whatever excellency is in the creature may be found in the higheſt perfection in Jeſus Chriſt, for he inherits all true perfection: creatures' glories are all imperfect, there are innumerable deficiencies, they are chargeable with, innumerable foibles that caſt a ſhade upon their excellencies, that they at times can ſcarce appear. But there is no mixture in Jeſus: his excellencies always ſhine with infinite luſtre, and are ever apparent to attract our eſteem, and raiſe our admiration. Wiſdom and knowledge, faithfulneſs and prudence, and the inward ornaments of the mind, humility, meekneſs and the like; theſe are what principally recommend us one to another, and engage our eſteem. But what are theſe to thoſe ſhining excellencies that are in Jeſus, and juſtly render him a ſuitable object of our eſteem? Behold him poſſeſſed of every divine qualification: As to wiſdom and knowledge, who can exceed him? He knows all the various caſes of his people, what their temptations, difficulties, and diſeaſes are; and what applications to make for their removal: "he has all treaſures of wiſdom " and knowledge," whereby he is able to govern every thing wiſely, to conduct every circumſtance ſo as to prevent the deſigns of Satan from taking effect, and to promote his own glory and the good of his people. Col. ii. 3. He is faithful and juſt in the execution of his threatenings, and in the fulfilment of his promiſes: his name is therefore emphatically ſtyled "faithful and true," Rev. xix. 11. being faithful in the management of every concern that is committed to him,

whether by his father or by his people. He is almighty and powerful, able to help in the moſt diſtreſſing caſe, to ſupport under, and to deliver out of the moſt deplorable circumſtances. His name is therefore " mighty to ſave." If. lxiii 1 He is unchangeable and everlaſting, " the ſame yeſterday, to-" day, and for ever;" he never alters his purpoſes nor changes his mind, Heb. xiii. 8. He is in ſhort poſſeſſed of a fulneſs of excellencies; " in him it hath pleaſed the Fa-" ther that all fulneſs ſhould dwell," Col. i. 19. He is kind and condeſcending, loving and compaſſionate, he is friendly and eaſy of acceſs, he is conſiderate and bountiful, meek and humble. " He is the only begotten of the Father, full " of grace and truth," John i. 14. Nay, he poſſeſſes every divine excellency, being " God over all bleſſed for ever-" more," Rom. ix. 5. Who then ſhall not adore ſuch excellencies? Certainly he that poſſeſſes them is a worthy object of our eſteem. What is there that can appear more amiable and lovely? It is indeed one thing to profeſs to believe thoſe excellencies in Chriſt, another to have a ſuitable ſenſe of them; ſuch a ſenſe as draws the admiration and affection of the ſoul. We may hear of all the excellencies of Jeſus, and yet find no real love to him: this is too frequently the caſe. The ſinner hears and gives his aſſent, but for want of a real ſpiritual view, his heart remains hardened, and he finds no workings of affection. But this is not your caſe, Chriſtians. Your underſtandings were once darkneſs, but now are they light in the Lord. You have had a ſpiritual diſcerning, by which you have ſeen the excellency and amiableneſs of Jeſus, and found your deſires drawn out after him. A view of his glory and ſuitableneſs has engaged your eſteem, and filled you with the moſt honourable thoughts of him. Oh how can I but love him, ſays the believer? Not love Jeſus! One ſo amiable, ſo ſuitable, ſo excellent and glorious! I cannot but adore his name, and admire his beauty; the whole creation is nothing when compared with him; he is fairer than all the children of men: and how amazing is it that my ſoul is no more employed in adoring his excellencies? Once I was ignorant, a ſtranger to every beauty; but now I cannot view Jeſus in any character in which he is repreſented, but I ſee a glory and comelineſs in him: and Oh ſtupid creatures that are not raiſed with the deſcriptions of his perſon, his righteouſneſs, his fulneſs, and his infinite excellencies!

2. The Chriſtian loves an unſeen Saviour becauſe of the relation which he ſtands in to him. This occaſions that love and eſteem oftentimes which we have one for another: the ties of nature and relation are ſtrong arguments and inducements to affection and eſteem; a mother muſt turn monſter if ſhe does not love her babe; and ſo muſt a child if he does not love and honour his parent: a huſband muſt act in direct oppoſition to his character, if he love not his wife, and a wife muſt be guilty of the ſame, if ſhe can remain void of affection to her huſband: children of the ſame family ought not to diſagree, but the tendereſt love and affection ſhould ſpread and be ever diffuſed. All theſe characters and relations lay a juſt foundation for the greateſt eſteem, and call for the tendereſt affection. And thus if we take a view of the relations which Chriſt and believers ſtand in to one another, we ſhall no longer wonder at the love which the Chriſtian has for Jeſus. Chriſt is repreſented as a bridegroom, as the huſband; and his people as the bride, (or the wife: the relation is as real as that of huſband and wife, and the greateſt advantages flow from it: as a bridegroom therefore Chriſt is ſaid to rejoice over his bride, and to love his ſpouſe; and muſt we not ſuppoſe the ſame in the church? The ſame affectionate temper, and the kindeſt thoughts of the unſeen Jeſus? The relation lays a foundation for the moſt cordial reſpect and eſteem, and the character which is given the church abundantly and clearly ſhows that her warmeſt affections are fixed upon the great Redeemer. When the Chriſtian comes to conſider that Jeſus has eſpouſed him unto himſelf for ever, and that he has taken the character of an huſband, his ſoul is full of the moſt cordial eſteem, and he rejoices in and longs after him, is filled with a tender concern for his honour, and bears a laſting reſpect to his glorious name. Again, Chriſt and the Chriſtian ſtand related as father and ſon: as it is neceſſary to act conſiſtently with that relation, that a child ſhould love his parent; ſo it is equally neceſſary that Chriſtians ſhould love Jeſus; Jeſus their compaſſionate father, who poſſeſſes all the kind affections of the moſt indulgent parent, and that in the utmoſt perfection. As a father he pities, he loves, he corrects, but

with affection; he instructs and advises; he longs, he yearns over his people: is afflicted in all their afflictions, and carries them ever upon his heart: as children therefore they are bound to love, to honour, and highly to esteem him; to entertain the most exalted thoughts of him; and to behave with the utmost respect to him. Again, Christ and his people are brethren: he took flesh and blood, and dwelt in human nature; so that he is one with us, flesh of our flesh, and bone of our bone. In such a relation how amiable must he appear to the Christian? As a brother he entertains the highest respect, lives in constant harmony, and is not willing to offend or grieve him. Again, Christ and his people are related as friends: he calls them frequently so, John xv. 14, 15. And he acts a most friendly part to them by administering to their necessities, comforting them, and sympathizing with them under all their afflictions: as friends therefore they must on their part respect, honour, and esteem him, bear a tender concern for his glorious name, and ever discover a sincere regard to his interest and kingdom. There are various other relations in which Christ and his people stand to one another, to fill up which there must be a constant, sincere and mutual love; but these few hints are sufficient to shew us, why Christians love an unseen Jesus.

3. The Christian is under the greatest obligations to Jesus for the wonders of his free and unmerited love to him: and no wonder then that he loves him though unseen. Where a person superior to us in outward circumstances, appears of a truly humane, generous and beneficent temper, condescends to the lowest offices in life to promote our advantage, calls us by the most affectionate titles, confers the highest favours upon us, and is continually studying our interest; such a person was he to be found amongst us, could not but be greatly valued and esteemed. It would discover the utmost ingratitude, to slight or despise him: such, nay an infinitely greater friend is Jesus to the Christian; his love exceeds all human compassion, it is infinitely great and glorious, and therefore cannot but raise the admiration of the humble soul; and engage his esteem. This brings us to the third general, namely,

III. To mention a few particulars which may serve to evince the reasonableness of the Christian's love to an unseen faviour. 1. Let us view the infinite glory of his perfon. 2. The amazing greatnefs of his condefcention for his people's advantage. 3. The bleffings which he has conferred upon the Chriftian. 4. The endearing titles he has given him. 5. The care he continually takes of him, and the glory he has prepared and will fecure for him. And 6. The freenefs of this love.

1. Let us view the infinite glory of the perfon of Chrift. A perfon of eminent rank greatly recommends himfelf to the efteem of his fellow-creatures, when he appears affable and friendly, and takes notice of thofe that are much inferior to him : whilft perfons of a haughty and infolent behaviour, are only fit objects of contempt, and are generally defpifed notwithftanding all their grandeur. And if it is fo amiable in an imperfect mortal to take notice of thofe who are below him ; how much more amiable muft it be in Jefus the fon of God, to take notice of thofe who are fo much beneath his notice ? Oh that every proud and haughty temper was moulded after the amiable temper of Jefus ! Behold him exalted above all created beings ; fee him poffeffed of every poffible excellency ; view him in dignity above angels and archangels, receiving all divine honours, from thofe glorious and exalted fpirits, and yet kindly taking notice of finful polluted creatures, creatures at fuch a diftance from him, and fo much beneath his regards, and unworthy of his care ! What amazing condefcention is this in the high and lofty one that inhabits eternity ? How glorious does he appear ? It cannot but draw the efteem of the Chriftian, when he fits down and views the dignity of the fon of God, and yet the notice which he is pleafed to take of fuch guilty polluted creatures as we. How can I but love an unfeen faviour, fays he ? Would it not appear the higheft ingratitude to take no notice of the kindnefs of thofe of fuperior rank and character amongft ourfelves ? And is it not more ungrateful to be infenfible of the notice which Jefus the mighty God takes of us ? Lord I will, nay, I cannot but love thee : what, thou fo glorious, fo happy in the bofom of thy father, and in the enjoyment of thine own excellencies, yet doft thou take notice of fuch a polluted wretch ! Haft thou notwithftanding thy greatnefs, thy glory in the midft of furrounding angels ; haft thou yet been pleafed to fet thy love upon fuch a poor polluted worm as me ? What honour is this thou haft con-

ferred upon me? Lord, I will ever love thee, I will ever adore thine infinite goodnefs; thy name fhall be ever precious to my foul, and I will give thee my whole heart.

2. The aftonifhing humiliation of Jefus Chrift, in human nature, is a moft powerful attractive to the Chriftian, and cannot but raife his efteem. To take the leaft notice of fuch unworthy creatures as we, is amazing condefcention, how much more when we confider what Jefus has done? He has done what angels wonder at, all heaven ftands aftonifhed; and yet finful man can hear and remain unmoved! He can hear the reprefentation without feeling one tender affection move; he can hear and yet be hardened; how wonderful that the ftones break not their native filence, and upbraid us with ingratitude! Do you wonder, finners, that the Chriftian difcovers fo tender an affection for Chrift? It is rather wonderful, it is abundantly more fo, that your hearts are fo much hardened againft him, when there is every thing that tends to raife your admiration, and engage your affection. Love is a powerful incentive to love: and Oh view the amazing love of Jefus Chrift in his humiliation, and then confider what returns fuch love requires. See him poffeffed of infinite excellencies and perfections, and yet difrobing himfelf of his glory, and coming in the likenefs of finful flefh! " Behold he who was in the form of God, " and thought it no robbery to be equal with God, took " upon him the form of a fervant, and was found in " fafhion as a man, and became obedient unto death, even " the death of the crofs!" Such condefcention as this is indeed aftonifhing; this is fomething the moft wonderful and amazing that was ever tranfacted. " Oh, great is the " myftery of godlinefs, God manifefted in the flefh," 1 Tim. iii. 16 And is not this enough to engage our warmeft affections? Was a fellow creature to lay down his life, and freely facrifice himfelf for our advantage, would it not be enough to render his memory ever precious to us? And fhould it not be much more the cafe here? Afk not the Chriftian why he loves an unfeen Jefus. It is apparent to all: he muft be the moft hardened creature that can refift the influence of fuch aftonifhing love, and not find his breaft filled with the moft honourable and exalted thoughts of him. It is ftrange, fays the Chriftian, if I fhould not love Jefus; Jefus, that kind, that generous friend, that wonder of an-

gels, who veiled his glory in a human form, stooped so low as to appear in flesh, in circumstances of poverty, meanness, and affliction, enduring the daring insolence and contradiction of prophane sinners, the buffetings of devils, and submitted to a most painful and ignominious death, even the death of the cross. I must love that dear name; I must honour his person, and give him my whole heart and mind, and soul, and strength: oh how unspeakably great my obligations? Did the mighty God appear in the character of a servant, did he submit to the law, and endure the greatest sufferings for my sake? Oh most ungrateful wretch, if I did not love him! The heavens and the earth would be as much astonished at my ingratitude, as they are at the greatness of his love. Lord, may it never be said that I despise thee: no; thy love has won all my soul. When I view it, especially under the kind influences of thy spirit, it appears so glorious, that I cannot possibly withstand it; it melts my soul, raises my admiration, wins my affections, curbs every rising thought against thy person and government, and makes me willing to be entirely thine. Highly reasonable is it, I should be wholly and ever thine.

3. The blessings which Jesus has conferred upon the Christian, fill him with the warmest love to him. Herein is his love abundantly manifested. He came into this lower world to purchase the most valuable and important blessings, and he accordingly bestows them on the Christian: this consideration cannot but engage the soul to love him with the strongest affection. How winning is the kindness of our fellow mortals? When we receive favours, especially some extraordinary tokens of esteem, we should be reckoned the most abandoned, ungrateful, and unworthy creatures, if we did not respect our benefactor. And would it not be much more so here? The blessings which Jesus has bestowed upon the Christian, are not trifling and inconsiderable, but of the most valuable kind: they are blessings we all absolutely stand in need of, and are sufficient to give us lasting and substantial happiness. Is it a small thing to have our sins forgiven, and be made the children of God? Is it a trifling matter to be delivered from the power of sin, and be adorned with the image of God? Is it of no concern to be introduced into the favour of God, and be made an object of infinite love and delight? Lo these are blessings which Jesus

bestows upon every Christian here! And how reasonable is it then that he should love and honour him? Christians, it was Jesus that put your names in his book; it was he that made satisfaction to infinite justice for your numerous sins, it was he that died, that you might live eternally. And oh it is this same Jesus that has actually redeemed your souls from the slavery of sin and Satan, and has made you the children of God: "he saw you in your blood, and said unto " you, live: and was not that a time of astonishing love? He saw you dead in trespasses and sins, and hurrying on to everlasting death, and he sent his spirit to quicken your souls and make you alive: he saw you wandering and running in the broad road to everlasting ruin, and he stopped you in the midst of your career, and brought you into the way to eternal peace. Oh well then, may you love him! it is he that has given you a new nature, lively hopes of a happy immortality, and a conformity to the divine image: he has clothed you with his perfect righteousness, cast that glorious robe around you, pardoned your sins and made you heirs of an immortal inheritance. No wonder that you love him! such a friend, such a generous friend and benefactor is most certainly deserving of the highest esteem: you cannot possibly exceed in your love to him. Oh, says the Christian, how great are my obligations? I had been now amongst the thoughtless crowd, running into all manner of excess of riot, or however absolutely ignorant and secure, every moment exposed to everlasting burnings; had it not been for Jesus, who saw me, pitied me, and plucked me as a brand out of the fire. I had now been deceiving myself with false hopes, crying peace, peace, when under the most dreadful guilt, had not Jesus kindly took hold of me, enlightened my understanding, led me into the knowledge of himself, and gave me some well grounded hopes of eternal life: and has he thus wonderfully changed my state? Raised me from a child of wrath to a child of God? Has he freely pardoned all my sins, passed by my rebellious carriage and behaviour, and made me an heir of eternal glory? And shall I not love him? Are not these most powerful arguments, the greatest attractives? I cannot withstand them: the consideration of what Christ has done for such an unworthy creature as I am, constrains me to love him, and to give up myself entirely unto him. Blessings so great, so excellent and glorious, cannot certainly be ever forgot. "Oh whom have I in " heaven but thee? And there is none upon earth that I " defire or efteem in comparifon of thee:" thou art all and in all to my foul, Pfal. lxxiii. 25.

4 The endearing titles which he/gives his people, fhew his love to them, and lay them under obligations to love him. He treats them in the kindeft and moſt affectionate manner, both in his words and actions, he addreſſes them in the fofteft language, and calls them by the moft endearing titles. Solomon reprefents Chrift fpeaking to the church in the moft tender manner, calling her " his fpoufe, his " love, his dove, his undefiled," Cant. v. 2. And making ufe of every title of endearment, to fhew his love and affection to her. Thus, in various other parts of fcripture, we have the moft affectionate titles given to believers. Chrift calls them *my people* to diftinguifh them from others, and to fhew what property he has in them, and how much he efteems them. He calls them his children, made fo by faith in his blood, and therefore as fuch lying near his heart. They are his jewels, his treafure, the apple of his eye; all which manifeft the peculiar tendernefs he has for them, and the care that he takes of them. This therefore is enough to recommend him ever to their efteem: how juftly would a perfon render himfelf an object of contempt amongſt men, who did not efteem the man that always addreffed him in the kindeft language, and that with the utmoft fincerity? He muſt be of an uncommonly ungrateful difpofition, who could remain churlifh under fuch affectionate treatment. Let none then wonder why the Chriftian loves an unfeen Jefus. It would be difcovering the moſt fordid temper to caſt contempt upon him as the proud prophane finner does. He cannot do it: he is loft and overwhelmed, when he comes to confider the titles which Jefus has given him, and confequently the love and tendernefs of which they are fo expreffive. Lord, doſt thou take fuch kind notice of me an unworthy creature? Doſt thou call me by fuch affectionate names? I who am fo vile, fo polluted, who might have felt the weight of thine everlafting fury and vengeance. Lord, I am aftonifhed, when I confider what honour thou doft put upon me, and fhall I not love thee? Lord what is my love? Art thou made the more happy by it? Doſt thou receive any benefit or advantage from it? No, far be from

me such a proud and self-flattering thought: yet, though thou art not rendered more glorious by it, still I love thee, it is my duty, it is my happiness, and whatever contempt others cast upon thee, I should be of all creatures the most ungrateful was I to do it: Lord I abhor the thought: behold thou knowest all things, and thou therefore knowest that I desire to love thee with all my heart, with all my soul, and with all my strength.

5. The care which Christ continually takes of his people, and the glory which he has purchased for, and will give unto them, abundantly shew the greatness of his love to them, and win their hearts and affections to him. He not only sends his Spirit at first to awaken, enlighten, and quicken them, but he manifests and discovers the utmost care of, and concern for them, while they are passing through this solitary wilderness, till he brings them to that glorious Canaan which he has purchased for them. They are surrounded with dangerous enemies, and consequently with innumerable temptations, by which they are liable to be led aside, to the dishonour of God, and wounding their souls: Jesus therefore takes them under his constant care, and acts the kindest part to them. As a shepherd, he continually watches over, guards, and protects them that no ravenous beast of prey break in upon them, and devour them, or lest they should wander from the fold, and be in danger of being eternally lost. Under a former head we have heard, that as a father he pities them under all their distresses, corrects their disobedience, and gives them the most affectionate instructions and advice. As the captain of their salvation he leads them on to the battle, encourages and animates them with the hopes of success, and brings them off complete conquerors. As their prophet he guides them by his word and spirit: as their priest he has offered himself a sacrifice to satisfy infinite justice for their sins; and as their advocate he sits above pleading their cause and making continual intercession for them. Thereby making up every breach, continuing them in the divine favour, and procuring them every needful supply. As their king he defends them in the enjoyment of their privileges and immunities, secures them from the power and malice of their enemies, governs them by his laws, and makes them happy in the enjoyment of his royal presence and favour. And thus he

difcovers a conftant care and concern for them He hands out of his inexhauftible fulnefs, continually for their abundant fupply; he is their righteoufnefs and ftrength; their wifdom, fanctification, and redemption; in fhort, he is their all and in all : they are nothing, they can do nothing without him. They are kept by his mighty power, through faith unto falvation : he continually heals their backflidings, forgives their iniquities and preferves them to his heavenly kingdom, which he has prepared for them, and where he will at length bring them. They are obliged to him for the bleffings they have already received, for their perfeverance in grace, and for the profpect of a glorious immortality; he not only gives them bleffings here, but he has prepared for them glories, glories of an immortal and exalted nature, and will put them into the full and everlafting poffeffion of them hereafter : and is not all this enough to win their love, and engage their efteem ? It is not poffible for the Chriftian to do otherwife than love his Redeemer. He muft do it : his engagements, his obligations are fo great, and his fenfe of them fo deep, that he is powerfully, though fweetly conftrained to love an unfeen faviour. Oh my foul, behold the love of thy great Redeemer: what are corn, and oil, and wine ? What are filver and gold, and all corruptible things ? They are not to be mentioned with the bleffings my Redeemer has given me, and has laid up for me : behold he has made me an heir of God, an heir of an incorruptible, immortal, and moft glorious inheritance; he has brought me out of my native darkne s into his marvellous light, he has clothed me with the robe of his righteoufnefs, and is daily acting the kindeft and tendere't part towards me. And behold what he has laid up in referve for me : fee, Oh my foul, look into eternity, thy Redeemer has made it all over to thee ; he has taken the fting out of death for thee, and purchafed heaven : fee how he defigns to exalt thee, to make thee a king and a prieft unto God, and to live with him for ever and ever ! Oh how can I then but love him ? Deny him my heart: no, I abhor the thought : Lord I would be thine, for ever thine, I would love thee more, and I would mourn before thee that I am fo defective.

6. A confideration of the freenefs of the love of Chrift, in all that he has done, and will do for the Chriftian, engages him to love and efteem him. Was a perfon to be-

stow valuable presents upon us in our necessitous circumstances, and have no advantage in view by so doing, but act from a mere principle of generosity and compassion, we could not but value and esteem so uncommon a friend: such a one is Christ to his people; he had no personal advantage in view, when he undertook the work of redemption; he was under no necessity to act so kind a part; none could compel him to it; he was perfectly free in whatever he has done. It was his own generous act; an act of the highest compassion, to display the riches of his distinguishing grace: we had nothing to recommend us to him, nothing to entitle us to his favour, but every thing that tended to fill him with an everlasting abhorrence of us: our circumstances were also the most distressing; poor and miserable, blind and naked; children of wrath and deserving of everlasting punishment: in these circumstances were we, when Jesus beheld us and loved us, and manifested himself unto us. What amazing grace, what astonishing love was this? When the soul comes to take a view of it, he is bewildered, overcome with the greatness of it, and raised in admiration: Oh why did Jesus put my name in his book? Why did he actually redeem me from sin and Satan? Why has he brought me into a state of favour with God, when many thousands around me, are buried in sin and exposed to everlasting burnings? Oh the love of Jesus is so astonishing that I cannot possibly entertain suitable conceptions of it! And how can I but love him who has done more for me than tongue can express, nay, than heart can conceive, and that freely, without the least obligation? Oh Lord, thy love overcomes my soul when I consider it: Oh that mine to thee was greater and more fervent. And thus we see the reasons why the Christian loves an unseen Jesus And how rational a part he acts in the greatest fervours of devotion.

1. Hence we learn the stupidity and degeneracy of human nature, that we should be naturally enemies to so lovely a Saviour. We are ready enough to esteem what appears excellent, except it is in spiritual cases. And here, instead of valuing what is really worthy, we find a hatred of, and an aversion to it; see how Jesus is despised: with what contempt does the proud sinner view him; he hates his person, he will not submit to his government, he despises his glorious characters. Is not this something asto-

nifhing? Alas how is human nature funk! Oh the dreadful effects of fin, it blinds our minds, it corrupts our judgements; we call good evil, and evil good: amazing ftupidity! That Jefus who fhould be the object of our efteem, is the object of our contempt! How is our nature changed! What ftrange, ignorant, perverfe creatures are we? Lament, Oh my foul: the crown is fallen from thy head, and the moft amiable object is defpifed.

2 Hence how fhould every Chriftian mourn that his love to Chrift is fo weak One fo lovely, fo glorious, one fo generous and kind certainly deferves the ftrongeft affection. The Chriftian is under the greateft obligations to Jefus; the bleffings he has received, the glories he has in profpect call for conftant returns of love. But Oh! how defective is the Chriftian himfelf? Do you love Jefus as you ought? Lament, Oh my foul: how wandering thy defires? How cool thy affections oftentimes to Jefus? What a fondnefs for prefent things? How earneftly do I purfue them? How feldom converfe with Jefus and his love? How bent to backflide? How often does my wicked heart ftart afide? How frequently do I difhonour Jefus? Lament and mourn, O my foul, over thy ingratitude! Strange that one's heart fhould be fo cold: ftrange that our fouls fhould be no more employed in converfing with Chrift's amiablenefs and excellencies!—Are you not all chargeable? Oh let us, as in the prefence of God, charge our fouls with neglect. And let us labour to grow in love to him.

3. How happy are all thofe who love an unfeen Saviour? Thofe who love Jefus he loves. Prov. viii. 17. And what a pleafing confideration fhould this be to the foul?—Chrift himfelf loves thee, Oh my foul! He has fet his heart upon thee; thou art an object of his favour: What an honour! What an encouragement is this! Happy it is when we can thus apply the love of Chrift to our fouls: and all that love Chrift may do it: for to whomfoever he is precious, they are precious to him; *we love him becaufe he firft loved us,* and from hence may moft comfortably conclude our affured intereft in him In fine,

4. How defirable a place is heaven, where we fhall have the cleareft views and greateft fenfe of the love of Chrift to us, and find our fouls filled with the ftrongeft love to him? May we all learn to love an unfeen Saviour. Amen.

END OF THE SERMONS.

THE

PLEASANTNESS

OF A

RELIGIOUS LIFE,

OPENED AND PROVED;

AND

RECOMMENDED TO THE CONSIDERATION OF ALL,

PARTICULARLY OF

YOUNG PEOPLE.

TO WHICH IS SUBJOINED,

A CHURCH IN THE HOUSE.

BEING A

SERMON

CONCERNING

FAMILY RELIGION.

BOTH BY THE LATE REVEREND

Mr. MATTHEW HENRY,

MINISTER OF THE GOSPEL IN CHESTER.

AIR:

PRINTED BY J. & P. WILSON, FOR THE PUBLISHER.

M,DCC,XCII.

TO THE

READER.

THAT diftinction which the learned Dr. Henry More infifts fo much upon, in his explanation of the Grand Myftery of Godlinefs, between the animal life, and the divine life, is certainly of great ufe to lead us into the underftanding of that myftery. What was the fall and apoftacy of man, and what is ftill his fin and mifery, but the foul's revolt from the divine life, and giving up itfelf wholly to the animal life? And what was the defign of our Redeemer, but to recover us to the divine and fpiritual life again by the influences of his grace? And to this his gofpel has a direct tendency; his religion is all fpiritual and divine, while all other religions favour of the animal life. Chriftianity, faith he, is that period of the wifdom and providence of God, wherein the animal life is remarkably infulted and triumphed over by the divine, book 1, chap. 7. And fo far, and no further, are we Chriftians indeed, than as this revolution is brought about in our fouls.

The conflict is between thefe two: Nothing draws more forcibly than pleafure; in order therefore to the advancing of the interests of the divine life in myself and others, I have here endeavoured, as God has enabled me, to make it evident, that the pleasures of the divine life are unspeakably better, and more deserving, than those of the animal life: Were people convinced of this, we should gain our point.

The substance of this was preached last year, in six sermons, in the ordinary course of my ministry, among many other reasons why we should be religious; I was then solicited to make it public, and now take this opportunity to prepare it for the press, when, through the good hand of my God upon me, I have finished my fifth volume of Expositions, before I go about the sixth. And herein, I confess, I indulge an inclination of my own; for this doctrine of the pleasantness of religion, is what I have long had a particular kindness for, and taken all occasions to mention. Yet I would not thus far have gratified either my friends request, or my own inclination, if I had not thought that, by the blessing of God, it might be of some service to the common interest of Christ's kingdom, and the common salvation of precious souls.

May 31st, 1714.   M. H.

THE
PLEASANTNESS
OF A
RELIGIOUS LIFE.

Prov. iii. 17.

Her ways are ways of pleasantness, and all her paths are peace.

TRUE religion and godliness are often in scripture, and particularly in this book of the Proverbs, represented, and so recommended to us, under the name and character of wisdom, Prov. i. 2, 7, 20.—ii. 2, 10.—iii. 13. Psal. cxi. 10. Because it is the highest improvement of the human nature, and the best and surest guide of human life. It was one of the first and most ancient discoveries of God's mind to the children of men, to the inquisitive part of them that are in search for wisdom, and would have it at any rate; then when God made a weight for the winds, and a decree for the rain, when he brought all the other creatures under the established rule and law of the creation, according to their respective capacities, then he declared this to man, a reasonable creature, as the law of his creation, Job. xxviii. 25,—28. " Behold, the fear of the Lord, that is wisdom; " and to depart from evil," the evil of sin, " is under-" standing."

The great men of the world, that engross its wealth and

honours, are pretenders to wisdom, and think none do so well for themselves as they do: But though their neighbours applaud them, and their posterity, that reap the fruit of their worldly wisdom, approve their sayings; yet this their way is their folly, Psal xlix. 13, 18. and so it will appear, when God himself shall call those fools, who said to their souls, take your ease, in barns full of corn, and bags full of money, Luke xii. 20 Jer xvii 11.

The learned men of the world were wellwishers to wisdom, and modestly called themselves *Philosophoi*, lovers of wisdom; and many wise principles we have from them, and wise precepts: And yet their philosophy failed them in that which man's great duty and interest lies in, acquainting himself with his maker, and keeping up communion with him; herein they that professed themselves to be wise, became fools, Rom. i. 22. " And the world by wisdom knew " not God," 1 Cor i. 21.

But true Christian's are, without doubt, the truly wise men, to whom Christ is made of God wisdom, 1 Cor. i. 30, in whom are hid, not from them, but for them, all the treasures of wisdom and knowledge, Col ii 3. They understand themselves best, and on which side their interest lies, who give up themselves to the conduct of Christ and his word and spirit; that consult his oracles, and govern themselves by them, which are indeed the truest oracles of reason, Prov ix. 10. Men never begin to be wise, till they begin to be religious; and they then leave off to be wise, when they leave off to do good, Psal. xxxvi 3.

Now, to recommend to us the study and practice of this true wisdom, to bring us into a willing subjection to her authority, and keep us to a conscientious observance of her dictates, the great God is here by Solomon reasoning with us, from those topics, which, in other cases, use to be cogent, and commanding enough. It is wonderful condescension, that he, who has an indisputable authority over us, thus vouchsafes to reason with us; to draw with the cords of a man, and the bands of love, Hos. xi. 4. when he might make use only of the cords of a God, and the bands of the law, Psal. ii. 3. to invite us to that by precious promises, which he enjoins upon us by his precepts, and those not grievous, 1 John v. 3.

Interest is the great governess of the world; which, when

men are once convinced of, they will be fwayed by more than by any thing elfe. Every one is for what he can get, and therefore applies himfelf to that which he thinks he can get by; the common inquiry is, "Who will fhew us any " good?" We would all be happy, would all be eafy.

Now, it is here demonftrated by eternal truth itfelf, that it is our intereft to be religious; and therefore religion deferves to be called wifdom, becaufe it teaches us to do well for ourfelves; and it is certain, that the way to be happy (that is, perfectly holy) hereafter, is to be holy (that is, truly happy) now. It is laid down for a principle here, "Hap-" py is the man that findeth wifdom," ver. 13. that finds the principles and habits of it planted in his own foul by divine grace; that, having diligently fought, has at length found that pearl of great price: "And the 'man that " getteth underftanding," reckons himfelf therein a true gainer. The man that draws out underftanding, fo the original word fignifies; that produceth it, and brings it forth, qui profert intelligentiam; and fo the Chaldee reads it.—— Happy is the man that, having a good principle in him, makes ufe of it both for his own and others benefit: that, having laid up, lays out.

It is neceffary to our being happy, that we have right notions of happinefs; the nature of it, wherein it confifts, what are the ingredients of it, and what the ways that lead to it: for many keep themfelves miferable by thinking themfelves happy, when really they are not; and we have reafon to fufpect their miftake concerning themfelves, becaufe they miftake fo grofsly concerning others: they call the proud happy, Mal. iii. 15. they "blefs the covetous, whom the " Lord abhors," Pfal. x. 4. It concerns us, therefore, to confider, whence we take our meafures of happinefs, and what rules we go by in judging of it; that we may not covet our lot with thofe, with whom we fhould dread to have our lot; that we may not fay as the pfalmift was tempted to fay, when he looked upon the outward profperity of worldly people, "Happy is the people that is in fuch a cafe;" but as he was determined to fay, when he looked upon the true felicity of good people, happy, thrice happy, for ever happy, is that people whofe God is the Lord, Pfal. cxliv. 15. And as God here faith, whofe judgement we are fure is according to truth, happy is the man that finds wifdom.

The happiness of those who are religious is here proved,.
1. From the true profit that is to be got by religion; Godliness is profitable to all things, 1 Tim. iv. 8. It is of universal advantage. Though we may be losers for our religion, yet we shall not only not be losers by it, but we shall be unspeakable gainers in the end. They that trade with wisdom's talents, will find the merchandise of it better than the merchandise of silver, and the gain thereof than fine gold, and that it is more precious than rubies. As long since as Job's time it was agreed, that the advantages of religion were such, that as they could not be purchased, so they could not be valued with the gold of Ophir, the precious onyx, or the sapphire; the topaz of Ethiopia could not equal them, Job. xxviii. 16, 19. Length of days is in wisdom's right hand, even life for evermore; length of days and no shortening of them; and in her left hand riches and honour, ver. 16. the unsearchable riches of Christ, and the honour that comes from God, which are true riches, and true honours, because durable, because eternal, and for ever out of the danger of poverty and disgrace.

In all labour there is profit, more or less, of one kind or other; but no profit like that in the labour of religion: They who make a business of it, will find great advantage by it. Its present incomes are valuable, and a comfortable, honourable maintenance for a soul; but its future recompences infinitely more so, above what we are able either to speak or think.

2. From the transcendent pleasure that is to be found in it. Here is profit and pleasure twisted, which completes the happiness: for all excel who mingle the pleasant with the useful. Those who pursue the gains of the world in wealth and riches, must be willing to deny themselves in their pleasures; and they that will indulge themselves in their pleasures, must be content not to get money, but to spend it. As they that are covetous, know they must not be voluptuous, so they that are voluptuous leave no room to be covetous; but it is not so in the profits and pleasures of religion: here a man may both get and save the spiritual riches of divine grace, and yet at the same time bathe in a full stream of divine consolations, and be nevertheless a holy epicure in spiritual delights, for his laying up treasures in heaven; the soul may even then dwell at ease, when it is

labouring most diligently for the meat that endures to eternal life.

This is that which the text speaks of; and both the profit and pleasure of religion are put together in the next words, "she is a tree of life," ver. 18. both enriching and delighting "to them that lay hold upon her." What gain or comfort like that of life?

First, We are here assured, that her ways are ways of pleasantness; not only pleasant ways, but in the abstract, ways of pleasantness, as if pleasantness were confined to those ways, and not to be found any where else: and the pleasantness ariseth not from any foreign circumstance, but from the innate goodness of the ways themselves. Or it notes the exceeding superlative pleasantness of religion; it is as pleasant as pleasantness itself; they are ways of pleasantness, this, in the original, is the word from which Naomi had her name in the day of her prosperity, which afterwards she disclaimed, Ruth i. 20. Call me not Naomi, pleasant; but Marah, bitter. Think you hear wisdom saying on the contrary, call me not Marah, bitter, as some have miscalled me, but call me Naomi, pleasant. The vulgar Latin reads it, viæ pulchræ, or her ways are beautiful ways; ways of sweetness, so the Chaldee.

Wisdom's ways are so; *i e.* the ways which she has directed us to walk in, the ways of her commandments, those are such, that if we keep close to, and go on in we shall certainly find true pleasure and satisfaction. Wisdom saith, This is the way, walk in it, and you shall not only find life at the end, but pleasure in the way. That which is the only right way to happiness, we must resolve to travel, and to proceed, and persevere in it, whether it be fair or foul, pleasant or unpleasant; but it is a great encouragement to a traveller, to know that his way is not only the right way, but a pleasant way; and such is the way to heaven.

God had told us, by Solomon, chap. ii. 3, 4. that we must cry after knowledge, must give our voice to understanding, that we must seek it, and search for it, must spare no cost or pains to get it: he had told us, that this wisdom would restrain us from the way both of the evil man, and of the strange woman, chap. ii. 12. 16. that it would keep us from all the forbidden pleasures of sense Now, lest these restraints from pleasure, and constraints to piety and labour, should discourage any from the ways of religion, he here assures us, not only that our pains will be abundantly recompensed with the profits of religion, but the pleasures we forego will be abundantly balanced with the pleasures we shall enjoy.

Secondly, It is added, that all her paths are peace. Peace is sometimes put for all good; here some take it for the good of safety and protection. Many ways are pleasant, they are clean and look smooth; but they are dangerous, either not found at bottom, or beset with thieves; now the ways of wisdom have in them a holy security, as well as a holy serenity; and they who walk in them have God himself for their shield as well as their sun, and are not only joyful in the hope of good, but are or may also be quiet from the fear of evil.

But we may take it for the good of pleasure and delight, and so it speaks the same with the former part of the verse: As there is pleasantness in wisdom's ways, so there is peace in all her paths.

1. There is not only peace in the end of religion, but peace in the way. There is not only peace provided as a bed, for good men to lie down in at night when their work is done and their warfare is accomplished; but they shall then enter into peace, rest in their beds, Isa. lvii. 2. Mark the perfect man, and behold the upright, for the end of that man is peace, Psal. xxxvii. 37. it is everlasting peace: but there is also peace provided as a shade, for good men to work in all day, that they may not only do their work, but do it with delight. For even the work of righteousness as well as its reward, shall be peace, Isa. xxxii. 17. and the immediate effect of righteousness, as well as its issue at last, quietness and assurance for ever.

It is possible, that war may be the way to peace: sic quærimus pacem, thus we pursue peace, is the best motto to be engraven on weapons of war. But it is the glory of those who are truly religious, that they not only seek peace but enjoy it. The peace of God rules their hearts, and by that means keeps them; and, even while they are travellers, they have peace, though they are not yet at home.

It is the misery of the carnal irreligious world, that the ways of peace they have not known, Rom. iii. 17. for they are like the troubled sea; there is no peace, saith my God, to the wicked, Ifa lvii. 20, 21. How can peace be fpoken to thofe who are not the fons of peace? Luke x. 4, 5. to thofe who have not grace for the word of peace to faften upon? They may cry peace to themfelves, but there is no true peace either in their way or in their end: To fuch I fay, as in 2 Kings ix 18 What haft thou to do with peace? turn thee behind me; while in God's name I fpeak peace to all who are in covenant with the God of peace, to all the faithful fubjects of the prince of peace: They have experimentally known the way of peace, and to them I fay, Go on, and profper; Go on in peace, for the God of love and peace is and will be with you.

2. There is not only this peace in the way of religion in general, but in the particular paths of that way. View it in the feveral acts and inftances of it, in the exercife of every grace, in the performance of every duty, and you will find that what is faid of the body of Chriftianity, is true of every part of it; it is peace.

The ways of religion are tracked as path-ways are, Cant. i. 8. we go forth by the footfteps of the flock. It is the good old way that all have walked in, who are gone to heaven before us; and this contributes fomething to the peace of it. Walk in the old way, and you fhall find reft to your fouls, Jer. vi. 16. We go on in our way with fo much the more affurance, when we fee thofe going before us, who, through faith and patience are now inheriting the promife; let us but keep the path, and we fhall not mifs our way.

The Chaldee reads it, Itinera ejus pacifica, that is, Her journeys are peace. The paths of wifdom are not like walks in a garden, which we make ufe of for diverfion only, and an amufement; but like tracks in a great road, which we prefs forward in with care and pains, as a traveller in his journey, ftill going on, till we come to our journey's end. We muft remember, that in the ways of religion we are upon our journey, and it is a journey of bufinefs, bufinefs of life and death, and therefore we muft not trifle, or lofe time, but muft lift up our feet, as Jacob did, Gen. xxix. 1. (Then Jacob went on his way, in the margin it is, he lift up his feet) and lift up our hearts as Jehofhaphat did in the ways of the Lord, 2 Chron. xvii. 6. and not take up fhort of the end of our faith and hope, not take up fhort of home: And though the journey is long, and requires all this care and application, yet it is pleasant, it is peace notwithstanding.

In the way of religion and godliness, taken generally, there are different paths, according to the different sentiments of wise and good men in the less weighty matters of the law; but, blessed be God, every different path is not a by-path; And if it be not, but keep within the same hedges of divine truths and laws, as to the essentials of religion, it may be, it shall be a way of peace; for both he that eateth and he that eateth not giveth God thanks, Rom. xiv. 6. and has comfort in it. If we rightly understand that the kingdom of God, the way of wisdom, is not meat and drink, and we shall find it to be, which indeed it is, righteousness and peace, and joy in the Holy Ghost, Rom. xiv. 17.

3. There is this peace in all the paths of wisdom, in all the instances of pure and undefiled religion; look into them all, make trial of them all, and you will find there is none to be excepted against, none to be quarrelled with; they are all uniform and of a piece: the same golden thread of peace and pleasure runs through the whole web of serious godliness.

We cannot say so of this world, that all its paths are peace, however some of them may pretend to give the mind a little satisfaction; its pleasures have their allays; that which one thing sweetens, another comes presently and embitters. But as there is a universal rectitude in the principles of religion, Psal cxix. 128. I have esteemed all thy precepts concerning all things to be right; and Prov. viii. 8 All the words of my mouth are in righteousness, saith wisdom, and there is nothing froward or perverse in them; so there is an universal peace and pleasure in the practice of religion: All our paths, if such as they should be, will be such as we could wish.

The doctrine, therefore, contained in these words, is,
That true piety hath true pleasure in it. Or thus;
The ways of religion are pleasant and peaceful ways.

CHAP. I.

The Explication of the Doctrine.

IT is a plain truth which we have here laid down, and there is little in it that needs explication: It were well for us, if we would but as readily subscribe to the certainty of it, as we apprehend the sense and meaning of it. Nor will any complain that it is hard to be understood, but those who know no other pleasures than those of sense, and relish no other, and therefore resolve not to give credit to it. Those who think, How can this be, that there should be pleasure in piety? will be ready to question what is the meaning of this doctrine? and call it a hard saying.

You know what pleasure is; I hope you know something what the pleasure of the mind is, a pleasure which the soul has the sensation of. And do you not know something what piety is? a due regard to a God above us, and having the eyes of the soul ever up unto him; and then you know what I mean when I say, that there is an abundance of real pleasure and satisfaction in the ways of religion and godliness.

But to help you a little in the understanding of it, and to prevent mistakes, observe,

First, That I speak of true piety, and of that as far as it goes.

1. Hypocrites are very much strangers to the delights and pleasures of religion; nay, they are altogether so, for it is joy which those strangers do not intermeddle with. Counterfeit piety can never bring in true pleasure. He who acts a part upon a stage, though it be the part of one who is never so pleasant, though he may humour the pleasantness well enough, he doth not experience it. The pleasures of God's house lie not in the outer courts, but within the veil. None know what the peace of God means, but those who are under the dominion and operation of his grace; nor can any who deny the power of godliness, expect to share in the pleasures of it. When wisdom enters into thine heart, takes possession of that, and becomes a living active principle there; then, and not till then, it is pleasant unto thy soul, Prov. ii. 19. Those who aim at no more than the credit of their religion before men, justly fall short of the comfort of it in themselves.

Hypocrites have other things that they delight in, the satisfactions of the world, the gratifications of sense, which put their mouths out of taste to spiritual pleasures, so that they have no pleasure in them. They that have their hearts upon their marketings, are weary of the New Moons and the Sabbaths, Amos viii. 5. With good reason, therefore, doth Job afk, " Will the the hypocrite delight himfelf in "the Almighty?" chap. xxvii. 10. No, his foul takes its eafe in the creature, and returns not to the Creator as its reft and home.

Some flafhy pleafure an hypocrite may have in religion, from a land-flood of fenfible affections, who yet has not the leaft tafte of the river of God's pleafures. There were thofe who " delighted to know God's ways." Ifa. lviii. 2. They met with fome pretty notions in them, that furprifed them, and pleafed their fancies; but they did not delight to walk in them. The ftony ground received the word with joy, and yet received no lafting benefit by it, Luke viii. 13. Herod heard John gladly, Mark vi. 20 He found fomething very agreeable in his fermons, and which natural confcience could not but embrace; and yet could not bear to be reproved for his Herodias. A florid preacher, fuch as Ezekiel was, may be to them as " a very lovely fong of one that " can play well on an inftrument," Ezek. xxxiii. 32. And yet, at the fame time, the word of the Lord, if it touch their confciences, and fhew them their tranfgreffions, is to them a reproach, Jer. vi. 10.

They whofe hearts are not right with God in their religion, cannot have the pleafure of communion with God; for it is the foul only which converfeth with God, and that he communicates himfelf to. " Bodily exercife profiteth lit- " tle," 1 Tim. iv. 8. and therefore pleafeth little. The fervice of God is a burden and a tafk to an unfanctified unrenewed heart; it is out of its element when it is brought into that air: and therefore, inftead of fnuffing it up, and faying, behold what a pleafure it is! It fnuffs at it, and faith, " Behold, what a wearinefs it is!" Mal. i. 13.

Nor can they take any pleafure in communing with their own confciences, or in their reflections; for they are ready upon all occafions to give them uneafinefs, by charging them with that which is difagreeable to their profeffion, and gives the lie to it: and though they cry, peace, peace; to themfelves, they have that within them that tells them, the God of heaven doth not fpeak peace to them; and this cafts a damp upon all their pleafure, that their religion itfelf gives them pain, God himfelf is a terror to them, and the gofpel itfelf condemns them for their infincerity. And, in time of trouble and diftrefs, none are fo much afraid as the finners in Zion, Ifa. xxxiii. 14. The secret sinners there; and fearfulness is the greatest surprise of all to the hypocrites, Amos vi. 1. that were at ease in Zion, and thought its strong holds would be their security.

And therefore it is, that hypocrites cast off religion, and discharge themselves of the profession of it, after they have a while disguised themselves with it; because it did not sit easy, and they are weary of it. Tradesmen, that take no pleasure in their business, will not stick to it long; no more will those who take no pleasure in their religion: Nor will any thing carry us through the outward difficulties of it, but the inward delights of it; if those be wanting, the tree is not watered, and therefore even its leaf will soon wither, Psal. i. 3. The hypocrite will not always call upon God, will not long do it, because " he will not delight himself in the " Almighty," Job xxvii. 9, 10. And this ought not to be a stumbling block to us. Thus hypocrites in religion prove apostates from it; and the reason is, because they never found it pleasant, because they were never sincere in it, which was their fault, and not the fault of the religion they professed.

Let us therefore " take heed, and beware of hypocrisy," Luke xii. 1. as ever we hope to find pleasure in religion. Counterfeit piety hath some other end in view, some other end to serve, than that which is the spring of true delight. They who rest in that " hew them out cisterns," Jer. ii. 13 that can hold but little water, and that dead, nay, " broken cisterns that can hold no water?" And how can they expect the pleasure which they have, that cleave to, and continually draw from, the " fountain of life and living " water?" No; as their principles are, such are their pleasures; as their aims are, such are their joys; they appeal to the world, and to the world they shall go. But let not the credit of religion suffer then, for the sake of those who are only pretenders to it, and so indeed enemies to it.

2. It is possible that true Christians may, through their own fault and folly, want very much of the pleasure of religion; and therefore, I say, true piety, as far as it goes, is very pleasant; as far as it has its due influence upon us, and is rightly understood, and lived up to.

We abide by it, that wisdom's ways are always pleasant; and yet must own, that wisdom's children are sometimes unpleafant, and therein come fhort of juftifying wifdom in this matter as they ought to do. Luke vii. 35. and rather give advantage to her accufers, and prejudice to her caufe. Either they mifs thefe ways, and turn afide out of them, and fo lofe the pleafure that is to be found in them; or (which is a common cafe) they " refufe to take the comfort" which they might have in thefe ways. They hamper themfelves with needlefs perplexities, make the yoke heavy which Chrift has made eafy, and that frightful which he defigned fhould be encouraging; they indulge themfelves, and then, as Jonah, when he was angry, juftify themfelves in caufelefs griefs and fears, and think they do well to " put themfelves into an " agony," to be " very heavy and fore amazed," and their fouls exceeding forrowful, even unto death, as Chrift's was; whereas Chrift put himfelf into fuch an agony to make us, eafy.

But let not true piety fuffer in its reputation becaufe of this: For though it be called a religious melancholy, it is not fo; for it is contrary to the very nature and defign of religion, while it fhelters itfelf under the colour of it, and pretends to take rife from it. It is rather to be called a fuperftitious melancholy, *deifidamonia,* arifing from fuch a flavifh fear of God, as the Heathen were driven by to their Demons and barbarous facrifices; which is a great injury to the honour of his goodnefs, as well as a great injury to themfelves.

If the profeffors of religion look for that in the world, which is to be had in God only, and that is perfect happinefs; or, if they look for that in themfelves, which is to be had in Chrift only, and that is a perfect righteoufnefs; or, if they look for that on earth, which is to be had in heaven only, and that is perfect holinefs; and then fret, and grieve, and go mourning from day to day, becaufe they are difappointed in their expectations, they may thank themfelves, " Why feek they the living among the dead?" Luke xxiv. 5, 17.

Let but religion, true and pure religion in all the laws and inftances of it, command and prevail, and thefe tears will foon be wiped away: Let but God's fervants take their work before them, allow each principle of their religion its due weight, and each practice of it its due place and proportion, and let them not dafh one precept of the gofpel, any more than one table of the law, in pieces against the other: let them lock upon it to be as much their duty to rejoice in Christ Jesus; as to mourn for sin; nay, and more, for this is in order to that; and then we shall not fear, that their sorrows will in the least shake the truth of our doctrine: for, as far as the religion is carried, it will carry this character along with it, and further it cannot be expected.

Secondly, In true piety, I say, there is a pleasure; there is that which we may find comfort in, and fetch satisfaction from. There is in it a good as well as an useful pleasure. That is pleasant which is agreeable, which the soul rejoiceth in, or at least reposeth in; or which it relisheth, pleaseth itself with, and desireth the continuance and repetition of. Let a man's faculties be in their due frame and temper, not vitiated, corrupted, or depraved; and there is that in the exercise of religion which highly suits them, and satisfies them: and this pleasure is such as is not allayed with any thing to cast a damp upon it.

1. The ways of religion are right and pleasant; they are pleasant without the allay of injury and iniquity. Sin pretends to have its pleasures, but they are the "perverting of that which is right," Job, xxxiii. 27 they are stolen waters, Prov ix. 17 Unjust, though pleasant; but the pleasures of godliness are as agreeable to the rectitude of our nature, as they are gratifying to the pure and undebauched desires of it. It is the way in which we should go, and the way in which, if we were not wretchedly degenerated, we would go of choice.

They are right; for they are marked out to us by our rightful Lord, who, having given us the being of rational creatures, has authority to give us a law suited to our being; and he has done it both by natural conscience, and by the written word: he hath said, "this is the way, walk in it," Isa. xxx. 21. It is not only permitted and allowed us, but charged and commanded for us to walk in; he hath sent us as messengers from him to travel this road upon his errand.

They are right; for they lead directly to our great end, have a tendency to our welfare here and for ever. They are the only right way to that which is the felicity of our being, which we shall certainly miss and come short of, if we do not walk in this way.

But that is not all, they are alfo pleafant: "Behold, how "good and how pleafant!" Pfal. cxxxiii. 1. It is the happinefs of thofe that fear God, that he not only teacheth them in the way that he fhall choofe, (and we may be fure that is the right way) but alfo that their "fouls fhall dwell "at eafe," Pfal. xxv. 12, 13. And juftly may they dwell at eafe, who have infinite Wifdom itfelf to choofe their way, and guide them in it. That may be right which is not pleafant, and that pleafant which is not right; but religion is both: Therefore in the next verfe it is compared to the tree of life. The tree of knowledge was indeed pleafant to the eyes, and a tree to be defired, but it was forbidden; and therefore religion is called a "tree of life," Gen. xxix. 6. which was not only pleafant, but was allowed till fin entered.

2. They are eafy and pleafant; pleafant without the allay of toil and difficulty, any more than arifeth from the corruption of our own nature: That indeed makes fuch oppofition, that we have need of arguments; and, bleffed be God, we have good arguments to prove the practice of religion eafy: But it is more than fo, it is pleafant.

Much lefs is faid than is intended, when we are told that "his commandments are not grievous," 1 John v. 3. They are not only not grievous and galling, but they are gracious and pleafing. His yoke is eafy, Mat. xi. 30. The word there ufed, *Chrefos*, fignifies more than fo, it is fweet and gentle: Not only eafy as a yoke is to the neck, when it is fo well fitted as not to hurt it; but eafy as a pillow is to the head when it is weary and fleepy. It is not only tolerable, but very comfortable. There is not only no matter of complaint in the ways of God, nothing to hurt us, but there is abundant matter of joy and rejoicing: It is not only work which is not wearinefs, but work which is its own wages; fuch a tree of life, as will not only fcreen us from the ftorm and tempeft, and feed us with neceffary food, but we may fit down under the fhadow of it with great delight, and the fruit of it will be "fweet unto our "tafte," Cant. ii. 3

3. They are gainful and pleafant, and have not the allay of expence and lofs. That may be profitable, which yet may be unpleafant; and that pleafant, which afterwards may prove very unprofitable and prejudicial. What fruit

have sinners from those things in which yet they said they had pleasure? Rom. vi. 21. But religion brings both pleasure with it, and profit after it: The pleasures of religion do not cost us dear; there is no loss by them, when the account comes to be balanced.

The gain of this world is usually fetched in by toil and uneasy labour, which is grievous to flesh and blood. The servants of this world are drudges to it; " they rise up " early, sit up late, eat the bread of sorrows," Psal. cxxvii. 2. in pursuit of its wealth. They " labour and be- " reave their souls of good," Eccl. iv. 8 But the servants of God have a pleasure even in the work they are to get by, and which they shall be recompensed for.

Besides the tendency that there is in the practice of serious godliness to our happiness in the other life, there is much in it that conduceth to our comfort in this life. David observes it to the honour of religion, Psal xix. 10. that not only after keeping, but in keeping God's commandments, there is a great reward; a present great reward of obedience in obedience. A " good man is satis- " fied in himself," Prov. xiv. 14. that is, in that which divine grace hath wrought in him; and the saints are said to " sing in the way of the Lord," Psal cxxxviii. 5. as those that find them pleasant ways

And the closer we adhere to the rules of religion, and the more intimate our converse is with divine things, the more we live with an eye to Christ and another world, the more comfort we are likely to have in our own bosoms. Great peace have they that love God's law, Psal. cxix, 165. and the more they love it, the greater their peace is; nay, it is promised to the church, that all her children shall be taught of the Lord, (and those whom he teacheth are well taught, and taught to do well) and then " great shall be " the peace of her children," Isa. liv. 13. it shall be entailed upon them; peace like a river, gliding with the ease of a bird.

Thirdly, I call it a true pleasure. As there is a science, falsely so called, 1 Tim. vi. 20. so there is a pleasure falsely so called. One of the ancients distinguishes between *Hedonas agetheis*, and *Hedonas Pseudeit, Damascen. Orthod. Fid l.* 2. pleasures that have some truth in them, and pleasures that deceive us with a lie in their right hand. Some have said that the school of Epicurus, which is commonly branded and condemned for making pleasure man's chief good, did not mean sensual pleasure, but the pleasure of the mind. And we should be willing enough to admit it, but that the other principles of his philosophy were so atheistical and irreligious. But this we are sure of, that it is a true pleasure which religion secures to us; a pleasure that deserves the name, and answers it to the full.

It is a true pleasure: For,

1. It is real, and not counterfeit. Carnal worldlings pretend a great satisfaction in the enjoyments of the world, and the gratifications of sense; Soul, take thine ease, faith one, Luke xii. 20. I have found me out substance, faith another, Hosea xii. 8 even the life of my hand; faith a third, "*I have seen the fire,*" Isa. lvii. 10. The wicked boasts of his heart's desire; but Solomon assures us, not only that the end of that mirth is heaviness, but that even "*in laughter the heart is sorrowful,*" Prov. xiv. 13. Both those that make a god of their belly, and those that make a god of their money, find such a constant pain and uneasiness attending their spiritual idolatries, that their pleasure is but from the teeth outward. Discontent at present, disappointments, and fear of worse ungoverned passions (which seldom are made less turbulent by the gratifications of the appetite) and above all, conscience of guilt, and dread of divine wrath, these give them the lie, when they boast of their pleasures, which, with such allays, are not to be boasted of; they would not be thought to be disappointed in that which they have chosen for their happiness, and therefore they seem to be pleased, they seem to be pleasant, when really their heart, if it knows its own wickedness, cannot but "*know its own bitterness,*" Prov. xiv. 10.

And many of the good things of this world, of which we said, These same shall comfort us, prove vexatious to us; and we are disappointed in that, wherein we most promised ourselves satisfaction; If we say our bed shall comfort us, perhaps it is not a bed to rest on, but a bed to toss on, as it was to poor Job, when wearisome nights were appointed to him. Nay, such strangers are we to real pleasure in the things of this life, and so oft do we deceive ourselves with that which is counterfeit, that we wish to live to those days of life which we are told will be evil days, and those years of which we are assured that we shall say, "*We have no pleasure in them,*" Eccl. xii. 1.

But the pleasures of religion are solid, substantial pleasures, and not painted; gold, and not gilded over: Those sons of pleasure inherit substance, Prov viii. 21. it is that which is (Job xv. 11) the foundation firm, the superstructure strong, the consolations of God not few, nor small, while a vain and foolish world "*cause their eyes to fly upon* "*that which is not,*" Prov xxiii. 5. Worldly people pretend to the joy they have not; but godly people conceal the joy they have, as he did that had found the treasure hid in the field. They have, like their Master, "*meat to eat,* "*which the world knows not of,*" John iv. 32.

2. It is rational, and not brutish. It is the pleasure of the soul, not of sense; it is the peculiar pleasure of a man, not that which we have in common with the inferior creatures. The pleasures of religion are not those of the mere animal life, which arise from the gratifications of the senses of the body, and its appetites; no, they affect the soul, that part of us by which we are allied to the world of spirits, that noble part of us, and therefore are to be called the true pleasures of a man.

The brute creatures have the same pleasures of sense that we have, and perhaps in some of them the senses are more exquisite, and consequently they have them in a much higher degree, nor are their pleasures liable to the correctives of reason and conscience as ours are. Who live such merry lives as the Leviathan, who plays in the deep? or the birds that sing among the branches? Psal. civ. 12, 26.

But what are these to a man who being " taught more " than the beasts of the earth, and made wiser than the fowls " of heaven," Job. xxxv. 10 11. and being dignified above the beasts, not so much by the powers of reason, as by a capacity for religion, is certainly designed for enjoyments of a more excellent nature, for spiritual and heavenly delights ? When God made man, he left him not to the enjoyments of the wide world, with the other creatures, but inclosed him a Paradise, a garden of pleasure (so Eden signifies) where he should have delights proper for him; signified indeed by the pleasures of a garden, pleasant trees, and their fruits, but really the delights of a soul, that was a ray of divine light, and a spark of divine fire, newly breathed into him from above, and on which God's image and likeness was imprinted. And we never recover our felicity, which we lost by our first parents indulging the appetite of the body, till we come to the due relish of those pleasures which man has in common with angels, and a due contempt of those which he has in common with the brutes.

The pleasures of wisdom's ways may at second-hand affect the body, and be an advantage to that; hence it is said, Prov. iii. 8. to he "health to the navel," and " marrow to the bones;" but its residence is in the " hidden man of the " heart," 1 Pet iii 4. and its comforts " delight the soul in " the multitude of its thoughts," Psal. xciv. 19. It is pleasant to the soul, and makes that like a watered garden. These are pleasures which a man, by the assistance of divine grace, may reason himself into, and not as it is with sensual pleasures, may reason himself out of.

There is no pleasure separate from that of religion, which pretends to be an intellectual pleasure, but that of learning, and that of honour : But as to the pleasure of a proud man in his dignities, and the respects paid him, as Herod, in the acclamations of the croud, it doth but affect the fancy; it is vain-glory, it is not glory : It is but the folly of him that receives the honour, fed by the folly of them that give it; so that it doth not deserve to be called a rational pleasure; it is a lust of the mind that is gratified by it, that is as much an instance of our degeneracy, as any of the lusts of the flesh are.

And as to the pleasure of a scholar, abstracted from religion, it is indeed, rational and intellectual; yet only the pleasure of the mind, in knowing truth, and not its enjoying good, Solomon, that had as much of this pleasure as ever any man had, and as nice a taste of it, yet hath assured us from his own experience, that in much wisdom of this kind is much grief, and he that increaseth knowledge, increaseth sorrow, Ec. i. 18.

But the pleasures which a holy soul hath in knowing God, and in communion with him, are not only of a spiritual nature, but they are satisfying, they are filling to the soul, and make a happiness adequate to its best affections.

3. It is remaining, and not flashy and transitory. That is true pleasure, and deserves the name, which will continue with us as a tree of life, and not wither as the green herb;. which will be not as the light of a candle, which is soon burnt, out, but as that of the sun, which is a faithful witness in heaven. We reckon that most valuable, which is most durable.

The pleasures of sense are fading and perishing. As the world passeth away, 1 John ii. 17. so do the lusts of it: That which at first pleaseth and satisfieth, after a while palls and surfeits. "As the crackling of thorns under a pot," Eccl. vii. 6. which make a great blaze, and a great noise for a little while, but soon end in soot and ashes; such is the "laughter of the fool; the end of his mirth is heaviness." Belshazzar's jollity is soon turned into the utmost consternation; "The night of my pleasure hath he turned into fear to me," Isa. xxi. 4. The pleasures of sin are said to be but for a season, Heb. xi. 25. for the "end of that mirth is heaviness." As they have no consistence, so they have no continuance.

But the pleasures of religion will abide; they wither not in winter, nor tarnish with time, nor doth age wrinkle their beauty: Frosts nip them not, nor do storms blast them; they continue through the greatest opposition of events, and despise that time and chance which happens to all things under the sun, Eccl ix. 11. Believers when they are sorrowful, appear only as sorrowful, for they are always rejoicing, 2 Cor. vi. 10. and ii. 14. Thanks be to God who always causeth us to triumph. If an immortal soul make an eternal God its chief joy, what should hinder but that it should rejoice evermore, 1 Thess. v. 16. for as the treasure, so the pleasure is laid up there, where neither moth nor rust can corrupt, nor thieves break through and steal. Christ's joy, which he gives to those who are his, is joy which no man taketh from them, John xvi 22. for it is their heart that rejoiceth. They are the beginning of everlasting pleasures, the earnest and foretaste of them; so that they are, in effect, pleasures for evermore.

So then, the great truth which I desire my heart and yours may be fully convinced of, is this: "That a holy, "heavenly life, spent in the service of God, and in commu- "nion with him, is, without doubt, the most pleasant and "comfortable life any man can live in this world."

CHAP. II.

The Pleasure of being Religious, proved from the Nature of True Religion; and many particular Instances of it.

THE doctrine needs no further explication, nor can have any better than our own experience of it; but the chief part of this undertaking is to prove the truth of it: And O that God, by me, would set it before you in a true light, so as that you may be all convinced of it, and embrace it as a faithful saying, and well worthy of all acceptation, that a godly life is a pleasant life; so as that we may be wrought upon to live such a life!

Pleasure is a tempting thing: What yields delight, cannot but attract desire; it is next to necessity, so strongly doth it urge. Surely, if we were but fully persuaded of this, that religion has pleasure on its side, we would be wrought upon by the allurement of that to be religious. It is certainly so, let us not be in doubt of it. Here is a bait that has no hook under it, a pleasure courting you which has no pain attending it, no bitterness at the latter end of it; a pleasure which God himself invites you to, and which will make you happy, truly and eternally happy: and shall not this work upon you?

But we may entertain ourselves and our hearers long enough with discourses of the pleasantness of wisdom's ways; but they will not profit, unless they are mixed with faith. O that we would all mix faith with this truth! that we would yield to the evidence of it!

To make way for the truth of it, I would only desire two things;

1. That you would lay aside prejudice, and give a fair and impartial hearing to this cause, and do not prejudge it. He who answers any matter before he hear it out, it is folly and shame to him, Prov. viii. 13, 14 especially if it be a matter of great importance and concern to himself; a matter of life and death. Be willing therefore to believe that it is possible there may, and then I doubt not but to make out that it is certain there is true pleasure in true religion.

You have got a notion, it may be, and are confirmed in it by the common cry of the multitude, that religion is a four melancholy thing, that it is to bid farewel to all pleafure and delight, and to fpend your days in grief, and your years in fighing: and if we offer any thing to the contrary, that it is a pleafant thing, and the beft entertainment that can be to the mind, you are ready to fay, as Ezekiel's hearers did of him, Doth he not fpeak parables? Ezek. xx. 49 Doth he not fpeak paradoxes? You ftartle at it, and ftart from it as a hard faying. Like Nathaniel, when he faid, Can any good thing come out of Nazareth? John i. 46. fo you are ready to fay, Can there be any pleafure in religion? Believe it, firs, there can be, there cannot but be pleafure in it.

Do not meafure religion by the follies of fome who profefs it, but do not live up to their profeffion nor adorn it: Let them bear their own burden, or clear themfelves as they can; but you are to judge of things not perfons, and therefore ought not to be prejudiced againft religion for their fakes. Nor fhould you meafure by the bad opinions which its adverfaries have of it, or the bad name which they endeavour to put it into, who neither know it nor love it, and therefore care not what unjuft things they fay to juftify themfelves in the contempt of it, and to hinder others from embracing it; but think freely of this matter.

2. That you would admit this as a principle, and abide by it, That the foul is the man. This is the demand I make in order to the proof of the doctrine; and I hope it will be readily granted me. That man is principally to be confidered as an intellectual, immortal being, endowed with fpiritual powers and capacities, allied to the world of fpirits, and accountable to the Father of fpirits; that there is a fpirit in man, which has fenfations and difpofitions of its own, active and receptive faculties diftinct from thofe of the body: and that this is the part of us, which we are and ought to be moft concerned about; becaufe it is really well or ill with us, according as it is well or ill with our fouls.

Believe, that, in man's prefent ftate, the foul and the body have feparate and contefting interefts. The body thinks it is its intereft to have its appetites gratified, and to be indulged in its pleafures; while the foul knows it is its intereft to have the appetites of the body fubdued and mortified, that fpiritual pleafures may be the better relifhed;

And we are here upon our trial which of thefe two we will fide with.

Be wife therefore, be refolute, and fhew yourfelves men who are actuated and governed by reafon, and are affected with things as reafon reprefents them to you. Not reafon as it is in the mere natural man, clouded, and plunged, and loft in fenfe; but reafon elevated and guided by divine revelation to us, and divine grace in us. Walk by faith, and not by fenfe; let the God who made you, and knows you, and wifhes you well, and from whom your judgement muft proceed, determine your fentiments in this matter, and the work is done.

Now I fhall, in the firft place, endeavour the proof of this doctrine, by fhewing you what religion is, wherein it confifts, and what thofe things are which conftitute ferious godlinefs; and then you may yourfelves judge whether it be not in its own nature pleafant. If you underftand religion aright, you will find that it has an innate fweetnefs in it, infeparable from it. Let it but fpeak for itfelf, and it will recommend itfelf. The very fhewing of this beauty in its own features and proportions, is enough to bring us all in love with it.

You fhall fee the pleafure of religion in twelve inftances of it.

Firft, To be religious is " to know the only true God, " and Jefus Chrift whom he hath fent," John xvii. 3. And is not that pleafant? This is the firft thing we have to do, to get our underftandings rightly informed, concerning both the object and the medium of our religious regards, to feek and to receive this light from heaven, to have it diffufed through our fouls as the morning light in the air, and to be turned to the impreffions of it, as the clay to the feal, Job xxxviii. 14 and this is a pleafure to the foul that underftands itfelf, and its own true intereft. " Truly the light is fweet, " and a pleafant thing it is for the eyes to behold the fun;" Eccl xi. 8. It " rejoiceth the heart," Prov xv. 30 Hence light is often put for joy and comfort; but no light is comparable to that of " the knowledge of the glory of God in " the face of Jefus Chrift," 2 Cor. iv. 6.

This is finding the knowledge we had loft, and muft for ever have defpaired of finding, if God had not made it known to us by his Spirit: It is finding the knowledge we are undone without, and happy, for ever happy in; for what is heaven but this knowledge in perfection? it is finding the knowledge which the foul would covet and reft in, if it had but recovered itfelf from the delirium which by the fall it is thrown into. They who fat in darknefs, when they begin to be religious, begin to fee a great light, Matth. iv 16. And it is a pleafing furprife to them; it is coming into a new world; fuch a pleafure as none could know fo well, as he who had his fight given him, though he was born blind. Matth. xiii. 16. "Bleffed are your eyes," faith Chrift to thofe whom he had brought into an acquaintance with himfelf, "for they fee. Apply thy heart to my knowledge," faith Solomon, Prov. xxii. 17, 18. "for it is a pleafant " thing if thou keep it within thee." Thou wilt " eat honey, " becaufe it is good, and the honey-comb, which is fweet " to the tafte; fo fhall the knowledge of wifdom be to thy " foul." Prov. xxiv. 13, 14. Could a learned man, who had hit upon a demonftration in mathematics, cry out in a tranfport of joy, *I have found, I have found*; and may not they much more boaft of the difcovery, who have found the knowledge of the moft high?

There is no pleafure in any learning like that of learning Chrift and the things that belong to our everlafting peace. For that which is known is not fmall and trivial, is not doubtful and uncertain, is not foreign to us, and which we are not concerned in; which are things that may much diminifh the pleafure of any knowledge: but it is great and fure, and of the laft importance to us, and the knowledge of it gives us fatisfaction; here we may reft our fouls. To know the perfections of the divine nature, the unfearchable riches of divine grace, to be led into the myftery of our redemption and reconciliation by Chrift; this is food, fuch knowledge as this is a feaft to the foul: It is meat indeed, and drink indeed; it is the knowledge of that which the angels defire to look into, 1 Pet i. 12. If the knowledge of the law of God was fo fweet to David, fweeter than honey to his tafte, Pfal xix. 10 and cxix. 103. how much more fhould the knowledge of the gofpel of Chrift be fo to us? When God gives this wifdom and knowledge, with it he gives joy to him who is good in his fight, Eccl. ii. 26.

I wonder what pleafure or fatisfaction thofe can have in themfelves, who are ignorant of God, and Chrift, and another world, though they are told there is such a knowledge to be had, and these are they who have it, and it is their continual entertainment. But thus do men stand in their own light, when they "love darkness rather than light."

Secondly, To be religious, is to return to God. "and re-" "pose in him as the rest of our souls:" And is not that pleasure? It is not only for our understandings to embrace the knowledge of him, but our affections to fasten upon the enjoyment of him? It is to love God as our chief good, and to rest in that love; to "love him with all our heart, and" "soul, and mind, and might," who is well worthy of all that love, and infinitely more; amiable in himself, gracious to us; who will accept our love, and return it; who hath promised to "love those that love him," Prov. viii .7. The love of God reigning in the soul (and that is true religion) is as much a satisfaction to the soul, as the love of the world is a vexation to it, when it comes to be reflected upon, and is found to be so ill bestowed.

How pleasant must it needs be, so far to recover ourselves, as to quit the world for a portion and happiness as it is utterly insufficient to be so, and to depend on him only, who has enough in him to answer our utmost expectations? when we have in vain sought our satisfaction where it is not to be had, to seek it and find it where it is? to come from doating upon "ly-" "ing vanities, and spending our money for that which is not" "bread," Isa. lv. 2. to live and live plentifully upon a God that is enough, a God all-sufficient, and in him to enjoy our own mercies? Did ever any thing speak a mind more easy and better pleased than that of David, "Return unto thy" "rest, O my soul?" Psal. cxvi. 7. to God as thy rest, for in him I am where I would be, I have what I would have: Or that, Psal. xvi. 2, 5, 6. "O my soul, thou hast said unto" "the Lord, Thou art my Lord. the portion of my inheri-" "tance, and of my cup?" And then, "the lines are fallen to" "me in pleasant places, and I have a goodly heritage?" Or that, Psal. lxxiii 25. "Whom have I in heaven but thee?" "and there is none upon earth that I desire in compari-" "son of thee; for when flesh and heart fail, thou art the" "strength and joy of my heart, and my portion for ever?"

We place not religion in raptures and transports; but, without doubt, those souls that are at home in God, that have "made the Most High their habitation," Psal. xci. 9. whose desires are towards him, whose delights are in him, who are in him as their centre and element, dwell at ease. None can imagine the pleasure that a believer has in his covenant-relation to God, and interest in him, and the assurance of his love. Have I taken " thy testimonies to be my heritage for " ever?" Psal. cxix. 111. surely they are the rejoicing of my heart; I cannot be better provided for. When king Asa brought his people to renew their covenant with God, it is said, " They sware unto the Lord with a loud voice, and " with shoutings, and with trumpets," 2 Chron. xv. 14, 15. " And all Judah rejoiced at the oath, for they had sworn with " all their heart." When we come to make it our own act and deed, to " join ourselves to the Lord in an everlasting " covenant," and are upright with him in it, we cannot but be pleased with what we have done; it is a marriage covenant, it is made with joy, Cant. ii. 16. " My beloved is " mine, and I am his."

Thirdly, To be religious, is to " come to God as a Father, " in and by Jesus Christ as mediator:" And is not this pleasant? We have not only the pleasure of knowing and loving God, but the pleasure of drawing nigh to him, and having by faith a humble freedom and intimacy with him, Psal. lxv. 4. " Blessed are they that dwell in his courts," they shall be " satisfied with the goodness of his house, " even of his holy temple." Religion is described by coming to God; and what can be more agreeable to a soul that comes from him?

It is to come to God as a child to his father, to his father's house, to his father's arms, and to cry, *abba father*. To come as a petitioner to his prince, is a privilege; but to come as a child to his father, is a pleasure: and this pleasure have all the saints, that have received the spirit of adoption. They can look up to the God that made them, as one that loves them, and has a tender compassion for them, " as a father hath for his children," Psal. ciii. 13. and delights to do them good, taking pleasure in their prosperity; as one whom though they have offended, yet is reconciled to them, owns them as his children, and encourages them to call him Father. When he afflicts them, they know it is in love, and for their benefit, and that still it is " their Father's good pleasure to give them the kingdom," Luke xii. 32. When Ephraim bemoaned himself as a bul-

lock unaccuftomed to the yoke, God bemoaned him "as a
" dear fon, as a pleafant child," Jer. xxxi. 18, 20. And, if
even prodigals when penitents become pleafant chil4ren to
God, furely they have no reafon to be unpleafant to themfelves.

But this is not all; it is not only to come to God as a
father, who himfelf loves us, John xvi. 27. but it is to come
to him in the name of Jefus Chrift, who is our advocate
with the Father; that by thefe two immutable things we
might have ftrong confolation, that we have not only a God
to go to, but an advocate to introduce us to him, and to fpeak
for us. Believing in Chrift is fometimes expreffed by rejoicing in him; for it is a complacency of foul in the methods which infinite wifdom has taken, of bringing God and
man together by a mediator. " We are the circumcifion,
" that rejoice in Chrift Jefus," Phil. iii. 3. not only rely
upon him, but triumph in him. Paul is not only not afhamed
of the crofs of Chrift, but he glories in it, Gal. vi. 14. And,
when the eunuch is brought to believe in Chrift with all his
heart, he goes on his way rejoicing, highly pleafed with what
he has done.

What a pleafure, what a fatisfaction is it, to lodge the great
concerns of our fouls and eternity (which, furely, we cannot
but have fome careful thoughts about) in fuch a fkilful faithful hand as that of our Lord Jefus? and this we do by faith.
To caft the burden on him who is able to fave to the uttermoft, and as willing as he is able, and thus to make ourfelves
eafy? How is bleffed Paul elevated at the thought of this?
" Who is he that condemneth? It is Chrift that died, yea,
" rather is rifen again," Rom. viii. 34. And with what
pleafure doth he reflect upon the confidence he had put in
Jefus Chrift? 2 Tim. i. 12. "I know whom I have believed,
" and he is able to keep that which I have committed to
" him againft that day." They that know what it is to be
in pain for fin, and in care to obtain the favour of God, cannot but know what a pleafure it is to believe in Chrift as
the propitiation for our fins, and our interceffor with God.

How can we live a more pleafant life, than to " live by the
" faith of the Son of God," Gal ii. 20. to be continually
depending on him, and deriving from him, and referring all
to him; and as we have received him, fo to walk in him?

It is in believing that we are filled with joy and peace, Rom. xv. 13.

Fourthly, To be religious, is to enjoy God in all our creature-comforts: and is not that pleasant? It is to take the common supports and conveniences of life, be they of the richest, or be they of the meanest, as the products of his providential care concerning us, and the gifts of his bounty to us, and in them to " taste and see that the Lord is good," Psal. xxxiv. 8. good to all, good to us, It is to look above second causes to the first, through the creature to the Creator, and to say, concerning every thing that is agreeable and serviceable to us, this I asked, and this I have, from the hand of my heavenly Father. What a noble taste and relish doth this put into all the blessings with which we are daily loaded, our health and ease, our rest and sleep, our food and raiment, all the satisfaction we have in our relations, peace in our dwellings, success in our callings? The sweetness of these is more than doubled, it is highly raised, when by our religion we are taught and enabled to see them all coming to us from the goodness of God as our great benefactor, and thus to enjoy them richly, 1 Tim. vi. 17. while those who look no further than the creature, enjoy them very poorly, and but as the inferior creatures do.

Carnal irreligious people, though they take a greater liberty in the use of the delights of sense than good people dare take, and therein think they have the advantage of them, yet I am confident they have not half the true delight in them that good people have; not only because all excesses are a force upon nature, and surfeits are as painful as hunger and thirst, but because, though they do not thus abuse God's good creatures, yet they deprive themselves of the comfort of receiving them from their father's hand, because they are not affected to him as obedient children. " They knew not " that I gave them corn, and wine, and oil," Hos. ii. 8. They make use of the creature, but, as in Isa. xxii. 11. " they have not looked unto the maker thereof, nor had " respect to him that fashioned it long ago," as good people do; and so they come short of the pleasure which good people have.

Is it not pleasant to taste covenant-love in common mercies? Very pleasant to see the hand of our heavenly Father spreading our table, filling our cup, making our houses safe, and our beds easy? This they do, that by faith have their eyes ever towards the Lord, that by prayer fetch in his blessing upon all their enjoyments, and by praise give the glory of them to that mercy of his which endureth for ever. And when thus a continual regard is had to that mercy, an abundant sweetness is thereby infused into all the comforts of this life: for as the wrath and curse of God is the wormwood and the gall, Lam. iii. 19. in all the afflictions and miseries of this life; so his loving kindness is the honey and oil in all the comforts and enjoyments of this life: that is it that is better than life, Psal. lxiii. 3. 5. and which is abundantly satisfying; which puts gladness into the heart beyond the joy of harvest, Psal iv. 6. 7. Then the nations are glad, and sing for joy, when not only the earth yields her increase, but with it God, even their own God, gives them his blessing, Psal. lxvii. 4, 6. And when the church is brought to such a sense of God's grace, as to cry out, " How great " is his goodness, and how great is his beauty!" Zech. ix. 17. it follows, that then corn shall make the young men cheerful; intimating that we have no joy of our enjoyments, no true joy of them, till we are led by these streams to the fountain. " To the pure all things are pure," Tit. i. 14. and the more pure they are, the more pleasant they are.

Fifthly, To be religious, is to " cast all our cares upon " God, and to commit all our ways and works to him, with " an assurance that he will care for us:" and is not this pleasant? It is a very sensible pleasure to be eased of some pressing burden which we are ready to sink under; and care is such a burden: It is a " heaviness in the heart of man, " which maketh it to stoop " Now, true religion enables us to " acknowledge God in all our ways," Prov. iii. 6. and then depend upon him to direct our steps, and follow his directions, not leaning to our own understanding: It is to refer ourselves, and the disposal of every thing that concerns us in this world, to God, and to his will and wisdom, with an entire acquiescence in his award and arbitration; " Here " I am, let the Lord do with me as seemeth good in his " eyes," 2 Sam. xv. 26.

To be truly godly, is to have our wills melted into the will of God in every thing, and to say *amen* to it, not only as a prayer, but as a covenant; " Father in heaven, thy will " be done; not as I will, but as thou wilt." It is to be fully reconciled to all the difpofals of the divine providence, and methods of divine grace, both concerning others and ourfelves: To be fatisfied that " all is well that God doth," and will appear fo at laft, when the myftery of God fhall be finifhed. And how doth the mind enjoy itfelf that is come to this! How eafy is it! It is not only freed from racking anxieties, but filled with pleafing profpects: Fears are hereby filenced, and hopes kept up and elevated. Nothing can come amifs to thofe who have thus been taught by the principles of their religion to make the beft of that which is, becaufe it is the will of God; which is making a virtue of neceffity.

What uncomfortable lives do they live, who are continually fretting at that which cannot be helped, quarrelling with the difpofals of providence when they cannot alter them, and thus, by contracting guilt as well as by indulging grief, doubling every burden? But how pleafantly do they travel through the wildernefs of this world, who conftantly follow the pillar of cloud and fire, and accommodate themfelves to their lot, whatever it is? That like Paul, through Chrift ftrengthening them, have learned in every eftate to be content, " know how to want and how to abound?" Phil. iv. 11, 12, 13.

Religion brings the mind to the condition, whatever it is, and fo makes it eafy, becaufe the condition, though it be not in every thing to our mind, it is according to God's mind, who in all occurrences " performeth the thing that " is appointed for us," Job xxiii. 14. and will make all " work for good to them that love him." When the Pfalmift had directed us to " delight ourfelves always in the " Lord," Pfal. xxxvii. 4, 5 that is, to make our religion a conftant pleafure to ourfelves; he directs us, in order thereunto, to commit our way unto the Lord, to truft alfo in him, that he will bring it to pafs, fo as that we fhall have the defire of our hearts. And when Paul had encouraged us to be careful for nothing, but in every thing to make our requefts known to God, he affures us that, if we do fo, the peace of God, which paffeth all underftanding, fhall keep our hearts and minds, Phil iv. 6, 7.

Sixthly, To be religious, is to rejoice in the Lord always. Phil. iii. 1, & iv. 4. And is not that pleafant? It is not only one of the privileges of our religion, that we may rejoice, but it is made one of the duties of it: We are defective in our religion, if we do not live a life of complacency in God, in his being, his attributes, and relations to us. It should be a constant pleasure to us, to think that there is a God; that he is such a one as the scripture has revealed him to be, a being infinitely wise and powerful, holy, just, and good; that this God governs the world, and gives law to all the creatures; that he is our owner and ruler; that in his hand our breath is, in his hand our times, our hearts, and all our ways are. Thus certainly it is, and thus it must be; and happy they who can please themselves with these thoughts; as those must needs be a constant terror to themselves, who could wish it were otherwise.

They who thus delight in God, have always something, and something very commanding too, to delight in; a fountain of joy that can never be either exhausted or stopped up, and to which they may always have access. How few are there who live many days and yet rejoice in them all! Eccl. xi. 8. such a thing is supposed indeed, but it is never found true in any, but those who make God their joy, the gladness of their joy, as the Psalmist expresses it, Psal. xliii. 4. their exceeding joy: And in him it is intended their joy should terminate, when we are bid to rejoice evermore, 1 Thess. v. 16.

The conversion of the nations to Christ and his holy religion is often prophesied of in the Old Testament, under the notion of their being brought into a state of holy joy, Psal. xcvi. 11, & xcvii. 1, & c. 1. "Let the earth rejoice that the "Lord reigns, and let the multitude of isles be glad there- "of; Rejoice ye gentiles with his people." The gospel is "glad tidings of great joy to all people," Rom. xv. 10. When Samaria received the gospel, there was great joy in that city, Acts viii 8 so essential is joy to religion.

And the conversation of those who are joined to the Lord, when it is as it should be, is cheerful and joyful: They are called upon to walk in the light of the Lord, Psal. cxxxviii. 5. and to sing in the ways of the Lord, Isa ii. 5. and to serve the Lord their God with joyfulness and gladness of heart in the abundance of all things, Deut xxviii 47. yea, and in the want of all things too, Hab iii 17. though the fig-tree do not blossom, and there be no fruit in the vine. Has God now accepted thee and thy works in Jesus Christ?

Go thy way, eat thy bread with joy, and drink thy wine with a merry heart, Eccl. ix 7. It is the will of God that his people fhould be a cheerful people, that his Ifrael fhould rejoice in every good thing which the Lord their God giveth them, Deut. xxvi 11. fo that it is their own fault if they have not a continual feaft, and be not made to rejoice with the out-goings of every morning and every evening; for the compaffions of that God, in whom they rejoice, are not only conftant, but new and freſh daily.

Seventhly To be religious, is to make a bufinefs of praifing God: And is not that pleafant? It is indeed very unpleafant, and much againft the grain, to be obliged continually to praife one that is not worthy of praife; but what can be more pleafant, than to praife him to whom all praife is due, and ours particularly? to whom we and all the creatures lie under all poffible obligations; who is worthy of, and yet exalted far above all bleffing and praife; from whom all things are, and therefore to whom all things ought to be?

There is little pleafure in praifing one, whom none praife who are wife and good, but only the fools in Ifrael; but, in praifing God, we concur with the bleffed angels in heaven, and all the faints, and do it in concert with them, who the more they know him, the more they praife him "Blefs " the Lord, ye his angels, and all his hofts;" and therefore, with what pleafure may I caft in my mite into fuch a treafury! " Blefs the Lord, O my foul."

There is little pleafure in praifing one, who will not regard our praifes, nor take notice of our expreffions of efteem and affection: but when we offer to God the facrifice of praife continually, according to the obligation which our religion lays upon us, that is, the " fruit of our lips, giving " thanks to his name," Heb. xiii. 15. we offer it to one that takes notice of it, accepts it, is well pleafed with it, fmells a favour of reft from it, Gen. viii. 21 and will not fail to meet thofe with his mercies, that follow him with their praifes: for he hath faid, that they that offer praife glorify him; fuch a favourable conftruction doth he put upon it, and fuch an high ftamp upon coarfe metal.

Now, what is it that we have to do in religion but to praife God? We are taken into covenant with God, that we fhould be to him for a name, and for a praife," Jer xiii. 11. are called into his marvellous light, that we fhould " fhew "forth the praises of him that called us," 1 Pet. ii. 9. and how can we be more comfortably employed? They are therefore blessed that dwell in God's house, for " they will " be still praising him," Psal. lxxxiv. 4. And it is a good thing, good in itself, and good for us, it is very pleasant, to " give thanks unto the Lord, and to shew forth his praises," Psal. cxxxv. 3, and xcii 1. for we cannot do ourselves a greater honour, or fetch in a greater satisfaction, than by " giving unto the Lord the glory due unto his name." it is not only a heaven upon earth, but it is a pledge and earnest of a heaven in heaven too; for if we be here every day blessing God, Psal. clxv. 2. we shall be praising him for ever and ever; for thus all that shall go to heaven hereafter, begin their heaven now. Compare the hellish pleasure which some take in profaning the name of God, and the heavenly pleasure which others take in glorifying it, and tell me which is preferable.

Eighthly, To be religious, is " to have all our inordinate " appetites corrected and regulated:" And is not that pleasant? To be eased from pain is a sensible pleasure; and to be eased from that which is the disease and disorder of the mind, is a mental pleasure. Those certainly live a most unpleasant uncomfortable life, that are slaves to their appetites, and indulge themselves in the gratifications of sense, though never so criminal; that lay the reins in the neck of their lusts, and withhold not their hearts from any joy. The drunkards and unclean, though they are said to give themselves to their pleasures, yet really they estrange themselves from that which is true pleasure, and subject themselves to a continual pain and uneasiness.

The carnal appetite is often overcharged and that is a burden to the body, and its distemper: when enough is as good as a feast, I wonder what pleasure it can be to take more than enough; and the appetite the more it is indulged, the more humoursome and troublesome it grows; it is surfeited, but not satisfied; it doth but grow more impetuous and more imperious. It is true of the body, what Solomon says of a servant, Prov. xxix. 21. " He that delicately bringeth " up his servant from a child, shall have him become his " son," nay his master, " at the length." If we suffer the body to get dominion over the soul, so that the interests of the soul must be damaged, to gratify the inclinations of the body, it will be a tyrant, as an ufurper generally i-, and will rule with rigour: and as God faid to the people, 1 Sam. viii. 18. when by Samuel he had fhewed them the manner of the king that they chofe, when they rejected his government, "You will cry out in that day becaufe of your king "which ye have chofen you, and the Lord will not hear;" fo it is with thofe that bring themfelves into diforders, difeafes and terrors by the indulgence of their lufts, who can pity them? they are well enough ferved for "fetting fuch a "king over them. Who hath wo? who hath forrow?" Prov. xxiii. 29. None fo much as they that tarry long at the wine, though they think themfelves to have the monopoly of pleafure. The truth is, they that live in thefe pleafures are dead while they live, 1 Tim v. 6. and, while they fancy themfelves to take the greateft liberty, really find themfelves in the greateft flavery; for they are "led captive "by Satan at his will," 2 Pet. ii. 19. and of "whom a "man is overcome, of the fame is he brought in bondage."

And if the carnal appetite have not gained fuch a complete poffeffion, as quite to extinguifh all the remains of reafon and confcience: thofe noble powers, fince they are not permitted to give law, will give diiturbance: and there are few that have fo full an enjoyment of the forbidden pleafures of fenfe, but that they fometimes feel the checks of reafon, and the terrors of confcience. which mar their mirth, as the hand-writing on the wall did Belfhazzar's, and make their lives uncomfortable to them, and juftly fo, which makes them the more fo.

Now, to be religious, is to have the exorbitant power of thofe lufts and appetites broken, and, fince they will not be fatisfied, to have them mortified, and brought into a quiet fubmiffion to the commanding faculties of the foul, according to the direction of the divine law; and thus the peace is preferved, by fupporting good order and government in the foul.

Thofe certainly live the moft eafy, healthful, pleafant lives, that are moft fober, temperate, and chafte; that allow not themfelves to eat of any forbidden tree, though pleafant to the eye; that live regularly, and are the mafters, not the fervants, of their own bellies, 2 Cor ix. 27. that "keep "under their bodies, and bring them into fubjection," to religion and right reafon; and by laying the axe to the root, and breaking vicious habits, difpofitions, and defires, in the ftrength of divine grace, have made the refraining of vicious acts very eafy and pleafant: Rom. viii. 13. "If through " the fpirit we mortify the deeds of the body," we live, we live pleafantly.

Ninthly, To be religious, is " to have all our unruly paf- " fions likewife governed and fubdued ;" and is not that pleafant? Much of our torment arifeth from our intemperate heats, difcontent at the providence of God, fretfulnefs at every crofs occurrence, fear of every imaginary evil, envy at thofe that are in better ftate than ourfelves, malice againft thofe that have injured us, and an angry refentment of every the leaft provocation: thefe are thorns and briers in the foul; thefe fpoil all our enjoyments, both of ourfelves, and of our friends, and of our God too; thefe make mens lives unpleafant, and them a terror to themfelves, and to all about them.

But when, by the grace of God, thefe roots of bitternefs are plucked up, which bear fo much gall and wormwood, and we have learned of our Mafter to be "meek and lowly " in heart," Matth. xi. 29. we find reft to our fouls, we enter into the pleafant land. There is fcarce any of the graces of a Chriftian, that have more of a prefent tranquillity and fatisfaction, both inherent in them, and annexed to them, than this of meeknefs. " The meek fhall eat and be fatis- " fied," Pfal. xxii. 26. they fhall " inherit the earth," Mat. v. 5. they fhall " delight themfelves in the abundance of " peace," Pfal xxxvii. 11. and they fhall " increafe their " joy in the Lord," Ifa. xxix. 19. which nothing diminifheth more than ungoverned paffion; for that grieves the fpirit of grace, the comforter, and provokes him to withdraw, Eph. iv. 30, 31.

How pleafant is it for a man to be mafter of his own thoughts, to have a calmnefs and ferenity in his own mind, as thofe have, that have rule over their own fpirits, and thereby are kept in peace, peace! That will break an angry man's heart, that will not break a meek man's fleep.

Tenthly, To be religious, is to dwell in love to all our brethren, and to do all the good we can in this world: and is not that pleafant! Love is the fulfilling of the law; it is the fecond great commandment, to love our neighbour as ourfelves, Rom. xiii. 10. All our duty is fummed up in one word, which, as it is a ſhort word, ſo it is a ſweet word, *love*. Behold " how good and how pleaſant it is to live in " holy love," Pſal. cxxxiii. 1. It is not only pleaſing to God, and amiable in the eyes of all good men, but it will be very comfortable to ourſelves; for they that " dwell in " love, dwell in God, and God in them," 1 John iv. 16,

Religion teacheth us to be eaſy to our relations, and to pleaſe them well in all things; neither to give nor reſent provocations; to bear with their infirmities; to be courteous and obliging to all with whom we converſe; to keep our temper, and the poſſeſſion and enjoyment of our own ſouls, whatever affronts are given us: and can any thing contribute more to our living pleaſantly?

By love we enjoy our friends, and have communion with them in all their comforts, and ſo add to our own; " Re-" joicing with them that do rejoice," 1 Theſſ. iii 9. By love we recommend ourſelves to their love; and what more delightful than to love, and be beloved? Love is the very element of a pure and ſanctified mind, the ſweet air it breathes in, the cement of the beſt ſociety, which contributes ſo much to the pleaſure of human life. The ſheep of Chriſt, united in flocks by the bond of holy love, lie down together in the green paſtures, by the ſtill waters, where there is not only plenty, but pleaſure. The apoſtle exhorting his friends to be of good comfort, 2 Cor. xiii. 11. and to go on cheerfully in their Chriſtian courſe, exhorts them, in order to that, to " be of one mind, and to live in peace;" and then " the God of love and peace will be with them."

And what pleaſure comparable to that of doing good? It is ſome participation of the pleaſure of the eternal mind, who delights to ſhew mercy, and to do good: Nay, beſides the divinity of this pleaſure, there is a humanity in it; the nature of man, if it be not debauched and vitiated, cannot but take pleaſure in making any body ſafe and eaſy. It was a pleaſure to Job, to think that he had " cauſed the widow's " heart to ſing for joy, had been eyes to the blind, and feet " to the lame; and a father to the poor," and that they had been " warmed with the fleece of his ſheep," Job xxix. 13, 15, 16. & xxxi 20. The pleaſure that a good man hath in doing good, confirms that ſaying of our Saviour's, that " it is more bleſſed to give than to receive," Acts xx 35.

Eleventhly, To be religious, is to " live a life of communion with God:" And is not that pleasant? Good Christians, being taken into friendship, have " fellowship with the " Father, and with his Son Jesus Chrift," 1 John iii. 3 and make it their bufinefs to keep up that holy converfe and correspondence. Herein confifts the life of religion, to converfe with God, to receive his communications of mercy and grace to us, and to return pious and devout affections to him; and can any life be more comfortable? Is there any converfation that can poffibly be fo pleafant as this to a foul that knows itfelf, and its own powers and interefts?

In reading and meditating upon the word of God, we hear God fpeaking with a great deal of condefcenfion to us and concern for us; fpeaking freely to us, as a man doth to his friend, and about our own bufinefs; fpeaking comfortably to us in compaffion to our diftrefsful cafe: And what can be more pleafant to thofe who have a value for the favour of God, and are in care about the interefts of their own fouls? Pfal. cxii. 6. " When their judges are over-" thrown in ftony places, they fhall hear my words for " they are fweet: The words of God will be very fweet to thofe who fee themfelves overthrown by fin, and fo they will be to all that love God. With what an air of pleafure doth the fpoufe fay, " It is the voice of my beloved," and he fpeaks to me! Cant. ii. 8. 10.

In prayer and praife we fpeak to God, and we have liberty of fpeech; have leave to " utter all our words before " the Lord," as Jephthah did his in Mizpeh, Judges xi. 11. we fpeak to one whofe ear is open, is bowed to our prayers, nay, to whom the prayer of the upright is a delight. Prov. xv. 8. which cannot but make it very much a delight to them to pray. It is not only an eafe to a burdened fpirit to unbofom itfelf to fuch a friend as God is, but a pleafure to a foul that knows its own extraction, to have fuch a boldnefs, as all believers have to enter into the holieft.

Nay, we may as truly have communion with God in providences as in ordinances, and in the duties of common converfation, as in religious excercifes; and thus that pleafure may become a continual feaft to our fouls. What can be more pleafant, than to have a God to go to, whom we may " acknowledge in all our ways," and whom our eyes are ever towards; Pfal. xxv 15. to fee all our comforts coming to us from his hand, and all our croffes too; to refer ourfelves,

and all events that are concerning us, to his difpofal, with an affurance that he will order all for the beft? What a pleafure is it to behold the beauty of the Lord in all his works, and to tafte the goodnefs of the Lord in all his gifts, in all our expectations to fee " every man's judgement pro-
" ceeding from him ;" to make God our hope, and God our fear, and God our joy, and God our life, and God our all? This is to live a life of communion with God.

Twelfthly, To be religious, is to " keep up a conftant be-
" lieving profpect of the glory to be revealed:" It is to fet eternal life before us as the mark we aim at, and the prize we run for, and to " feek the things that are above," Col. iii. 1. And is not this pleafant? It is our duty to think much of heaven, to place our happinefs in its joys, and thitherward to direct our aims and purfuits; and what fubject, what object can be more pleafing! We have need, fometimes, to frighten ourfelves from fin, with the terrors of eternal death; but it is much more a part of our religion, to encourage ourfelves in our duty, with the hopes of that eternal life which God hath given us, that " life which is in
" his Son," 1 John v. 11.

What is Chriftianity, but " having our converfation in
" heaven," Phil. iii. 20 trading with the new Jerufalem, and keeping up a conftant correfpondence with that better country, that is, the heavenly, as the country we belong to, and are in expectation of, to which we remit our beft effects and beft affections; where our head and home is, and where we hope and long to be?

Then we are as we fhould be, when our minds are in a heavenly frame and temper; then we do as we fhould do, when we are employed in the heavenly work, as we are capable of doing it in this lower world: and is not our religion then a heaven upon earth? If there be a fulnefs of joy and pleafure in that glory and happinefs, which is grace and holinefs perfected; there cannot but be an abundance of joy and pleafure in that grace and holinefs, which is glory and happinefs begun. If there will be fuch a complete fatisfaction in vifion and fruition, there cannot but be a great deal in faith and hope, fo well founded, as that of the faints is. Hence we are faid, " Believing to rejoice with joy un-
" fpeakable," 1 Pet. i 8. and to be " filled with joy and peace
" in believing," Rom. xv. 13.

It is the character of all God's people, that they are born from heaven, and bound for heaven, and have laid up their treasure in heaven; and they that know how great, how rich, how glorious, and how well secured that happiness is to all believers, cannot but own, that, if that be their character, it cannot but be their unspeakable comfort and delight.

Now, lay all this together, and then tell me, whether religion be not a pleasant thing indeed, when even the duties of it themselves are so much the delights of it: and whether we do not serve a good master, who has thus made our work its own wages, and has graciously provided two heavens for those who never deserved one.

CHAP. III.

The pleasantness of Religion proved, from the provision that is made for the comfort of those that are religious, and the privileges they are entitled to.

WE have already found by inquiry, (O that we could all say we had found by experience!) that the very principles and practices of religion themselves have a great deal of pleasantness in them, and the one half of that has not been told us; and yet the comfort that attends religion, and follows after it, cannot but exceed that which is inherent in it, and comes with it. If the work of righteousness be peace, much more is the effect of righteousness so, Isa. xxxii. 17. If the precepts of religion have such an air of sweetness in them, what then have the comforts of it? Behold, happy is the people, even in this world, whose God is the Lord.

We must conclude, that they that walk in the ways of holy wisdom, have, or may have, true peace and pleasure; for God hath both taken care for their comfort, and given them cause to be comforted: so that, if they do not live easily and pleasantly, it is their own fault.

First, The God whom they serve, hath, in general, taken care for their comfort, and has done enough to convince them, that it is his will they should be comforted; that he not only gives them leave to be cheerful, but would have them to be so: for what could have been done more to the satisfaction of his family, than he has done in it?

1. There is a purchase made of peace and pleasure for them, so that they come to it fairly, and by a good title. He that purchased them a peculiar people to himself, took care they should be a pleasant people, that their comforts might be a credit to his cause, and the joy of his servants in his work might be a reputation to his family. We have not only " peace with God through our Lord Jesus Christ," Rom v. 1, 2, 3. but peace in our own consciences too; not only peace above, but peace within; and nothing less will pacify an offended conscience, than that which satisfied an offended God. Yet this is not all; we have not only inward peace, but we rejoice in the hope of the glory of God, and triumph over, nay, we triumph in tribulation.

Think what a vast expence (if I may so say) God was at, of blood and treasure, to lay up for us, and secure to us, not only a future bliss, but present pleasure, and the felicities not only of our home, but of our way. Christ had trouble, that we might have peace; pain, that we might have pleasure; sorrow, that we might have joy. He wore the crown of thorns, that he might crown us with roses, and a lasting joy might be upon our heads. He put on the spirit of heaviness that we might be arrayed with the garments of praise. The garden was the place of his agony, that it might be to us a garden of Eden; and there it was that he indented with his persecutors for the disciples, upon his surrendering himself, saying in effect to all agonies, as he did to them, "If ye seek me, let these go their way," John xviii. 8. if I be resigned to trouble, let them depart in peace

This was that which made wisdom's ways pleasantness, the everlasting righteousness which Christ, by dying, wrought out, and brought in. This is the foundation of the treaty of peace, and consequently the fountain of all those consolations which believers are happy in. Then it is, that all the seed of Israel glory, when they can each of them say, "In the Lord have I righteousness and strength," Isa. xlv. 24, 25. and then Israel shall dwell safely, in a holy security, when they have learned to call Christ by this name, " The " Lord our righteousness," Jer. xxiii. 6. If Christ had not gone to the Father, as our High Prieſt, with the blood of ſprinkling in his hand, we could never have rejoiced, but muſt have been always trembling.

Chriſt is our peace, Eph ii. 14. 17. not only as he made peace for us with God, but as he preached it to them " that " were afar off, and to them that were nigh ;" and has engaged that his people, whenever they may have trouble in the world, ſhall have peace in him, John xvi 33. upon the aſſurance of which they may be of good cheer, whatever happens. It is obſervable, that in the cloſe of that ordinance which Chriſt inſtituted in " the night wherein he was betrayed," to be a memorial of his ſufferings, he both ſung a hymn of joy, and preached a ſermon of comfort ; to intimate that which he deſigned in dying for us, was to give us " ever-" laſting conſolation, and good hope through grace," 2 Theſſ. ii. 16. and that we ſhould aim at, in all our commemorations of his death.

Peace and comfort are bought and paid for : If any of thoſe who were deſigned to have the beneſit of this purchaſe, deprive themſelves of it, let them bear the blame ; but let him have the praiſe who intended them the kindneſs, and who will take care, that though his kindneſs be deferred, it ſhall not be defeated : For, though his diſciples may be ſorrowful for a time, " their ſorrow ſhall be turned into joy," John xvi. 20.

2 There are promiſes made to believers of peace and pleaſure ; the benefits Chriſt bought for them are conveyed to them, and ſettled upon them in the covenant of grace, which is well ordered in all things, 2 Sam. xxiii. 5. for the comfort and ſatisfaction of thoſe, who have made that covenant " all their ſalvation, and all their deſire." There it is that light is ſown for the righteous. and it will come again in due time ; the promiſes of that covenant are the wells of ſalvation, out of which they draw water with joy ; the breaſts of conſolation, out of which, by faith, they ſuck, and are ſatisfied, Iſa. xxii. 3. and xvi. 12.

The promiſes of the Old Teſtament, that point at goſpel-times, ſpeak moſtly of this as the bleſſing reſerved for thoſe times, that there ſhould be great joy and rejoicing ; Iſa. xxxv. 1. & lx. 1. " The deſert ſhall rejoice and bloſſom as the " roſe ;" Ariſe, ſhine, for the light is come : For the deſign of the goſpel was to make religion a more pleaſant thing than it had been by freeing it both from the burdensome services which the Jews were under, and from the superstitious fears which the heathen kept themselves and one another in awe with; and by enlarging the privileges of God's people, and making them easier to come at.

Every particular believer is interested in the promises made to the church, and may put them in suit, and fetch in the comfort contained in them, as every citizen has the benefit of the charter, even the meanest. What a pleasure may one take in applying such a promise as that " I will " never leave thee, nor forsake thee?" or that, " All things " shall work for good to them that love God?" These and such as these, " guide our feet in the ways of peace;" and as they are a firm foundation on which to build our hopes, so they are a full fountain from which to draw our joys By the " exceeding great and precious promises, we partake of " a divine nature," 2 Pet. i. 4. of this instance of it as much as any, a comfortable enjoyment of ourselves; and by all the other promises that promise is fulfilled, Isa. lxv. 14, 15. " My servants shall eat, but ye shall be hungry; " my servants shall drink, but ye shall be thirsty; my ser- " vants shall rejoice, but ye shall be ashamed; my servants " shall sing for joy of heart, but ye shall cry for sorrow of " heart:" and the encouragement given to all the church's faithful friends is made good, " rejoice ye with Jerusalem, " and be glad with her, all ye that love her," Isa. lxvi. 10.

3. There is provision made for the application of that which is purchased and promised to the saints. What will it avail that there is wine in the vessel, if it be not drawn out? that there is a cordial made up, if it be not administered? Care is therefore taken, that the people of God be assisted in making use of the comforts treasured up for them in the everlasting covenant.

A religious life, one may well expect, should be a very comfortable life; for infinite wisdom has devised all the means that could be to make it so. " What could have " been done more for God's vineyard," Isa. v. 4. to make it flourishing as well as fruitful, than what he has done in it? There is not only an overflowing fulness of oil in the good olive, but golden pipes (as in the prophet's vision, Zech. iv 12.) for the conveyance of that oil to the lamps, to keep them burning. When God would himself furnish a paradife for a beloved creature, there was nothing wanting that might contribute to the comfort of it; in it was planted " every tree that was pleafant to the fight, and good for " food," Gen. ii. 8, 9. So in the gofpel there is a paradife planted for all the faithful offspring of the fecond Adam : A Canaan, a land flowing with milk and honey, a pleafant land, a reft for all the fpiritual feed of Abraham. Now, as God put Adam into paradife, and brought Ifrael into Canaan; fo he has provided for the giving of poffeffion to all believers, of all that comfort and pleafure that is laid up for them. As, in the garden of Eden, innocency and pleafure were twifted together; fo, in the gofpel of Chrift, grace and peace, " righteoufnefs and peace have kiffed each other," Pfal. lxxxv. 10. and all is done that could be wifhed, in order to our entering into this reft, this bleffed fabbatifm," Heb. iv. 3, 9. So that, if we have not the benefit of it, we may thank ourfelves; God would have comforted us, and we would not be comforted, our fouls refufed it.

Four things are done with this view, that thofe who live a godly life, may live a comfortable pleafant life ; and it is a pity they fhould receive the grace of God herein in vain.

(1.) The bleffed Spirit is fent to be the Comforter ; he doth alfo enlighten, convince, and fanctify; but he hath his name from this part of his office, John xiv. 16. " he is the " Comforter." As the fon of God was fent to be " the " Confolation of Ifrael." Luke ii. 25. to provide matter for comfort ; fo the Spirit of God was fent to be the Comforter, to apply the confolation which the Lord Jefus has provided. Chrift came to make peace, and the Spirit to fpeak peace, and to make us to hear joy and gladnefs, even fuch as will caufe broken bones themfelves to rejoice, Pfal. li. 8. Chrift having wrought out the falvation for us, the work of the Spirit is to give us the comfort of it; hence the joy of the faints is faid to be the " joy of the Holy Ghoft," 1 Theff i. 6. becaufe it is his office to adminifter fuch comforts as tend to the filling of us with joy.

God by his Spirit moving on the face of the waters, made the world according to the word of his power ; and by his Spirit moving on the fouls of his people, even when they are a perfect chaos, he " creates the fruit of the lips, peace," Ifa. lvii 19 the production of the word of his promife ; and if he did not create it, it would never be : And we muft not only attend to the word of God fpeaking to us, but fubmit to the Spirit of God working upon us with the word.

The Spirit, as a Comforter, was given not only for the relief of the faints in the fuffering ages of the church, but to continue with the church always to the end, for the comfort of believers, in reference to their conftant forrows both temporal and fpiritual; and what a favour is this to the church! no lefs needful, no lefs advantageous than the fending of the Son of God to fave us, and for which, therefore, we fhould be no lefs thankful. Let this article never be left out of our fongs of praife, but let us always give thanks to him, who not only fent his Son to make fatisfaction for us, for his mercy endureth for ever, but fent his Spirit to give fatisfaction to us, for his mercy endureth for ever; fent his Spirit not only to work in us the difpofition of children towards him; but alfo to witnefs to our adoption, and feal us to the day of redemption.

The Spirit is given to be our teacher, and to lead us into all truth; and, as fuch, he is a comforter: For by rectifying our miftakes, and fetting things in a true light, he filenceth our doubts and fears, and fets things in a pleafant light. The Spirit is our remembrancer, to put us in mind of that which we do know; and, as fuch, he is a comforter; for, like the difciples, we diftruft Chrift in every exigence, becaufe we " forget the miracles of the loaves," Mat. xvi. 9. The Spirit is our fanctifier; by him fin is mortified, and grace wrought and ftrengthened; and, as fuch, he is our comforter; for nothing tends fo much to make us eafy, as that which tends to make us holy. The Spirit is our guide, and we are faid to be led by the Spirit; and, as fuch, he is our comforter: for, under his conduct, we cannot but be led into ways of pleafantnefs, to the green paftures, and ftill waters.

(2.) The Scriptures are written " that our joy may be full," 1 John i. 4. that we may have that joy which alone is filling, and hath that in it which will fill up the vacancies of other joys, and make up their deficiencies; and that we may be full of that joy, may have more and more of it, may be wholly taken up with it, and may come at length to the full perfection of it in the kingdom of glory: Thefe things are written to you, not only that you may receive the word with joy, at firft, when it is a new thing to you, but that your joy may be full and conſtant. The word of God is the main pipe, by which comfort is conveyed from Chriſt, the fountain of life, to all the ſaints. That book which the Lamb, that was ſlain, took out of the right hand of him, that ſat on the throne, is that which we are by faith to feed upon and digeſt, and to fill our ſouls with; and we ſhall find that it will, like Ezekiel's roll, Ezek. iii. 3. " be in our " mouths as honey for ſweetneſs," and the opening of its ſeals will put a " new ſong into our mouth," Rev. v. 9.

Scripture-light is pleaſant, much more ſweet, more pleaſant, than for the eyes to behold the ſun. The manner of its conveyance is ſuch, as makes it abundantly more ſo; for God ſpeaks to us after the manner of men, in our own language. The comforts which the ſcripture ſpeaks to us, are the ſure mercies of David, ſuch as we may depend upon; and it is continually ſpeaking. The ſcriptures we may have always with us, and whenever we will, we may have recourſe to them; ſo that we need not be to ſeek for cordials at any time. The word is nigh thee, Rom x. 8. in thy houſe, and in thy hand; and it is thy own fault if it be not in thy mouth, and in thy heart. Nor is it a ſpring ſhut up, or a fountain ſealed; thoſe that compare ſpiritual things with ſpiritual, will find the ſcripture its own interpreter, and ſpiritual pleaſure to flow from it as eaſily, and plentifully, to all that have ſpiritual ſenſes exerciſed, as the honey from the comb.

All the ſaints have found pleaſure in the word of God, and thoſe who have given up themſelves to be led and ruled by it. It was ſuch a comfort to David in his diſtreſs, that, if he had not had that for his delight he would have periſhed in his affliction, Pſal. cxix 92. Nay, he had the joy of God's word to be his continual entertainment, Pſal. cxix. 54. " Thy ſtatutes have been my ſongs in the houſe of my " pilgrimage"—Thy words were found, faith Jeremiah, and I did eat them, feaſt upon them with as much pleaſure, as ever any hungry man did upon his neceſſary food, or epicure upon his dainties: I perfectly regaled myſelf with them; and " thy word was unto me the joy and rejoicing of my " heart," Jer. xv 16. And we not only come ſhort of their experiences, but fruſtrate God's gracious intentions, if we do not find pleaſure in the word of God; for, " whatſoever things were written aforetime, were written " for our learning, that we through patience and comfort " of the ſcriptures, might have hope," Rom. xv. 4.

(3.) Holy ordinances were instituted for the furtherance of our comfort and to make our religion pleasant unto us. The conversation of friends with each other is reckoned one of the greatest delights of this world; now ordinances are instituted for the keeping up of our communion with God, which is the greatest delight of the soul that is allied to the other world. God appointed to the Jewish church a great many feasts in the year (and but one fast, and that but for one day) on purpose for this end, that they might rejoice before the Lord their God, they and their families, Deut. xvi. 11.

Prayer is an ordinance of God, appointed for the fetching in of that peace and pleasure which is provided for us. It is intended to be not only the ease of our hearts, by casting our burden upon God, as it was to Hannah, 1 Sam. i. 18. who, when she had prayed, "went her way, and did " eat, and her countenance was no more sad;" but to be the joy of our hearts, by putting the promises in suit, and improving our acquaintance with heaven; " Ask and ye " shall receive, that your joy may be full," John xvi. 24. There is a throne of grace erected for us to come to; a mediator of grace appointed, in whose name to come; the Spirit of grace given to help our infirmities, and an answer of peace promised to every prayer of faith; and all this, that we might fetch in not only sanctifying, but comforting grace in every time of need, Heb. iv. 16. God's house, in which wisdom's children dwell, is called a house of prayer; and thither God brings them, on purpose to make them joyful, Isa. lvi. 7.

Singing of plalms is a gospel-ordinance, that is designed to contribute to the pleasantness of our religion; not only to express, but to excite, and to increase our holy joy: in singing to the Lord, we make a joyful noise to the rock of our salvation, Psal. xcv. 2. When the apostle had warned all Christians to take heed of drunkenness, be not drunk with wine, wherein is excess; lest they should think that thereby he restrained them from any mirth that would do them good, he directs them instead of the song of the drunkard, when the heart is merry with wine, to entertain themselves with the songs of angels, Eph. v. 18, 19. Speaking to yourselves (when you are disposed to please yourselves) in psalms, and hymns, and spiritual songs, singing and making melody in your hearts to the Lord. There is no more of substance in this ordinance, but the word and prayer put together: but the circumstance of the voice and tune being a natural means of affecting our hearts, both with the one and with the other; God, in condescension to our state, hath been pleased to make a particular ordinance of it, to shew how much it is his will that we should be cheerful, Jam. v. 13. "Is any merry? let him sing psalms." Is any vainly merry? let him suppress the vanity and turn the mirth into a right channel; he need not banish or abjure the mirth, but let it be holy, heavenly mirth, and in that mirth let them sing psalms. Nay, is any afflicted, and merry in his afflictions? let him shew it by singing psalms, as Paul and Silas did in the stocks, Acts xvi. 25.

The Lord's day is appointed to be a pleasant day, a day of holy rest, nay, and a day of holy joy; a thanksgiving-day, Psal. cxviii. 24. "This is the day which the Lord hath "made, we will rejoice and be glad in it." The psalm and song for the Sabbath-day begins thus, "It is a good thing "to give thanks unto the Lord," Psal. xcii. 1. So far were the primitive Christians carried in this notion, that the Lord's day was designed for holy triumph and exultation, that they thought it improper to kneel in any act of worship on that day.

The Lord's supper is a spiritual feast; and a feast (Solomon saith, Eccl. x. 19.) was made for laughter, and so was this for holy joy. We celebrate the memorials of his death, that we may rejoice in the victories that he obtained, and the purchases he made by his death; and may apply to ourselves the privileges and comforts, which by the covenant of grace are made ours. There we cannot but be glad and rejoice in him, where we "remember his love more than "wine," Cant i 4.

(4) The ministry is appointed for the comfort of the saints; and their guides in the ways of wisdom are instructed, by all means possible, to make them ways of pleasantness, and to encourage them to go on pleasantly in those ways. The priests of old were ordained for men, Heb. iii. 1, 2. and were therefore taken from among men, that they might have compassion upon the mourners. And the prophets had this particularly in their commission, "Comfort ye, "comfort ye my people, faith your God, speak ye comfort- "ably to Jerusalem," Isa. xl. 1.

Gofpel-minifters, in a fpecial manner, are appointed to be the helpers of the joy of the Lord's people; to be Barnabas's, fons of confolation; to ftrengthen the weak hands, and the feeble knees, and to fay to them who are of a "fearful heart, be ftrong," Ifa. xxxv. 3, 4. The tabernacles of the Lord of hofts being amiable, the care of all that ferve in thofe tabernacles muft be to make them appear fo; that they who compafs the altars of God, may find him God their exceeding joy.

Thus hath God taken care for the comfort of his people, fo that he is not to be blamed if they be not comforted: but that is not all,

Secondly, There are many particular benefits and privileges which they are entitled to, who walk in the ways of religion, that contribute very much to the pleafantnefs of thofe ways. By the blood of Chrift, thofe benefits and privileges are procured for them, which fpeaks them highly valuable; and by the covenant of grace they are fecured to them, which fpeaks them unalienable.

1. Thofe that walk in wifdom's ways are "difcharged "from the debts of fin," and that is pleafant: They are privileged from arrefts, Rom. viii. 33. "Who fhall lay any "thing to their charge?" while it is God that juftifies them, and will ftand by his own act, againft hell and earth: And, he is always near that juftifies them, Ifa. l. 8. and fo is their advocate, that pleads for them nearer than their accufer, (though he ftand at their right hand to refift them) and able to caft him out, and all his accufations.

Surely, they put a force upon themfelves, that are merry and pleafant under the guilt of fin; for, if confcience be awake, it cannot but have a fearful looking for of wrath: But, if fin be done away, the burden is removed, the wound is healed, and all is well; Son, be of good cheer, Mat. ix. 2 though fick of a palfy, yet be cheerful, for thy fins are forgiven thee; and therefore, not only they fhall not hurt thee, but God is reconciled to thee, and will do thee good: Thou mayeft enjoy the comforts of this life, and fear no fnare in them; mayeft bear the croffes of this life, and feel no fting in them; and mayeft look forward to another life without terror or amazement.

The pain which true penitents have experience of, in their reflections upon their fins, makes the pleafure and fatisfaction they have in the affurance of the pardon of them doubly fweet; as the forrow of a woman in travail is not an allay, but rather a foil to the joy, that a child is born upon it into the world. No pain more acute than that of broken bones, to which the forrows of a penitent finner are compared; but when they are well fet, and well knit again, they are not only made eafy, but they are made to rejoice, to which the comforts of a pardoned finner are compared. "Make me to hear joy and gladnefs, that the bones which " thou haft broken may rejoice," Pfal. li. 8. All our bones, when kept, that none of them were broken, muft fay, Lord, who is like unto thee? But there is a more fenfible joy for one difplaced bone reduced, than for the multitude of bones that were never hurt; as for one loft fheep brought home, than for ninety and nine that went not aftray: fuch is the pleafure which they have, that know their fins are pardoned.

When God's prophets muft fpeak comfortably to Jerufalem, they muft tell her that her iniquity is pardoned, Ifa xl. 2. Such a pleafure there is in the fenfe of the forgivenefs of fins, that it enables us to make a light matter of temporal afflictions, particularly that of ficknefs, Ifa. xxxiii. 24. " The inhabitant fhall not fay, I am fick; for the people " that dwelleth therein fhall be forgiven their iniquity:" And to make a great matter of temporal mercies when they are thus fweetened and fecured, particularly that of recovery from ficknefs, Ifa. xxviii. 17. " Thou haft in love to my " foul, cured my body, and delivered it from the pit of " corruption; for thou haft caft all my fins behind thy " back." If our fins be pardoned, and we know it, we may go out and come in in peace, nothing can come amifs to us; we may lie down and rife up with pleafure, for all is clear between us and heaven: Thus, " bleffed is the man whofe " iniquity is forgiven."

2. They have " the Spirit of God witneffing with their " fpirits, that they are the children of God," Rom. viii 16. and that is pleafant Adoption accompanies juftification; and if we have an affurance of the " forgivenefs of our fins " according to the riches of God's grace," Eph. i, 5. 7. we have an affurance of this further comfort, that we were " pre-" deftinate unto the adoption of children by Jefus Chrift." The fame evidence, the fame teftimony that is given of our being pardoned, ferves as an evidence and teftimony of our being preferred, our being thus preferred. Can

the children of princes and great men pleafe themfelves with the thoughts of the honours and expectations that attend that relation? and may not the children of God think with pleafure of the adoption they have received, Gal. v. 6. the Spirit of adoption? and that fpirit is witnefs to their adoption. And the pleafure muſt be the greater, and make the ſtronger impreſſion of joy, when they remember, that they were by nature not only ſtrangers and foreigners, but children of wrath, and yet thus highly favoured.

The comfort of relations is none of the leaſt of the delights of this life: But what comfort of relations comparable to this of being related to God as our father; and to Chriſt, as our elder brother; and to all the faints and angels too, as belonging to the fame family, which we are happily brought into relation to? The pleafure of claiming and owning this relation, is plainly intimated in our being taught to cry, Abba, Father, Rom. viii. 15. Why ſhould it be thus doubled, and in two languages, but to intimate to us the unaccountable pleafure and ſatisfaction, with which good Chriſtians call God Father? it is the ſtring they harp upon, Abba, Father.

With what pleafure doth David's own fpirit witnefs to this? "O my foul, thou haſt faid unto the Lord, Thou art my "Lord," Pfal. xvi. 2. and it is more to me that God is mine, than if all the world were mine: But when, with our fpirits, the fpirit of God witneffeth this too, faying to thy foul, Yea, he is thy God, and he owns thee as one of his family; witnefs what he has wrought both in thee, and for thee, by my hand: what joy doth this fill the foul with! joy unfpeakable! efpecially confidering that, as the prophet fpeaks, in the place, in the fame heart and confcience, where it was faid (and by the fpirit too, when he convinced as a fpirit of bondage) "Ye "are not my people, even there it ſhall be faid unto them," by the fpirit when he comforts as a fpirit of adoption, "Ye are the fons of the living God," Hof. i. 10.

3. They have an acceſs with boldnefs to the throne of grace, and that is pleafant. Prayer not only fetcheth in peace and pleafure, but it is itfelf a great privilege; and not only an honour, but a comfort; one of the greateſt comforts of our lives, that we have a God to go to at all times, fo that we need not fear coming unfeafonably, or coming too often; and in all places, though as Jonah in the fiſhes belly, or as

David in the depths, or in the ends of the earth, Pfal. cxxx. 1. & lxi. 2.

It is a pleasure to one who is full of care and grief to unbosom himself; and we are welcome to pour out our complaint before God, and to shew before him our trouble, Pfal. cxlii. 1, 2. and to one who wants, or fears wanting, to petition one who is able, and willing to supply these wants. And we have great encouragement to "make our requests "known unto God;" we have an "access with confidence," Eph. iii. 12. not an access with difficulty, as we have to great men, not an access with uncertainty of acceptance, as the Ninevites. "Who can tell if God will return to us?" But we have an access with an assurance: whatsoever we ask in faith, according to his will, "we know that we have "the petitions that we desired of him," 1 John v. 15.

It is a pleasure to talk to one we love, and that we know loves us, and, though far above us, yet takes notice of what we say, and is tenderly concerned for us: What a pleasure is it then to speak to God? to have not only a liberty of access, but a liberty of speech, freedom to utter all our mind, humbly, and in faith; "boldness to enter into the holiest "by the blood of Jesus," Heb. x. 19, 20. and not with fear and trembling, as the high priest, under the law, entered into the holiest; but boldness to pour out our hearts before God, PfaL lxii. 8. as one who, though he knows our case better than we ourselves, yet will give us the satisfaction of knowing it from us, according to our own shewing. Beggars, who have good benefactors, live as pleasantly as any other people: It is the case of God's people; they are beggars, but they are beggars to a bountiful benefactor, who is "rich in mercy to all who call upon him." Blessed are they that "wait daily at the posts of wisdom's doors," Prov. viii. 34. If the prayer of the upright be God's delight, it cannot but be theirs, Cant. ii. 14.

4. They have a sanctified use of all their creature comforts, and that is pleasant. "The Lord knows the way of "the righteous," and takes cognizance of all their concerns, Pfal. xxxvii. 23. The steps, yea, and the stops too, of a good man are ordered by the Lord; both his successes when he goes forwards, and his disappointments when he goes backwards: He "blesseth the work of their hands," and his blessing "makes rich, and adds no sorrow with it," Prov.

x 27. more is implied than is expressed, it adds joy with it, infuseth a comfort into it.

What God's people have, be it little or much, they have it from the love of God, and with his blessing; and then, " behold all things are clean *and sweet* to them," Luke x. 41. They come from the hand of a Father, by the hand of a Mediator, not in the channel of common providence, but by the golden pipes of the promises of the covenant. Even the unbelieving husband, though not sanctified himself, yet is " sanctified by the believing wife," 1 Cor. vii. 14. and so is the comfort of other relations; for to those who please God, every thing is pleasing, or should be so, and is made so by his favour. And hence it is, Psal. xxxvii. 16. that a " little that a righteous man has," having a heart to be content with it, and the divine skill of enjoying God in it, is better to him than the " riches of many wicked" were to them; and that " a dinner of herbs where love is," and the " fear of the Lord," is better, and yields abundantly more satisfaction, than " a stalled ox, and hatred and trouble " therewith," Prov. xv. 16, 17.

5. They have the testimony of their own consciences for them in all conditions, and that is pleasant. A good conscience is not only a brazen wall, but a continual feast; and all the melody of Solomon's instruments of music of all sorts, were not to be compared to that of the bird in the bosom, when it sings sweet. If Paul has a conscience void of offence, though he be as sorrowful, yet he is always rejoicing ; nay, and even when he is " pressed above measure," 2 Cor. i. 8, 12. and has " received a sentence of death within him- " self, his rejoicing is this, even the testimony of his consci- " ence" concerning his integrity.

As nothing is more painful and unpleasant, than to be smitten and reproached by our own hearts, to have our consciences fly in our faces, and give us our own; so there is nothing more comfortable, than to be upon good grounds reconciled to ourselves, to " prove our own work," Gal. vi. 4. by the touchstone of God's word, and to find it right; for then have we " rejoicing in ourselves alone, and not in an- " other: For if our hearts condemn us not," 1 John iii. 21. " then have we confidence towards God; may lift up our " face without spot" unto him, and comfortably appeal to his omniscience: " Thou, O Lord, knowest me, thou haft " feen me, and tried my heart towards thee," Jer. xii 3.

This will not only make us eafy under the cenfures and reproaches of men, as it did Job: " my heart fhall not re- " proach me," though you do; and Paul: " it is a very " fmall thing with me to be judged of man's judgement;" But it will be a continual delight to us, to have our own hearts fay, Well done. For the voice of an enlightened, well informed confcience is the voice of God, it is his deputy in the foul: The thoughts of the fober heathen between themfelves, when they did not accufe, yet the utmoft they could do was but to excufe, which is making the beft of bad; but they who have their hearts fprinkled from an evil confcience by the blood of Chrift, Rom. ii. 15. are not only excufed, but encouraged and commended; for their praife is not of men, but of God.

It is eafy to imagine the holy, humble pleafure that a good man has, in the juft reflection upon the fuccefsful refiftance of a ftrong and threatening temptation; the feafonable fuppreffing and croffing of an unruly appetite or paffion, and a check given to the tongue when it was about to fpeak unadvifedly. What a pleafure is it to look back upon any good word fpoken, or any good work done, in the ftrength of God's grace, to his glory, and any way to the advantage of our brethren, either for foul or body! With what a fweet fatisfaction may a good man lie down in the clofe of the Lord's Day, if God has enabled him, in fome good meafure, to " do the work of the day in the day, according as the " duty of the day requires?" We may then " eat our " bread with joy, and drink our wine with a merry heart," when we have fome good ground to hope, that God now accepteth our works through Jefus Chrift, Ecclef. ix. 7.

6. They have the earnefts and foretaftes of eternal life and glory, and that is pleafant indeed. They have it not only fecured to them, but dwelling in them, in the firftfruits of it, fuch as they are capable of in their prefent imperfect ftate, 1 John v. 13. " Thefe things are written unto " you that believe on the name of the Son of God, that ye " may know, not only that you fhall have, but that you " have eternal life; you are fealed with that holy fpirit of " promife," Eph. i. 13, 14. marked for God, which is the earneft of our inheritance, not only a ratification of the grant, but part of the full payment.

Canaan, when we come to it, will be a land flowing with milk and honey; "In God's prefence there is a fulnefs of "joy, and pleafures for evermore," Pfal. xvi. 11. But, left we fhould think it long ere we come to it, the God whom we ferve has been pleafed to fend to us, as he did to Ifrael, fome clufters of the grapes of that good land to meet us in the wildernefs; which if they were fent us in excufe of the full enjoyment, and we were to be put off with them, that would put a bitternefs into them; but, being fent us in earneft of the full enjoyment, that puts a fweetnefs into them, and makes them pleafant indeed.

A day in God's courts, an hour at his table in communion with him, is very pleafant, better than a thoufand days, than ten thoufand hours, in any of the enjoyments of fenfe; but this very much increafeth the pleafantnefs of it, that it is the pledge of a bleffed eternity, which we hope to fpend within the veil, in the vifion and fruition of God. Sabbaths are fweet, as they are earnefts of the everlafting fabbatifm, or keeping of a fabbath (as the apoftle calls it, Heb. iv. 9.) which remains for the people of God.—Gofpel feafts are therefore fweet, becaufe earnefts of the everlafting feaft, to which we fhall fit down with Abraham, and Ifaac, and Jacob. The joys of the Holy Ghoft are fweet, as they are earnefts of that joy of our Lord, into which all Chrift's good and faithful fervants fhall enter. Praifing God is fweet, as it is an earneft of that bleffed ftate, in which we fhall not reft day or night from praifing God. The communion of faints is fweet, as it is an earneft of the pleafure we hope to have in the "general affembly, and church of the firft-"born," Heb. xii. 23.

They who travel wifdom's ways, though fometimes they find themfelves walking in the low and darkfome valley of the fhadow of death, where they can fee but a little way before them, yet at other times they are led with Mofes to the top of Mount Pifgah, and thence have a pleafant profpect of the land of promife, and the glories of that good land; not with fuch a damp upon the pleafure of it as Mofes had, Deut xxxiv. 4 "Thou fhalt fee it with thine eyes, but thou "fhalt not go over thither;" but fuch an addition to the pleafure of it as Abraham had, when God faid to him, Gen. xiii. 14, 15. "All the land which thou feeft, to thee will "I give it" Take the pleafure of the profpect, as a pledge of the poffeffion fhortly.

CHAP. IV.

The Doctrine further proved by Experience.

HAVING found religion in its own nature pleasant, and the comforts and privileges so with which it is attended; we shall next try to make this truth more evident, by appealing to such as may be thought competent witnesses in such a case. I confess, if we appeal to the natural man, the mere animal, (as the word signifies, 1 Cor. ii. 14.) that looks no further than the things of sense, and judgeth by no other rule than sense, and "receiveth not the "things of the spirit of God, for they are foolishness to him;" such a one will be so far from consenting to this truth, and concurring with it, that he will contradict and oppose it. Our appeal must be to those who have some spiritual senses exercised; for otherwise "the brutish man knows not, nei- "ther doth the fool understand this," Psal. xcii. 6.

We must therefore be allowed to look upon convinced sinners, and comforted saints. Wicked people whom the Spirit hath rowsed out of a sinful security, and godly people whom the Spirit has put to rest in a holy serenity, are the most competent proper witnesses to give evidence in this case; and to their experience we appeal.

First, Ask those who have tried the ways of sin and wickedness, of vice and profaneness, and begin to pause a little, and to consider whether the way they are in be right; and let us hear what are their experiences concerning those ways: And our appeal to them is in the words of the apostle, "What fruit had ye then in those things, whereof ye are "now ashamed?" Rom. vi. 21. Not only, What fruit will ye have at last, when the end of these things is death? or, as Job xxi. 21. "What pleasure hath he in his house af- "ter him, when the number of his months is cut off in "the midst?" but, What fruit, what pleasure had ye then, when you were in the enjoyment of the best of it?

Those that have been running to an excess of riot, that have laid the reins in the neck of their lusts, have rejoiced with the "young man in his youth, and walked in the way "of their hearts, and the sight of their eyes," have taken a boundless liberty in the gratifications of sense, and have

made it their bufinefs to extract out of this world, whatever
may pafs under the name of pleafure: but when they begin to think (which they could not find in their hearts to do
while they were going on in their purfuit) afk them now
what they think of thofe pleafures which pretend to vie
with thofe of religion; and they will tell you:

1. That " the pleafure of fin was painful and unfatisfying
" in the enjoyment," and which then they had no reafon to
boaft of. It was a fordid pleafure, and beneath the dignity of a man, and which could not be had, but by yielding up
the throne in the foul to the inferior faculties of fenfe, and
allowing them the dominion over reafon and confcience,
wh ch ought to command and give law. It was the gratifying of an appetite, which was the difeafe of the foul, and
which would not be fatisfied, but, like the daughters of
the horfe-leech, ftill cry, give, give.

What poor pleafure hath the covetous man in the wealth
of the world? It is the luft of the eye that is thereby humoured; for " what good hath the owner thereof, fave the
" beholding thereof with his eyes?" 1 John ii 16 and
what a poor fatisfaction is that? And yet even that is no
fatisfaction neither; for he that loveth filver, will find, that
the more he has, the more he would have, fo that he fhall
not be fatisfied with filver; nay, it faftens upon the mind
a burden of care and perplexity, fo that " the abundance
" of the rich will not fuffer him to fleep," Eccl. v. 10, 11,
12.

Drunkennefs paffeth for a pleafant fin, but it is a brutifh
pleafure; for it puts a force upon the powers of nature, difturbs the exercife of reafon, and puts men out of the poffeffion and enjoyment of their fouls; and fo far is it from
yielding any true fatisfaction, that the gratifying of this bafe
appetite is but bringing oil to a flame: " When I awake, I
" will feek it yet again," is the language of the drunkard,
Prov. xxiii. 35.

Contention and revenge pretend to be pleafant fins too,
eft vindicta bonum vita jucundis ipfa; but it is fo far from
being fo, that it is, of all other fins, the moft vexatious: It
kindles a fire in the foul, puts it into a hurry and diforder;
where they are, there is confufion and every evil work.
The lufts, from whence not only wars and fightings come,
Jam. iv. 1. but other fins are faid to war in the members;

they not only war againſt the ſoul, 1 Pet ii. 11. and threaten the deſtruction of its true intereſts, but they war in the ſoul, and give diſturbance to its preſent peace, and fill it with continual alarms.

They that have made themſelves ſlaves to their luſts, will own, that it was the greateſt drudgery in the world, and therefore is repreſented in the parable of the prodigal, by a young gentleman hiring himſelf to one that "ſent him in-" to his field to feed ſwine," Luke xv 16. where he was made a fellow commoner with them, and "would fain" "have filled his belly with the huſks," that they did eat; ſuch a diſgrace, ſuch a diſſatisfaction is there in the pleaſures of ſin; beſides the diverſity of maſters which ſinners are at the back of, and their diſagreement among themſelves; for they that are diſobedient to that God who is one, are deceived, ſerving divers luſts and pleaſures, and therein led captive by Satan, their ſworn enemy, at his will, Tit. iii. 3

2. That the pleaſure of ſin was very bitter and tormenting in the reflection. We will allow that there is a pleaſure in ſin for a ſeaſon, Heb. xi. 25. but that ſeaſon is ſoon over, and is ſucceeded by another ſeaſon that is the reverſe of it; the ſweetneſs is ſoon gone, and leaves the bitterneſs behind in the bottom of the cup; the wine is red, and gives its colour, its flavour very agreeable; but at the laſt it "bites" "like a ſerpent, and ſtings like an adder," Prov. xxiii. 32. Sin is that ſtrange woman, whoſe flatteries are charming, but "her end bitter as wormwood," Prov. v. 3, 4.

When conſcience is awake, and tells the ſinner he is very guilty; when his ſins are ſet in order before him in their true colour, and he ſees himſelf defiled and deformed by them: when his own wickedneſs begins to correct him, and his backſlidings to reprove him, and his own heart makes him "loath himſelf for all his abominations," Jer. ii. 19. where is the pleaſure of his ſin then? As the thief is aſhamed when he is diſcovered to the world, ſo are the drunkards, the unclean, when diſcovered to themſelves; and ſay, "Where ſhall I cauſe my ſhame to go?" there is no remedy but I muſt lie down in it. If the pleaſure of any ſin would laſt, ſurely that of ill got gain would, becauſe there is ſomething to ſhew for it; and yet though that wickedneſs be ſweet in the ſinner's mouth, though he "hide it un-

" der his tongue, yet in his bowels it is turned into the gall
" of afps," Job. xx. 11, &c He hath fwallowed down
riches, but fhall be forced to vomit them up again.

Solomon had fkimmed the cream of fenfual delights, and pronounced not only vanity and vexation concerning them all, even the beft, but concerning thofe of them that were finful, the forbidden pleafures into which he was betrayed; that the reflection upon them filled him with horror and amazement: " I applied my heart," faith he, " to know " the wickednefs of folly, even of foolifhnefs and mad- " nefs;" fo he now calls the loofes he had taken: he cannot fpeak bad enough of them; for " I find more bitter than " death, the woman whofe heart is fnares and nets, and her " hands as bands," Eccl. vii. 26.

And is fuch pleafure as this worthy to come in competition with the pleafures of religion, or to be named the fame day with them? What fenfelefs creatures are the fenfual, that will not be perfuaded to quit the pleafures of brutes, when they fhall have in exchange the delights of angels?

Secondly, Afk thofe that have tried the ways of wifdom, what are their experiences concerning thofe ways. " Call " now if there be any that will anfwer you, and to which " of the faints will you turn?" Job. v. 1. Turn you to which you will, and they will agree to this, that " wifdom's " ways are pleafantnefs, and her paths peace." However about fome things they may differ in their fentiments, in this they are all of a mind, that God is a good mafter, and his fervice not only perfect freedom, but perfect pleafure.

And it is a debt which aged and experienced Chriftians owe both to their mafter and to their fellow-fervants, both to Chrift and Chriftian, to bear their teftimony to this truth; and the more explicitly and folemnly they do it, the better. Let them tell others " what God has done for " their fouls," and how they have " tafted that he is gra- " cious," Pfal lxvi 16. Let them own to the honour of God and religion, that, as in 1 Kings viii. 56. there " has " not failed one word of God's good promife," by which he defigned to make his fervants pleafant; that what is faid of the pleafantnefs of religion, is really fo: let them " fet to " their feal that it is true," 1 John i. 1. Let it have their *probatum eft*; we have found it fo.

The ways of religion and godlinefs are the good old ways, Jer. vi. 16. Now, if you would have an account of the way you have to go, you muſt inquire of thoſe that have travelled it; not thoſe who have occaſionally ſtept into it now and then, but thoſe whoſe buſineſs had led them to frequent it. Aſk the ancient travellers, whether they have found reſt to their ſouls in this way; and there are few you ſhall inquire of, but they will be ready to own theſe four things from experience:

1. That they have found "the rules and dictates of reli-" "gion very agreeable both to right reaſon, and to their" "true intereſt," and therefore pleaſant. They have found the word nigh them, and accomodated to them, and not at ſuch a mighty diſtance as they were made to believe. They have found "all God's precepts concerning all things to be" "right," and reaſonable, and highly equitable; and, when they did but ſhew themſelves men, they could not but conſent, and ſubſcribe "to the law, that it was good," Rom. vii. 16. and there is a wonderful decorum in it.

The laws of humility and meekneſs, ſobriety and temperance, contentment and patience, love and charity; theſe are agreeable to ourſelves when we are in our right mind: They are the rectitude of our nature, the advancement of our powers and faculties, the compoſure of our minds, and the comfort of our lives, and carry their own letters of commendation along with them. If a man underſtood himſelf, and his own intereſt, he would comport with theſe rules, and govern himſelf by them, though there were no authority over him to oblige him to it. All that have throughly tried them, will ſay, they are ſo far from being chains of impriſonment to a man, and as fetters to his feet, that they are as chains of ornament to him, and as the girdle to his loins.

Aſk experienced Chriſtians, and they will tell you what abundance of comfort and ſatisfaction they have had in keeping ſober, when they have been in temptation to exceſs; in doing juſtly, when they might have gained by diſhoneſty as others do, and no-body know it; in forgiving an injury, when it was in the power of their hand to revenge it; in giving alms to the poor, when perhaps they ſtraitened themſelves by it; in ſubmitting to an affliction, when the circumſtances of it were very aggravating; and in bridling their paffion under great provocations. With what comfort does Nehemiah reflect upon it, that though his predeceffors in the government had abufed their power, yet fo did not I, (faith he, Neh. v. 15.) becaufe of the fear of God? And with what pleafure doth Samuel make his appeal, 1 Sam. xii. 3. " Whofe ox have I taken, or whom " have I defrauded?" and Paul his; " I have coveted no " man's filver, or gold, or apparel." If you would have a regifter of experiences to this purpofe, read the 119th Pfalm, which is a collection of David's teftimonies to the fweetnefs and goodnefs of God's law, the equity and excellency of it, and the abundant fatisfaction that is to be found in a conftant confcientious conformity to it.

2. That they have found the exercifes of devotion to be very pleafant and comfortable; and, if there be an heaven upon earth, it is in communion with God in his ordinances; in hearing from him, in fpeaking to him, in receiving the tokens of his favour and communications of his grace, and returning pious affections to him, pouring out the heart before him, lifting up the foul to him.

All good Chriftians will fubfcribe to David's experience, Pfal. lxxiii. 28. "It is good for me to draw near to God;" the nearer the better; and it will be beft of all, when I come to be neareft of all, within the veil, and will join with him in faying, " Return unto thy reft, O my foul!" Pfal. cxvi. 7. to God as to thy reft, and repofe in him. I have found that fatisfaction in communion with God, which I would not exchange for all the delights of the fons of men, and the peculiar treafures of kings and provinces.

What a pleafure did thofe pious Jews in Hezekiah's time find in the folemnities of the Paffover, who, when they had kept feven days according to the law in attending on God's ordinances, " took counfel together to keep other " feven days; and they kept other feven days with glad- " nefs," 2 Chron. xxx. 23. And, if Chrift's hearers had not found an abundant fweetnefs and fatisfaction in attending on him, they would never have continued their attendance three days in a defert place, as we find they did, Matth. xv. 32. No wonder then that his own difciples, when they were fpectators of his transfiguration, and auditors of his difcourfe with Mofes and Elias in the holy mount, faid, " Mafter, it is good for us to be here;" here let us make tabernacles, Matth. xvii. 4.

I appeal to all, that know what it is to be inward with God in an ordinance, to worship him in the Spirit, whether they have not found abundant satisfaction in it? They will say with the spouse, Cant. ii. 3 " I sat down under " his shadow with delight, and his fruit was sweet unto my " taste:" And with the noble Marquis of Vico, " Let " their money perish with them, that esteem all the wealth " and pleasure of this world worth one hour's communion " with God in Jesus Christ." They will own, that they never had that true delight and satisfaction in any of the employments or enjoyments of this world, which they have had in the service of God, and in the believing relishes of that loving-kindness of his, which is better than life, Psal. lxiii. 3, 5. These have put gladness into their hearts, more than the joy of harvest, or theirs that divide the spoil. If in their preparations for solemn ordinances they have gone forth weeping, bearing precious seed; yet they have " come again with rejoicing, bringing their sheaves with " them," Psal cxxvi. 5, 6.

3. That they have found the pleasure of religion sufficient to overcome the pains and trouble of sense, and to take out the sting of them, and take off the terror of them. This is a plain evidence of the excellency of spiritual pleasures, that religious convictions will soon conquer sensual delights, and quite extinguish them, so that they become as songs to a heavy heart; for a wounded spirit who can bear? But it has often been found, that the pains of sense have not been able to extinguish spiritual delights, but have been conquered and quite overbalanced by them. Joy in spirit has been to many a powerful allay to trouble in the flesh.

The pleasure that holy souls have in God, as it needs not to be supported by the delights of sense, so it fears not being suppressed by the grievances of sense. They can rejoice in the Lord, and joy in him as the God of their salvation, even then, when the " fig-tree doth not blossom, " and there is no fruit in the vine," Hab. iii. 17, 18. for even then, when in the world they have tribulation, Christ has provided that in him they should have satisfaction.

For this we may appeal to the martyrs, and other sufferers for the name of Christ: How have their spiritual joys made their bonds for Christ easy, and made their prisons their delectable orchards, as one of the martyrs called his?

Animated by these comforts, they have not only taken patiently, but "taken joyfully the spoiling of their goods, " knowing in themselves that they have in heaven a better " and a more enduring substance," Heb. x 34 Ask Paul, and he will tell you, 2 Cor. vi 4, 5 that even then when he was troubled on every side, when without were fightings, and within were fears, yet he was filled with comfort, and was exceeding joyful in all his tribulation; and that as his sufferings for Christ did increase, his consolation in Christ increased proportionably, 2 Cor i. 5. And though he expects no other but to finish his course with blood, yet he doubts not but to finish his course with joy.

Nay, we may appeal to the sick-beds and death-beds of many good Christians for the proof of this; when wearisome nights have been appointed to them, yet God's " sta- " tutes have been their songs, their songs in the night," Psal. cxix. 54. I have pain said one, but I bless God I have peace; weak and dying, said another, but *sat lucis intus*, light and comfort enough within. The delights of sense forsake us, when we most need them to be a comfort to us; when a man is " chastened with pain upon his bed, and the " multitude of his bones with strong pain. he abhorreth " bread and dainty meat," and cannot relish it, Job. xxxiii. 19, 20. But then the bread of life and spiritual dainties have the sweetest relish of all. Many of God s people have found it so: this is my " comfort in mine affliction, that thy word " hath quickened me," Psal. cxix 50. This has made all their bed in their sickness, and made it easy.

The pleasantness of wisdom's ways hath sometimes been remarkably attested by the joys and triumphs of dying Christians, in reflecting upon that divine grace which hath carried them comfortably through this world, and is then carrying them more comfortably out of it to a better. " What is " that light which I see?" said an eminent divine upon his death bed; " It is the sun shine," said one that was by: No, replied he, " it is my Saviour's shine; O the joys! O the " comforts that I feel! Whether in the body, or out " of the body, I cannot tell; but I see and feel things that " are unutterable, and full of glory. O let it be preached " at my funeral, and tell it when I am dead and gone, that " God deals familiarly with man. I am as full of comfort

" as my heart can hold." Mr. Joseph Allein's life, and Mr. John Janeway's have remarkable inftances of this.

4. They have found, that " the clofer they have kept to " religion's ways, and the better progrefs they have made " in thofe ways, the more plea'ure they have found in them." By- this it appears, that the pleafure takes its excellency from the religion; that the more religion prevails, the greater the pleafure is. What difquiet and difcomfort wifdom's children have, is owing, not to wifdom's ways, thofe are pleafant, but to their deviations from thofe ways, or their flothfulnefs and trifling in thefe ways; thofe indeed are unpleafant, and fooner or later will be found fo.

If good people are fometimes drooping and in forrow, it is not becaufe they are good, but becaufe they are not fo good as they fhould be; they do not live up to their profeffion and principles, but are too much in love with the body, and hanker too much after the world: though they do not turn back to Sodom, they look back towards it, and are too mindful of the country from which they came out; and this makes them uneafy, this forfeits their comforts, and grieves their comforter, and difturbs their peace, which would have been firm to them, if they had been firm to their engagements. But, if we turn afide out of the ways of God, we are not to think it ftrange if the confolations of God do not follow us

But if we " cleave to the Lord with full purpofe of " heart," then we find the "joy of the Lord our ftrength." Have we not found thofe duties moft pleafant, in which we have taken moft pains, and moft care? and that we have had the moft comfortable fabbath-vifits made to our fouls then, when we have been moft " in the Spirit on the Lord's " day?" Rev. i. 10

And the longer we continue, and the more we mend our pace in thefe ways, the more pleafure we find in them. This is the excellency of fpiritual pleafures, and recommends them greatly, that they increafe with ufe; fo far are they from withering or going to decay. The difficulties which may at firft be found in the ways of religion wear off by degrees, and the work of it grows more eafy, and the joys of it more fweet.

Afk thofe that have backflidden from the ways of God, have left their firft love, and begin to bethink themfelves,

and to remember whence they are fallen, whether they had not a great deal more comfort when they kept clofe to God, than they have had fince they turned afide from him; and they will fay with that adulterefs, when fhe found the way of her apoftacy hedged up with thorns, " I will go, and re-
" turn to my firft hufband; for then it was better with me
" than now," Hof. ii 7. There is nothing got by departing from God, and nothing loft by being faithful to him.

CHAP. V.

The doctrine illuftrated by the fimilitude ufed in the Text, of a pleafant way or journey.

THE practice of religion is often, in fcripture, fpoken of as a way, and our walking in that way: it is the way of God's commandments, it is a high-way, the king's high-way, the king of kings high-way; and thofe that are religious are travelling in that way. The fchool-men commonly call Chriftians in this world *viatores*, travellers when they come to heaven, they are *comprehenfores*, they have then attained, are at home; here they are in their journey, there at their journey's end. Now, if heaven be the journey's end, the prize of our high calling, and we are fure, if we fo run as we ought, that we fhall obtain that, it is enough to engage and encourage us in our way, though it be never fo unpleafant; but we are told *ex abundanti*, that we have alfo a pleafant road.

Now, there are twelve things which help to make a journey pleafant; and there is fomething like to each of them which may be found in the way of wifdom, and thofe who walk in that way.

Firft, It helps to make a journey pleafant, to go upon a good errand. He that is brought up a prifoner in the hands of the minifters of juftice, whatever conveniences he may be accommodated with, cannot have a pleafant journey, but a melancholy one: and that is the cafe of a wicked man; he is going on, in this world, towards deftruction; the way he is in, though wide and broad, leads directly to it; and, while he perfifts in it, every ftep he takes is fo much nearer hell: and therefore he cannot have a pleafant journey; it is absurd and indecent to pretend to make it so: though the way may seem right to a man, yet there can be no true pleasure in it, while " the end thereof is the ways of death, and " the steps take hold on hell," Prov. v 5.

But he that goes into a far country to receive for himself a kingdom, whatever difficulties may attend his journey, yet the errand he goes on is enough to make it pleasant: And on this errand they go that travel wisdom's ways; they look for a kingdom which cannot be moved, and are pressing forwards in the hopes of it. Abraham went out of his own country, not knowing whither he went, Heb. xi. 8. but those that set out and hold on in the way of religion, know whither it will bring them, that it leads to life, Mat. vii. 14. eternal life; and therefore in the way of righteousness is life, Prov. xii. 28 because there is such a life at the end of it.

Good people go upon a good errand, for they go on God's errand, as well as on their own; they are serving and glorifying him, contributing something to his honour, and the advancement of the interests of his kingdom among men; and this makes it pleasant: And that which puts so great a reputation upon the duties of religion, as that by them God is served and glorified, cannot but put so much the more satisfaction into them. With what pleasure doth Paul appeal to God, as the God whom " he served with his spirit " in the gospel of his son?" Rom i. 9.

Secondly, It helps to make a journey pleasant, to have strength and ability for it. He that is weak, and sickly, and lame, can find no pleasure in the pleasantest walks; how should it be, when he takes every step in pain? But a strong man rejoiceth to run a race, while he that is feeble trembles to set one foot, before another. Now, this makes the ways of religion pleasant, that they who walk in those ways are not only cured of their natural weakness, but are filled with spiritual strength; they travel not in their own might, but in the greatness of his strength, who is mighty to save, Isa. lxiii. 1.

Were they to proceed in their own strength, they would have little pleasure in the journey, every little difficulty would foil them, and they would tire presently; but they go forth, and go on in the strength of the Lord God, Psal. lxxi. 16. and upon every occasion, according to his promise, he renews that ftrength to them, and they " mount, up with wings like eagles, " they go on with cheerfulnefs and alacrity, they run and are not weary, they walk and do not faint, Ifa xl. 31. God, with his comforts, enlargeth their hearts; and then they not only go but run the way of his commandments, Pfal. cxix. 32.

That which to the old nature is impracticable and unpleafant, and which therefore is declined, or gone about with reluctancy, to the new nature is eafy and pleafant: And this new nature is given to all the faints, which puts a new life and vigour into them, " ftrengthens them with all " might in the inner man, Col. i. 11 unto all diligence in doing work, patience in fuffering work, and perfeverance in both; and fo all is made pleafant. They are ftrong in the Lord, and in the power of his might, Eph. vi. 10. and this not only keeps the fpirit willing, even then when the flefh is weak, but makes even the lame man to leap as an hart, and the tongue of the dumb to fing, Ifa. xxxv. 6. I can do all things through Chrift ftrengthening me, Phil. iv. 13.

Thirdly, It helps to make a journey pleafant, to have daylight. It is very uncomfortable travelling in the night, in the black and dark night; " He that walketh in darknefs," fays our faviour, " knows not whither he goes," John xii. 35. right or wrong, and that is uncomfortable: And in another place, " If a man walk in the night, he ftumbleth, be-" caufe there is no light in him," John xi. 10. And this is often fpoken of as the miferable cafe of wicked people, " They know not, neither will they underftand, they walk on " in darknefs, Pfal. lxxxii. 5. They are in continual danger, and fo much the more, if they be not in continual fear.

But wifdom's children are all " children of the light, and " of the day," 1 Theff. v. 5. They were darknefs, but are now " light in the Lord, and walk as children of the light," Eph. ii. 8. Truly the light is fweet, even to one who fits ftill, but much more fo to one who is in a journey; and doubly fweet to thofe who fet out in the dark, as we all did. But this great light is rifen upon us, not only to pleafe our eyes, but to " guide our feet into the paths of peace," Luke i 79. And then they are indeed paths of peace, when we are guided into them, and guided in them by the light of the gofpel of Chrift. And all that walk in the light of gofpel-conduct, cannot fail to walk in the light of gofpel-comforts.

And it adds to the pleafure of having day-light in our travels, if we are in no danger of lofing it, and of being benighted: And this is the cafe of thofe who walk in the light of the Lord; for the Sun of righteoufnefs, that is rifen upon them with healing under his wings, fhall no more go down, but fhall be their everlafting light, Ifa. lx. 20.

Fourthly, It helps to make a journey pleafant, to have a good guide, whofe knowledge and faithfulnefs one can confide in. A traveller, though he has day light, yet may mifs his way, and lofe himfelf, if he have not one to fhew him his way, and go before him, efpecially if his way lie, as ours does, through a wildernefs, where there are fo many by-paths; and though he fhould not be guilty of any fatal miftake, yet he is in continual doubt and fear, which makes his journey uncomfortable.

But this is both the fafety and the fatisfaction of all true Chriftians, that they have not only the gofpel of Chrift for their light, both a difcovering and directing light, but the Spirit of Chrift for their guide: It is promifed, " that he " fhall lead them into all truth," John xvi. 13. fhall "guide " them with his eye," Pfal. xxxii. 8. Hence they are faid to " walk after the Spirit, and to be led by the Spirit," Rom. viii. 1, 14. as God's Ifrael were led through the wildernefs of old by a pillar of cloud and fire, and the Lord was in it.

This is that which makes the way of religion fuch a highway, as that the way-faring men, though fools, fhall not err therein, Ifa xxxv. 8. There are fools indeed, wicked ones, who walk after the flefh, that mifs their way, and wander endlefsly; " The labour of the foolifh wearieth " every one of them, becaufe he knoweth not how to go to " the city," Eccl. x. 15 but thofe fools that fhall not err therein are weak ones, the foolifh things of the world, who in a fenfe of their own folly are fo wife, as to give up themfelves entirely to the conduct of the Spirit, both by confcience and the written word; and, if they have done this in fincerity, they know whom they have depended upon to " guide them by his counfel, and afterwards to receive " them to his glory," Pfal lxxiii. 24. Thefe may go on their journey pleafantly, who are promifed, that whenever they are in doubt, or in danger of miftaking, or being mifled, they shall "hear a voice saying to them, This is the "way, walk in it," Isa. xxx. 2.

Fifthly, It helps to make a journey pleasant, to be under a good guard, or convoy, that one may travel safely. Our way lies through an enemy's country, and they are active subtle enemies; the road is infested with robbers that lie in wait to spoil and to destroy; we travel by the lions dens, and the mountains of the leopards; and our danger is the greater, that it ariseth not from flesh and blood, but spiritual wickednesses, 1 Pet. v. 8. Satan, by the world and the flesh, way-lays us, and seeks to devour us; so that we could not with any pleasure go on our way, if God himself had not taken us under his special protection.

The same spirit that is a guide to these travellers, is their guard also; for whoever are sanctified by the Holy Ghost, are by him "preserved in Christ Jesus," Jude 1. preserved blameless; and shall be "preserved to the heavenly king- "dom," 2 Tim. iv. 18 so as that they shall not be robbed of their graces and comforts, which are their evidences for and earnests of eternal life; they are kept "by the power "of God, through faith unto salvation," 1 Pet. i. 5. and therefore may go on cheerfully.

The promises of God are a writ of protection to all Christ's good subjects in their travels, and give them such a holy security, as lays a foundation for a constant serenity. Eternal truth itself hath assured them, that no evil shall befal them, Psal. xci. 10. nothing really and destructively evil, no evil but what God will bring good to them out of: God himself hath engaged to be their keeper, and to preserve their going out and coming in, from henceforth and for ever, which looks as far forwards as eternity itself; and by such promises as these, and that grace which is conveyed through them to all active believers, "God carries them, "as upon eagles wings, to bring them to himself," Deut. xxxii. 1..

Good angels are appointed for a guard to all that walk in wisdom's ways, to bear them in their arms where they go, Psal. xci. 11. and to pitch their tents round about them where they rest, Psal. xxxiv. 7. and so to keep them in all their ways. How easy may they be that are thus guarded, and how well pleased under all events! "as Jacob was, "who went on his way, and the angels of God met him," Gen. xxxii. 1.

Sixthly, It helps to make a journey pleasant, to have the way tracked by those that have gone before in the same road, and on the same errand. Untroden paths are unpleasant ones; but, in the way of religion, we are both directed and encouraged by the good examples of those that have chosen the way of truth before us, and have walked in it. We are bidden to follow them, who are now through faith and patience (those travelling graces of a Christian) inheriting the promises, Heb. vi. 12.

It is pleasant to think that we are walking in the same way with Abraham, and Isaac, and Jacob, with whom we hope shortly to sit down in the kingdom of God. How many holy, wise, good men have governed themselves by the same rules that we govern ourselves by, with the same views, have lived by the same faith that we live by, looking for the same blessed hope, and have by it " obtained a good report?" Heb. xi. 2. And we " go forth by the footsteps of the flock," Cant. i. 8.

Let us therefore, to make our way easy and pleasant, " take the prophets for an example," Jam. v. 10. And " being compassed about with so great a cloud of witnesses," that are like the cloud in the wilderness that went before Israel, not only to shew them the way, but to smooth it for them; let us run with patience, and cheerfulness, the " race " that is set before us, looking unto Jesus," the most encouraging pattern of all, who has " left us an example, " that we should follow his steps," Heb. xii. 1. And what more pleasant than to follow such a leader, whose word of command is, Follow me!

Seventhly, It helps to make a journey pleasant, to have good company: this deceives the time, and takes off the tediousness of a journey as much as any thing; *amicus pro vehiculo*. It is the comfort of those who walk in wisdom's ways, that though there are but few walking in those ways, yet there are some, and those the wisest and best, and more excellent than their neighbours; and it will be found there are more ready to say, " We will go with you, for we have " heard that God is with you," Zech. viii. 23.

The communion of saints contributes much to the pleasantness of wisdom's ways. We have many fellow-traveliers, that quicken one another, by the fellowship they have one with another, as "companions in the kingdom and "patience of Jesus Christ,' Rev. i. 9 It was a pleasure to them, who were going up to Jerusalem to worship, that their numbers increased in every town they came to, and so they went from strength to strength, they grew more and more numerous, "till every one of them in Zion appeared "before God," Psal. lxxxiv, 7. and so it is with God's spiritual Israel, to which we have the pleasure of seeing daily additions of such as shall be saved.

They that travel together make one another pleasant by familiar converse; and it is the will of God that his people should by that means encourage one another, and strengthen one another's hands; "They that fear the Lord shall speak "often one to another," Mal. iii 17. exhort one another daily, and communicate their experiences. And it will add much to the pleasure of this, to consider the kind notice God is pleased to take of it; He hearkens, and hears, and a book of remembrance is written for those that fear the Lord, and think on his name.

Eighthly, It helps to make a journey pleasant, to have the way lie through green pastures, and by the still waters; and so the ways of wisdom do. David speaks his experience herein, Psal. xxiii. 2. that he was led into the green pastures, the verdure whereof was grateful to the eye; and by the still waters, whose soft and gentle murmurs were music to the ear: And he was not driven through these, but made to lie down in the midst of these delights, as Israel when they encamped at Elim, where there were "twelve wells "of water, and three-score and ten palm trees," Exod. xv. 27.

Gospel ordinances, in which we deal much in our way to heaven, are very agreeable to all the children of God, as these green pastures, and still waters; they call the sabbath a delight, and prayer a delight, and the word of God a delight. These are their pleasant things, Isa. lxiv. 11. There is a river of comfort in gospel ordinances, the "streams whereof make glad the city of God, the holy "place of the tabernacles of the most High," Psal. xlvi. 4. and along the banks of this river their road lies.

Those that turn aside from the ways of God's commandments, are upbraided with the folly of it, as leaving a pleafant road for an unpleafant one. Will a man, a traveller, be fuch a fool as to leave my fields, which are fmooth and even, for a rock that is rugged and dangerous, or for the the fnowy mountains of Lebanon? Jer. xviii. 14. in the margin, " Shall the running waters be forfaken for the ftrange cold " waters?" Thus are men enemies to themfelves, and the foolifhnefs of man perverteth his way.

Ninthly, It adds to the pleafure of a journey, to have it fair over head. Wet and ftormy weather takes off very much of the pleafure of a journey; but it is pleafant travelling when the fky is clear, and the air calm and ferene: And this is the happinefs of them that walk in wifdom's ways, that all is clear between them and heaven; there are no clouds of guilt to interpofe between them and the Sun of righteoufnefs, and to intercept his refrefhing beams; no ftorms of wrath gathering that threaten them.

Our reconciliation to God, and acceptance with him, makes every thing pleafant. How can we be melancholy, if heaven fmile upon us? " Being juftified by faith, we " have peace with God," Rom. v. 1, 2. and peace from God, peace made for us, and peace fpoken to us; and then we rejoice in tribulation. Thofe travellers cannot but rejoice all the day, " who walk in the light of God's coun" tenance," Pfal. lxxxix. 15.

Tenthly, It adds likewife to the pleafure of a journey, to be furnifhed with all needful accommodations for travelling. They that walk in the way of God, have wherewithal to bear their charges; and it is promifed them that they fhall want no good thing, Pfal. xxxiv. 10. If they have not an abundance of the wealth of this world, which perhaps will but overload a traveller, and be an incumbrance rather than any furtherance, yet they have good bills; having accefs by prayer to the throne of grace whereever they are, and a promife that they fhall receive what they afk; and accefs by faith to the covenant of grace, which they may draw upon, and draw from, as an inexhauftible treafury. Jehovah Jireh, The Lord will provide.

Chrift our " Melchizedec brings forth bread and wine," as Gen. xiv. 18. for the refrefhment of the poor travellers, that they may not faint by the way. 1 Kings xix. 8. when Elijah had a long journey to go, he was victualled accordingly; God will give grace sufficient to his people for all their exercises, 2 Cor. xii 9. " strength according to the " day; Verily they shall be fed." And since travellers must have baiting places, and resting places, Christ has provided rest at noon, Cant. i. 7. in the heat of the day, for those that are his; and rest at night too : " Return to thy " rest, O my soul."

Eleventhly, It adds something to the pleasure of a journey, to sing in the way, This takes off something of the fatigue of travelling, exhilarates the spirits ; pilgrims used it; and God has put a song, a new song, into the mouths of his people, Psal. xl. 3. even praises to their God, and comfort to themselves. He hath given us cause to be cheerful, and leave to be cheerful, and hearts to be cheerful, and has made it our duty to rejoice in the Lord always.

It is promised to those, who are brought to praise God, by hearing the words of his mouth, that they shall sing in the ways of the Lord, Psal cxxxviii. 5. and good reason, for great is the glory of the Lord. How pleasantly did the released captives return to their own country, when they came with singing unto Zion! Isa. li. 11. And much more Jehoshaphat's victorious army, when they came to Jerusalem, " with psalteries and harps to the house of the " Lord; for the Lord had made them to rejoice over their " enemies," 2 Chr. xx. 28. With this the travellers may revive one another; " O come, let us sing unto the Lord."

Twelfthly, It helps to make a journey pleasant, to have a good prospect. The travellers in wisdom's ways may look about them with pleasure, so as no travellers ever could ; for they can call all about them their own, even the " world, " and life, and death, and things present, and things to " come;" in this state, all is yours, if you be Christ's, 1 Cor. iii. 22. The whole creation is not only at peace with them, but at their service.

They can look before them with pleasure; not with anxiety and uncertainty, but a humble assurance; not with terror, but joy. It is pleasant in a journey, to have a prospect of the journey's end; to see that the way we are in leads directly to it, and to see that it cannot be far off; every step we take is so much nearer it, nay, and we are within a few steps of it: We have a prospect of being shortly with Christ in paradise; yet a little while, and we shall be at home, we shall be at rest; and whatever difficulties we may meet with in our way, when we come to heaven all will be well eternally well.

CHAP. VI.

The Doctrine vindicated from what may be objected against it.

"SUFFER me a'little, (faith Elihu to Job, Job. xxxvi. 2.) "and I will shew thee that I have yet to speak on "God's behalf," something more to say in defence of this truth, against that which may seem to weaken the force of it. We all ought to concern ourselves for the vindication of godliness, and to speak what we can for it; for we know that it is every where spoken against. And there is no truth so plain, so evident, but there have been those who have objected against it: The prince of darkness will raise what mists he can to cloud a truth, that stands so directly against his interest; but great is the truth, and will prevail.

Now, as to the truth of the pleasantness of religion,

First, It is easy to confront the reproaches of the enemies of religion, that put it into an ill name. There are those who make it their business, having perverted their own ways, to pervert the right ways of the Lord, and cast an odium upon them; as Elymas the sorcerer did, with design to turn away the deputy from the faith. Acts xiii. 8, 10. They are like the wicked spies, that brought up an evil report upon the promised land, Numb. xiii. 23. as a land that did eat up the inhabitants thereof; and neither could be conquered nor was worth conquering.

The scoffers of the latter days speak ill of religion, as a task and a drudgery; they dress it up in frightful formidable colours, but very false ones, to deter others from piety, and to justify themselves in their own impiety. They suggest, that Christ's yoke is heavy, and his commandments grievous, and that to be religious is to bid adieu to all pleasure and delight, and to turn tormentors to ourselves; that God is a hard master, "reaping where he has not sown, and "gathering where he has not strawed," Matth. xxv. 24.

There were thofe of old who thus reproached the ways of God, and flandered religion; for they faid, "It is vain to "ferve God," Mal. iii. 13 there is neither credit nor comfort in it; and what profit is it that we have kept his ordinances, and (obferve their invidious defcription of religion) that we have walked mournfully before the Lord of hofts? as if to be religious was to walk mournfully, whereas indeed it is to walk cheerfully.

Now, in anfwer to thefe calumnies, we have this to fay, that the matter is not fo. They who fay thus of religion, "fpeak evil of the things which they know not," 2 Pet. ii. 12 while "what they know naturally as brute beafts, in "thofe things they corrupt themfelves," Jude 10 The devil, we know, was a liar from the beginning, and a falfe accufer of God and religion, and in this particularly reprefented God to our firft parents, Gen. iii. 5. as having dealt hardly and unjuftly with them in tying them out from the tree of knowledge; as if he envied them the happinefs and pleafure they would attain to by eating of that tree: and the fame method he ftill takes to alienate men's minds from the life of God, and the power of godlinefs. But we know, and are fure, that it is a groundlefs imputation; for wifdom's ways are ways of pleafantnefs, and all her paths are peace.

Secondly, It is eafy alfo to fet afide the mifreprefentations of religion, which are made by fome who call themfelves its friends, and profefs kindnefs for it. As there are enemies of the Lord who blafpheme, 2 Sam. xii. 14. fo there are among the people of the Lord thofe who give them great occafion to do fo, as David did. How many wounds doth religion receive in the houfe of her friends? falfe friends they are, or foolifh ones, unworthy to be called wifdom's children, for they do not juftify her as they ought; but, through miftake and indulgence of their own weaknefs, betray her caufe, inftead of pleading it, and witneffing to it; and confirm people's prejudices againft it, which they fhould endeavour to remove.

Some who profefs religion are morofe and four in their profeffion, peevifh and ill humoured, and make the exercifes of religion a burden and tafk, and terror to themfelves and all about them, which ought to fweeten the fpirit, and make it eafy, and candid, and compaffionate to the infirmities of the weak and feeble of the flock.

Others are melancholy and forrowful in their profeffion and go mourning from day to day, under prevailing doubts, and fears, and difquietments about their fpiritual ftàte. We know, fome of the beft of God's fervants have experienced trouble of mind to a great degree.

But as to the former, it is their fin; and let them bear their own burden, but let not religion be blamed for it : and as to the latter, though there are fome very good people that are of a forrowful fpirit, yet we will abide by it, that true piety has true pleafure in it notwithftanding.

But, (1.) God is fometimes pleafed for wife and holy ends, for a time, to fufpend the communication of his comforts to his people, and to hide his face from them, to try their faith, that it may be " found to praife, and honour, " and glory at the appearing of Chrift," 1 Pet. i. 6, 7. and fo much the more for their being a while in heavinefs through manifold temptations. Thus he correƈts them for what has been done amifs by them, and takes this courfe to mortify what is amifs in them; even winter feafons contribute to the fruitfulnefs of the earth. Thus he brings them to a clofer and more humble dependence upon Chrift for all their comfort, and teacheth them to live entirely upon him. And though for a fmall moment he thus forfakes them, Ifa. liv. 7, 8. it is but to magnify his power fo much the more in fupporting them, and to make his returns the fweeter, for he will gather them with everlafting loving kindnefs. Light is fown for them, and it will come up again.

(2.) This, as it is their afflicƈion, God's hand muft be acknowledged in it, his righteous hand; yet there is fin in it, and that is from themfelves. Good people have not the comforts they might have in their religion; and whofe fault is it? they may thank themfelves, they run themfelves into the dark, and then fhut their eyes againft the light. " My " wounds ftink and corrupt," faith David, Pfal. xxxviii. 5. The wounds of fin which I gave myfelf are unhealed, not bound up, or mollified with ointment. And why? Is it for want of balm in Gilead, or a phyfician there ? No, he owns it is becaufe of my foolifhnefs; I did not take the right method with them. God fpeaks joy and gladnefs to them, but they turn a deaf ear to it; like Ifrael in Egypt, that hearkened not to Mofes for "anguifh of fpirit and fore "bondage," Exod. vi. 9 But let not the blame be laid upon religion, which has provided comfort for their fouls; but let them bear the blame whofe fouls refufe to be comforted, or who do not take the way appointed for comfort, who do not go through with their repenting and believing. David owns, the reafon why he wanted comfort, and was in pain, and in a tofs, was becaufe he kept filence: he was not fo free with God as he might, and fhould have been; but when he faid, "I will confefs my tranfgreffion unto the Lord," he was forgiven, and all was well, Pfal. xxxii. 3, 4, 5.

Thofe do both God and Chrift, and themfelves, and others, a deal of wrong, who look upon him with whom they have to do in religion, as one that feeks an occafion againft them, and counts them for his enemies, and is extreme to mark what they think, or fay, or do amifs; whereas he is quite otherwife, is flow to anger, fwift to fhew mercy, and willing to make the beft of thofe whofe hearts are upright with him, though they are compaffed about with infirmity: he "will not always chide; he doth not delight in the death "of them that die," but would rather they fhould "turn "and live," Ezek. xxxiii. 11. Nor doth he delight in the tears of them that weep, doth not afflict willingly, nor "grieve the children of men," Lam. iii. 33. much lefs his own children, but would rather they fhould be upon good grounds comforted Religion then clears itfelf from all blame, which fome may take occafion to caft upon it, from the uncomfortable lives which fome lead that are religious.

But, *thirdly*, It will require fome more pains to reconcile this truth of the pleafantnefs of religion's ways, with that which the word of God itfelf tells us of, the difficulties which the ways of religion are attended with. We value not the mifapprehenfions of fome, and the mifreprefentations of others, concerning religion's ways; but we are fure the word of God is of a piece with itfelf, and doth not contradict itfelf Our mafter hath taught us to call the way to heaven a narrow way, *odos tethlimmene*, an afflicted way, a diftreffed way.; and we have in fcripture many things that fpeak it fo. And it is true; but that doth not contradict this doctrine, that the ways of wifdom are pleafant: for the pleafantnefs that is in wifdom's ways is intended to be a balance, and it is very much an over-balance, to that in them which is any way diftafteful or incommodious. As for the imaginary difficulties which the fluggard dreams of, " a lion in the way, a lion in the ftreet," we do not regard them: but there are fome real difficulties in it, as well as real comforts; for " God hath fet the one over againft the " other," Eccl. vii. 14. that we might ftudy to comport with both, and might fing, and fing unto God of both, Pfal. ci. 1.

We will not, we dare not make the matter better than it is, but will allow there is that in religion which at firft view may feem unpleafant; and yet doubt not but to fhew that it is reconcileable to, and confiftent with, all that pleafure which we maintain to be in religion, and fo to take off all exceptions againft this doctrine. *Amicæ fcripturarum lites, utinam & noftra!* It were well if we could agree with one another, as well as fcripture doth with itfelf.

There are four things which feem not well to confift with this doctrine, and yet it is certain they do.

Firft, It is true, that to be religious, is to live a life of repentance; and yet religion's ways are pleafant notwithftanding. It is true, we muft mourn for fin daily, and reflect with regret upon our manifold infirmities; fin muft be bitter to us, and we muft even loath and abhor ourfelves for our corruptions that dwell in us, and the many actual tranfgreffions that are committed by us. We muft renew our repentance daily, and every night muft make fome forrowful reflections upon the tranfgreffions of the day. But then,

1. It is not our walking in the way of wifdom that creates us this forrow, but our trifling in that way, and our turning afide out of it. If we would keep clofe to thefe ways, and pafs forwards in them as we ought, there would be no occafion for repentance. If we were as we fhould be, we fhould be always praifing God, and rejoicing in him; but we make other work for ourfelves by our own folly, and then complain that religion is unpleafant; and whofe fault is that? If we would be always loving and delighting in God, and would live a life of communion with him, we fhould have no occafion to repent of that; but if we leave the fountain of living waters, and turn afide to broken cif-

terns, or the brooks in the fummer, and fee caufe, as doubtlefs we fhall, to repent of that, we may thank ourfelves.

What there is of bitternefs in repentance, is owing, not
to our religion, but to our defects and defaults in religion;
and it proves not that there is bitternefs in the ways of God,
but in the ways of fin, which make a penitential forrow neceffary for the preventing of a forrow a thoufand times
worfe, for fooner or later fin will have forrow. If repentance be bitter, we muft fay, not that this comes of being
godly, but this comes of being finful. Jer. iv. 18. " This is
" thy wickednefs becaufe it is bitter." If by fin we have
made forrow neceffary, it is certainly better to mourn now,
than mourn at the laft Prov v. 11. To contiaue impenitent, is not to put away forrow from thy heart, but to put it
off to a worfe place.

2. Even in repentance, if it be right, there is a true pleafure, a pleafure accompanying it. Our Saviour hath faid
of them who thus mourn, not only that they fhall be comforted, but that they are bleffed, Mat. v. 4. When a man
is confcious to himfelf that he has done an ill thing, and
what is unbecoming him and may be hurtful to him, it is
incident to him to repent of it. Now religion hath found
a way to put a fweetnefs into that bitternefs. Repentance,
when it is from under the influence of religion, is nothing
but bitternefs and horror, as Judas's was; but repentance,
as it is made an act of religion, as it is one of the laws of
Chrift, is pleafant, as it is the raifing of the fpirit, and the
difcharging of that which is noxious and offenfive.

Our religion has not only taken care, that penitents be
not overwhelmed with an excefs of forrow, 2 Cor ii 7. and
fwallowed up by it; that their forrow do not work death,
as the forrow of the world doth; but it has provided, that
even this bitter cup fhould be fweetened; and therefore we
find that, under the law, the facrifices for fin were commonly attended with expreffions of joy; and while the
priefts were fprinkling the blood of the facrifices to make
atonement, 2 Chron xxix. 24, 25 the Levites attended with
pfalteries and harps, for fo was the commandment f the
Lord by his prophets. Even the day to afflict the foul is the
day of atonement; and when we receive the atonement, we
" joy in God, through our Lord Jefus Chrift," Rom. v. 1. In
giving confent to the atonement we take the comfort of it.

In forrowing for the death of fome dear friend or relation, thus far we have found a pleafure in it, that it hath given vent to our grief which our fpirits were full of; fo, in forrow for fin, the fhedding of juft tears is fome fatisfaction to us. If it is a pleafure to be angry, when a man thinks, with Jonah, he doth well to be angry; much more is it a pleafure to be forry, when a man is fure he doth well to be forry. The fame word in the Hebrew, fignifies both confolari and pœnitere, both to comfort and to repent, becaufe there is comfort in true repentance.

3. Much more after repentance, there is a pleafure attending it, and flowing from it It is a way of pleafantnefs, for it is the way of pleafantnefs. To them that mourn in Zion, that forrow after a godly fort, God hath appointed " beauty for afhes, and the oil of joy for mourning." Ifa. lxi. 3. And the more the foul is humbled under the fenfe of fin, the more fenfible will the comfort of pardon be; it is wounding in order to be healed. The jubilee trumpet founded in the clofe of the day foul-affliction, Lev. xxv 9. which proclaimed the acceptable year of the Lord, the year of releafe; and an acceptable year it is indeed, to thofe who find themfelves tied and bound with the cords of their fins.

True penitents go weeping, it is true, but it is to feek the Lord of Hofts, Jer l. 4, 5. To feek him as their God, and to enter into covenant with him: And let their hearts rejoice that feek the Lord, Pfal. cv. 3. for they fhall find him, and find him their bountiful rewarder. They forrow not as thofe that have no hope, but good hope that their iniquities are forgiven; and what joy can be greater than that of a pardon to one condemned?

Secondly, It is true, that to be religious is to take care, and to take pains, and to labour earneftly, Luke xiii. 25 and yet wifdom's ways are ways of pleafantnefs. It is true, we muft ftrive to enter into this way, muft be in an agony, fo the word is. There is a violence which the kingdom of heaven fuffers, and the violent take it by force, Mat. xi. 12. And, when we are in that way, we muft run with patience, Heb. vii. 1. The bread of life is to be eaten in the fweet of our face; we muft be always upon our guard, and keep our hearts with all diligence Bufinefs for God and our fouls is what we are not allowed to be flothful in, but fervent in fpirit, ferving the Lord. Rom. xii. 11. We are foldiers of

Jesus Christ, and we must endure hardness, must war the good warfare till it be accomplished, 2 Tim. ii. 3.

And yet even in this contention there is comfort. It is work indeed, and work that requires care; and yet it will appear to be pleasant work, if we consider how we are enabled for it, and encouraged in it.

1. How we are enabled for it, and strengthened with strength in our souls to go on in it, and go through with it. It would be unpleasant, and would go on very heavily, if we were left to ourselves, to travel in our own strength; but if we be actuated and animated in it by a better spirit, and mightier power than our own, it is pleasant. If God " work " in us both to will and to do of his own good pleasure," Phil. ii. 12, 13. we shall have no reason to complain of the difficulty of our work; for God ordains peace for us, true peace and pleasure, by " working all our works in us," Isa. xvi. 12.

We may sing at our work, if our minds be by the Spirit of God brought to it, our hands strengthened for it, and our infirmities helped, Rom. viii. 26. and particularly our infirmities in prayer; that by it we may fetch in strength for every service, strength according to the day. Daniel at first found God's speaking to him a terror, he could not bear it; but when one like " the appearance of a man came and " touched him," (who could be no other but Christ the Mediator) and put strength into him, saying, " Peace be " unto thee, be strong, yea, be strong," it was quite another thing with him, then nothing more pleasant; " Let my Lord " speak, for thou hast strengthened me," Dan. x. 17, 18, 19.

Though the way to heaven be up hill, yet, if we be carried on in it as upon eagles wings, it will be pleasant; and those are so that wait upon the Lord, for to them it is promised that they shall renew their strength. That is pleasant work, though against the grain to our corrupt natures, for the doing of which we have not only a new nature given us, inclining us to it, and making us habitually capable of application to it, but actual supplies of grace sufficient for the doing of it, promised us, 2 Cor xii. 9, 10. by one who knows what strength we need, and what will serve, and will neither be unkind to us, nor unfaithful to his own word.

And it is obfervable, that when God, though he eafed not Paul of the thorn in the flefh, yet faid that good word to him, " My grace is fufficient for thee," immediately it follows, therefore " I take pleafure in infirmities, in re-
" proaches, in diftreffes for Chrift's fake; for when I am
" weak, then I am ftrong." Sufficient grace will make our work pleafant, even the hardeft part of it.

2. How we are encouraged in it. It is true, we muft take pains, but the work is good work, and is to be done, and is done by all the faints from a principle of holy love, and that makes it pleafant 1 John v. 3. as Jacob's fervice for Rachel was to him, becaufe he loved her. It is an unfpeakable comfort to induftrious Chriftians, that they are working together with God, and he with them; that their mafter's eye is upon them, and a witnefs to their fincerity; he fees in fecret, and will reward openly, Mat. vi. 6. God now accepteth their works, fmiles upon them, and his Spirit fpeaks to them " good words, and comfortable words," Zech. i. 13. witneffeth to their adoption. And this is very encouraging to God's fervants, as it was to the fervants of Boaz, to have their mafter come to them, when they were hard at work reaping down his own fields, and with a pleafant countenance fay to them, " The Lord be with you," Ruth ii 4. Nay, the Spirit faith more to God's labourers, " The Lord is with you."

The profpect of the recompence of reward is in a fpecial manner encouraging to us in our work, and makes it pleafant, and the little difficulties we meet with in it to be as nothing. It was by having an eye to this, that Mofes was encouraged not only to bear the reproach of Chrift, but to " efteem it greater riches than the treafures of Egypt," Heb. xi. 26. In all labour there is profit; and if fo, there is pleafure alfo in the profpect of that profit, and according to the degree of it. We muft work, but it is to work out our falvation, a great falvation, which, when it comes, will abundantly make us amends for all our toil. We muft ftrive, but it is to enter into life, eternal life We muft run, but it is for an incorruptible crown, the prize of our high calling. And we do not run at an uncertainty, nor " fight
" as thofe that beat the air ;" for to him that " fows righ-
" teoufnefs there is a fure reward," Prov. xi. 18. and the

assurance of that harvest will make even the seed-time pleasant.

Thirdly, It is true, that to be religious, is to " deny our- " selves in many things that are pleasing to sense;" and yet wisdom's ways are pleasantness for all that. It is indeed necessary, that beloved lusts should be mortified and subdued, corrupt appetites crossed and displeased, which, to the natural man, is like " plucking out a right eye, and cutting off a " right hand," Mat. v. 29 . There are forbidden pleasures that must be abandoned, and kept at a distance from : the flesh must not be gratified, nor provision made to fulfil the lusts of it, Rom. xiii. 14 but on the contrary we must keep under the body, and bring it into subjection, Cor. ix. 27. we must crucify the flesh, must kill it and put it to a painful death . The first lesson we are to learn in the school of Christ, is to deny ourselves, Mat. xvi. 24. and this must be our constant practice; we must use ourselves to deny our- selves, and thus take up our cross daily.

Now, will not this spoil all the pleasure of a religious life ? No, it will not; for the pleasures of sense, which we are to deny ourselves in, are comparatively despicable, and really dangerous.

1. These pleasures we are to deny ourselves in are com- paratively despicable : How much soever they are valued and esteemed by those who live by sense, and know no bet- ter, they are looked upon with a generous contempt by those who live by faith, and are acquainted with spiritual and di- vine pleasures. And it is no pain to deny ourselves in these pleasures, when we know ourselves entitled to better, more rational, and noble, and agreeable, the delights of the blessed spirits above.

The garlic and onions of Egypt were doated upon by those that knew not how to value either the manna of the wilderness, or the milk and honey of Canaan, Numb. xi. 5. So the base and sordid pleasures of sense are relished by the depraved and vicious appetites of the carnal mind; but when a man has learned to put a due estimate upon spirit- ual pleasures, those that are sensual have lost all their sweet- ness, and are become the most insipid things in the world; have no pleasure in them, in comparison with that far greater pleasure which excelleth.

Is it any diminution to the pleasure of a grown man, to deny himself the toys and sports which he was fond of when he was a child? No, when he became a man, he "put away those childish things;" he is now past them, he is above them, for he is acquainted with those entertainments that are manly and more generous Thus mean and little do the pleasures of sense appear to those that have learned to delight themselves in the Lord.

2. They are really dangerous, they are apt to take away the heart. If the heart be set upon them, they blind the mind, debauch the understanding and conscience, and in many quench the sparks of conviction, and of that holy fire, which comes from heaven, and tends to heaven They are in danger of drawing away the heart from God; and the more they are valued and covered, the more dangerous they are of piercing us through with many sorrows, and of drowning us in destruction and perdition. To deny ourselves in them, is but to avoid a rock, upon which multitudes have fatally split themselves.

What diminution is it to the pleasure of a safe and happy way on sure ground, which will certainly bring us to our journey's end, to deny ourselves the false and pretended satisfaction of walking in a fair but dangerous way, that leads to destruction; Is it not much pleasanter travelling on a rough pavement, than on a smooth quicksand? Where there is a known peril, there can be no true pleasure; and therefore the want of it is no loss or uneasiness.

What pleasure can a wife or considerate man take in those entertainments, in which he has continual reason to suspect a snare and a design upon him, any more than he that was at a feast could relish the dainties of it, when he was aware of a naked sword hanging directly over him by a single thread? The foolish woman, indeed calls the stolen waters sweet, and bread eaten in secret pleasant, Prov. v. 17, 18. But those find no difficulty or uneasiness in denying them, who know " that the dead are there, and her guests are already in the depths of hell Therefore, however the corrupt heart may find some reluctancy in refusing those forbidden pleasures, we may say of it, as Abigal did of David's denying himself the satisfaction of being revenged on Nabal, Afterwards this shall be no grief unto us, nor offence of heart, 2 Sam. xxv. 31.

Fourthly, It is true, that through many tribulations we muſt enter into the kingdom of God, Acts xiv. 23 that we muſt not only deny ourſelves the pleaſures of ſenſe, but muſt ſometimes expoſe ourſelves to its pains; we muſt take up our croſs when it lies in our way, and bear it after Chriſt: We are told, that all that will live godly in Chriſt Jeſus, muſt ſuffer perſecution, at leaſt they muſt expect it, and get ready for it? bonds and afflictions abide them, loſſes in their eſtates, balks in their preferment, reproaches and contempts, baniſhments and deaths muſt be counted, upon: And will not this ſpoil the pleaſure of religion? No, it will not; for,

1. It is but light affliction at the worſt, that we are called out to ſuffer, and but for a moment, compared with the far more exceeding and eternal weight of glory that is reſerved for us, 2 Cor. iv. 17 with which the ſufferings of this preſent time are not worthy to be compared, Rom. viii. 18. All theſe troubles do but touch the body, the outward man, and the intereſts of that, they do not at all affect the ſoul; they break the ſhell, or pluck off the huſk; but do not bruiſe the kernal.

Can the brave and courageous ſoldier take pleaſure in the toils and perils of the camp, and in jeoparding his life in the high places of the field, in the eager purſuit of honour, and in the ſervice of his prince and country; and ſhall not thoſe who have the intereſts of Chriſt's kingdom near their hearts, and are carried on by a holy ambition of the honour that comes from God, take a delight in ſuffering for Chriſt when they know that thoſe ſufferings tend to his honour, and their own hereafter? They that are perſecuted for righteouſneſs ſake, that are reviled, and have all manner of evil ſaid againſt them falſely, becauſe they belong to Chriſt, are bidden not only to bear it patiently, but to rejoice in it, and to be exceeding glad, " for great is their reward in heaven," Mat. v. 11, 12. Every reproach we endure for Chriſt, will be a pearl in our crown ſhortly.

2. As thoſe afflictions abound for Chriſt, ſo our " conſo-
" lations in Chriſt do much more abound," 2 Cor. i. 4, 5. The more the waters increaſed, the higher was the ark lifted up; the more we ſuffer in God's cauſe, the more we partake of his comforts; for he will not be wanting to thoſe whom he calls out to any hardſhips more than ordinary for his name's

fake. The Lord was with Jofeph in the prifon, when he lay there for a good confcience; and thofe went from the council " rejoicing, that were counted worthy to fuffer " fhame for Chrift's name;" were honoured to be difhonoured for him, Acts v. 41.

Thus the extraordinary fupports and joys which they experience, that patiently fuffer for righteoufnefs fake, add much more to the pleafantnefs of the ways of wifdom, than the fufferings themfelves do, or can derogate from it: for the fufferings are human, the confolations are divine; they fuffer in the flefh, but they rejoice in the fpirit; they fuffer for a time, but they rejoice evermore, and " this their joy " no man taketh from them."

C H A P. VII.

The application of the Doctrine.

CONCERNING this doctrine of the pleafantnefs of religion's ways, I hope we may now fay as Eliphaz doth of his principle, " Lo, this, we have fearched it, fo it " is," Job. v. 27. it is inconteftibly true; and therefore we may conclude as he doth, " Hear it, and know thou it for " thy good;" know thou it for thyfelf; fo the margin reads it; apply it to thyfelf, believe it concerning thyfelf, not only that it is good, but that it is good for me to draw near to God, Pfal. lxxiii. 28 And then only we hear things, and know them for our good, when we hear them, and know them for ourfelves.

Three inferences, by way of counfel and exhortation we fhall draw from this doctrine.

Firft, Let us all then be perfuaded, and prevailed with, to enter into, and to walk in thefe paths of wifdom, that are fo very pleafant. This is what I principally intend in opening and proving this truth; moft people would rather be courted than threatened to their duty. Much might be faid to frighten you out of the ways of fin and folly, but I would hope to gain the fame point another way, by alluring you into the ways of wifdom and holinefs. This comes to invite you to a feaft which the Lord of hofts hath, in the gospel, made to all nations, Isa. xxv. 6 and to all in the nations, and to you among the rest (for none are excluded, that do not by their unbelief exclude themselves) a feast of fat things full of marrow, of wines on the lees well refined; delights for souls infinitely transcending the delicacies of sense. You are welcome to this feast; come, for all things are now ready; " Come, eat of wisdom's bread, " and drink of the wine that she has mingled," Prov. ix. 5.

Is a life of religion such a sweet and comfortable life, why then should not we be religious? If such as these be the ways of wisdom, why should not we be travellers in those ways? Let this recommend to us a life of sincere and serious godliness, and engage us to conform to all its rules, and give up ourselves to be ruled by them. It is not enough to have a good opinion of religion, and to give it a good word; that will but be a witness against us, if we do not set ourselves in good earnest to the practice of it, and make conscience of living up to it.

I would here, with a particular and pressing importunity, address myself to you that are young; to persuade you, now in the days of your youth, now in the present day, to make religion your choice and your business: And I assure you, if you do so, you will find it your delight. God, by his grace, convince you of the real comforts that are to be had in real godliness, that you may be drawn cheerfully to Christ with these cords of a man, and held fast to him with these bands of love. My son (saith Solomon to his little scholar, Prov. xxiv. 13, 14.) eat thou honey because it is good; and the honey comb, which is sweet to thy taste; (he doth not forbid him the delights of sense, he may use them soberly and moderately, and with due caution; but remember that) " so shall the knowledge of wisdom be to " thy soul, when thou hast found it:" Thou hast better pleasures than these to mind and pursue, spiritual and rational ones; and, instead of being made indifferent to those, we should rather be led to them, and quickened in our desires after them, by these delights of sense, which God gives us to engage us to himself and his service.

The age of youth is the age of pleasure. You think you may now be allowed to take your pleasure; O that ye would take it, and seek it there where alone it is to be had, and that is in a strict observance of the laws of virtue and god-

3 A

liness! Would you live a pleafant life, begin betimes to live a religious life; and the fooner you begin, the more pleafant it will be; it is beft travelling in a morning. Would you rejoice, O young people, in your youth? " and " have your hearts to cheer you in the days of your youth," Eccl. xi. 9. do not walk in the way of your corrupt and carnal hearts, but in the way of God's commandments; for he knows what is good for you, better than you do yourfelves: Do not walk in the fight of your eyes, for the eyes are apt to fly upon that which is not, Prov. xxiii. 5. but live by faith, that faith which being the fubftance of things hoped for, and the evidence of things not feen, will lead you to that which is; " for wifdom makes thofe that love " her to inherit fubftance, and fills their treafures," Prov. viii. 21. and thence arifeth their true fatisfaction.

That which I would perfuade you to is, to walk in the way of wifdom, to be fober minded, to be thoughtful about your fouls and your everlafting ftate, and get your minds well principled, and well affected, and well inclined; " Wifdom is the principal thing, therefore get wifdom, and, " with all thy gettings, get underftanding," Prov. iv. 7. That which I would perfuade you with, is the pleafantnefs of this way; you cannot do better for yourfelves than by a religious courfe of life. " My fon, if thine heart be " wife, my heart fhall rejoice, even mine," Prov. xxiii. 15, 16. yea my reins fhall rejoice if thy lips (out of the abundance of thine heart) fpeak right things: But that is not all; not only my heart fhall rejoice, but thy own fhall.

I wifh you would fee, and ferioufly confider, the two rivals that are making court to you for your fouls, for your beft affections, Chrift and Satan; and act wifely in difpofing of yourfelves, and make fuch a choice as you will afterwards reflect upon with comfort You are now at the turning time of life; turn right now, and you are made for ever. Wifdom faith, Prov. ix. 4, 16. Whofo is fimple, let him turn in to me, and fhe will cure him of his fimplicity; Folly faith, Whofo is fimple, let him turn in to me, and fhe will take advantage of his fimplicity: Now let him come whofe right your hearts are, and give them him, and you fhall have them again more your own.

That you may determine well between thefe two compe-
titors for the throne in your fouls:

1ft, See the folly of carnal finful pleafures, and abandon them. You will never be in love with the pleafures of
religion, till you are perfuaded to fall out with forbidden
pleafures. The enjoyment of the delights of fenfe fuits
beft with that age, the appetite towards them is then moft
violent: Mirth, fport, plays, dainties are the idols of young
people; they are therefore called youthful lufts. Eccl. xii.
1. The days will come, the evil days, when they themfelves will fay they have no pleafure in them; like Barzillai,
2 Sam. xix. 35. who, when he is old, can no more relifh
what he eats and what he drinks. O that reafon, and wifdom, and grace, might make you as dead to them now, as
time and days will make you after a while!

Will you believe one that tried the utmoft of what the
pleafures of fenfe could do towards making a man happy:
" He faid of laughter, It is mad; and of mirth, What
" doth it? and that forrow is better than laughter," Eccl.
ii. 2. and vii 3. Mofes knew what the pleafures of the
court were, and yet chofe rather to fuffer affliction with the
people of God, than to continue in the fnare of them,
Heb. xi. 25. And you muft make the fame choice; for
you will never cordially embrace the pleafures of religion,
till you have renounced the pleafures of fin: Covenant
againft them, therefore, and watch againft them.

If you would live, " and go in the way of underftand-
" ing, you muft forfake the foolifh," Prov. ix. 6. take heed
of the way both of the evil man, and of the ftrange woman; " Avoid it, pafs not by it, turn from it, and pafs
" away," Prov. ii. 12, 16. Look upon finful pleafures as
mean, and much below you; look upon them as vile, and
much againft you; and do not only defpife them, but
dread them, and hate even the garments fpotted with the
flefh.

2dly, Be convinced of the pleafure of wifdom's ways,
and come and try them. You are, it may be, prejudiced
againft religion as a melancholy thing; but as Philip faid to
Nathaniel, John 1. 46. " Come and fee." Believe it
poffible that there may be a pleafure in religion, which you
have not yet thought of. When religion is looked upon at
a diftance, we fee not that pleafure in it, which we fhall

certainly find when we come to be better acquainted with it. Peter Martyr, in a sermon, illustrated this by this comparison (and it proved a means of the conversion of the Marquis of Vico): He that looks upon persons dancing at a distance, would think they were mad; but let him come nearer, and observe how they take every step by rule, and keep time with the music, he will not only be pleased with it, but inclined to join with them.

Come and take Christ's yoke upon you, and you will find it easy. Try the pleasure there is in the knowledge of God and Jesus Christ, and in converse with spiritual and eternal things; try the pleasure of seriousness and self-denial, and you will find it far exceeds that of vanity and self indulgence. Try the pleasure of meditation on the word of God, of prayer, and praise, and Sabbath sanctification, and you will think you have made a happy change of the pleasure of vain and carnal mirth for these true delights.

Make this trial by these four rules:

1. " That man's chief end is to glorify God, and enjoy " him." Our pleasures will be according to that which we pitch upon and pursue as our chief end. If we can mistake so far, as to think it is our chief end to enjoy the world and the flesh, and our chief business to serve them, the delights of sense will relish best with us: But, if the world was made for man, certainly man was made for more than the world; and, if God made man, certainly he made him for himself: God then is our chief good; it is our business to serve and please him, and our happiness to be accepted of him.

And if so, and we believe so, nothing will be a greater pleasure to us, than that which we have reason to think will be pleasing to him. If we do, indeed, look upon God as our chief good, we shall make him our chief joy, our exceeding joy, Psal. xciii. 4. If we consider that we were made capable of the pleasure of conversing with God in this world, and seeing him and enjoying him in another; we cannot but think that we wretchedly disparage ourselves, when we take up with the mean and sordid pleasures of sense as our felicity, especially if we forego all spiritual and eternal pleasures for them; as certainly we do, and give up all our expectations of them, if we place our happiness in these present delights: And we are guilty of a greater absurdity than that which profane Esau was guilty of, who for a mess of pottage sold his birthright, Heb. xii. 26.

2. That the soul is the man; and that is best for us, that is best for our souls. Learn to think meanly of this flesh, by which we are allied to the earth and the inferior creatures; it is formed out of the dust, it is dust, and it is hastening to the dust; and then the things that gratify it will not be much esteemed as of any great moment: "Meats for the "belly, and the belly for meats, but God shall destroy both it "and them;" and therefore let us not make idols of them.

But the soul is the noble part of us, by which we are allied to heaven and the world of spirits; those comforts therefore which delight the soul, are the comforts we should prize most, and give the preference to, for the soul's sake. Rational pleasures are the best for a man.

3. That the "greatest joy is that which a stranger doth "not intermeddle with," Prov. xiv. 10. The best pleasure is that which lies not under the eye and observation of the world, but which a man has and hides in his own bosom; and by which he enjoys himself, and keeps not only a peaceable, but a comfortable possession of his own soul, though he doth not by laughter, or other expressions of joy, tell them the satisfaction he has. Christ had meat to eat which the world knew not of, John iv 32. and so have Christians to whom he is the bread of life

4. That all is well that ends everlastingly well. That pleasure ought to have the preference, which is of the longest continuance. The pleasures of sense are withering and fading, and leave a sting behind them to those that placed their happiness in them; but the pleasures of religion will abide with us: In these is continuance, Isa. lxiv 5. they will not turn with the wind, nor change with the weather, but are meat which endures to everlasting life.

Reckon that the best pleasure which will remain with you, and stand you in stead when you come to die; which will help to take off the terror of death, and allay its pains. The remembrance of sinful pleasures will give us killing terrors, but the remembrance of religious pleasures will give us living comforts in dying moments. They that live over Belshazzar's revels, may expect to receive the summons of death with the same confusion that he did, when "the joints of his "loins were loosed, and his knees smote one against another," Dan. v. 6. but they that live over Hezekiah's devotions, may receive them with the fame compofure that he did, when with a great deal of fatisfaction he looked back upon a well fpent life,: " Now, Lord, remember how I have " walked before thee in truth, and with an upright heart," Ifa. xxxviii. 3.

Secondly, " Let us, that profefs religion, ftudy to make it " more and more pleafant to ourfelves." We fee how much is done to make it fo, let us not receive the grace of God herein in vain. Let them, that walk in wifdom's ways, tafte the fweetnefs of them and relifh it. Chrift's fervice is perfect freedom, let us not make a drudgery of it, nor a toil of fuch a pleafure. We fhould not only be reconciled to our duty, as we ought to be to our greateft afflictions, and to make the beft of it; but we fhould rejoice in our duty, and fing at our work. if God intended that his fervice fhould be a pleafure to his fervants, let them concur with him herein, and not walk contrary to him.

Now, in order to the making of our religion pleafant to us, more and more fo, I fhall give feven directions.

1. " Let us always keep up good thoughts of God, and " carefully watch againft hard thoughts of him." As it is the original error of many that are loofe and carelefs in religion, that they think God altogether fuch a one as themfelves, Pfal. l. 21. as much a friend to fin as themfelves, and as indifferent whether his work be done or no; fo it is the error of many that are fevere in their religion that they think God, like themfelves, a hard mafter; they have fuch thoughts of him, as Job had in an hour of temptation, when he looked upon God as " feeking occafions againft him, num- " bering his fteps, and watching over his fins, and taking " him for his enemy," Job xiii. 24 and xiv. 16. as if he were extreme to mark iniquities, and implacable to thofe that had offended, and not accepting any fervice that had in it the leaft defect or imperfection.

But the matter is not fo, and we do both God and ourfelves a great deal of wrong, if we imagine it to be fo. What could have been done more than God has done, to convince us that he is gracious, and merciful, flow to anger, and ready to forgive fin when it is repented of? (I faid, I will confefs mine iniquity unto thee; and thou forgaveft, Pfal. xxxii. 5) and as ready to accept the fervices that come from an upright heart. He will not always chide, nor contend for ever. So far is he from taking advantages againſt us, that he makes the beſt of us : Where the ſpirit is willing, he accepts that, and overlooks the weakneſs of the fleſh. Let us deal with him accordingly : Look upon God as love, and the God of love ; and then it will be pleaſant to us to hear from him, to ſpeak to him, to converſe with him, and to do him any ſervice.

It is true, God is great, and glorious, and jealous, and to be worſhipped with reverence and holy fear ; but is he not our Father, a tender gracious Father ? have we not an Advocate with the Father ? was not God, in Chriſt, reconciling the world to himſelf, 2 Cor. v. 19. and to all his attributes and relations to us, by ſhewing himſelf willing to be reconciled to us, notwithſtanding our provocations ? See him, therefore, upon a throne of grace, and come boldly to him, and that will make your ſervice of him pleaſant.

2. Let us dwell much, by faith, upon the promiſes of God. What pleaſant lives ſhould we lead, if we were but more intimately acquainted with thoſe declarations which God has made of his good will to man, and the aſſurances he has given of his favour, and all the bleſſed fruits of it, to thoſe who ſerve him faithfully ? The promiſes are many, and exceeding great and precious, ſuited to our caſe, and accommodated to every exigence; there are not only promiſes to grace, but promiſes of grace, grace ſufficient ; and theſe promiſes all yea and amen in Chriſt.

What do theſe promiſes ſtand in our bibles for, but to be made uſe of ? Come then, and let us apply them to ourſelves, and inſert our own names in them by faith ; what God ſaid to Abraham, " I am thy ſhield," Gen. xv. 1. I am *El-ſhaddai*, " a God all ſufficient," Gen. xvii. 1. what he ſaid to Joſhua, " I will never fail thee nor forſake thee," Joſh. i. 5. he ſaith to me What he ſaith to all that love him, " that all things ſhall work for good to them," Rom. viii. 28. and to all that fear him, that no good thing ſhall be wanting to them, Pſal xxxiv. 10. he ſaith to me ; and why ſhould not I take the comfort of it ?

Theſe promiſes and the like, are wells of ſalvation, from which we may draw water with joy; and breaſts of conſolation from which we may ſuck, and be ſatisfied; they will be both our ſtrength and our ſong in the houſe of our pilgrimage. So well ordered is the covenant of grace in all things, and so sure, 2 Sam. xxiii. 5. that if having laid up our portion in it, and so made it all our salvation, we would but fetch our maintenance from it, and so make it all our defire and delight, we should have in it a continual feast, and should go on our way rejoicing. See Psal cxix 111.

3. Let us order the affairs of our religion with discretion. Many make religion unpleasant to themselves, and discouraging to others, by their imprudent management of it; making that service to be a burden by the circumstances of it, which in itself would be a pleasure; doing things out of time, or tasking themselves above their strength, and undertaking more than they can go through with, especially at first, which is like "putting new wine into old bottles," Mat ix. 17. or like "over-driving the flocks one day," Gen. xxxiii. 13. If we make the yoke of Christ heavier than he has made it, we may thank ourselves that our drawing in it becomes unpleasant. Solomon cautions us, Eccl. vii. 16. against being righteous overmuch, and making ourselves overwise, as that by which we may destroy ourselves, and put ourselves out of conceit with our religion; there may be over-doing in well-doing, and then it becomes unpleasant.

But let us take our religion as Christ hath settled it, and we shall find it easy. When the ways of our religion are ways of wisdom, then they are ways of pleasantness; for the more wisdom, the more pleasantness; that wisdom which dwells with prudence. Wisdom will direct us to be even and regular in our religion, to take care that the duties of our general and particular calling, the business of our religion, and our necessary business in the world, do not interfere or intrench upon one another. It will direct us to time duty aright; for every thing is beautiful and pleasant in its season, Eccl. iii. 11. and work is then easy when we are in a frame for it.

4. Let us live in love, and keep up Christian charity, and the spiritual communion of saints; if we would be of good comfort, we must be of one mind, 2 Cor. xiii. 11. and therefore the apostle presseth brotherly love upon us, with an argument taken from the consolations in Christ, Phil. ii 1. i e the comfort that is in Christianity: As ever you hope to have the comfort of your religion, submit to that great law of it, "Walk in love:" for behold how good and how

pleafant it is, how good in itfelf, and pleafant to us, for brethren to dwell together in unity.

The more pleafing we are to our brethren the more pleafant we fhall be to ourfelves.

Nothing makes our lives more uncomfortable than ftrife and contentions: " Wo is me that I dwell among thofe that " hate peace," Pfal. cxx. 5. it is bad being among thofe that are difpofed to quarrel and worfe having in ourfelves a difpofition to quarrel. The refentments of contempt put upon us are uneafy enough, and contrivances to revenge it much more fo And nothing makes our religion more uncomfortable than ftrifes and contentions about that We forfeit and lofe the pleafure of it, if we entangle ourfelves in perverfe difputings about it.

But by holy love we enjoy our friends, which will add to the pleafure of enjoying God in this world. Love itfelf fweetens the foul and revives it, and, as it is the loadftone of love, it fetcheth in the further pleafure and fatisfaction of being beloved, and fo it is a heaven upon earth; for what is the happinefs and pleafure of heaven, but that there love reigns in perfection? Then we have moft peace in our bofoms, when we are moft peaceably difpofed towards our brethren.

5. Let us be much in the exercife of holy joy, and employ ourfelves much in praife. Joy is the heart of praife, as praife is the language of joy; let us engage ourfelves to thefe, and quicken ourfelves in thefe. God has made thefe our duty, by thefe to make all the other parts of our duty pleafant to us; and for that end we fhould abound much in them, and attend upon God with joy and praife. Let us not croud our fpiritual joys into a corner of our hearts, nor our thankful praifes into a corner of our prayers, but give both fcope and vent to each.

Let us live a life of delight in God, and love to think of him as we do of one whom we love and value. Let the flowing in of every ftream of comfort lead us to the fountain; and, in every thing that is grateful to us, let us tafte that the Lord is gracious. Let the drying up of every ftream of comfort drive us to the fountain; and let us rejoice the more in God for our being deprived of that which we ufed to rejoice in.

Let us be frequent and large in our thankfgivings. It

will be pleasant to us to recount the favours of God, and thus to make some returns for them; though poor and mean, yet such as God will gracioufly accept. We should have more pleasure in our religion, if we had but learned in every thing to give thanks, 1 Thess. v 18. for that takes out more than half the bitterness of our afflictions, that we can see cause even to be thankful for them; and it infuseth more than a double sweetness into our enjoyments, that they furnish us with matter for that excellent heavenly work of praise; " Sing praises unto his name, for it is " pleasant; comfortable, as well as comely," Psal. cxxxv. 3.

6. Let us act in a constant dependence upon Jesus Christ Religion would be much more pleasant, if we did but cleave more closely to Christ in it, and do all in his name: The more precious Christ is to us, the more pleasant will every part of our work be; and therefore believing in Christ is often expressed by our rejoicing in him, Phil. iii. 5. We may rejoice in God, through Christ, as the Mediator between us and God; may rejoice in our communion with God, when it is kept up through Christ; may rejoice in hope of eternal life, when we see this life in the Son: " He that hath the Son of God, hath life," i. e. he has comfort, 1 John v. 11, 12.

There is that in Christ, and in his undertaking and performances for us, which is sufficient to satisfy all our doubts, to silence all our fears, and to balance all our sorrows He was appointed to be the consolation of Israel, and he will be so to us, when we have learnt not to look for that in ourselves, which is to be had in him only, and to make use of his mediation in every thing wherein we have to do with God. When we rejoice in the righteousness of Christ, and in his grace and strength; rejoice in his satisfaction and intercession; rejoice in his dominion and universal agency and influence, and in the progress of his gospel, and the conversion of souls to him, and please ourselves with prospects of his second coming; we have then a joy, not only which no man taketh from us, but which will increase more and more: And of the increase of Christ's government, and therefore of that peace, there shall be no end, Isa. ix. 7. Our songs of joy are then most pleafant, when the burden of them is, none but Chrift, none but Chrift.

7. Let us converfe much with the glory that is to be revealed. They that by faith fend their hearts and beft affections before them to heaven, while they are here on this earth, may in return fetch thence fome of thofe joys and pleafures that are at God's right hand. That which goes up in vapours of holy defire, though infenfible, in groanings which cannot be uttered, will come down again in dews of heavenly confolations, that will make the foul as a watered garden.

Let us look much to the end of our way, how glorious it will be, and that will help to make our way pleafant. This abundantly fatisfies the faints, and is the fatnefs of God's houfe on earth, Pfal. xxxvi. 8, 9. This makes them now to drink of the river of God's pleafures, that with him is the fountain of life, whence all thefe ftreams come, and in his light they hope to fee light, everlafting light. By frequent meditations on that reft which remains for the people of God, Heb. iv. 3. we now enter into that reft and partake of the comfort of it.

Our hopes of that happinefs through grace would be very much ftrengthened, and our evidences for it cleared up infenfibly, if we did but converfe more with it, and the difcoveries made of it in the fcripture. We may have foretaftes of heavenly delights while we are here on earth, clufters from Canaan while we are yet in this wildernefs; and no pleafure comparable to that which thefe afford. That is the fweeteft joy within us, which is borrowed from the joy fet before us ; and we deprive ourfelves very much of the comfort of our religion, in not having our eye more to that joy. We rejoice moft triumphantly, and with the greateft degrees of holy glorying, when we " rejoice in " hope of the glory of God," Rom vi. 2. In this our heart is glad, and our glory rejoiceth," Pfal. xvi. 4.

Thirdly, Let us make it appear, that we have, indeed, found wifdom's ways to be pleafantnefs, and her paths peace. If we have experienced this truth, let us evidence our experiences, and not only in word, but in deed, bear our teftimony to the truth of it. Let us live as thofe that believe the fweetnefs of religion, not becaufe we are told it, but becaufe we have tafted it, 1 John i 1.

If so be then (to borrow the apostle's words, 1 Pet. ii. 3.) " we have tasted that the Lord is gracious," if we have, indeed, found it a pleasant thing to be religious;

1. Let our hearts be much enlarged in all religious exercises, and all instances of gospel obedience. The more pleasant the service of God is, the more we should abound in it. When God enlargeth our hearts with his consolations, he expects that we should run the way of his commandments, that we should exert ourselves in our duty with more vigour, and press forward the more earnestly towards perfection.

This should make us forward to every good work, and ready to close with all opportunities of serving God, and doing good That which we take a pleasure in, we need not to be twice called to. If indeed the hearts of those rejoice that seek the Lord, as in Psal cv. 3. then when God saith, seek ye my face, how steadily should our hearts answer at the first word, " Thy face, Lord. will we seek?" Psal. xxvii 8. and how glad will they be, when it is said unto us, " Let us go to the house of the Lord?" Psal. cxxii 1. This should make us forward to acts of charity, that there is a pleasure in doing good; and we shall reflect with comfort upon it, that we have done something that will turn to the honour of God, and our own account.

This should make us lively in our duty; the heart fixed in hearing the word, and in prayer and praise. Those that take delight in music, how doth it engage them? how do all the marks of a close application of mind appear in their countenance and carriage? And shall not we, by our attending on the Lord without distraction, make it to appear, that we attend upon him with delight, and are in our element when we are in his service? Let this be my rest for ever; here let me dwell all the days of my life, Psal. xxvii. 4.

This should keep us constant and unwearied in the work and service of God. What is really our delight, we are not soon weary of. If we delight in approaching to God, we will seek him daily, and make it our daily work to honour him. If meditation and prayer be sweet, let them be our daily excercise; and let this bind our souls with a bond to God, and the " sacrifice as with cords to the horns of the " altar." With this we should answer all temptations to apoſtacy; Shall I quit ſo good a maſter, ſo good a ſervice? " Intreat me not to leave Chriſt, or to turn from following " after him; for it is good to be here Here let us make " tabernacles," Matth xvii. 4. Whither elſe ſhall we go, but to him that has the words of eternal life?

2. Let our whole converſation be cheerful, and melancholy be baniſhed. Are the ways of religion pleaſant? let us be pleaſant in them, both to ourſelves, and to thoſe about us As for thoſe who are yet in a ſtate of ſin and wrath, they have reaſon to be melancholy, let the ſinners in Zion be afraid; be afflicted, joy is forbidden fruit to them, What have they to do with peace? Rejoice not, O Iſrael, for joy as other people, for thou haſt gone a whoring from thy God, Hoſ. ix. 1.

But thoſe who, through grace, are called out of darkneſs into a marvellous light, have cauſe to be cheerful, and ſhould have hearts to be ſo. " Ariſe, ſhine, for thy light is " come," Iſa. lx. 1. Is the ſun of righteouſneſs riſen upon us? let us ariſe and look forth as the morning with the morning. That comfort which Chriſt directs to our ſouls, let us reflect back upon others. And as our light is come, ſo is our liberty. Art thou " looſed from the bands of thy " neck? O captive daughter of Zion awake, awake, put " on thy ſtrength, put on thy beautiful garments, and ſhake " thyſelf from the duſt, ariſe and ſit down," O Jeruſalem, Iſa. lii 1, 2

Though vain and carnal mirth is both a great ſin, and a great ſnare, yet there is a holy cheerfulneſs and pleaſantneſs of converſation which will not only conſiſt very well with ſerious godlineſs, but greatly promotes it in ourſelves, and greatly adorns it, and recommends it to others. A merry heart (Solomon ſaith) doth good like a medicine, Prov. xvii. 22. and maketh fat the bones; while a broken ſpirit doth hurt like a poiſon, and drieth the bones. Chriſtians ſhould endeavour to keep up a cheerful temper, and not indulge themſelves in that which is ſadning and diſquieting, to the ſpirit; and they ſhould ſhew it in all holy converſation, that thoſe they converſe with may ſee they did not renounce pleaſure, when they embraced religion.

I am ſure, none have ſo much reaſon to rejoice as good people have, nor ſo much done for them to encourage their joy; and therefore to allude to that of Jonadab to Amnon,

"Why art thou, being the king's son, lean from day to day?" 2 Sam. xiii. 4. Are we in prosperity? therefore let us be cheerful, in gratitude to the God of our mercies, who expects that we should serve him with joyfulness, and gladness of heart, in the abundance of all things, Deut. xxviii. 47. and justly takes it ill if we do not.

Tristis es, & fælix? sciat hoc fortuna caveto,
Ingratum dicet te (lupe) si scierit   Mart.

Are we in affliction? yet let us be cheerful, that we may make it appear our happiness is not laid up in the creature, nor our treasures on earth. If it is the privilege of Christians to rejoice in tribulation, let them not throw away their privilege, but glory in it, and make use of it. Let the joy of the Lord, that hath infused itself into our hearts, diffuse itself into all our converse. Go thy way, eat thy bread with joy, Eccl. ix 7. and drink thy wine, nay, if thou shouldst be reduced to that, drink fair water, with a merry heart, if thou hast good ground to hope that, in Christ Jesus, God now accepteth thy works; and this joy of the Lord will be thy strength

3. Let us look with contempt upon the pleasures of sense, and with abhorrence upon the pleasures of sin. The more we have tasted of the delights of heaven, the more our mouths should be put out of taste to the delights of this earth. Let not those who have been feasted with the milk and honey of Canaan, hanker after the garlic and onions of Egypt.

Let us keep at a distance from all forbidden pleasures. There is a hook under those baits, a snake under the green grass; a rock under those smooth waters, on which multitudes have split. We must so dread the drunkard's pleasures, as not to "look upon the wine when it is red," Prov. xxiii. 31. so dread the pleasures of the adulterer, as not to " look upon a woman to lust after her," Mat. v. 28. for these pleasures of sin not only are but for a season, but at the last they " bite like a serpent, and sting like an adder." Either spiritual pleasures will deaden the force of the pleasures of sin, or the pleasures of sin will spoil the relish of spiritual pleasures.

Let us keep up a holy indifferency even to the lawful delights of sense, and take heed of loving them more than God. The eye that has looked at the sun is dazzled to every thing elfe : have we beheld the beauty of the Lord? let us fee and own, how little beauty there is in other things. If we be tempted to do any thing unbecoming us, by the allurements of pleafure; we may well fay, offer thefe things to thofe that know no better; but we do, and will never leave " fountains of living waters, for cifterns of puddle " water"

4. Let not our hearts envy finners. Envy arifeth from an opinion that the ftate of others is better than our own, which we grudge and are difpleafed at, and wifh ourfelves in their condition. Good people are often cautioned againft this fin; " Be not envious againft evil men, nor defire to " be with them," Prov. xxiv 1. Pfal. xxxvii. 1. for if there be all this pleafure in religion, and we have experienced it, furely we would not exchange conditions with any finner, even in his beft eftate.

Envy not finners their outward profperity, their wealth and abundance, which puts them into a capacity of having all the delights of fenfe wound up to the heights of pleafureablenefs. Though they lie " upon beds of ivory," Amos vi. 4, 5, 6. and " ftretch themfelves upon their couches, and " eat the lambs out of the flocks, and the calves out of the " midft of the ftall; though they chant to the found of the " viol, drink wine in bowls, and anoint themfelves with the " chief ointments;" yet thofe have no reafon to envy them, whofe fouls dwell at eafe in God, who are fed with the bread of life, the true manna, angels food, and drink of the water of life freely, and make melody with their hearts to the Lord, and are made to hear from him joy and gladnefs, and have received the anointing of the Spirit. If we have relifhed the delights of religion, we will fay as David, Let us not eat of their dainties, Pfal. cxli. 4.

Envy not finners the liberty they take to fin; that they can allow themfelves in the full enjoyment of thefe pleafures, which we cannot think of without horror. But have we not then the enjoyment of thofe pleafures which are infinitely better, and which they are ftrangers to? We cannot have both; and, of the two, are not ours, without difpute, preferable to theirs? and why then fhould we envy them? Their pleafures are enflaving, ours enlarging; theirs debafing to the foul, ours ennobling; theirs furfeiting, ours fatisfying; theirs offenfive to God, ours pleafing to him; theirs will end in pain and bitternefs, ours will be perfected in endlefs joys: and what reafon then have we to envy them?

5 Let not our fpirits fink, or be dejected, under the afflictions of this prefent time. We difparage our comforts in God, if we lay too much to heart our croffes in the world: And therefore, hereby let us evidence, that, being fatisfied of God's loving kindnefs, we are fatisfied with it. Let us look upon that as fufficient to balance all the unkindneffes of men They that value themfelves upon God's fmiles, ought not to vex themfelves at the world's frowns. The light of God's countenance can fhine through the thickeft clouds of the troubles of this prefent time; and therefore we fhould walk in the light of the Lord, even then, when as to our outward condition we fit in darknefs.

We manifeft that we have found true delight and fatisfaction in the fervice of God, and communion with him, when the pleafure of that will make the bittereft cup of affliction, that our Father puts into our hand, not only paffable, but pleafant; fo that, like bleffed Paul, when we are as forrowful, yet we may be always rejoicing, and may take pleafure in infirmities and reproaches, becaufe, though for the prefent they are not joyous but grievous, yet, when afterwards they yield the peaceable fruits of righteoufnefs, they become not grievous, but truly joyous. Bleffed is the man whom thou chaftencft.

6. Let the pleafure we have found in religion, difpofe us to be liberal and charitable to the poor and diftreffed. The pleafing fenfe we have of God's bounty to us, by which he has done fo much to make us eafy, fhould engage us bountifully to diftribute to the neceffities of faints, according to our ability; not only to keep them from perifhing, but to make them eafy; and that they may rejoice as well as we. Cheerfulnefs that enlargeth the heart, fhould open the hand too. Paul obferves it concerning the churches of Macedonia, who were ready to give for the relief of the poor faints at Jerufalem, that it was the abundance of their joy, their fpiritual joy, their joy in God, that abounded unto the riches of their liberality, 2 Cor. viii. 2.

When the people of Ifrael are commanded to rejoice in every good thing which God had given them, Deut. xxvi.

11, 12. they are commanded alfo to give freely to the Levite, the ftranger, the fatherlefs, and the widow, that they may eat, and be filled. And when upon a particular occafion they are directed to eat the fat, and drink the fweet, Neh. viii 10. at the fame time they are directed to fend portions to them for whom nothing is prepared: and then the joy of the Lord will be their ftrength. By our being charitable, we fhould fhow that we are cheerful; that we cheerfully tafte God's goodnefs in what we have, and truft his goodnefs for what we may hereafter want.

7. Let us do what we can, to bring others to partake of the fame pleafures in religion that we have tafted, efpecially thofe that are under our charge. It adds very much to the pleafure of an enjoyment, to communicate of it to others; efpecially when the nature of it is fuch, that we have never the lefs, but the more rather, for others fharing in it. What good tidings we hear that are of common concern, we defire that others may hear them, and be glad too. He that has but found a loft fheep, " calls his friends " and neighbours to rejoice with him," Luke xv. 6. much more he that has found Chrift, and found comfort in him; who can fay, not only, come and rejoice with me, but, come and partake with me: for yet there is room enough for all, though never fo numerous; enough for each, though never fo neceffitous and craving.

When Samfon had found honey in the carcafs of the lion, Judges xiv. 8. he brought fome of it to his parents, that they might partake with him: thus, when we have found a " day in God's courts better than a thoufand," we fhould invite others into thofe courts, by telling them what " God has done for our fouls," Pfal lxvi 16. and how willing he is to do the fame for theirs, if they in like manner apply themfelves to him. When Andrew, with a furprifing pleafure, had found the Meffiah, John i. 41, 45. he cannot reft till he has brought his brother Peter to him; nor Philip, till he hath brought his friend Nathaniel. They that are feafted with the comforts of God's houfe, fhould not covet to eat their morfel alone, but be willing to communicate of their fpiritual things.

8. Let us be willing to die, and leave this world. We have reafon to be afhamed of ourfelves, that we who have not only laid up our treafure above, but fetch our pleafures

thence, yet are as much in love with our present state, and as loth to think of quitting it, as if our treasure, and pleasure, and all, were wrapt up in the things of sense and time. The delights of sense entangle us, and hold us here; " These are the things that make us loth to die," as one once said, viewing his fine house and gardens. And are these things sufficient to court our stay here, when God calls to " arise, and depart, for this is not our rest ?" Mic. ii. 10.

Let us not be afraid to remove from a world of sense to a world of spirits, since we have found the pleasures of sense not worthy to be compared with spiritual pleasures. When in old age, which is one of the valleys of the shadow of death, we can no longer relish the delights of the body, but they become sapless and tasteless, as they were to Barzillai; yet we need not call those evil days, and years in which we have no pleasure, if we have walked and persevered in wisdom's ways; for, if so, we may then in old age, look back with pleasure on a life well spent on earth, as Hezekiah did, and look forward with more pleasure, upon a life to be better spent in heaven.

And when we have received a sentence of death within ourselves, and see the day approaching, the pleasure we have in loving God, and believing in Christ, and in the expressions of holy joy and thankfulness, should make even a sick-bed and a death-bed easy. The saints shall be joyful in glory, and shall " sing aloud upon their beds," Psal. cxlix. 5. those beds to which they are confined, and from which they are removing to their graves, their beds in the darkness. Our religion, if we be faithful to it, will furnish us with living comforts in dying moments, sufficient to balance the pains of death, and take off the terror of it; and to enable us to triumph over it, " O death! where is thy sting ?" Let us then evidence our experiences of the pleasures of religion, by living above the inordinate love of life, and fear of death.

Lastly, Let us long for the perfection of these spiritual pleasures in the kingdom of glory When we come thither, and not till then, they will be perfected. While we are here, as we know and love but in part, so we rejoice but in part; even our spiritual joys here have their damps and allays; we mix tears and tremblings with them: but, in heaven, there is a fulness of joy without mixture, and pleasures for evermore withot period or diminution. Christ's servants will there enter into the joy of their Lord, and it shall be everlasting joy, Isa. xxxv. 10.

And what are the pleasures in the way of wisdom, compared with those at the end of the way? If a complacency in the divine beauty and love be so pleasant while we are in the body, and are absent from the Lord; what will it be when we have put off the body, and go to be present with the Lord? If a day in God's courts, and a few minutes spent there in his praises, be so pleasant; what will an eternity within the veil be, among them that dwell in his house above, and are still praising him? If the earnest of our inheritance be so comfortable, what will the inheritance itself be? Now, wherever there is grace, it will be aiming at, and pressing towards, its own perfection; it is a " well of " water springing up to eternal life," John iv. 14. This therefore we should be longing for. Our love to God in this world is love in motion, in heaven it will be love at rest. O when shall that sabbatism come, which remains for the people of God.? Here we have the pleasure of looking towards God; O when shall we come, and appear before him! Our Lord, Jesus, when at his last passover, which he earnestly desired to eat with his disciples, he had drunk of the fruit of the vine, he speaks as one that longed to " drink " it new in the kingdom of his Father," Mat. xxvi. 19. It is very pleasant to serve Christ here; but to " depart " and to be with Christ, is far better. Now are we the " sons of God," 1 John iii. 2 and it is very pleasant to think of that: but it doth not yet appear what we shall be; something there is in reserve, which we are kept in expectation of: we are not yet at home, but should long to be there, and keep up holy desires of that glory to be revealed, that we may be quickened, as long as we are here, to press " towards the mark for the prize of the high calling."

A CHURCH IN THE HOUSE,

A

SERMON

CONCERNING

FAMILY RELIGION.

PUBLISHED AT THE REQUEST OF SOME WHO
HEARD THE SUBSTANCE OF IT PREACHED
IN LONDON, APRIL 16, 1704.

1 COR. xvi. 19.

——*With the Church that is in thine House.*

SOME very good interpreters, I know, understand this of a "settled, stated, solemn meeting of Christians at the house of Aquila and Priscilla, for public worship; and they were glad of houses to meet in, where they wanted those better conveniences, which the church was afterwards, in her prosperous days, accommodated with. When they had not such places as they could wish, they thankfully made use of such as they could get.

But others think it is meant only of their own family, and the strangers within their gates; among whom there was so much piety, and devotion, that it might well be called a church or religious house. Thus the ancients generally understand it. Nor was it only Aquila and Priscilla, whose house was thus celebrated for religion here, and Rom. xvi. 5. but Nymphas also had a church in his house, Col. iv. 15. and Philemon, verse 2. Not but that others, to whom and from whom salutations are sent in Paul's epistles, made conscience of keeping up religion in their families; but these are mentioned, probably because their families were more numerous than most of those other families were, which made their family devotions more solemn, and consequently more taken notice of.

In this sense I shall choose to take it; from hence to recommend family religion to you, under the notion of a church in the house. When we see your public assemblies so well filled, so well frequented, we cannot but thank God, and take courage; your diligent attendance on the ministry of the word and prayers, is your praise, and I trust, through grace, it redounds to your spiritual comfort and benefit: But my subject at this time will lead me to inquire into the state of religion in your private houses, whether it flourish or wither there? whether it be upon the throne, or under foot there? Herein I desire to deal plainly and faithfully with your consciences, and I beg you will give them leave to deal so with you.

The pious and zealous endeavours both of magistrates and ministers for the reformation of manners, and the suppression of vice and prophaneness, are the joy and encouragement of all good people in the land, and a happy indication that God hath yet mercy in store for us: "If the Lord had "been pleased to kill us, he would not have shewed us such "things as these." Now I know not any thing that will contribute more to the furtherance of this good work, than the bringing of family religion more into practice and reputation. Here the reformation must begin. Other methods may check the disease we complain of; but this, if it might universally obtain, would cure it. Salt must be cast into these springs, and then the waters would be healed.

Many a time, no doubt, you have been urged to this part of your duty; many a good sermon perhaps you have heard, and many a good book has been put into your hands with this design, to persuade you to keep up religion in your families, and to assist you therein: But I hope a further attempt to advance this good work, by one who is a hearty well-wisher to it, and to the prosperity of your souls and families, will not be thought altogether needless, and that by the grace of God it will not be wholly fruitless; at least it will serve to remind you of what you have received and heard to this purpose, that you may hold fast what is good, and repent of what is amiss, Rev. iii. 3.

The lesson then which I would recommend to you from the text is this:

That *the families of Christians should be little churches.* Or thus, *That wherever we have a house, God should have a church in it.*

Unhappy contests there have been, and still are, among wise and good men, about the constitution, order, and government of churches: God by his grace heal these breaches, lead us into all truth, and dispose our minds to love and peace; that, while we endeavour herein to walk according to the light God hath given us, we may charitably believe that others do so too; longing to be there where we shall be all of a mind

But I am now speaking of the churches concerning which there is no such controversy. All agree that masters of families, who profess religion and the fear of God themselves, should, according to the talents they are entrusted with, maintain and keep up religion and the fear of God in their families, as those that must give account; and that families, as such, should contribute to the support of Christianity in a nation, whose honour and happiness is to be a Christian nation. As nature makes families little kingdoms, and perhaps œconomics were the first and most ancient politics; so grace makes families little churches: and those were the primitive churches of the Old Testament, before " men " began to call upon the name of the Lord in solemn as- " semblies, and the sons of God came together to present " themselves" before him

Not that I would have these family-churches set up and kept up in competition with, much less in contradiction to, public religious assemblies, which ought always to have the preference: (The Lord loves the gates of Sion, more than all the dwellings of Jacob, Psal. lxxxvii. 2. and so must we; and must not forsake the assembling of ourselves together, under colour of exhorting one another daily at home;) far be it from us to offer any thing that may countenance the

A CHURCH IN THE HOUSE. 391

invading of the office of the miniftry, or laying it in common, and the ufurping or fuperfeding of the adminiftration of facraments: No, but thefe-family churches (which are but figuratively fo) muft be erected and maintained in fubordination to thofe more facred and folemn eftablifhments.

Now, that I may the more diftinctly open to you, and prefs upon you this great duty of family religion, from the example of this and other texts of a church in the houfe, I fhall endeavour, (1.) To fhew you what this church in the houfe is, and when our families may be called churches. And, (2.) To perfuade you, by fome motives, thus to turn your families into churches. And then, (3.) To addrefs to you upon the whole matter, by way of application.

I am, in the firft place, to tell you what that family religion is, which will be as a church in the houfe, and wherein it doth confift; that you may fee what it is we are perfuading you to.

Churches are facred focieties, incorporated for the honour and fervice of God in Chrift, devoted to God, and employed for him; fo fhould our families be.

1. Churches are focieties devoted to God, called out of the world, taken in out of the common to be inclofures for God: He hath fet them apart for himfelf; and, becaufe he hath chofen them, they alfo have chofen him, and fet themfelves apart for him. The Jewifh church was feparated to God for a peculiar people, a kingdom of priefts.

Thus our houfes muft be churches; with ourfelves we muft give up our houfes to the Lord, to be to him for a name, and a people. All the intereft we have, both in our relations, and in our poffeffions, muft be confecrated to God; as, under the law, all that the fervant had was his mafters for ever, after he had confented to have his ear bored to the door-poft. When God effectually called Abram out of Ur of the Chaldees, his family put on the face of a particular church; for, in obedience to God's precept, and in dependence on God's promife, they took all the fubftance they had gathered, and the fouls they had gotten, and put themfelves and their all under a divine conduct and government, Gen xii. 5. His was a great family; not only numerous, but very confiderable; the father of it was the father of all them that believe: But even little families, jointly and entirely given up to God, fo become churches.

When all the members of the family yield themselves to God, " subscribe with their hands to be the Lord's," and " surname themselves by the name of Israel," and the master of the family, with himself, gives up all his right, title, and interest in his house, and all that belongs to it, unto God, to be used for him, and disposed of by him, here is a church in the house.

Baptism was ordained for the discipling of nations, Mat. xxviii. 19. that the kingdoms of the world, as such, might, by the conversion of their people to the faith of Christ, and the consecration of their powers and governments to the honour of Christ, become his kingdoms, Rev. xi. 15. Thus by baptism households likewise are discipled, as Lydia's, and the Jailor's, Acts xvi. 15, 33. and in their family-capacity are given up to him, who is in a particular manner the God of all the families of Israel, Jer. xxx. 1. Circumcision was at first a family ordinance; and in that particular, as well as others, baptism doth somewhat symbolize with it: When the children of Christian parents are by baptism admitted members of the universal church, as their right to baptism is grounded upon, so their communion with the universal church, is, during their infancy, maintained and kept up chiefly by their immediate relation to these churches in the house; to them therefore they are first given back, and in them they are deposited, under the tuition of them, to be trained up till they become capable of a place and a name in particular churches of larger figure and extent. So that baptized families, that own their baptism, and adhere to it, and in their joint and relative capacity make profession of the Christian faith, may so far be called little churches

More than once, in the Old Testament, we read of the dedication of private houses. It is spoken of as a common practice, Deut. xx. 5. " What man is there that hath built " a new house, and hath not dedicated it?" i. e. taken possession of it: In the doing of which, it was usual to dedicate it to God by some solemn acts of religious worship. The thirtieth Psalm is intitled, a psalm or song at the dedication of the house of David. It is a good thing, when a man hath a house of his own, thus to convert it into a church, by dedicating it to the service and honour of God, that it may be a Bethel, a house of God, and not a Beth-aven, a house of vanity and iniquity. Every good Christian that is a householder, no doubt, doth this habitually and virtually; having firſt given his own ſelf to the Lord, he freely ſurrenders all he hath to him : but it may be of good uſe to do it actually and expreſsly, and often to repeat this act of reſignation; "this " ſtone which I have ſet for a pillar, ſhall be God's houſe," Gen. xxviii. 22. Let all I have in my houſe, and all I do in it, be for the glory of God ; I own him to be my great landlord, and I hold all from and under him ; to him I promiſe to pay the rents, the quitrents, of daily praiſes and thankſgivings, and to do the ſervices, the eaſy ſervices, of goſpel obedience. Let holineſs to the Lord be written upon the houſe, and all the furniture of it ; according to the word which God hath ſpoken, Zech. xiv. 20, 21. that every pot in Jeruſalem, and Judah " ſhall be holineſs to the Lord of " hoſts." Let God by his providence diſpoſe of the affairs of my family, and by his grace diſpoſe the affections of all in my family, according to his will, to his own praiſe. Let me and mine be only, wholly, and for ever his.

Be perſuaded, brethren, thus to dedicate your houſes to God, and beg of him to come and take poſſeſſion of them. If you never did it, do it to-night with all poſſible ſeriouſneſs and ſincerity. " Lift up your heads, O ye gates, and be " ye lift up, ye everlaſting doors, and the king of glory " ſhall come in." Bring the ark of the Lord into the tent you have pitched, and oblige yourſelves, and all yours, to attend it. Look upon your houſes as temples for God, places for worſhip, and all your poſſeſſions as dedicated things, to be uſed for God's honour, and not to be alienated or profaned.

2. Churches are ſocieties employed for God, purſuant to the true intent and meaning of this dedication.

There are three things neceſſary to the well being of a church, and which are moſt conſiderable in the conſtitution of it. Thoſe are doctrine, worſhip, and diſcipline. Where the truths of Chriſt are profeſſed and taught, the ordinances of Chriſt adminiſtred and obſerved, and due care taken to put the laws of Chriſt in execution among all that profeſs themſelves his ſubjects, and this under the conduct and inſpection of a goſpel-miniſtry ; there is a church : and ſomething anſwerable hereunto there muſt be in our families, to denominate them little churches.

Masters of families, who preside in the other affairs of the house, must go before their households in the things of God. They must be as prophets, priests, and kings, in their own families; and, as such, they must keep up family-doctrine, family-worship, and family-discipline: then is there a church in the house, and this is the family religion I am persuading you to.

First, Keep up family-doctrine. It is not enough that you and yours are baptised into the Christian faith, and profess to own the truth as it is in Jesus; but care must be taken, and means used, that you and yours be well acquainted with that truth, and that you grow in that acquaintance, to the honour of Christ, and his holy religion, and the improvement of your own minds, and theirs that are under your charge. You must dwell with your families as men of knowledge, 1 Pet iii. 7. *i. e.* as men that desire to grow in knowledge yourselves and to communicate your knowledge for the benefit of others, which are the two good properties of those that deserve to be called men of knowledge.

That you may keep up family-doctrine,

1. You must read the scriptures to your families, in a solemn manner, requiring their attendance on your reading, and their attention to it; and inquiring sometimes whether they understand what you read? I hope, there are none of you without bibles in your houses, store of bibles, every one a bible: thanks be to God, we have them cheap and common, in a language that we understand. The book of the law is not such a rarity with us, as it was in Josiah's time. We need not fetch this knowledge from afar, nor send from sea to sea, and from the river to the ends of the earth, to seek the knowledge of God; no, the word is nigh us. When popery reigned in our land, English bibles were scarce things; a load of hay, it is said, was once given for one torn leaf of a bible. But now bibles are every one's money. You know where to buy them; or, if not able to do that, perhaps in this charitable city, you may know where to beg them. It is better to be without bread in your houses, than without bibles; for the words of God's mouth are, and should be to you, more than your necessary food.

But what will it avail you to have bibles in your houses,

if you do not use them? To have the great things of God's law and gospel written to you, if you count them as a strange thing? You look daily into your shop-books, and perhaps converse much with the news-books; and shall your bibles be thrown by as an almanack out of date? It is not now penal to read the scriptures in your families, as it was in the dawning of the day of reformation from popery, when there were those that were accused and prosecuted for reading in a certain great heretical book, called an English bible. The Philistines do not now stop up these wells, as Gen. xxvi. 18. nor do the shepherds drive away your flocks from them, Exod. ii. 17. nor are they as a " spring shut up, or a fountain " sealed:" but the gifts given to men have been happily employed in rolling away the stone from the mouth of these wells. You have great encouragements to read the scripture; for notwithstanding the malicious endeavours of atheists to vilify sacred things, the knowledge of the scripture is still in reputation with all wise and good men. You have also variety of excellent helps to understand the scripture, and to improve your reading of it; so that if you or yours perish for lack of this knowledge, as you certainly will if you persist in the neglect of it, you may thank yourselves, the guilt will lie wholly at your own doors.

Let me therefore with all earnestness press it upon you, to make the solemn reading of the scripture a part of your daily worship in your families. When you speak to God by prayer, be willing to hear him speak to you in his word, that there may be a complete communion between you and God. This will add much to the solemnity of your family-worship, and will make the transaction the more awful and serious, if it be done in a right manner; which will conduce much to the honour of God, and your own and your families edification It will help to make the word of God familiar to yourselves, and your children and servants, that you may be ready and mighty in the scriptures, and may from thence be thoroughly furnished for every good word and work. It will likewise furnish you with matter and words for prayer, and so be helpful to you in other parts of the service. If some parts of scripture seem less edifying, let those be more frequently read that are most so. David's psalms are of daily use in devotion, and Solomon's proverbs in conversation; it will be greatly to your advantage to be well versed in them. And, I hope, I need not press any Christian to the study of the New Testament, nor any Christian parents to the frequent instructing of their children in the pleasant and profitable histories of the Old Testament. When you only hear your children read the bible, they are tempted to look upon it as no more than a school book; but when they hear you read it to them in a solemn, religious manner, it comes, as it ought, with more authority. Those masters of families who make conscience of doing this daily, morning and evening, reckoning it part of that which the duty of every day requires, I am sure, have comfort and satisfaction in so doing, and find it contributes much to their own improvement in Christian knowledge, and the edification of those that dwell under their shadow; and the more, if those that are ministers expound themselves, and other masters of families read some plain and profitable exposition of what is read, or of some part of it.

It is easy to add, under this head, that the seasonable reading of other good books will contribute very much to family instruction. In helps of this kind, we are as happy as any people under the sun, if we have but hearts to use the helps we have, as those that must give an account shortly of them, among other the talents we are intrusted with.

2. You must also catechise your children and servants, so long as they continue in that age of life which needs this milk. Oblige them to learn some good catechism by heart, and to keep it in remembrance, and, by familiar discourse with them, help them to understand it, as they become capable. It is an excellent method of catechising, which GOD himself directs us to, Deut. vi. 7. To teach our children the things of GOD, by talking of them as we do sit in the house, and go by the way, when we lie down, and when we rise up. It is good to keep up stated times for this service, and be constant to them, as those that know how industrious the enemy is to sow tares, while men sleep. If this good work be not kept going forward, it will of itself go backward. Wisdom also will direct you to manage your catechising, as well as the other branches of family religion, so as not to make it a task and a burden, but as much as may be a pleasure to those under your charge, that the blame may lie wholly upon their own impiety, and not at all upon your imprudence, if they should say, Behold what a weariness is it?

This way of inſtruction by catechiſing, doth in a ſpecial manner belong to the church in the houſe; for that is the nurſery in which the trees of righteouſneſs are reared, that afterwards are planted in the courts of our God. Public catechiſing will turn to little account without family catechiſing. The labour of miniſters in inſtructing of youth, and feeding the lambs of the flock, therefore proves to many labour in vain, becauſe maſters of families do not do their duty, in preparing them for public inſtruction, and examining their improvement by it. As mothers are children's beſt nurſes, ſo parents are, or ſhould be, their beſt teachers. Solomon's father was his tutor, Prov. iv. 3. 4. And he never forgot the leſſons his mother taught him. Prov. xxxi. 1.

The baptiſm of your children, as it laid a ſtrong and laſting obligation upon them to live in the fear of God, ſo it brought you under the moſt powerful engagements imaginable to bring them up in that fear. The child you gave up to God to be dedicated to him, and admitted a member of Christ's viſible church, was in God's name given back to you, with the ſame charge that Pharaoh's daughter gave to Moſes' mother, Take this child, and nurſe it for me; and, in nurſing it for God, you nurſe it for better preferment than that of being called the ſon of Pharaoh's daughter. It is worth obſerving, that he to whom God firſt did the honour of entailing the ſeal of the covenant upon his ſeed, was eminent for this part of family religion; "I know Abraham, "ſaith God, that he will command his children, and his "houſehold after him, to keep the way of the Lord," Gen. xviii. 19 Thoſe therefore who would have the comfort of God's covenant with them and their ſeed, and would ſhare in that bleſſing of Abraham which comes upon the Gentiles, muſt herein follow the example of faithful Abraham. The entail of the covenant of grace is forfeited and cut off, if care be not taken with it to tranſmit the means of grace. To what purpoſe were they diſcipled, if they be not taught? Why did you give them a Chriſtian name, if you will not give them the knowledge of Chriſt and Chriſtianity? God has owned them as his children, and born unto him, Ezek. xvi. 20. and therefore he expects they ſhould be brought up for him; you are unjuſt to your God, unkind to your children, and unfaithful to your truſt, if having by baptiſm entered your children in Christ's School, and lifted them under his banner, you do not make confcience of training them up in the learning of Christ's fcholars, and under the difcipline of his foldiers.

- Confider what your children are now capable of, even in the days of their childhood. They are capable of receiving impreffions now, which may abide upon them while they live; they " are turned as clay to the feal," and now is the time to apply to them the feal of the living God. They are capable of honouring God now, if they be well taught, and by their joining, as they can, in religious fervices, with fo much reverence and application as their age will admit, God is honoured, and you in them prefent to him living facrifices, holy and acceptable. The hofannas even of children well taught, will be the perfecting of praife, and highly pleafing to the Lord Jefus.

- Confider what your children are defigned for (we hope) in this world: they muft be a " feed to ferve the Lord," which fhall be " accounted to him for a generation." They are to bear up the name of Chrift in their day, and into their hands muft be tranfmitted that good thing, which is committed to us. They are to be praifing God on earth, when we are praifing him in heaven. Let them then be brought up accordingly, that they may anfwer the end of their birth and being. They are defigned for the fervice of their generation, and to do good in their day; confult the public welfare then, and let nothing be wanting on your parts to qualify them for ufefulnefs, according as their place and capacity is.

Confider efpecially what they are defigned for in another world. They are made for eternity. Every child thou haft, hath a precious and immortal foul, that muft be forever either in heaven or hell, according as it is prepared in this prefent ftate; and perhaps it muft remove to that world of fpirits very fhortly; and will it not be very fad, if, through your carelefnefs and negleƈt, your children fhould learn the ways of fin, and perifh eternally in thofe ways? Give them warning, that, if poffible, you may deliver their fouls, at leaft that you may deliver your own, and may not bring their curfe and God's too, their blood and your own too, upon your heads.

I know you cannot give grace to your children, nor is a religious converſation the conſtant conſequent of a religious education: "the race is not always to the ſwift, nor the "battle to the ſtrong;" but if you make conſcience of do- ing your duty, by keeping up family doctrine, if you teach them the good and the right way, and warn them of by-paths if you reprove, exhort, and encourage them as there is occaſion, if you pray with them and for them, and ſet them a good example, and at laſt conſult their ſoul's welfare in the diſpoſal of them, you have done your part, and may comfortably leave the iſſue and ſucceſs with God.

Secondly, Keep up family worſhip. You muſt not only, as prophets, teach your families, but as prieſts, muſt go before them, in offering the ſpiritual ſacrifice of prayer and praiſe Herein likewiſe you muſt tread in the ſteps of faithful Abraham; (whoſe ſons you are while thus you do well) you muſt not only like him, inſtruct your houſehold, but like him, you muſt with them." call on the name of the " Lord the everlaſting God," Gen. xxi. 33. Wherever he pitched his tent, " there he built an altar unto the Lord," Gen. xii. 7, 8, 13 vii. 18. Though he was yet in an unſettled ſtate, but a ſtranger and a ſojourner; though he was among jealous and envious neighbours, for the Canaanite and the Perizzite dwelled then in the land; yet wherever Abraham had a tent, God had an altar in it, and he himſelf ſerved at that altar. Herein he has left us an example.

Families, as ſuch, have many errands at the throne of grace, which furniſh them with matter and occaſion for family prayer every day; errands which cannot be done ſo well in ſecret or public, but are fitteſt to be done by the family in concert, and apart from the other families. And it is good for thoſe that go before the reſt in family-devotion, ordinarily to dwell moſt upon the concerns of thoſe that join in their family capacity, that it may indeed be a family prayer, not only offered in and by the family, but ſuited to it. In this and other ſervices, we ſhould endeavour not only to ſay ſomething, but ſomething to the purpoſe.

Five things eſpecially you ſhould have upon your heart in your family prayer, and ſhould endeavour to bring ſomething of each, more or leſs, into every prayer with your families.

1. You ought to make family acknowledgements of your dependence upon God and his providence, as you are a fa-

mily. Our great bufinefs in all acts of religious worfhip is, " to give unto the Lord the glory due unto his name;" and this we muft do in our family worfhip. Give honour to God as the founder of families by his ordinance, becaufe " it was not good for man to be alone ;" as the founder of your families by his providence, for he it is that " buildeth " the houfe, and fetteth the folitary in families." Give honour to him as the owner and ruler of families; acknowledge that you and yours are his, under his government, and at his difpofal, as the fheep of his pafture. Efpecially adore him as the God of all the families of Ifrael, in covenant-relation to them, and having a particular concern for them above others, Jer. xxxi. 1. Give honour to the great Redeemer, as the head of all the churches, even thofe in your houfes; call him the mafter of the family, and the great upholder and benefactor of it; for he it is " in whom " all the families of the earth are bleffed," Gen. xii 3. All family bleffings are owing to Chrift, and come to us through his hand and his blood. Own your dependence upon God, and your obligations to Chrift, for all good things pertaining both to life and godlinefs, and make confcience of paying homage to your chief Lord, and never fet up a title to any of your enjoyments in competition to his.

2. You ought to make family confeffions of your fins againft God; thofe fins you have contracted the guilt of in your family capacity. We read in fcripture of the iniquity of the houfe, as of Eli's, 1 Sam. iii. 13, 14. Iniquity vifited upon the children; Sins that bring wrath upon families, and a curfe that " enters into the houfe, to confume it with " the timber thereof, and the ftones thereof, Zech. v. 4. How fad is the condition of thofe families that fin together, and never pray together; that by concurring in frauds quarrels, and exceffes, by ftrengthening one another's hands in impiety and profanenefs, fill the meafure of family guilt, and never agree together to do any thing to empty it!

And even religious families that are not polluted with grofs and fcandalous fins, yet have need to join every day in the folemn acts and expreffions of repentance before God for their fins of daily infirmity. Their vain words and unprofitable converfe among themfelves; their manifold defects in relative duties, provoking one another's lufts and paffions, inftead of provoking one another to love and to good works. These ought to be confessed and bewailed by the family together, that God may be glorified, and what has been amiss may be amended for the future. It was not only in a time of great and extraordinary repentance that families mourned apart, Zech. xii. 11. but in the stated returns of the day of expiation the priest was particularly to " make atonement for his houshold," Lev. xvi. 17. In many things we all offend God, and one another, and a penitent confession of it in prayer together, will be the most effectual way of reconciling ourselves both to God, and to one another. The best families, and those in which piety and love prevail most, yet in many things come short, and do enough every day to bring them upon their knees at night.

3. You ought to offer up family thanksgivings for the blessings which you, with your families, receive from God. Many are the mercies which you enjoy the sweetness and benefit of in common; which, if wanting to one, all the family would be sensible of it. Hath not God " made a " hedge of protection about you and your houses, and all " that you have ?" Job i. 10. Hath he not created a defence upon every dwelling place of Mount Zion, as well as upon her assemblies ? Isa. iv. 5. The dreadful alarms of a storm, and the desolations made as by a fire once in an age, should make us sensible of our obligations to the divine providence, for our preservation from tempests and fire every day, and every night. It is of the Lord's mercies that we are not consumed, and buried in the ruins of our houses. When the whole family comes together safe in the morning, from their respective retirements, and when they return safe at night, from their respective employments, there having been no disaster, no adversary, no evil occurrent, it is so reasonable, and (as I may say) so natural for them to join together in solemn thanksgivings to their greater Protector, that I wonder how any that believe a God, and a providence, can omit it. Have you not health in your family, sickness kept or taken from the midst of you ? Doth not God bring plentifully into your hands, and increase your substance ? Have you not your table spread, and your cup running over, and manna rained about your tents ? And doth not the whole family share in the comfort of all this ? Shall not then the voice of thanksgiving be in

3 E

those tabernacles, where the voice of rejoicing is? Pſal. cxviii. 15. Is the vine by the houſe ſide fruitful and flouriſhing, and the olive plants round the table green and growing? Are family relations comfortable and agreeable, not broken, nor imbittered? And ſhall not that God be acknowledged herein, who makes every creature to be that to us that it is? Shall not the God of your mercies, your family mercies, be the God of your praiſes, your family praiſes, and that daily?

The benefit and honour of your being Chriſtian families, your having in God's houſe, and within his walls, a place, and a name, better than that of ſons and daughters, and the ſalvation this brings to your houſe, furniſheth you with abundant matter for joint thankſgivings. You hath he known above all the families of the earth, and therefore he expects, in a ſpecial manner, to be owned by you. Of all houſes, the houſe of Iſrael, the houſe of Aaron, and the houſe of Levi, have moſt reaſon to bleſs the Lord, and to ſay, that his mercy endureth for ever.

4. You ought to preſent your family petitions for the mercy and grace which your families ſtand in need of. Daily bread is received by families together, and we are taught not only to pray for it every day, but to pray together for it, ſaying, Our Father, give it us. There are affairs and employments which the family is jointly concerned in the ſucceſs of, and therefore ſhould jointly aſk of God wiſdom for the management of them, and proſperity therein. There are family cares to be caſt upon God by prayer, family comforts to be ſought for, and family croſſes which they ſhould together beg for the ſanctification and removal of. Hereby your children will be more effectually poſſeſſed with a belief of, and regard to, the divine providence, than by all the inſtructions you can give them, which will look beſt in their eye, when thus reduced to practice by your daily acknowledging God in all your ways.

You deſire that God will give wiſdom and grace to your children, you travail in birth again till you ſee Chriſt formed in them, you pray for them; it is well, but it is not enough; you muſt pray with them; let them hear you pray to God for a bleſſing upon the good inſtructions and counſels you give them; it may perhaps put them upon praying for themſelves, and increaſe their eſteem both of you, and of the good leſſons you teach them. You would have your ſervants diligent and faithful, and this perhaps would help to make them ſo. Maſters do not give to their ſervants that which is juſt and equal, if they do not continue in prayer with them.

There are ſome temptations which families, as ſuch, lie open to: buſy families are in temptation to worldlineſs, and neglect of religious duties; mixed families are in temptation to diſcord, and mutual jealouſies; decaying families are in temptation to diſtruſt, diſcontent, and indirect courſes, to help themſelves; they ſhould therefore not only watch but pray together, that they be not overcome by the temptations they are expoſed to.

There are family bleſſings which God hath promiſed, and for which he will be ſought unto, ſuch as thoſe on the houſe of Obed-Edom for the Ark's ſake; " or the mercy " which Paul begs for the houſe of Oneſiphorus," 2 Tim. i. 16. Theſe joint bleſſings muſt be ſued out by joint prayers. There is a ſpecial bleſſing which God commands upon families that dwell together in unity, Pſal. cxxxiii. 1, 3. which they muſt ſeek for by prayer, and come together to ſeek for it, in token of that unity which qualifies for it. Where God commands the bleſſing, we muſt beg the Bleſſing. God by promiſe bleſſeth David's houſe, and therefore David by prayer bleſſeth it too, 2 Sam. vi. 20.

5. You ought to make family interceſſions for others alſo. There are families you ſtand related to, or which by neighbourhood, friendſhip or acquaintance, you become intereſted in, and concerned for, and theſe you ſhould recommend in your prayers to the grace of God, and your family, that are joined with you in the alliances, ſhould join with you in thoſe prayers. Evil tidings perhaps are received from relations at a diſtance, which are the grief of the family; God muſt then be ſought unto by the family for ſuccour and deliverance. Some of the branches of the family are perhaps in diſtant countries, and in dangerous circumſtances, and you are ſolicitous about them; it will be a comfort to yourſelves, and perhaps will be of advantage to them, to make mention of them daily in your family prayers. The benefit of prayer, will reach far, becauſe he that hears prayer can extend his Hand of power and

mercy to the utmost corners of the earth, and to them that are afar off upon the sea.

In the public peace likewise, we and our families have peace; and therefore, if we forget thee, O Jerusalem, we are unworthy ever to stand in thy courts, or dwell within thy walls. Our families should be witnesses for us, that we pray daily for the land of our nativity, and the prosperity of all its interests; that praying every where, we make supplication for the King, and all in authority, 1 Tim. ii. 2, 8 That we bear upon our hearts the concerns of God's church abroad, especially the suffering parts of it. Thus keeping up a spiritual communion with all the families that in every place call on the name of the Lord Jesus.

In a word, Let us go by this rule in our family devotions; whatever is the matter of our care, let it be the matter of our prayer: and let us allow no care which we cannot in faith spread before God: and whatever is the matter of our rejoicing, let it be the matter of our thanksgiving; and let us withhold our hearts from all those joys, which do not dispose us for the duty of praise.

Under this head of family worship, I must not omit to recommend to you the singing of psalms in your families, as a part of daily worship, especially Sabbath worship. This is a part of religious worship, which participates both of the word and prayer; for therein we are not only to give glory to God, but to teach and admonish one another; it is therefore very proper to make it a transition, from the one to the other. It will warm and quicken you, refresh and comfort you, and perhaps, if you have little children in your houses, they will sooner take notice of it, than of any other part of your family devotion; and some good impressions may thereby be fastened upon them insensibly.

Thirdly, Keep up family discipline, that so you have a complete church in your house, though in little. Reason teacheth us, " that every man should bear rule in his own " house," Esther i. 22. And since that, as well as other power, is of God, it ought to be employed for God; and they that so rule, must be just, ruling in his fear. Joshua looked further than the acts of religious worship, when he made that pious resolution, " as for me and my house, we

"will ferve the Lord," Joſhua xxiv. 15 For we do not ferve him in fincerity and truth (which is the fervice he there ſpeaks of, verſe. 14.) if we and ours ferve him only on our knees, and do not take care to ferve him in all the inſtances of a religious converſation. Thoſe only that have clean hands and a pure heart, are accounted "the ge-
" neration of them that feek God," Pſal. xxiv. 4, 6. And without this, thoſe that pretend to feek God daily, do but mock him, Iſa. lviii. 2.

The authority God hath given you over your children and fervants, is principally defigned for this end, that you may thereby engage them for God and godlineſs. If you ufe it only to oblige them to do your will, and fo to ferve your pride, and to do your buſineſs, and fo to ferve your worldlineſs, you do not anſwer the great end of your being inveſted with it: You muſt uſe it for God's honour, by it to engage them as far as you can, to do the will of God, and mind the buſineſs of religion. Holy David not only bleſſed his houſehold, but took care to keep good order in it; as appears by that plan of his family difcipline, which we have in the ci. pſalm. A pſalm which Mr. Fox tells us, that bleſſed martyr biſhop Ridley often read to his family, as the rule by which he reſolved to govern it.

You are made keeper of the vineyard; be faithful to your truſt, and carefully watch over theſe that are under your charge, knowing you muſt give account.

1. Countenance every thing that is good and praiſeworthy in your children and fervants. It is as much your duty to commend and encourage thoſe in your family that do well, as to reprove and admoniſh thoſe that do amiſs; and if you take delight only in blaming that which is culpable, and are backward to praiſe that which is laudable, you give occaſion to fuſpect fomething of an ill nature not becoming a good man, much leſs a good Chriſtian. It ſhould be a trouble to us, when we have a reproof to give, but a pleaſure to us to ſay with the apoſtle, 1 Cor. ii. 2. Now I praiſe you.

Moſt people will be eafier led than driven, and we all love to be ſpoken fair: When you fee any thing that is hopeful and promiſing in your inferiors, any thing of a towardly and tractable diſpoſition, much more any thing of a pious affection to the things of God, you ſhould therefore contrive to encourage it. Smile upon them when you see them set their faces heavenwards, and take the first opportunity to let them know you observe it, and are well pleased with it, and do not despise the day of small things This will quicken them to continue and abound in that which is good, it will hearten them against the difficulties they see in their way, and perhaps may turn the wavering, trembling scale the right way, and effectually determine their resolutions to cleave to the Lord. When you see them forward to come to family worship, attentive to the word, devout in prayer, industrious to get knowledge, afraid of sin, and careful to do their duty, let them have the praise of it; for you have the comfort of it, and God must have all the glory. Draw them with the cords of a man, hold them with the bands of love, so shall your rebukes, when they are necessary, be more acceptable and effectual. The great Shepherd gathers the lambs in his arms, and carries them in his bosom, and gently leads them, and so should you.

2. Discountenance every thing that is evil in your children and servants. Use your authority for the preventing of sin, and the suppressing of every root of bitterness, lest it spring up, and trouble you, and thereby many be defiled. Frown upon every thing that brings sin into your families, and introduceth any ill words, or ill practices. Pride and passion, strife and contention, idleness and intemperance, lying and slandering, these are sins which you must not connive at, nor suffer to go without a rebuke. If you return to the Almighty, this among other things is required of you, that you put away iniquity, all iniquity, these and other the like iniquities, far from your tabernacles, Job xxii. 23. Make it to appear, that, in the government of your families, you are more jealous for God's honour, than for your own authority and interest; and shew yourselves more displeased at that which is an offence to God, than at that which is only an affront or damage to yourselves.

You must indeed be careful not to provoke your children to wrath, lest they be discouraged; and, as to your servants, it is your duty to forbear or moderate threatening; yet you must also, with holy zeal and resolution, and the meekness of wisdom, keep good order in your families, and set no wicked thing before your eyes, but witness against it. A little leaven leaveneth the whole lump. Be afraid of having wicked fervants in your houfes, left your children learn their way, and get a flfare to their fouls. Drive away with an angry countenance all that evil communication which corrupts good manners, that your houfes may be habitations of righteoufnefs, and fin may never find fhelter in them.

I come now, fecondly, to offer fome motives to perfuade you thus to turn your families into little churches. And O that I could find out acceptable words, with which to reafon with you fo as to prevail! "Suffer me a little, and I will " fhew you what is to be faid on God's behalf," which is worth your confideration.

Firft, If your families be little churches, " God will " come to you, and dwell with you in them ;" for he hath faid concerning the church, " This is my reft for ever, here " will I dwell." It is a very defirable thing to have the gracious prefence of God with us in our families, that prefence which is promifed, where " two or three are gathered to- " gether in his name." This was it that David was fo defirous of, Pfal. ci. 2. " O when wilt thou come unto me!" His palace, his court, would be as a prifon, as a dungeon, to him, if God did not come to him, and dwell with him in it; and cannot your hearts witnefs to this defire? You that have houfes of your own, would you not have God to come to you and dwell with you in them? Invite him then, beg his prefence, court his ftay. Nay, he invites himfelf to your houfes, by the offers of his favour and grace; " Behold he " ftands at your door and knocks:" It is the voice of your beloved, open to him, and bid him welcome: meet him with your hofannas; bleffed is he who cometh. He cometh peaceably, he brings a bleffing with him, a bleffing which he will caufe to reft upon the habitations of the righteous, Ezek. xliv. 30. He will command a bleffing which fhall amount to no lefs than life for evermore, Pfal. xxxiii. 3. This prefence and bleffing of God will make your relations comfortable, your affairs fuccefsful, your enjoyments fweet, and behold by it all things are made clean to you. This will make your family comforts double comforts; and your family croffes but half croffes; it will turn a tent into a temple, a cottage into a palace. Beautiful for fituation, the joy of the whole earth, are the houfes in which God dwells.

Now the way to have God's prefence in your houfes with you is, to furnifh them for his entertainment. Thus the good Shunammite invited the prophet Elisha to the chamber she had prepared for him, by accommodating him there with " a bed and a table, a stool and a candlestick," 2 Kings iv. 10. Would you furnish your houses for the presence of God, it is not expected that you furnish them as his tabernacle was of old furnished, with blue, and purple, and scarlet, and fine linen; but set up and keep up for him a throne and an altar, that from the altar you and yours may give glory to him, and from the throne he may give law to you and yours; and then you may be sure of his presence and blessing, and may solace yourselves from day to day in the comfort of it. God will be with you in a way of mercy, while you are with him in a way of duty: If you seek him he will be found of you: The secret of God shall be in your tabernacle, as it was on Job's, chap xxix. 4. as it is with the righteous, Psal. xxv. 14. Prov. iii. 32, 33.

Secondly. If you make your houses little churches, God will make them little sanctuaries; nay, he will himself be to you as a little sanctuary, Ezek xi. 16. The way to be safe in your house is, to keep up religion and the fear of God in your houses; so shall you dwell on high, and the " place of your defence shall be the munition of rocks," Isa. xxxiii. 16. The law looks upon a man's house as his castle, religion makes it truly so. If God's grace be the glory in the midst of the house, his providence will make a wall of fire round about it, Zech. ii 5. Satan found it to his confusion, that God made a hedge about pious Job, about his house, and about all that he had on every side, so that he could not find one gap by which to break in upon him, Job i. 10. Every dwelling place of Mount Sion shall be protected, as the tabernacle was in the wilderness; for God hath promised, to " create upon it a cloud and smoke by " day, and the shining of a flaming fire by night, which " shall be a defence upon all the glory," Isa. iv. 5. If we thus " dwell in the house of the Lord all the days of our " life," by making our houses his houses, we shall be " hid " in his pavilion, in the secret of his tabernacle shall he " hide us," Psal. xxvii. 4, 5.

Wherever we encamp, under the banner of Christ, the angels of God will encamp round about us, and pitch their tents, where we pitch ours; and we little think how much we owe it to the ministration of the good angels, that we and ours are preserved from the malice of evil angels, who are continually seeking to do mischief to good people. There are terrors that fly by night and by day, which they only that abide under the shadow of the Almighty can promise themselves to be safe from, Psal. xci 1, 5. Would you insure your houses by the best policy of insurance, turn them into churches, and then they shall be taken under the special protection of him that keeps Israel, and neither slumbers nor sleeps; and, if any damage come to them, it shall be made up in grace and glory. The way of duty is without doubt the way of safety.

Praying families are kept from more mischiefs than they themselves are aware of. They are not always sensible of the distinction which a kind providence makes between them and others; though God is pleased sometimes to make it remarkable, as in the story which is credibly related of a certain village in the canton of Bern in Switzerland, consisting of ninety houses, which in the year 1584, was all destroyed by an earthquake, except one house, in which the good-man and his family were at that time together praying. That promise is sure to all the seed of faithful Abraham, Fear not, I am thy shield, Gen. xv. 1. wisdom herself hath past her word for it, Prov. i. 33. Whoso hearkeneth to me, wherever he dwells safely, and shall be quite from all real evil itself, and from the amazing tormenting fear of evil. Nothing can hurt, nothing needs frighten, those whom God protects.

Thirdly, If you have not a church in your house, it is to be feared Satan will have a seat there. If religion do not rule in your families, sin and wickedness will rule there. I know where thou dwellest, (saith Christ to the angel of the church of Pergamos, Rev ii. 13.) even where Satan's seat is; that was his affliction; but there are many whose sin it is; by their irreligion and immorality they allow Satan a seat in the houses, and that seat a throne. They are very willing that the strong man armed should keep his palace there, and that his goods should be at peace; and the surest way to prevent this is by setting up a church in the house. It is commonly said, That where God hath a church, the devil will have his chapel; but it may more truly be said in this case, Where God hath not a church, the devil will have his chapel. If the unclean spirit find

3 F

the houſe in this ſenſe empty empty of good, though it be ſwept and garniſhed, he taketh to himſelf ſeven other ſpirits more wicked than himſelf, and they enter in and dwell there.

Terrible ſtories have been told of houſes haunted by the devil, and of the fear people have had of dwelling in ſuch houſes; verily thoſe houſes in which rioting and drunkenneſs reign, in which ſwearing and curſing are the language of the houſe, or in which the more ſpiritual wickedneſs of pride, malice, covetouſneſs and deceit, have the aſcendant, may truly be ſaid to be haunted by the devil, and they are moſt uncomfortable houſes for any man to live in: They are holds of foul ſpirits, and cages of unclean and hateful birds, even as Babylon the great will be when it is fallen, Rev xviii 2.

Now the way to keep ſin out of the houſe is, to keep up religion in the houſe, which will be the moſt effectual antidote againſt Satan's poiſon. When Abraham thought concerning Abimelech's houſe, Surely the fear of God is not in this place, he concluded no leſs, but they will ſlay me for my wife's ſake," Gen. xx. 11. Where no fear of God is, no reading, no praying, no devotion, what can one expect but all that is bad? Where there is impiety, there will be immorality; they that reſtrain prayer, caſt of fear, Job, xv. 4. But, if religious worſhip have its place in the houſe, it may be hoped that vice will not have a place there. There is much of truth in that ſaying of good Mr. Dod, " Either " praying will make a man give over ſinning, or ſinning " will make a man give over praying " There remains ſome hope concerning thoſe who are otherwiſe bad, as long as they keep up prayer. Though there be a ſtruggle between Chriſt and Belial in your houſes and the inſults of ſin and Satan are daring and threatening, yet as long as religion keeps the field, and the weapons of its warfare are made uſe of, we may hope the enemy will loſe ground.

Fourthly, A church in the houſe will make it very comfortable to yourſelves. Nothing more agreeable to a gracious ſoul, than conſtant communion with a gracious God; it is the one thing it deſires, to dwell in the houſe of the Lord; here it is as in its element, it is its reſt for ever. If therefore our houſes be houſes of the Lord, we ſhall for that reaſon love home, reckoning our daily devotions, the ſweeteſt of our daily delights; and our family-worſhip, the moſt valuable of our family comforts. This will ſanctify to us all the conveniences of our houfe, and reconcile us to the inconveniences of it. What are Solomon's gardens and orchards, and pools of water, and other the delights of the fons of men, Ecclef. ii. 5, 6, 8. in comparifon with thefe delights of the children of God?

Family religion will help to make our family relations comfortable to us, by promoting love, preventing quarrels, and extinguifhing heats that may at any time happen. A family living in the fear of God, and joining daily in religious worfhip, truly enjoys itfelf; "Behold how good, and "how pleafant a thing it is for brethren thus to dwell to-"gether;" it is not only like ointment and perfume which rejoice the heart, but like the holy ointment, the holy perfume, wherewith Aaron, the faint of the Lord, was confecrated: Not only like the common dew to the grafs, but like the dew which defcendeth upon the mountains of Sion, the holy mountains, Pfal. cxxxiii. 1, 2. The communion of faints in that which is the work of faints, is without doubt the moft pleafant communion here on earth, and the livelieft reprefentation, and fureft pledge of thofe everlafting joys, which are the happinefs of the fpirits of juft men made perfect, and the hopes of holy fouls in this imperfect ftate.

Family religion will make the affairs of the family fuccefsful; and though they may not in every thing iffue to our mind, yet we may by faith forefee that they will at laft iffue to our good. If this beauty of the Lord our God be upon us and our families, it will profper the work of our hands unto us, yea the work of our hands it will eftablifh; or however it will eftablifh our hearts in that comfort which makes every thing that occurs eafy, Pfal. xc. 17. cxii. 8.

We cannot fuppofe our mountain to ftand fo ftrong, but that it will be moved; trouble in the flefh we muft expect, and affliction in that from which we promife ourfelves moft comfort; and when the divine providence makes our houfes houfes of mourning, then it will be comfortable to have them houfes of prayer, and to have had them fo before. When ficknefs, and forrow, and death come into our families, and fooner or later they will come, it is good that they fhould find the wheels of prayer agoing, and the family accuftomed to feek God; for, if we are then to begin this good work when diftrefs forceth us to it, we fhall drive heavily in it. They that pray conftantly when they are well, may pray comfortably when they are fick.

Fifthly, A church in the house will be a good legacy; nay, it will be a good inheritance to be left to your children after you. Reason directs us to consult the welfare of posterity, and to lay up in store a good foundation for those that shall come after us to build upon; and we cannot do this better, than by keeping up religion in our houses. A family altar will be the best entail; your children shall for this, rise up and call you blessed; and it may be hoped, they will be praising God for you, and praising God like you, here on earth, when you are praising him in heaven.

You will hereby leave your children the benefit of many prayers put up to heaven for them, which will be kept, as it were, upon the file there, to be answered to their comfort when you are silent in the dust. It is true of prayer, what we say of winter, "It never rots in the skies." The seed of Jacob know they do not seek in vain, though perhaps they live not to see their prayers answered. Some good Christians, that have made conscience of praying daily with and for their children, have been encouraged to hope that the children of so many prayers should not miscarry at last; and thus encouraged, Joseph's dying words have been the language of many a dying Christian's faith, "I die, but God " will surely visit you," Gen. l. 24. I have heard of a hopeful son, who said, " He valued his interest in his pious fa- " ther's prayers, far more than his interest in his estate, " though a considerable one."

You will likewise hereby leave your children a good example, which you may hope they will follow when they come into houses of their own. The usage and practice of families is commonly transmitted from one generation to another; bad customs are many times thus entailed: They who " burnt incense to the queen of heaven, learned it of " their fathers," Jer. xliv. 17. And a " vain conversation was " thus received by tradition," 1 Pet. i. 18. And why may not good customs be in like manner handed down to posterity? Thus we should make known the ways of God to our children, that they may " arise and declare them to their " children," Psal. lxxviii. 6. and religion may become an heir loom in our families; let your children be able to say, when they are tempted to sit loose to religion, " that it was " the way of their family, the good old way in which their " fathers walked, and in which they themselves were edu-

"cated and trained up:" And with this they may answer him that reproacheth them. Let family worship, besides all its other pleas for itself, be able in your houses to plead prescription. And though to the acceptableness of the service requisite, that it be done from a higher and better principle, than purely to keep up the custom of family, yet better so than not at all: And the form of godliness may, by the grace of God, at length prove the happy Vehicle of its power; and dry bones, while unburied, may be made to live. Thus a good man leaves an inheritance to his children; and the generation of the upright shall be blessed.

Sixthly, A church in the house will contribute very much to the prosperity of the church of God in the nation. Family religion, if that prevail, will put a face of religion upon the land, and very much advance the beauty and peace of our English Jerusalem. This is that, which I hope we are all hearty well-wishers to; setting aside the consideration of parties and separate interests, and burying all names of distinction in the grave of Christian charity, we earnestly desire to see true catholic Christianity, and serious godliness, in the power of it, prevailing and flourishing in our land; to see knowledge filling the land, as the waters cover the sea; to see holiness and love giving law, and triumphing over sin and strife; we would see cause to call your city a city of righteousness, a faithful city, its walls salvation, and its gates praise. Now all this would be effected, if family-religion were generally set up and kept up.

When the wall was to be built about Jerusalem, it was presently done by this expedient, every one undertook to repair over against his own house. See Neh. iii. 10, &c. And, if ever the decayed walls of the gospel Jerusalem be built up, it must be by the same method. Every one must sweep before his own door, and then the street will be clean. If there were a church in every house, there would be such a church in our land, as would make it a praise throughout the whole earth. We cannot better serve our country, than by keeping up religion in our families.

Let families be well catechised, and then the public preaching of the word will be the more profitable, and the more successful. For want of this, when we speak never so plainly of the things pertaining to the kingdom of God, to the most we do but speak parables. The book of the

Lord is delivered to them that are not catechised, saying, Read this, and they say, We are not learned; learned enough in other things, but not in the one thing needful, Isa. xxix. 12. But our work is easy with those that from their childhood have known the holy scriptures.

If every family were a praying family, public prayers would be the better joined with, more intelligently, and more affectionately; for the more we are used to prayer, the more expert we shall be in that holy and divine art of entering into the holiest on that day And public reproofs and admonitions would be as a nail in a sure place, if masters of families would second them with their family discipline, and so clench those nails

Religious families are blessings to the neighbourhood they live in, at least by their prayers. A good man thus becomes a public good, and it is his ambition to be so. Though he see his childrens children, he has small joy of that, if he do not see peace upon Israel, Psal. cxxviii. 5, 6. And therefore postponing all his own interests and satisfactions, he sets himself to seek the good of Jerusalem all the days of his life. Happy were we, if we had many such. That which now remains is, to address myself to you upon the whole matter by way of exhortation; and I pray you, let my counsel be acceptable to you; and while I endeavour to give every one his portion, let your consciences assist me herein, and take to yourselves that which belongs to you.

First, Let those masters of families who have hitherto lived in the neglect of family religion, be persuaded now to set it up and from henceforward to make conscience of it. I know, it is hard to persuade people to begin even a good work that they have not been used to; yet if God by his grace set in with this word, who can tell but some may be wrought upon to comply with the design of it? We have no ill design in urging you to this part of your duty: We aim not at the advantage of a party, but purely at the prosperity of your families. We are sure we have reason on our side, and, if you will but suffer that to rule you, we shall gain our point, and you will all go home firmly resolved, as Joshua was, that whatever others do themselves, and whatever they say of you, you and your houses will serve the Lord God put it into, and keep it in the imagination of the thought of your heart, and establish your way therein before him.

Proceed in the right method; First, Set up Christ upon the throne in your hearts, and then set up a church for Christ in your house. Let Christ dwell in your hearts by faith, and then let him dwell in your houses; you do not begin at the right end of your work, if you do not first give your own selves unto the Lord; God had respect first to Abel, and then to his offering. Let the fear and love of God rule in your hearts, and have a commanding sway and empire there, and then set up an altar for God in your tents; for you cannot do that acceptably, till you have first consecrated yourselves as spiritual priests to God, to serve at that altar.

And when your hearts, like Lydia's, are opened to Christ, let your houses, like hers, be opened to him too, Acts xvi. 14, 15. Let there be churches in all your houses; let those that have the stateliest, richest, and best furnished houses, reckon a church in them to be their best ornament Let those that have houses of the greatest care and business, reckon family religion their best employment, and not neglect the one thing needful, while they are careful and cumbered about many things: Nor let those who have close and mean habitations be discouraged; the ark of God long dwelt in curtains. Your dwelling is not so strait but you may find room for a church in it. Church-work uses to be chargeable, but you may do this church-work cheap: You need not make silver shrines as they did for Diana, nor lavish gold out of the bag, as idolaters did in the service of their dunghill gods, (Isa. xlvi. 6.) No, an 'altar of earth " shall you make to your God," Exod. xx. 24 and he will accept it Church work uses to be slow work, but you may do this quickly Put on resolution, and you may set up this tabernacle to-night, before to-morrow.

Would you keep up your authority in your family? you cannot do it better than by keeping up religion in your family. If ever the master of a family looks great. truly great, it is when he is going before his house in the service of God, and presiding among them in holy things. Then he shews himself worthy of double honour, when he teacheth them the good knowledge of the Lord, and is their mouth to God in prayer, blessing them in the name of God.

Would you have your family relations comfortable, your affairs successful, and give an evidence of your professed subjection to the gospel of Christ? Would you live in God's fear, and die in his favour, and escape that curse which is entailed on prayerless families? Let religion, in the power of it, have its due place; that is, the uppermost place in your houses.

Many objections your own corrupt hearts will make against building these churches, but they will appear frivolous and trifling to a pious mind, that is steadfastly resolved for God and godliness; you will never go on in your way to heaven, if you will be frightened by lions in the street. Whatever is the difficulty you dread, the discouragement you apprehend in it, I am confident it is not insuperable, it is not unanswerable. But he that observes the wind, shall not sow; and he that regards the clouds, shall not reap.

Be not loth to begin a new custom, if it be a good custom, especially if it be a duty, as certainly this is, which while you continue in the neglect of, you live in sin; for omissions are sins and must come into judgement. It may be you have been convinced that you ought to worship God in your families, and that it is a good thing to do so; but you have put it off to some more convenient season. Will you now at last take occasion from this sermon to begin it? and do not defer so good a work any longer. The present season is without doubt the most convenient season: Begin this day; let this be the day of your laying the foundation of the Lord's temple in your house; and then consider from this day and upward, as God by the prophet reasons with the people who neglected to build the temple, Hag. ii. 18, 19. take notice whether God do not from this day remarkably bless you, in all that you have and do.

Plead not your own weakness and inability to perform family worship; make use of the helps that are provided for you: Do as well as you can, when you cannot do so well as you would, and God will accept of you. You will write what is necessary for the carrying on of your trade, though you cannot write so fine a hand as some others can; and will you not be as wife in the work of your Christian calling, to do your best, though it be far short of the best, rather than not do it at all? To him that hath but one talent, and trades with that, more shall be given; but from him that buries it, it shall be taken away. Be at some pains to make the scriptures familiar to you, especially David's psalms; and then you cannot be to seek for a variety of apt expressions proper to be used in prayer, for they will be always at your right hand. Take with you those words, words which the Holy Ghost teaches; for you cannot find more acceptable words.

And now, shall I prevail with you in this matter? I am loth to leave you unresolved, or but almost persuaded; I beg of you, for God's sake, for Christ's sake, for your own precious souls' sake, and for the childrens sake of your own bodies, that you will live no longer in the neglect of so great, and necessary, and comfortable a duty as this of family worship is. When we press upon you the more inward duties of faith and love, and the fear of God, it cannot be so evident that we succeed in our errand, as it may be in this. It is certain you get not good by this sermon, but it is wholly lost upon you, if, after you have heard it or read it, you continue in the neglect of family religion, and if still you cast off fear and restrain prayer before God. Your families will be witnesses against you, that it was not for want of being called to do it, but for want of a heart to do it when you were called. But I hope better things of you, my brethren, and things that accompany salvation, though I thus speak.

Secondly, Let those who have kept up family worship formerly, but of late have left it off, be persuaded to revive it. This perhaps is the case of some of you; you remember the kindness of your youth, and the love of your espousals: Time was when you sought God daily, and delighted to know his ways, as families that did righteousness, and forsook not the ordinances of your God; but now it is otherwise. The altar of the Lord is broken down and neglected, the daily sacrifice is ceased; and God hath kept an account how many days it has ceased, whether you have or no, Dan. viii. 13, 14. Now God comes into our houses seeking fruit, but he finds none, or next to none; you are so eager in your worldly pursuits, that you have neither hearts nor time for religious exercises. You began at first frequently to omit the service, and a small matter served for an excuse to put it by, and so by degrees it came to nothing.

O that those who have thus left their first love, would now remember whence they are fallen, and repent, and do their first works! Inquire how this good work came to be neglected; was it not because your love to God cooled, and the love of the world prevailed? Have not you found a manifest decay in the prosperity of your souls, since you let fall this good work? Hath not sin got ground in your hearts and in your houses? And though, when you dropt your family worship, you promised yourselves that you would make it up in secret worship, because you were not willing to allow yourselves time for both; yet, have you not declined in that also? Are you not grown less frequent, and less fervent in your closet devotions too? Where is now the blessedness you have formerly spoken of? I beseech you lay out yourselves to retrieve it in time: Say, as that penitent adulteress, Hof. ii. 7. " I will go and return to my first " husband, for then it was better with me than now." Cleanse the sanctuary, put away the strange gods: Is money the god, or thy belly the god that has gained possession of thy heart and house? whatever it is, cast it out. Repair the altar of the Lord, and begin again the daily sacrifice and oblation. Light the lamps again, and burn the incense. Rear up the tabernacle of David which is fallen down, lengthen its cords, and strengthen its stakes; and resolve it shall never be neglected again as it has been. Perhaps you and your families have been manifestly under the rebukes of providence since you left off your duty, as Jacob was while he neglected to pay his vow: I beseech you at length to hear the voice of the rod, and of him that hath appointed it; for it minds you of your forgotten vows, saying, " Arise, go up to Bethel, and dwell there," Gen. xxxv. 1. Let the place thou dwellest in ever be a Bethel, so shall God dwell with thee there.

Thirdly, Let those that are remiss and negligent in their family worship, be awakened to more zeal and constancy. Some of you perhaps have a church in your house, but it is not a flourishing church; it is like the church of Laodicea, neither cold nor hot; or like the church of Sardis, in which the things that remain are ready to die: So that it hath little more than a name to live. Something of this work of the Lord is done for fashion-sake, but it is done deceitfully: You have in your flock a male, but you vow and sacrifice to the Lord a corrupt thing: You grow customary in your accustomed services, and bring the torn and the blind, the lame and the sick for sacrifice: And you offer that to your God, which you would scorn to offer to your governor: And though it is but little you do for the church in your houfe, you think that too much, and fay, "Behold, what a wearinefs is it!" You put it off with a fmall and inconfiderable fcantling of your day, and that with the dregs and refufe of it. You can fpare no time at all for it in the morning, nor any in the evening till you are half afleep It is thruft into a corner, and almoft loft in a crowd of worldly bufinefs, and carnal converfe. When it is done, it is done fo flightly, in fo much hafte, and with fo little reverence, that it makes no impreffion upon yourfelves or your families The bible lies ready, but you have no time to read: your fervants are otherwife employed, and you think it is no matter for calling them in: You yourfelves can take up with a word or two of prayer, or reft in a lifelefs, heartlefs tale of words Thus it is every day, and perhaps little better on the Lord's days; no repetition, no catechifing, no finging of pfalms, or none to any purpofe.

Is it thus with any of your families? Is this the prefent ftate of the church in your houfe? My brethren, thefe things ought not to be fo. It is not enough that you do that which is good, but you muft do it well God and religion have, in effect, no place in your hearts or houfes, if they have not the innermoft and uppermoft place. Chrift will come no whither to be an underling; he is not a gueft to be fet behind the door. What comfort, what benefit can you promife to yourfelves from fuch trifling fervices as thefe; from an empty form of godlinefs, without the power of it?

I befeech you, firs, make a bufinefs of your family religion, and not a by bufinefs. Let it be your pleafure and delight, and not a tafk and drudgery. Contrive your affairs fo, as that the moft convenient time may be allotted both morning and evening for your family worfhip, fo as that you may not be unfit for it, or difturbed and ftraitened in it; herein wifdom is profitable to direct. Addrefs yourfelves to it with reverence and ferioufnefs, and a folemn paufe, that thofe who join with you may fee and fay, That God is with you of a truth, and may be ftruck thereby into a like holy awe. You need not be long in the fervice, but you ought to be lively in it; not flothful in this bufinefs, becaufe it is bufinefs for God and your fouls, but fervent in fpirit, ferving the Lord.

Fourthly, Let thofe who have a church in their houfe, be

very careful to adorn and beautify it in their converfation. If you pray in your families, and read the fcriptures, and fing pfalms, and yet are paffionate and froward with your relations, quarrelfome and contentious with your neighbours, unjuſt and deceitful in your dealings, intemperate and given to tippling, or allow yourfelves in any other finful way, you pull down with one hand, what you build up with the other. Your prayers will be an abomination to God, and to good men too, if they be thus polluted. Be not deceived. God is not mocked.

See that you be univerfal in your religion, that it may appear you are fincere in it. Shew that you believe a reality in it, by acting always under the commanding power and influence of it Be not Chriftians upon your knees, and Jews in your fhops. While you feem faints in your devotions, prove not yourfelves finners in your converfations. Having begun the day in the fear of God, be in that fear all the day long. Let the example you fet your families be throughout good ; and by it teach them not only to read and pray, for that is but half their work, but by it teach them to be meek and humble, fober and temperate, loving and peaceable, juſt and honeſt : So fhall you adorn the doctrine of God our Saviour ; and thofe that will not be won by the word, fhall be won by your converfation. Your family-worfhip is an honour to you ; fee to it, that neither you nor yours be in any thing a difgrace to it.

Fifthly, " Let thofe that are fetting out in the world, fet " up a church in their houfe at firſt, and not defer it." Plead not youth and bafhfulnefs ; if you have confidence enough to rule a family, I hope you have confidence enough to pray with a family. Say not, " the time is not come, the " time that the LORD's houfe fhould be built," as they did that dwelt in their cieled houfes, while God's houfe lay wafte, Hag. i. 2, 4. It ought to be built prefently ; and the longer you put it off, the more difficulty there will be in the doing of it, and the more danger that it will never be done.

Now you are beginning the world as you call it, is it not your wifdom, as well as duty, to begin with God ? can you begin better? or can you expect to profper, if you do not begin thus? The fuller your heads are of care about fetting up houfe and fhop, and fettling in both, the more need you have of daily prayer, that by it you may caſt your care on God, and fetch in wifdom and direction from on high.

Sixthly, " In all your removes, be sure you take the church
" in your house along with you " Abraham oft removed
his tent; but wherever he pitched it, there the first thing
he did was to build an altar. It is observable concerning
Aquila, and Prifcilla, of whose pious family my text speaks,
that when Paul wrote his epistle to the Romans, they were
at Rome ; for he sends salutations to them thither, and there
it is said they had a church in their house, Rom. xvi. 5.
But now, when he wrote this epistle to the Corinthians, they
were at Ephesus, for thence it should seem this epistle bore
date, and here he sends salutations from them ; and at Ephe-
fus also they had a church in their house. As wherever
we go ourselves, we must take our religion with us; so whereever we take our families, or part of them, we must take
our family religion with us ; for in all places we need divine
protection, and experience divine goodness. I will therefore that men pray every where.

When you are in your city houses, let not the business of
them crowd out your family religion ; nor let the diversions
of your country houses indispose your minds to these serious
exercises. That care and that pleasure are unseasonable
and inordinate, which leave you not both heart and time
to attend the service of the church in your house.

Let me here be an advocate also for those families whose
masters are often absent from them, for their health or pleasure, especially on the Lord's day, or long absent upon bufinefs: And let me beg thefe abfent mafters to confider with
whom they leave those few sheep in the wildernefs, 1 Sam.
xvii. 28. and whether they do not leave them neglected
and exposed. Perhaps there is not a just cause for your ab-
fence so much, nor can you give a good answer to that queftion, What dost thou here, Elijah? But, if there be a just cause,
you ought to take care that the church in your house be not
neglected when you are abroad, but that the work be done
when you are not at home to do it.

Seventhly, " Let inferior relations help to promote reli-
" gion in the families where they are." If family worship
be not kept up in the houses where you live, let so much the
more be done in your closets for God and your souls : If it
be, yet think not that will excuse you from secret worship :
All is little enough to keep up the life of religion in your
hearts, and help you forwards towards heaven.

Let the children of praying parents, and the servants of

praying masters, account it a great privilege to live in houses that have churches in them, and be careful to improve that privilege. Be you also ready to every good work; make the religious exercises of your family easy and pleasant to those that perform them, by shewing yourselves forward to attend on them, and careful to attend to them; for your backwardness and mindlessness will be their greatest discouragement. Let your lives also be a credit to good education, and make it appear to all with whom you converse, that you are every way the better for living in religious families.

Eighthly, " Let solitary people, that are not set in families, " have churches in their chambers, churches in their " closets." When every man repaired the wall of Jerusalem over against his own house, we read of one that repaired over against his chamber, Neh. iii. 10. These that live alone out of the way of family worship, ought to take so much the more time for their secret worship; and, if possible, add the more solemnity to it. You have not families to read the scriptures to; read them so much the more to yourselves. You have not children and servants to catechise, nor parents or masters to be catechised by; catechise yourselves then, that you may hold fast the form of sound words, which you have received. Exhort one another.——So we read it, Heb. iii. 13. *parakaleite eautous*——Exhort yourselves. So it might as well be read. You are not made keepers of the vineyards, and therefore the greater is your shame if your own vineyard you do not keep. When you are alone, yet you are not alone; for the Father is with you, to observe what you do, and to own and accept you if you do well.

Ninthly, " Let those that are to choose a settlement, con- " sult the welfare of their souls in the choice." If a church in the house be so necessary, so comfortable, then be ye not unequally yoked with unbelievers, who will have no kindness for the church in the house, nor assist in the support of it, but, instead of " building this house, pluck it down with " their hands," Prov. xiv. 1. Let apprenticeships and other services be chosen by this rule, That that is best for us, which is best for our souls; and therefore it is our interest to go with those, and be with those, with whom God is. When Lot was to choose a habitation, he was determined therein purely by secular advantages, Gen. xiii. 11, 14. and God justly corrected his sensual choice; for he never had a quiet day in the Sodom he chose, till he was fired out of it. The

Jewish writers tell of one of their devout Rabbins, who being courted to dwell in a place which was otherwise well accommodated, but had no synagogue near, he utterly refused to accept the invitation, and gave that text for his reason, Psal. cxix. 27. "The law of thy mouth is better to me than thousands of gold and silver."

Tenthly, "Let religious families keep up friendship and fellowship with each other, and as they have opportunity assist one another in doing good." The communion of churches hath always been accounted their beauty, strength, and comfort; and so is the communion of these domestic churches. We find here, and in other of Paul's epistles, kind salutations sent to and from the houses that had churches in them. Religious families should greet one another, visit one another, love one another, pray for one another, and, as becomes households of faith, do all the good they can one to another, forasmuch as they all meet now daily at the same throne of grace, and hope to meet shortly at the same throne of glory; to be no more as they are now divided in Jacob, and scattered in Israel.

Lastly, Let those houses that have churches in them, flourishing churches, have comfort in them. Is religion, in the power of it, uppermost in your houses? and are you and yours serving the Lord, serving him daily? Go on and prosper, for the Lord is with you, while you are with him. See your houses under the protection and blessing of heaven, and be assured, that all things shall work together for good to you. Make it to appear by your holy cheerfulness, that you find God a good Master, wisdom's ways pleasantness, and her paths peace; and that you see no reason to envy those that spend their days in carnal mirth for you are acquainted with better pleasures than any they can pretend to.

Are your houses on earth God's houses? are they dedicated to him, and employed for him? Be of good comfort, his house in heaven shall be yours shortly: In my Father's house there are many mansions; and one you may be sure for each of you, that thus, by a patient continuance in well-doing, seek for glory, honour, and immortality.

F I N I S.

SUBSCRIBERS NAMES.

A

WILLIAM Aird mason, Wigton
John Aiken, Kirkland
James Armstrong, Minnigaff
Andrew Adam tailor, Wood of Cree
John Adam, Carbynows
James Affleck, Barbuchany, Penningham
Alex. Armour weaver, Kilmaurs
William Auld, Nethertonholm, Kilmarnock
Robert Alexander merchant Girvan
James Alexander labourer, do.
Andrew Andrew, Stonykirk parish
William Affleck blacksmith, Barhill Colmonell
Walter Anderson in Dowes
John Anderson, Landbreck, Mochrum
Robert Andrew wheet miller, Creek, Sorbie
Quintin Andrew herd to the Countess of Crawford
Robert Alexander dier, Air
Robert Allan shoemaker, Newton upon Air
Robert Anderson overseer, Newton Coalwork, 18 copies
Hugh Andrew, Pack Mill, Tarbolton
Adam Anderson, parish of Air

B

THE rev. Mr. William Boyd, Minister, Fenwick
The rev. Mr. John Blair minister, Colmonell
John Black malster, Bladnock
—— Bruce merchant, Wigton
Hugh Baron
Jas. Black shoemaker, Glenturk
John Brown Craigincalie, Minnigaff
Samuel Brown, Craiginell, do.
William Burnet, Kilhubbel, Penningham
James Broadfoot wright, Causeyend, do.
Alexander Brown
James Black, gardener
Thomas Bell, bricklayer
Hugh Bone labourer Barwharren
John Blair miller, Daily
David Blair, do. do.
—— Braiden, coal cutter
Hamilton Baird, Dalquharran coal work
John Bell
William Brown manufacturer, Kilmarnock
Rob. Bowie, Kenning, Riccarton
James Boyd, Kamsehill, do.
—— Brown labourer Kilmarnock
William Brown shoemaker, do.
John Bell dier, do.
John Blair junior, Girvan
Wal. Bell blacksmith, Corsephairn
Hugh Bone, Straiton
Charles Bell, Kirkmichael
John Blain, do.
Hugh Bell dier, do.
Thomas Beggs blacksmith, Inch
James Bennoch, Inch
Tho. Baird Balneloch, Ballentrae
Andrew Baird, Auchincrosh, do.
William Baird, do.
Alexander Bruce, St Quivox
John Borland, do
David Blair miller, Newton upon Air
Joseph Boyd sailmaker, Air
Andrew Broadfoot, Whitehorn
John Broadfoot mason, do.

Alex Broadfoot shoemaker, do.
David Broadfoot weaver, do.
Alexander Bell Glasserton
Agnes Boyd, Drumrea
John Boyd, Kirkinner
James Brown, Barwharrie, do.
Charles Bell, Kirkmichael
John Blain, do.
Hugh Bell dier, do.
James Beattie, Dumfries
John Bryden, do.
—— Biggar, do.
—— Brair, farmer, do.
James Bowman gardener, do
George Broadfoot shipmaster, do.
Alex. Brown, Sorby parish
Edward Blackwood, do.
William Broadfoot farmer in Inch
Charles Broadfoot, Whitehills
William Bell, Smithston
Laurie Bryce merchant, Kirkmabreck
John Brett farmer do.
—— Bratner sailor, do.
Matthew Brear farmer in Backbie, do.
George Bell smith, Milton, Kirkinner
Robert Baverlie, Baldoon
John Baeth, Annoth parish
Patrick Bydson, do.
John Brown, do.
Peter Black carrier, Kirkcudbright
Samuel Bean slater, do.
Charles Bell, do. do
John Brydson buckle maker, do.
John Brown, Rerrick
William Brown junior, Linhins, do
Ephraim Black, Port Mary, do.

C

THE rev Mr John Curtis Quarrelwood
Richard Cosh tailor, Wigton
David Christian, Hervanie

John Costly, Glenturk
David Chambers in Holm, Minigaff
Mrs Chambers, Bargally, do.
Robert Cunningham Whitelaggen, do
John Elcherdie Pith, do.
William Clark, Killhabbee Peninghan
William Clark, Glenriddel, do.
David Coke, Pensioner, do.
George Campbell, do.
Robert Caw, do.
James Crawford shoemaker, Kirkinner
James Clark labourer, Daily
Mrs. Card, Kirkland
Baillie William Cumming Kilmarnock
Henry Crawford distiller, bridgeend, do.
William Campbell tailor, Corsephairn
James Clark, Glenhead, Straiton
Samuel Clark junior, do.
James Clark, Glenala, Kirkmichael
Andrew Cunningham chapman Inch
John Cumming, Ballantrae
Robert Carswell mason, Colmonell
William Campbell, Sorbie
David Clumpha, Sorbie
Peter Clumpha, do.
John Carson miller, Whithorn
James Cunningham tailor, do.
Alex Cumming merchant, Whithorn
Stewart Credie weaver, Down, do
Robert Carr, Rupin, do.
John Carr, Crachdow, Glaserton
Anthony Coultron, Arrock, do.
William Cumming merchant, Port William
John Cubbin merchant, do.
Samuel Clark weaver, Kirkinner

3 H

William Cumming, Kirkinner
Alex Cowan, do.
Eliz. Cowan, do.
John Cary weaver, do.
Thomas Cunningham innkeeper, Kirkmabreck
Samuel Carson failor, do.
John Crofbie, do. do.
John Crookshanks gardener, do.
Alex. Carson weaver Creetown
James Campbell, miner
John Credie, Garliefton
Sarah Cleland, Orchardtown
William Corchie Calfcadam
John Cunningham, Anwoth parish
William Carson, Girthon parish
John Comlin mufician Kirkudbright
Al Charters joiner, Landfide, do.
Thomas Culbert labourer, do do.
Nath Craig. Rerrick, 2 copies
Robert Cochran, Port Mary, do.
Robert Carnochan, Rerrick
Robert Collart, do.
James Cuthbert, Ochiltree parish
John Calderwood wright, Catrine
Robert Campbell, Dumfries par.
Thomas Cowan, do.
William Clark, do.
John Curry, Daily parish
—— Chalmers, do.
Dav. Culbert, Kirkland, Maybole
Andrew Crawford, Daily parish

D

ANTHONY Drinnan ftaymaker, Wigton
Andrew Donaldson baker
George Dunn, Cairndarrie
William Douglas Dramadaw
Robert Dalrymple merchant Minigaff
Mrs Dornan, Knockaffreck
Andrew Dickie, Kilmarnock
David Dale, Drum muir Dreghorn

David Davidson tailor, Girvan
Robert Dempfter shoemaker Carfephairn
Robert Dinn, Cadgerhole, do.
Mrs. Dick Dalkarnie, Straiton
Serjeant James Dick, do.
Andrew Dick, Kirkmichael
Hugh Dick, do.
Robert Dunlop Efq. of Dalkirk, do.
John Dick weaver, Lochall do.
William Donnan Auchleach Stonykirk parish
Andrew Donnan Bilkar, Inch pa.
William Donnan *Killorpeter*, do
Archibald Dormont, Port of Shital do
Adam Douglas miller, in Undermain, do.
Andrew Davidson, Inch parish
William Drinnan, Knochdollan, Colmonell
David Drinnan dier, Kildonan do.
James Douglas, Sorby parish
Hugh Bennifton, do
William Dalrymple Coalnog Sorby parish
Alex. Donnan in Revans, do.
Alex. Douglas miller in Dinnens, Whithorn
John Douglas merchant Whithorn
John Donnan blackfmith, do.
Alex Dunie in Chipperherring do
—— Dobie
Agnes Douglafs, Mochrum
John Dunn in Corfeduchan
Mary Donald in Barwharry, Kirkinner, parish
John Donnan farmer in Stories do
William Dalrymple do. Kirkown
William Dalrymple weaver, do.
John Duncan tailor, Kirkmabreck, parish
John Donaldson Anwoth
Robert Dennifton, Girthon par.
James Douglas mafon, Kirkudbright

William Duncan merchant Newton upon Air
John Donald Glenfide, Maybole
Robert Dow, Adamton mill
James Dinnidie, Dumfries par.
Tho Dixon, Dalton parish
John Donald, Slohabert, Kirkinner
Serjeant James Dick, Straiton
David Dick, Daily parish
Andrew Dick, Kirkmichael
Hugh Dick, do.

E

WILLIAM Erskine Penningham
John Earl in Mackerwhat, Ballentrae
Alex. Edgar tailor, Kirkown pa.

F

ALEXANDER Fullarton weaver, Wigton
Robert Fleming sheriff officer, Wigton
Thos. Findlay, Holm
John Fairfool excise officer Girvan
Alex. Fer barber, Stonykirk, pa.
Mr. John Forty comptroller at Lochryan
Anthony Farmer, Mount in Craigeaf
John Frazer weaver, Kirkcolm, Inch parish
John Findlay mason, Stranraer
David Fergusson, Ballantrae pa.
James Fallows, Daily parish
William Finlay, Sorby parish
Margaret Fleming in Billfeir, do.
James Finlay dier, Whithorn
John Frizzle cartwright Morieth
Andrew Fleming, Bow of Raventon
Andrew Fullarton farmer Whitedyke

Alex. Fullarton weaver, Kirkinner parish
John Forgie, Ballantrae parish
James Ferish, Lochrigg
Mrs Fergufon, Little Shalloch
John Forfyth wright, Maybole

G

JOHN Gilchrist, Wigton
Thomas Gibfon
Robert Guthrie, Chapman
Mrs. Gordon, Cardarken
James Gordon, Fintilloch, Penningham
William Graham shoemaker.
William Girvan mailter, Dashwood
James Grierfon merchant, Daily
Adam Grieve, Kirkmichael
Mr. William Grieve, Barlach 5 copies
Hugh Gilchrist weaver, Kilmarnock
Hugh Gebbie, Dikenook, do.
Alex. Graham
Thomas Gluig, Girvan
James Gray, Ballantrae
John Galloway, Smerton, do.
David Geddes weaver, Kells pa.
Alex Gifford farmer, Barwhinnock, Castle Stuart
Robert Gordon, shoemaker, Mochrum parish
Martin Gibfon cooper, do.
John Gregg, Ochiltree parish
John Gordon labourer
Archibald Gibfon, do.
Alex. Gowrly, Anwoth
Mrs. Galloway, Girthon parish
John Guthrie, Port Mary, Rerrick parish
William Gowdie, do do.
Robert Gibfon, Rerrick
George Gibfon, Air parish
George Girvan, St. Quivox pa.
John Green, Ochiltree parish

George Gregg blackfmith
James Grierfon, Dumfries pa.
Robert Gordon shoemaker, Glenthryplock
David Graham, Daily parish
Alex. Grant Kilkerran, do.
William Gowdie, Kirkofwald

H

BAILLIE john Hawthorn, Wigton
William Hannah carter, do.
Robert Hannah, Redbrae
john Heron merchant, Wigton
William Hallowday chapman
Alex Haiflip, do
William Heron merchant, N. S.
Peter Hannah Barwharran
Mrs. Heron, Keppinock, Kirkinner
Mr. john Hunter merchant, Air
James Henderfon
Robert Hay farmer Symington
James Henderfon shoemaker Kilmarnock
Adam Harris smith, Riccarton
William Hope, Girvan
William Haftings junior, Caftlemaddy, Carfphairn
William Hunter Trochane, Kirkmichael
William Hannah tailor, Sorby pa.
John Herbert, Garlieston, do
Mr. Hawthorn in Claunch, do.
William Hannah, Billfmith, Whithorn parish
Robert Hardy
John Hannah farmer in Knock, Glaferton
Matthew Heron
Peter Heron in Caftleftewart
Peter Heron farmer, Kirkmabreck
Alex. Hughan, do. do.
David Hannah joiner, do.
John Hunter failor, do.
Alex. Hannah, Millmofs, Sorby parish

William Hannah, Innerwell do.
Margaret Hannah, Midtown, do.
Robert Henning, Anwoth
Hugh Hannay, do.
john Hyndfon wright, Newton upon Air.
David Hutchifon farmer, Dalrymple
james Hutchifon in Coilton
john Hutchifon, Greenfield, Air parish
Mr. james Hall, merchant Whitehaven
George Hendry, St. Quivox par.
William Hannah, Slohabert Kirkinner
John Hunter Daily parish
Adam Hunter, do.

I

THE rev. Mr John Inglis, D. D. minifter of Kirkmabreck
Andrew Ignue
Michael Ignue
———Jardine, cartwright Whithorn p.
Tho. Jackfon, Waterhead, Corfephairn parish
Gilbert Jackfon, Kirkmichael p.
Janet Ignue, Sorbie p.
Tho. Irvine, Mochrum p. 5 cop.
W Jardine, Littlehills, Kirkinner
J of Irvine, Nockroon, Auchinleck
Samuel Ingram, Sanquhar
Will. Ingram, chapman, do.
James Johnfton shoemaker, Kirkmabreck
John Jolly failor, Creetown
Dan. Johnfton Kirkland Kirkcudbright
Will. Johnfton merchant, do.
George Irvine, Whitehaven
Gilbert Jackfon, Kirkmichael p.

K

PETER Kennan of Mill park, Efq.

David Kennedy of Craig. Efq.
Patrick Kaven, fhoemaker, Wig.
Alex. Kavend farmer, Grange of Cree
Robert Kelly, Blacklaggen Minigaff
William Kelly, Drunkmorn
Helen Kevand, Barns
David Kennedy weaver, Kilmar.
John Kirkland labourer, do.
William Kennedy, Kirkmichael
James Kennedy, Cafgrove, Glenluce parifh
John Kennedy, Gleneron, do.
John Kelly, fhoemaker Stonykirk parifh
William Kevan, Inch parifh
Thomas Kerr labourer, do.
—— Kevan tailor, Stranraer
Andrew Kennedy, do.
Alex. Kennedy in Drumfkeoch, Colmonell
William Kevand flater, Sorby p.
Alex. Keachie do.
Anthony Keachie, do.
James Kennedy weaver, Whithorn parifh
Alex Kevan, Mochrum parifh
Samuel Kelly fhoemaker, Kirkinner parifh
James Kelly in Ring, Kirkown p.
John Kelly, do. do.
Simon Kevand ftocking maker, Barglafs
John Kingan, Garliefton
John Kirlie, Yetton, Sorbie par.
Robert Kerr, Kifhin, Whithorn
Thomas Kirkpatrick, Rerrick
William Kirkpatrick, do.
John Keachie weaver, Air.
Mr Thomas Kilpatrick Whitehaven
Andrew Kay, Srair parifh
William Kae, Dumfries parifh
James Kerr, do.
William Kennedy, Kirkmichael, parifh

L

MR. JAMES LAING Bookfeller, Kilmarnock, 3 copies
Robert Lambie, Kilmaurs
Alex. Leith weaver, Girvan
Andrew Lamb dier, do.
John Logan in Garizzle, Colmonell
Edward Lewis, Sorby parifh
Peter Logan fhoemaker, Garliefton
Sarah Lockhart, Whithorn
John Lockhart, do. 8 copies
James Lawfon gardener
—— Lyon, Dalrymple, 2 cop.
—— Logan wright, Alloa, Air p.
Alex. Lauder gardener, Auchincruive
Mifs Lydia Laurie, Larg
A Little fannermaker, Newton S.

M

REV. Mr. James M'Kinlay, one of the minifters of Kilmarnock
The Rev. Mr. Alex. Moodie, Minifter, Riccartown
James M·Guffag Innkeeper, Wigton
William Mitchell, do.
Andrew M·Credie, merchant do. 6 copies
John M·William weaver, Wigton
Peter M'Guffag mafon, do.
Thomas ——— ———, Bladnock
John M'Gown, Mill of Torry
Alex. Milroy, Newmills
Jean Milligen
Alex. M'Handles dier, Torhoufe
John M'Launachan fkinner at Spittal
George M'Gill Tanner in Barrachan
John M'Gown, Wigton
James Murdoch Shoemaker
William Macadam Currier

Mr. James M'Kie, Pilgown Minigaff
Alex. Murray Clackmallack, do.
John Macmillan in Squanchando
James Makaw Killidarrach, do.
John M'Redie Storie, do.
James M'Kie, do. do.
Alex M'Gown, Buchan do.
Charles M'Cutcheon, Machermore mill
James M'Cawl, miner, do.
John Murray in Kirkcallah, Pennigham
Peter M'Culloch, Garthrow do.
—— Murray labourer, do.
William M'Gill, Barr, do.
James M'Clure weaver Dashwood
Alex. M'Kie Flesher
Samuel M'Kean, Batterson
James M'Jarrow, Shallow
Alex. M'Geoch shoemaker, 6 cop.
John M'Kie, Borland
Robert M'Clelland, Grange
—— Millmarrow, Downing
William M'Geoch, Crows Kirkinner
John M'Clymont, Balaird, do.
Eliz. M'Clymont there
Alex M'Cannachan weaver, do.
James M'Clure weaver, Clootock, do
Hugh M'Clellan farmer do. do.
Alex. M'Clellan do do. do.
John M'Guffig, Waterside do.
—— M'Dowall, Cassilis
Peter M'Kinnel, Slochabert
John M'Neily
—— M'Aulay
Peter M Geoch
—— Murray farmer, Tachall
James M'Fadzen in Catildones, Minigaff
Mrs. Murray in Sheegarland, do.
James Marmuldroch tailor
—— M'Dougal, Bargrinnan
Anthony M'cmuldroch, Dalna
James M'Cornick in Larg

Robert Millroy, Lagbees
Mrs. M'Cullochan, Borland do.
—— Millken, Black Craig
Anthony M Gown do.
Thomas M'Whinnel weaver
Peter Martin Carse Snow
John M'Clure weaver, Blackcraig, do.
Elizabeth Maxwell
Agnefs M Whirter
Gilbert M'Kenzie weaver do.
William M'Kennah do. do.
James M'Lauchlan blackfmith do
Robert Milroy, Corsesnow
Hugh Makennah, there
Gilbert M'Narin Machermore do.
William Milnrick, there
John M'Nairn, Brochfield
Thomas M Cornair
John M'Carnie labourer, Daily
Robert Murray weaver, Lauchrie
Peter M'Clurg, Catrine
William M'Micken wright, and miller in Acres mill
Alex. M'Clelland
Matthew Miller, Riccarton mill
William Mair weaver, Kilmaurs
James M'Lean manufacturer, Kilmarnock
John M'Fie cloth printer do.
Archd M'Fie print cutter, do.
John Morton Excise officer, do.
William Macfarlen linen printer, do.
Hugh M'Clymont merch. Girvan
Ham. Macmoreland vintner, do
Thomas M'Cowl weaver, do.
James M Credie junior, do.
Robert M'Cord mason, do.
Charles Mean, do.
William M'Connel wright, do.
Hugh M Ilwraith, Trehorg, do.
Charles Maitland farmer, do.
Hugh Macmillan, Tormichael, do
David M'Gill thatcher, do.
Abraham M Lean weaver, do.

SUBSCRIBERS NAMES.

Alexander M'Clymont junior, blacksmith, do.
James M Cracken, Ardwall, do.
Mrs. M'Ilwraith, Traweir, do.
Jean M'Ilwraith, do. do.
John M'Rae, Corsephairn
William Macmillan, do.
James Miller, do.

See page 434.

N

ROBERT Neil
Alex. Neilson, Culgroot, Stonykirk parish
Benjamin Nicholson, baker Stranraer
James Neilson nailer, Garlieston
—— Nicholson, Sorbie p.
Gilbert Nairn smith, do.
William Neilson, Clovehill
Hugh Niven mason, Maybole

O

JAs. Ogilvie merchant Wigton
Wil. Orr, Whatrigs Dreghorn
James Orr innkeeper, Greenhead Corsephairn
David Owens, Anwoth parish

P

DAVID Petrie dier, Kilmarnock
John Paul, Bargeenie Coal Work
—— Paterson carter, Stranraer
William Purie in Whitehills, Sorby parish
John Peerie mason, Glenthriplock, Mochrum parish
Alex Paterson, Port William
John Paterson in Carseriggan, Kirkown parish
Thomas Paine, Girthon parish
Jams Park weaver, Newton upon Air
Thomas Phinn merchant, do.

Q

GARNET Quoid in Muirmains, Mochrum parish

R

THE Rev. Mr James Robertson one of the Ministers of Kilmarnock
The Rev. Mr John Russel, do.
Neil Robertson, Drungan Coalwork
Thos. Rankine dier, Kilmarnock
William Rankine, do. do.
Alex. Robertson, coppersmith, do
James Rankine, manse, do.
—— Richmond, Riccarton
—— Ross shoemaker, Girvan
John Ramsay, do. do.
Robert Rened weaver, Straiton
Hugh Roddie, Gilfillan. Glenluce
Alex. Riggs sailor, Garlieston
George Rerlie, Engleton Sorby p.
Robert Rankin, Smithston
James Rolison, New Luce
Miss Harriet Reid, milliner, Kirkmabreck
Agnes Rigg, Galloway house
Robert Ramsay, Anwoth parish
Alex Rae, Lochfergus, Kirkudbright
John Reid, Rerrek
Alex Ross Kirkudbright 5 copies
Andrew Reid Coiltown
John Russel, Daily parish
Adam Rankine, Kirkland, Maybole

S

MARGARET Sloan, Knockgray Corsephairn
Alex Sloan, Glenhead, do.
John Stillie, Kirkmichael
James Stevenson, do
William Sinclair, Glastrown, do.
Archibald Stevenson, Glengaw, Inch parish

William Sloan in Garrery, Kells parish
Alex. Stewart wright, Sorby par.
James Skimming in Cornar, do.
John Stewart in Balerosh, do.
—— Stevenson, Whithorn par.
Mr Alex. Stewart Arrow. do.
William Stevenson shoemaker, Isle. do.
John Scamble, do.
Ann Stuart in Drumfad
Charles Stuart, Port William Mochrum parish
Jas Stuart in Drumtroddan, do.
—— Sloan weaver in Merton. do.
John Simpson in Landbreck, do.
Thomas Simpson, do. do.
Gilbert Stroyan in Eldrick Kirkown parish
Robert Smith weaver, Quarrelwood
Adam Smith, Whiteside, Dunsore
Campbell Stewart merchant Kirkmabreck
George Spark gardener, do.
David Shaw shoemaker, do.
Peter Skimming, Barglass
Thomas Spence, Garlieston
Alexander Scambell, Wigton
William Stewart mason, Wigton
Archibald Stewart, do. do.
Mrs Stewart, Kursedown
James Smith, blacksmith
An. Stewart, Leneway Minigaff
P. Strachan miner Blackcraig, do
John Shaw, Kiseknow, do.
Ardrew Stewart weaver, do.
Tho. Stroyan, Bla krack, Penningham
Samuel Shaw, Barhill do.
Alexander Stroyan, Dashwood
—— Simpson
And Smith weaver, Kilmarnock
Thomas Steven Crookedholm, do
Robert Stevenson, do.
Peter Seton

Mr. Nicholas Sloan, preacher of the gospel, Riccarton
Mr John Sinclair schoolmaster, do
Quintin Stevenson merch Girvan
James Scott shoemaker, do.
S. Shaw, Cullinoch, Corsephairn
Robert Shaw, Corsephairn p.
—— Smith weaver, Kirkcud.
Robert Shinnan, Rerrick
Wiliam Sharp, do.
—— Stevenson, Air parish
Charles Smith, Ochiltree
John Smith, Morktoun. 3 copies
Robert Sloan, Dumfries parish
John Stewart, Daily parish
—— Stillie, Kirkmichael
James Stevenson, do.

T

JANET Tait
James Thomson, Carwath
Jean Thomson, Millhabbel, Penningham
Andrew Thomson, Barwhinnie
John Thomson, Midclose, Minigaff
James Thomson, Northcraig,
—— —— manufac. Kilmck.
—— Tannahill, Nethertonholm
—— Taylor Girvan
William Thorburn, Inch parish
James Thomson, Lowcult, Sorbie
Andrew Tee, Port William
Walter Thomson gardener at Mairton
James Traffic Kirkinner parish
W. Tait, watchmaker, Kirkmabreck
W. Thomson schoolmaster, do.
Jas. Tait weaver, Kirkcudbright
Robert Thomson joiner, do.
W Turner, Chappelton, Rerrick
H. Turner farmer, Dalrymple p.
And. Torrance, merch. Catrine
James Turner Dumfries parish
—— Thomson, blacksmith, do
—— Todd, Cumbertrees par.

SUBSCRIBERS NAMES.

U

WALTER Uthers, Dumfries

V

JOHN Vernon tenant, Baldoon

W

WILLIAM Weir, shoemaker, Wigton
John White gardener, Bladnock
Eben. Wilson Miniwick, Minigaff
William Wilson, Auchinleck
Robert Walker miner, Blackcraig
John Wilson, Glenhaple, Penningham
Samuel Wilson, Glassock, do.
Alex. Wilson, Knockbrax
Peter Wither miner, Dashwood
Robert Wilson Nethertonholm Kilmarnock
William Wyllie, Newmills, do.
Thomas Wallace, Todhill, do.
Will. Wallace distiller, Nether tonholm, do.
Thomas Wright smith, Girvan
John Wallace, Knockgray, Corsephairn
John Wilson in Undermason Inchp
—— Wallace, servant in Halfmark, do.
Edward Wallace junior, cartwright, do.
Mr. John Waugh watch maker, Stranraer
William White miller in Creek, Sorby parish
John White, Whithorn parish
Peter Wyllie, Garlieston
William Walker, Girthon, par.
Samuel Wilson, Rerrick, 7 cop.
John Wither, Barmore, Stonykirk parish
James Wither, Carnwell, do.
James Wither, Port Patrick par.
Peter Wither Scalegill Hall

Andrew Walker, Arwhat, Sorby parish
John White Maybole
—— Wilson, do. parish

Y

THOMAS Young junior, wright Girvan

M

JOHN M'Turk merchant Corsephairn.
John M'Kenzie, Whiteburn do.
—— M Clymont, Straiton
Andrew M'Cosh, Corsekeoch, do.
Robert M'Caul. do.
—— M'William, do.
Mrs M'Clymont, Glenclack, Kirkmichael
Alex Murray Laight, Inch par.
Thos. Millinick, Carngarroch, do.
Jas. Mount weaver in Drummucloch, do.
James Murray, Corseclays, Ballentrae parish
John Murray, Backhills, Kells p.
William Murray, Sorby parish
Peter Mitchell, Whitehills, do.
William Morison in Inch
Alex Marshall innkeeper, Whithorn
Andrew M'Cawl joiner, do.
John M'Clure shoemaker, do.
Alex. M'Credie in Drumaston, do.
John M'Clemna, farmer in Aldbreck. do
John M'Clymont do. in Presstree do
James M'Gill tanner, do.
John Muir. Roonin, do.
James M'Culm, .sle, do'
John M'Jerrow, Glaserton parish
—— Mitchell
—— Muir
Margaret M'Haffie in Drumfad

SUBSCRIBERS NAMES.

Grizzel M'Guffag
Alex. M'Cormack miller at Morieth
Vance M'Bryde blackfmith
William M'Culloch in Domes
Mrs. Milnoe Barrolloch, Mochrum parifh
Eliz. Millhanch, do.
Alex. Milroy, do.
John M'Geoch, Altiery, do.
Robert M'Geoch, Drumblair, do.
Pat. Millhanch tailor, Port Wm.
John Murray in Muirmains
John Macmeekin, Girthon parifh
—— Macminn, do.
—— Muir, do.
William Macminn, do.
Samuel M'Taggart, do.
John M'Lauchlan Anwoth par.
James M'Bryde, do 28 copies
John Maxwell nailer, Kirkudbright
Peter M'Kellar weaver, do.
Samuel M'Naught, do. do.
John M Keachie mafon, do.
David M'Caig carpenter, do.
Anthony M'Kenzie merchant, do
Peter Macmillan, Borland, do.
Edward M'Clure, Parkgate, do.
Robert M'Adam merchant, Whitehaven
David M'Girr tydewaiter, Rerrick
William M'Douall, Kirkcud.
Ja. M Clelland flocking weaver do
James M'Naught Port Mary, Kerrick parifh
David Macminn, Rerrick
Alex M'Cartney, do.
James Maxwell, do.
William Macmeekan, do.
John M'Cartney, do
Robert M'Naught, do.
Thomas Macminn, do.
Hen Murdoch farmer, Dalrymple
Alex. Millwain in Thornhoufe, Stonykirk parifh

James M'Geoch, Stranraer
William M'Clelland, Air parifh
James Muckle,
John Morton, do.
Alex. Murdoch do.
James Macmurtrie, do.
James Muir tailor, do.
Agnes M'Cleve, Barneil, do.
John M'Corman, Trowhaine, do.
Andrew M'Lauchlan, Glenhole, Glenluce
William M'Croferie, Auchenmalg, do.
John M'Bride fhoemaker, do.
Fergus Macmafter, Drochdool do.
John Macmeeken dyke builder, Newluce
Thomas Macmafter, Maxwellan, Stonykirk parifh
John M'Craken, Barber, do.
Robert M'William in Ruckle, do.
William M'Donald, Killbran, do
John M'Clymont, Glack, do.
—— M'Dowal, Blaick, Inch p.
Mrs. M'Corock, Lochryan
Pat. M'Neily, Inch parifh
John M'Credie, do.
—— M'Broadin Little tongue do
Thos. M'Bryde in Big tongue do
James M'Clymont in Sleechan do.
Bruce M'William
James M'Coual Velveteer, do.
Pat. Macmeeken in Beoch, do.
Hugh M'Alexander in Billyate, do
Alex M'William farmer in Lothwol. do.
John M'Gill in Cornwal, do.
William M'Gaw, do.
James M'Dowal, do.
William M'Dowal, do.
Mary M'Neily
Robert M'Crule, fervant, do.
Andrew M'Credie teacher, Cairn, do.
James M'Geoch wright Lochend
Andrew M'Cloch tailor in Port,

SUBSCRIBERS NAMES. 435

Thomas M'Blain in Blairſhinnock, do.
William M'Clelland teacher, Pt. William
John M'Guffag blackſmith, Kirkinner pariſh
William M'Lauchlan in mill of Airie, do
Thomas M'Adam in Barwharrie Margaret M'Kie, do do.
Hugh Martin in Slohabert, do.
William M'Fier weaver, do. do.
Alex. Milligen in Airleſs, do.
John M'Loggan do. do.
—— M'Dowal in Barneſs, do.
James M'Geoch in Blairmachen,
Samuel M'Dowal in Barns
William M'Dowal, do. do.
—— M'Gill, do
David M'Culloch ſhoemaker, Barglaſs, do.
John M'Cornick, Kirkown par.
Samuel M'Clyre in Dirry, do.
Gilbert M'Craken in Barnharrow, do.
John M'Clelland weaver, do.
James Maxwell, do. do.
Alex. M'Nairn
John Milroy dier, do.
Gilbert M'Neily, do.
John Macmaſter ſhoemaker Stranraer
John M'Hiſlop in Garſar, Ballentrae pariſh
Thomas M'Craken ſchoolmaſter
John M'Ilraith, do.
Andrew M'Kiſſock junior, do
John M'Culloch of Glenduſk, Eſq
Gilbert M'Quay in Palreoch, Colmonell
Pet M'Craken in Bowgang, do.
John M'Whirter in Drumſkioch do
Andrew M'Cornick in Barwhinnock, Colmonell pariſh
Grizzel M'Guffag in Corwar, do.
John M'Reath miller, Kildonnan do.

Thomas M'Neily chapman, do.
Alex M'Kie
Robert M'Kiſſock in Tamgunroch, do.
James M'Craken, Sorby pariſh
John M'Whirter, do.
Robert M'Croſkie lintdreſſer, do.
John M'Kinnel, Little Acres, do.
Thomas M'Clelland farmer in Orchardton, do.
William M'Adam junior, Townhead, do.
Mrs. M'Dowal, Coalwoag, do.
And. M'Keerly in Kalmallet, do
Peter M'Kie weaver, do.
Mr. M'Guffag, Better, do.
Anthony M'Credie, Whithorn, p.
William M'Conky, Drumaſk, do.
Alex M'Nairn, do.
George M'Credie Broughton, do
William M'Dowal maſon, do.
—— M'Gill tailor, do.
Sarah M'Kie, Broughton, do.
Peter M'Kie farmer in Muroch, do
James M'Ghee maſon, Smithſton
William M'Skimminin Lamachlee, Morton
John M'Culloch of Barholm, Eſq.
Alex. M'Lean of Mark, Eſq.
John Milligen, church officer, Kirkmabreck
John M'Dowal innkeeper, do.
William Murray dier, do.
Samuel M'Kean joiner, do.
Robert Mitchell tailor, do.
James M'Croſkie joiner, do.
Patrick M'Kean maſon, do.
John M'Kie tydewaiter, do.
Alex. M'Kie
Nath. Martin teacher, do.
Alex Murray miller, Miln driggan
Anthony M'Taggart ſewer
John M'Kean
Anthony M'Lurg ſhoemaker
William M'Gown, Garlieſton
Joſeph M'Kinch, do.

John M‘Adam, Innerwell
Alex. Minnoch, Ironkiln
James M‘Cormick, Orchardtown
Thos. M‘Nae, Anwoth parish
John Milligen, do.
William Murray, do.
Alex. M‘Heuchan, do.
Jean Murray, do.
James M‘Nae, do.
Samuel Murphy, do.
Andrew M‘Clymont, do.
John M‘Fadzen, Alloa mill
Peter Mitchell, Broomberry yard
John M‘Clure wright, Maybole p.
Thomas M‘Caul, Sandwith
William M‘Credie, Auchinleck
Thomas M‘Ilwraith, Catrine
John M‘Hutcheon wright, do.
—— M‘Craken jenny spinner, do
—— M‘Ilwraith, Penvale
———————— Dalquharran
———————— Dunmurchie
—— M‘Culloch, Lamdouchty
—— Macmurtrie, Knockwhine
—— Muir, Carnfore

Alexan. Murray, Rountree toll
James M Harg, Dumfries par.
William M‘Vitae, do
Matthew Mitchell, do.
Samuel Marrin, do.
Robert Murray, do.
George M‘Culloch, Slohabert, Kirkinner
Andrew M‘Haffie, do. do.
———— M‘Credie, do. do.
Alex. M‘Geoch, Dalregal, do.
John M‘Kinnel, do.
Robert M‘William, Straiton, do.
———— M‘Caul, do.
David M‘Kie, Maybole
———— M‘Clure tanner, Daily
Alex. Murdoch, Kirkmichael, par.
James Muir, do.
———— Macmurtrie, do.
Gilbert Mein, Daily parish
John M‘Clymont, do.
Will ————————— do.
James Muckle, Kirkmichael par.
Gilbert M‘Clymont, do.
John Morton, Kirkmichael

there were many Subscribers Names which were
—d when the Printing was finished, it is hoped they
— excuse the omission of their names, as they will
— get their copies at the price stipulated in the Pro-

www.ingramcontent.com/pod-product-compliance
Lightning Source LLC
Chambersburg PA
CBHW051733300426
44115CB00007B/552